GERMAN MEN OF LETTERS
VOLUME V

Twelve Literary Essays

GERMAN
MEN OF LETTERS

VOLUME V

Twelve Literary Essays

edited by
ALEX NATAN

DUFOUR EDITIONS

1969

© 1969 OSWALD WOLFF (PUBLISHERS) LIMITED, LONDON

Library of Congress Card Number: 66-28772

Printed in Great Britain

CONTENTS

Introduction

by ALEX NATAN

The poet's word will always be the starting-point for any literary criticism. All the more so when a dozen neglected poets and writers are presented of whom the first died in 1825 and the last was interred in 1924. They belonged to the nineteenth century which resists even intelligent generalisation in a few words. Too variegated was the plenitude of phenomena, trends, problems and achievements which it produced. Under the impact of the French Revolution and of Napoleon life itself in Germany underwent tremendous changes. This historical process was beset with far-reaching tensions and radical contradictions. Far remote from the highly intellectual tide of the classical and early romantic period, this century witnessed writers of world-weary resignation and poets of outspoken nihilistic rebellion. Others tried to come to terms with time in their own, personalised way while the last of the writers, presented here, wrote the first psycho-analytical novel, expressing the same urges and impulses as the oldest had done quite unconsciously a century earlier.

They were all poets and writers of disillusionment who defy classification, and not founders of literary "schools". However, they are linked by a feeling of spiritual loneliness. The idealism of their early work gave way before the exigencies of the realistic demands of life. They had tried to escape into uncharted realms of mockery, of nightmares and ghoulish visions, of distorted fantasies, of resignation and capsuled introspection. They had died the death of burnt-out lives. Their remarkable work revolves around the disparity between the ideal and the actual, the appearance and the reality, between man's opinion of himself and his true worth. They all could state, as one of them, Jean Paul, said in *Quintus Fixlein*: "And I walked without aim through woods, through valleys, and over brooks, and through sleeping villages, to enjoy the great Night like a Day. I walked, and still looked like the magnet, to the region of midnight, to strengthen my heart at the gleaming twilight, at this upstretching Aurora of a morning beneath our feet ... The distant village-clock struck midnight, mingling, as it were, with the ever-pealing tone of ancient Eternity.

7

...I walked silently through little hamlets, and close by their outer churchyards, where crumbled upcast coffin-boards were glimmering, while the once bright eyes that had lain in them were mouldered into grey ashes... Cold thought! clutch not like a cold spectre at my heart : I look up to the starry sky, and an everlasting chain stretches thither, and over and below; and all is life, and Warmth, and Light..." Today phenomena occur in the firmament which would find none of the poets and writers presented in this volume unprepared.

Each generation must discover JEAN PAUL afresh. Reappraisals of the poet have of course been undertaken since his death. His reputation has oscillated more than that of any other outstanding German poet. "He has produced some of the most brilliant examples of virtuoso comic writing and some of the finest rhapsodic prose in German, he has given us a gallery of eccentrics equalled perhaps only by Dickens."[1] But no prophet is accepted in his own country. It was symptomatic that the Bavarian government refused permission to the Jean-Paul-Society in 1963, the bi-centenary of the poet's birth, to have his bust put in Walhalla, the German Pantheon. Certainly Jean Paul is today not read in Germany with the same genuine enthusiasm of the Biedermeierzeit nor with the somewhat exaggerated fervour of Stefan George's circle.[2] Ernst Jünger once confessed that "the Order of the Readers and Admirers of Jean Paul proved to be more arcane and secluded than the secret Society of Tristram-Shandy Readers. But it exists and will always exist". Stifter, Gotthelf, Conrad Ferdinand Meyer, Hugo von Hofmannsthal[3] and Hermann Hesse remained great admirers of him throughout their lives. Goethe, Schiller and Heine viewed him with disfavour, while Nietzsche called him "ein Verhängnis im Schlafrock".[4]

The influence of Jean Paul proved far more impressive in French literature.[5] Those pages which Madame de Stael devoted to the poet in her book De l'Allemagne (1814) were the prelude to a popularity of Jean Paul which has never ceased until the present day. With uncanny intuition this intelligent observer quotes the famous dream passage from Jean Paul's novel Siebenkäs where the dead Christ preaches to a dead congregation in the ruins of a church that God was no longer alive. The vision of the dead Christ is no blasphemy but the cry of a lonely soul in the wilderness of a suffering world. This agonising experience of Jean Paul made a deep impression on many French writers. Alfred de Vigny hailed the German poet as his "brotherly friend" while Alfred de Musset called him "our Jean Paul". Michelet and Balzac, Baude-

laire, Renan, Gobineau, Villiers de l'Isle-Adam all read the vision of the dead Christ. It inspired such French novels as *Vigny's "Le Mont des Oliviers", de Nerval's "Le Christ aux Oliviers"*, part of *Victor Hugo's "La Fin de Satan"* and *Leconte de Lisle's "La Recherche de Dieu"*. *Leon Daudet* has drawn attention to *Proust's* work with its close similarities to that of Jean Paul, although it is not at all certain that Proust ever read Jean Paul. The "surrealist" elements in Jean Paul are finding wider recognition in France than elsewhere, as the *"Contes de Cristel"* by *Daniel-Rops* (1966), *"La moto-cyclette"* by the avant-gardist *Pieyre de Mandiargues* (1965), and particularly *Louis Aragon's* last novel *"La mise à mort"* (1965) have shown. The last novel echoes once more the oration of the dead Christ.

In England the interest in Jean Paul was stimulated by an essay by Carlyle which appeared in 1827, after he, too, had read Madame de Stael's book. Carlyle showed much critical acumen when he wrote about Jean Paul's novels : "There is solid metal enough in them to fit out whole circulating libraries, were it beaten into the usual filigree." Professor Roy Pascal uses this dictum to support his own view that Jean Paul was not a great writer of novels because of his disregard for the established forms of the genre.[6] It was also Madame de Stael's book which caused Dostoevski to read Jean Paul. The existentialist kinship between the Oration of the dead Christ and the Russian "Grand-Inquisitor" underlines how much thought Jean Paul anticipated of Kierkegaard. Jean Paul was the archetype of a poet who broke out of his petty bourgeois environment and soared into the universe of his eccentric dreams and once admired ideals.

CLEMENS BRENTANO is one of the many tragic figures in German literature. Caroline Schlegel once called him "Demens Clemens" and was of the opinion that "all the Brentanos are extremely unnatural characters". From infancy the poet grew up to fear his father, an Italian merchant who had produced nineteen children and written sonnets in his native tongue. His mother, Maximiliane Laroche, Goethe's early friend, sought by her son in an almost Freudian manner, died before the young man had grown up. Brentano was an unstable, unreliable person, restless, "haltlos", without an anchor in life. In his young days the poet was "the jester of the Romanticists, the wayward knave and wag who cannot refrain from doing what he knows will cost him the friends he has made, nor from disturbing and destroying the emotions and illusions which he himself has skilfully produced" (Georg Brandes). In a letter Brentano once stated : "Every day I feel more clearly

that I can only find rest in the most fantastic, most romantic life."
His first wife, Sophie Mereau, was convinced that "our prosaic
world never carried a greater Don Quixote". No wonder that this
arch-romantic developed the gift of boundless imagination stronger
than all his other rich talents. In another letter Brentano wrote :
"Oh, my child! We had nourished nothing but imagination, and
it, in return, had half devoured us." Steffens, another romantic
writer, remarks of Brentano that he was the only one of the
Romanticists who seems to be thoroughly aware that life has no
aim. He calls him an ironical, sportive Kronos, who fantastically
demolishes every one of his definite utterances by means of its
successor, in this manner devouring his own children. The life of
this "enfant perdu of the Romantic School" is a remarkable
example of the truth of the words of Mephistopheles in Goethe's
Faust :

> Yes, despite reason and science,
> the highest possessions of man,
> let yourself be persuaded by the spirit of lies
> to believe in hallucinations and magic,
> and you are mine without fail.

Hallucinations and magic played no small part in Brentano's
existence, and the man who had begun by sneering at rationalism
as dull and barren, fell a prey to ideas far duller and more barren
than the emptiest rationalism, when he, for example, produced
what was irreverently called "the Fifth Gospel according to Brentano", the alleged visions of the stigmatised and hysterical nun
Anna Katherina Emmerick.[7]

Still, as a lyric poet and a writer of fairy-tales Brentano has
produced works of art, few in number, but of permanent value.
"It all bustles along in the most delightful confusion and only the
air of madness that informs it all lends it a certain unity." Heinrich
Heine continues in *Die Romantische Schule* to liken Brentano's
talents to a Chinese princess, in whose little tittering heart nested
the maddest fancies. In all his works Brentano showed himself
the perpetual adolescent in search of his lost childhood or, symbolically speaking, in quest of the lost paradise of the Middle Ages
which, to the poet, represented an age of unsophisticated happiness.
Thus Brentano's fairy-tales became a flight from himself and his
incapacity to cope with his own times to a fancy-free world of
make-believe and soaring fantasies. As a lyrical poet Brentano
created verses of enchanting beauty whose meaning however is often
obscured by their musical sound and variation. Not unlike Rilke,

who also preferred an orphic musicality to clear, lyrical thought, Brentano's stream of emotions is only too rapidly turned into a mere cascade of spell-binding words. Not without reason it has been said that Clemens Brentano was "one of the most significant victims of the peculiarly Romantic schizophrenia, known as 'Zerrissenheit', being unable to lose himself fully in sensual or intellectual enjoyment".[8]

The Romantic movement was not content with the mere glorification of past history, with the idea of a previous existence, or with speculating about future potentialities. The Romanticists blazed a remarkable trail for modern psychology. They explored the Ego into its remotest corners and dissolved it into its very elements. They pursued this Ego without any regard to the laws of time and space. Self-consciousness leads to self-duplication. Such a situation is only too often morbid and unhealthy. "He who indulges in self-contemplation separates himself from himself, observes himself from the point of view of a spectator, and ere long experiences the horrible feeling of the prisoner who, when he looks up, sees the eye of the warder at the little peep-hole in the door of his cell" (Georg Brandes). In the case of introspective natures the eye is never removed from the little glass panel. The more the beholder stares through it, the nearer he drifts towards the abyss of madness. This preoccupation with the Ego gave birth to the "Doppelgänger", an idea which Jean Paul already touched upon in his *Leibgeber-Schoppe* and which Brentano used for his ironical treatment of *Die mehreren Wehmüller*. Such a confrontation with the wraith of one's own self became a dominant theme in almost all E. T. A. HOFFMANN's *tales*. To him the Ego was merely a mask which camouflaged deeper-seated layers of disguise. To explore them, to lay them bare, fascinated the writer who, however, remained always aware of the contrast between a dull and humdrum world and his floating realm of dreams and daring fantasies.

It was almost inevitable that such a painstaking observer of his own moods, such an inquisitive analyst of the human mind, should become convinced that an evil power was always lurking in the background to paralyse the good intentions in man. Dreams, dipsomania, hallucinations, madness, crime, all the powers which disintegrate the Ego played a major part in Hoffmann's tales. He created most of his characters in his own image. His whole life resolved itself into moods which were carefully set down in his diaries. It only signified a logical step in this irrational world of nightmares and ghoulish horrors to create fantastic Egos, once the own Self was corroded. One important medium of this transmutation was the role music played as a major key to the magic realm of beauty and poetry.

It would however be a mistake to look for the quintessence of E. T. A. Hoffmann solely in this world of phantoms and to overlook his sharp appreciation of reality, though tucked away with uncanny technique. From his own experience he knew the secrets of a split-mind and its consequences. But he also knew love, the antidote, correctly gauged the liberating force of humour, and understood the curative effects of reality itself. One ignores too readily that Hoffmann also wrote stories which do not show the slightest trace of any preoccupation with the transcendental. With E. T. A. Hoffmann Romanticism was becoming an exploded idea. "Das Reich des Positivismus und des Naturalismus, das Gespenst der undurchsichtig werdenden Welt glimmt hier bei Hoffmann zum erstenmal unübersehbar auf."[9]

E. T. A. Hoffmann was the first modern creator of characters who were tormented by neurotic fears and misgivings, and persecuted by delusions. His influence on foreign literature proved of continuing strength. Gérard de Nerval, Victor Hugo, E. A. Poe, Baudelaire, Gogol, Dostoevski, Chekhov, the Surrealists, the Criminal Story have all used Hoffmannesque motifs of the horrific and the gruesome. The expressionist film which Germany produced after the First World War occasionally reminded one of those visionary reflections of the poet which he perceived while intoxicated and watching the darkness suddenly illuminated by phosphorescent spectres. His prose stimulated musicians because Hoffmann, no mean composer himself, always found inspiration and peace in the world of sound. Berlioz's "Symphonie Fantastique" owed much to the composer's reading of Hoffmann's tales. Robert Schumann composed musical pieces which he called "Kreisleriana", and Jacques Offenbach incorporated motifs from the poet's stories in his opera "The Tales of Hoffmann". Tchaikovsky's "Nutcracker" suite and Delibes' "Coppélia" ballet were inspired by the stories of Hoffmann. Even in our own days Busoni's "Die Brautwahl" and, particularly, Hindemith with his opera "Cardillac" have shown their indebtedness to E. T. A. Hoffmann. He remains a living force who deserves to be better known in this country.

The inclusion of CHRISTIAN DIETRICH GRABBE in the present volume needs justification, either by reference to his isolated position as a dramatist, or as a creator or interpreter of important ideas. Whoever becomes absorbed in a study of the development of German tragedy as a dramatic expression cannot help noticing the

tragic aspects of this historical process itself which follow succes-
sively with logical consistency.[10] As a subject matter man's existence,
once borne with optimistic pride and boundless faith, becomes increasingly doomed, to sink finally into an abyss of hopelessness and
shifting sands. "The tragedy of theodicy is replaced by the tragedy
of nihilism." Hence the inquiry into the nature of this "nothing".

"What is a tragedy? ... Surely nothing that can be captured in
five acts and measured out to the audience in scenes! It is a human
life which wants to be lived out ... a life long." This is Grabbe's
own definition and goes far as a clue to the appreciation of his
writings and to the understanding of the far-reaching identification of the poet with the dramatic figures of his imagination. A
knowledge of Grabbe's life is necessary to understand the dark,
sinister, evil-boding background of a pathological existence which
permeated his works. Not unlike Kleist and Grillparzer Grabbe's
predisposition for tragedy can be discovered in himself. "What shall
become of a man whose earliest memory was the escorting of an
aged murderer into fresh air!" Immermann's well-known description of the poet's physiognomy permits conclusions which shed an
ambivalent light on the schizophrenic aspects of Grabbe's mental
make-up. With reference to Faust's confession to the two souls
living in his heart Grabbe once spoke of the "five souls dwelling
in his head". A chequered career, a disastrous marriage anticipating
every ounce of marital torment Strindberg revealed half a century
later, incurable illness and utter despair, soaked and drowned in
alcohol, set the seal to the perdition of this late descendant of
"*Sturm und Drang*".

Grabbe, a true outcast of society, was torn to pieces between the
realisation of his physical inferiority and the creative forces within
himself striving for the creation of dramatic supermen and for the
cineramic magnification of their heroic deeds. But Grabbe was
overwhelmed by his conviction that an almighty malevolence was
guiding the fate of man over whose destiny Hell would always
triumph. He tried to combat this inescapable conclusion by con-
juring up images of lusty men of action who would restore a sense
for greatness, power, and sublimity to the world. But since Grabbe
himself was deeply corroded by his awareness of human impotence,
all his titanic supermen, in whom some writers care to recognise
the precursors of German expressionist drama, fail because they
too are nothing but mere sport of the Fates.

Grabbe's lasting contribution to German literature is to be found
in his *Hannibal* and in his *Napoleon*. The latter introduces the
masses as a vital factor into German drama. Both plays transcend

the strict definition of drama. Grabbe attempted an epic dramatisation which points to the first subconscious realisation of visions
only to be adequately expressed through the medium of the film
and superbly suitable for television treatment. The theme of
Hannibal, his best play, is not a superman but a failing hero whose
life and ambitions are wrecked on the limitations of the age. In
this play Grabbe dramatises the tragedy of a nation which realised
its historical hour too late and was doomed to perdition because it
betrayed the great leader who was destined to be its saviour. Hence
the reason why the Nazis resuscitated the forgotten plays of Grabbe,
was, because they hailed in him the first author of a "Führerdrama".
They had moreover good reason for this bizarre choice, for their
dramatic propagandist Hans Johst had written a play, "Der
Einsame", in the palmy days of expressionism, whose hero was
Grabbe. The anti-semitic attacks of Grabbe on his contemporary
Heine appealed to the Zeitgeist of the thirties. Martin Esslin calls
Grabbe one of "the poètes maudits" who have influenced the
Theatre of the Absurd. Grabbe's comedy *Scherz, Satire, Ironie und
tiefere Bedeutung,* in which the Devil visits the Earth and is mis-
taken for a maiden-lady novelist, is an early masterpiece of "black
humour".[11] Martin Esslin emphasises "the line of development
which leads from Grabbe and Büchner straight to Wedekind, the
Dadaists, German Expressionism and early Brecht".

Among the German poets of the nineteenth century who are
today almost forgotten but do not deserve such a harsh fate,
AUGUST VON PLATEN, the German master of the sonnet, must be
singled out. His remains a case of particular literary and psychological interest because it reflects not only the transitional period
following the Romantic Movement but underlines also vividly the
frightening ambivalence and disastrous consequences of what the
late Professor Elsie Butler called the tyranny of Greece over German literature. There once was a time when almost every educated
German knew Platen's *Tristan* by heart. It remains one of the
finest poems because here a true poet found profound expression
for his quest for beauty. What Thomas Mann had to say about
the true meaning of this poem and the sorrows of the poet can be
read in one of his essays, a worthy attempt to enlist sympathy for
the forgotten poet. Occasionally one comes across one of his ballads
in German school anthologies; but these ballads were nothing but
rhymed paraphrases of historical events, lacking true lyrical feeling
and overflowing painfully with educative knowledge. The rest of
his considerable work has vanished.

Platen's fate was to be born a nobleman at a time when the

aristocracy everywhere had to yield ground to a bourgeoisie which asserted its ascendency through money and property. His destiny was to be known as a homosexual at an age where such inclinations were still regarded as an unmentionable aberration of nature. Platen's diaries, hardly obtainable nowadays, bear witness to his ambivalence, to his inner torments and fights, and to his courage with which he fought against his fate. The nobleman in him made him a classicist at a time of Philistinism, who stood up against it because it was so conspicuously yielding to the softening influence of a Romanticism which disdained form and all self-discipline. It was, however, this inspiration, combined with an ardent love for form, which forced a renunciation of any realistic appreciation of life upon Platen who retired into an ivory tower of make-believe. And yet he knew only too well that his craving for classicism was nothing but an alien mask destined to hide the torments of his soul and the longings of his body. For Platen, in his assiduous cultivation of foreign forms, followed just as much in the footsteps of the Romanticists when he tried his hand at the oriental ghazel, at the southern sonnet, at Aristophanic comedy and at the Pindaric ode as other poets of his time did. "He thus fell into l'art pour l'art, not for lack of profundity, but in order to conquer the tragedy of his spiritual and physical existence" (August Closs).

Platen's thirst for beauty, his loneliness, his yearning for understanding, friendship and love drew him to Italy in quest of that unobtainable Hellas which brought so often unmitigated disaster to German writers. This search for an ideal which assumed tyrannical power over Platen ended with an over-dose of drugs. Buried in a grave in foreign soil he shares the destiny of his implacable rival and enemy Heine; but also of Stefan George whose poetry shows Platen's influence in form and imagery. Strange, Heine and George stipulated in their last wills that they should never be interred in Germany.

Platen's feud with Heine, admittedly of episodic character, throws nevertheless a significant light on the spiritual crisis of their age. The treatment Platen received from Heine was not undeserved; scorn was returned for scorn, and his arrogant under-estimation of Heine was cruelly avenged. The fact that the names of Heine and Platen came to form a constellation of hate was actually due to the similarity of their natures, to their supreme mastery of polemics, to the feeling of solitariness which, combined with a self-esteem that was always on the alert, made them prone to proclaim their own praises and to attack others with undue bitterness and with insufficient understanding. Heine was justified in all arguments against Platen except in the decisive one : his mockery of the formalism of Platen's verse, his satire of the calculability of its metres were identical with denying him the right to be a poet. Yet to be a poet was the most precious mainstay in Platen's life. In one of his poem's he had vowed :

> Ich schwöre den schönen Schwur, getreu stets zu sein
> Dem hohen Gesetz, und will, in Andacht vertieft,
> Voll Priestergefühl verwalten
> Dein gross Prophetenamt[12]

August von Platen does not deserve the cruel fate of being forgotten : his sonnets can stand comparison with Shakespeare's in their Platonism and homo-erotic response to beauty.

While Platen was preoccupied with classical form and metre NIKOLAUS LENAU displayed little inclination to submit to the rigid self-discipline of a poet. He remained the man of ever-changing moods, tossed about by unbridled passions, and a life-long seeker for a spiritual home which the undercurrents of approaching madness denied him. "He was a poète maudit in the late-romantic Byronic tradition, and his mind would veer erratically from vehement concern with himself to a gloomy resignation and indifference" (R. Thymms).

Compared with Platen who aimed at effacing every trace of personal experience from his work, Lenau's life formed the prime constituent of his creative activities. In this respect Lenau was more closely associated with Heine than with Platen. But as a personality he seemed to be a stranger to both.

Lenau was the only one among the three poets who did not hail from Germany. Through his Hungarian birth and upbringing he acquired a problem which Heine and Platen only faced and settled at later stages of their development. All three found themselves in opposition to the police regime of the day and emigrated to other countries. Lenau's sensitive spirit was roused to wrath by the tyranny of the Metternich system. He was consumed with a fiery indignation against the attempt to fetter by censorship thought and its expression. As Heine was driven to Paris and Platen to Italy, so Lenau sought escape from the gloom about him by emigration to the United States, only to find disillusionment there and to return to Germany.

In 1832, after the abortive rising of the Poles had been crushed by Russia, when the thoughts of excitable Germans were diverted from their own woes by the call for sympathy with Poland, Platen and Lenau poured forth Polish laments. This poetry abounded with sentimentality, and was mercilessly satirised by Heine in his *Krapulinski und Waschlapski*. Lenau's prime philosophy was almost the same as that of Platen : life is identical with sorrows and torment. The poet drew the ultimate conclusion from this outlook : his basic occupation remained with death and the transitoriness of life. Lenau was the poet of grief and woe. As a wholly subjective poet who roamed through two continents without finding peace or satisfaction he was one of the last Romanticists. But true romantic notions and romantic mythology were absent from his work. In a period of transition Lenau was an unstable sceptic, incapable of taking any committed stand, "a product of an age of pre-stabilised disharmony" (J. Klein).

Lenau's lament was the grievance of many sensitive minds in of his inner restlessness amounting often to a challenging doubt of God. In his sorrows he took flight into Nature because, to him, Nature reflected the melancholy of his own soul. But it is not so much in the *Schilflieder* or *Waldlieder* that Lenau survives but in those poems which give such a vivid account of the gipsies and Magyars of Hungary or the Red Indians of the United States. His sensitive feelings for the wide plains of the Danube or the mighty ocean gave his poetry its characteristics.

Lenau's laments was the grievance of many sensitive minds in those pre-1848 years to whom "a foundering in a sea of dreams amounted to an intimate shipwreck". This was the lament of Leopardi and Manzoni in Italy, of Pushkin and Lermontov in Russia, of Byron in England. After the exhausting experience of Napoleonic disorders this listlessness and this tired mood of resignation came as no surprise. The simultaneous publication of some books expressing this Europe-wide spiritual mood must be taken as a sign of the times. In the same year 1836, when Lenau published his *Faust,* Immermann's *Epigonen* appeared and Alfred de Musset confessed his satiety of life in *Confession d'un enfant du siècle.* Schopenhauers's expounding of his philosophy of pessimism and his yearning for redemption coincided with the publication of the last edition of Leopardi's poems. In Russia Pushkin created his *Eugen Onegin,* "the Mazurka-dancing dandy who knew how to feign pining melancholy and to parade his idleness in the theatre, in restaurants and in the ball-room". The Russian literature of this time is rich in such characters, as Lermontov so vividly portrays them in his *A Hero of Our Time.* This weariness of life was most brilliantly described by Gontcharov in his well-known novel of indolence *Oblomov.* Lenau's "Weltschmerz" found its Russian counterpart in "Oblomovchina".

In one of the early editions of ADALBERT STIFTER'S collected
works his biographer, Otto Stoessl, could still write : "Die Zeit kann
dem Dichter sein Geistiges anfechten, seine Ideen altern machen,
aber die Kunst, der Zauber der Stimmung, die Anmut der Gestalten
bleibt bestehen. . . . Es gibt Stunden, wo den Menschen jener Trost
der Einfalt, Ruhe, Treue, des Beharrens, der Stille not tut, wo
ihnen die Kunst das Gebet ersetzt. Da sind solche fromme, herzliche
Bücher froh begrüsst und Lächeln Trost. Zu diesen treuherzigen
Dichterseelen gehört Adalbert Stifter. Aus einfachem Herzen, aus
einem engen Leben in armen Land hat er uns Bedeutendes und
Bleibendes gegeben."[13]

This image of Stifter as the superb landscape painter in prose,
reflecting the guileless and innocent Biedermeier of an Austria,
where, at his time of life, centralism meant everything and a pro-
vincial exile threatened the very roots of creative existence, has
lost all its validity for modern criticism.

Who reads Stifter today cannot but hear a tragic undertone
which literary critics of the past brushed aside as a mere but attractive nuance. Behind the snug façade of the Austrian Biedermeier
the strands of an extremely unsettled, psychic disposition lay hidden
whose apparent harmony rested on the shifting sands of repression.
In Stifter's personality characteristics of self-disintegration and of
cruelty against himself and other people can be discovered. The
melancholy of a fading summer becomes so heavy that the inner
kinship to Trakl is undeniable, only that Stifter would still con-
ceal what Trakl later openly expressed. Stifter's work was still
aiming at achieving some sort of compensation. Therefore his
efforts to create a "Gegenwelt". A modern student of Stifter will
soon shed the traditional opinion of seeing in him a representative
of a cosy realism. The world as Stifter described it never really
existed.

A study of Stifter's life and letters reveals a completely different
and most problematic character, almost a split-personality. He was
a type of a writer who could have only existed in Austria, as his
affinities with Grillparzer, von Saar and Trakl show. While it was
asserted in the past that Stifter was a non-political writer, his
letters prove the contrary. Those political events, for example,
which are not mentional in *Nachsommer*, made Stifter physically
ill. His course of development contradicts the literary assessment of
the past. Born as the son of a linen-weaver he lost his father at the
age of twelve. Intended for the Church, he studied jurisprudence
and natural sciences. He himself wanted to try his luck as a painter
but began writing from sheer necessity of earning a living. He

lived the life of a true "bohemian" and contracted debts like Balzac and Dostoevski. Pressed by creditors and threatened with distraints Stifter began to gamble, to buy shares and to speculate recklessly and unsuccessfully. He lived an extremely unhappy double-existence and married an unloved woman who brought two nieces into his house, one of whom died young, while the other committed suicide soon afterwards. Could such a man believe in an unscathed world on the strength of such experiences? Would he indeed only narrate the effects of what he called the "gentle law"?

Although Stifter spent some time as a tutor in the house of Prince Metternich he was twice compelled to experience his censorship when he was forbidden to make public speeches and then consequently forfeited a licence to publish a *Lesebuch zur Förderung humaner Bildung*. During the last years of his life Adalbert Stifter suffered continuously from depressions, from vertigo and anxiety neuroses. When finally the pains of his incurable disease—cancer of the liver—exceeded all that was humanly bearable, he took a razor and finished his life by his own hand in mental derangement. The life of such a writer certainly does not correspond with the idealised picture of a harmonious and well-balanced poet in an ivory tower.

A similar misjudgment prevailed for a long time in the literary assessment of EDUARD MÖRIKE whom Gottfried Keller once called "a son of Horace and of an exquisite Swabian". There was a period when critics accepted Mörike as a good-natured parson who also wrote occasional but surprisingly good poetry. But behind this façade of an apparently idyllic existence, a man struggled with a complex and burdensome life and succeeded at last in finding some sort of equilibrium between the tensions of art and daily toil, of vocation and profession, and in bringing the bitterness of many dark hours and inner distress to poetic fruition.

The harvest of Mörike's long life consisted of only a small oeuvre: a novel, a few short stories, some fairy-tales and a volume of poetry. Mörike's oldest friend Hartlaub testified already in their youth that "He never said anything commonplace". In his poetry Mörike set out for his imaginary island of Orplid which was identical with the journey's end of all Romanticists. However, Mörike's embarkation was neither a daring venture of an unbridled mind nor a flight from reality, as so many romantic life stories had revealed before. Mörike did not shirk the everyday routine of his ministry and teaching but could, at the same time, not escape from the inner "Wanderlust" which put an end to the peaceful idyll of his

parsonage. Of his poetry Theodor Storm remarked : "It was as if
one was peering through these poems as through magic glasses
into the life of the poet himself. There were depth and grace and
German tenderness often fused with classical plasticity." Rightly
Professor Closs points out that "Mörike leads unruly romanticism
over the threshold of a new classical ideal and transfuses the latter
with a daemonic element".

Throughout his life the poet had been able to reflect the world
in two or three verses : the world of our earth, the world of love,
the world of suffering, the world of God. He had attempted a
psychological "Bildungsroman"—*Maler Nolten,* the formation of the
personality of a painter. Driven by a classical duty of obedience to
form and measure he had conceived one of the finest short stories
in German literature. Only a truly lyrical mind could write *Mozart
auf der Reise nach Prag,* for the entire story bears the stamp of
imaginative inspiration. It abounds with themes of a lyrical character associated throughout the story with the same persons, situations
and sentiments but always striving to get back to the starting point.
This mixture of realistic traits with the true ingredients of a fairy-
tale show that the unlimited domain of the legend appealed more
strongly to Mörike than the reality of the short story.

Hebbel once wrote to Mörike that he admired the art with which
he had caused a whole world to evolve out of a grain of mustard-
seed. Music plays a decisive part in this Mozart story. When
Susanna's aria from "Le Nozze di Figaro" is sung, it is sheer beauty
which serves to express the elegance of the Rococo period. Later, the
gala dinner is like "a painted symphony". When Mozart finally
begins to narrate the story of "Don Giovanni" and begins to
accompany himself on the piano, evening turns to dark night. The
frivolous atmosphere of the Rococo gives way to the premonition of
an inescapable tragedy. Mörike always perceived the deep affinities
between music and death. For Mörike Mozart became the symbol
of artistic genius. As a "Künstlernovelle" Mörike's story is only
rivalled by Thomas Mann's *Death in Venice.*

It was this close relationship between great music and the finality
of all things which induced Hugo Wolf to set to music over forty
poems of Mörike and thus assured the poet's immortality. The
composer perfected the often unspoken word, for his music could
give free vent to all elementary passions. Maybe Mörike would
have objected to Hugo Wolf's compositions as not Mozartian
enough, but then the composer intuitively perceived Mörike's
"daemonic element". But even the unmusical will find consolation
in those words which Gottfried Keller wrote after the writer's

death : *"Wenn sein Tod nun seine Werke nicht unter die Leute bringt, so ist ihnen nicht zu helfen. Nämlich den Leuten"*.

JEREMIAS GOTTHELF opens the chapter of modern Swiss literature. Even if much of his subject matter belongs to a world which no longer exists, Gotthelf's awareness of the problems of his time carries still today a tang of freshness and urgency which turns the past into the present. Gotthelf too had to overcome prejudice and misjudgment of literary criticism in the nineteenth and twentieth century before he met with a more impartial assessment in our own days. The writer introduced the peasant and the farmer into literature which, at the time, was not yet ready to recognise the true nature of the peasantry as a literary subject. Moreover, Gotthelf met with fierce opposition when he began his stubborn fight against a portentous *Zeitgeist* in politics and philosophy. Lastly, since he wrote his stories unconcernedly in a mixture of literary German and Bernese dialect the average reader found it difficult to get accustomed to this peculiar style. "Thus the memorable case happened that perhaps the greatest epic genius of the German tongue was considered to be a writer of village stories, not without talents but certainly disorderly and unruly" (Werner Günther).

It has often been stated that Jeremias Gotthelf, a country parson by profession, invites comparison with his two famous contemporaries Balzac in France and Trollope in England. Certainly Balzac wrote *Les Chouans,* a novel about the peasants of Britanny, in 1829, and Trollope showed many affinities with Gotthelf in his creation of small town characters. But Gotthelf limited his range to the narrow experience of the people of the Bernese Oberland with its almost exclusively agrarian activities. Certainly, like Dickens and Trollope, Gotthelf inclined to moralising as a strong weapon of social criticism. He always remained the prudish parson, and every comparison must stop here, as he could have never written any of Trollope's parliamentary novels nor Balzac's Rabelaisian *Contes Drôlatiques*. Even in his best work Gotthelf, the preacher, will remain didactic. He felt wedded to the old peasant customs and attacked bitterly those of his country-men who were alienated from true and simple Swiss country life or wavered in their loyalty to Christian beliefs. His hatred was directed against everything superficial, everything rotten, against the new-fangled Liberalism, against atheism, and, most of all, against encroaching materialism. Therefore he did not spare intellectuals of every description from his venom and did not even exempt priests and parsons. His

language was outspoken and unmistakable, for his country readers
would never accept evasive words or ambiguous expressions.

Gotthelf is a story-teller of the first rank and his descriptions of
the rural life of absorbing interest. Here he proves his outstanding
artistry. Whether he is concerned with following up the rise of a
peasant lad to a prosperous farmer, or in portraying a materialist
world, there is unity in the story, just as the Protestant parson used
to be the centre of the village life, a chronicler of reality, a rock
of faith and confidence.

Gotthelf is the great plein-air painter in the nineteenth-century
prose. Nature will always indicate through hail and rain, through
thunder and lightning when a man has become unfaithful to his
traditions, to his homeland, to the eternal laws. Gotthelf is not
afraid to point to the approaching struggles of the future from
which his Swiss peasants cannot escape. But they will be prepared
and well armed if they succeed in keeping intact their sane instincts
and their Christian ideals, surrounded by mountain air and involved
in a hard struggle for existence and for the preservation of ancient
traditions.

WILHELM RAABE, frequently regarded to be Jean Paul's legitimate
heir in German literature, represents a curious case of great
promise which he never fulfilled. He possessed the gift to be an
impassionate social writer at a period when decisive changes in her
social structure compelled Germany to steer a course which proved
so disastrous. Raabe who lacked the sweeping range and compassionate depth of a Balzac or a Tolstoy, impeded his own progress
by juxtaposing a strangely unreal perception of reality to the realism
of the everyday bourgeois world. His intellectual insight at a time
when Germany was reaching out to become a world power seemed
to be rather blurred by a predilection for Jean Paul's romantic
sentimentality and by Schopenhauer's pessimism which, in his case,
may have been just disappointed idealism. But it remains a strange
phenomenon that a writer, who only died in 1910, showed no understanding for such great social novelists and dramatists like Zola,
Ibsen, Shaw, and could not even muster sympathy for his native
naturalists.

Perhaps a clue to this puzzling behaviour can be discovered in
Raabe's style. He employed the methods of romantic irony in order
to destroy the romantic illusions of his own age. He knew well how
to mislead his readers by interrupting his stories by didactic digressions and by apparently pointless interpolations. Yet ultimately
Raabe always revealed his partisan sympathy for every brand of
fighters for untimely or lost causes, for cranks and crackpots, who

were sheltering from the cold winds of materialistic ascendancy, for misunderstood eccentrics, out of touch and tune with all their world stood for. As Raabe himself felt acutely the uneasiness of his time it becomes more intelligible why he sided so passionately with those of his characters who showed themselves unable to withstand the pressures of modern times. "His acceptance of change is not so much the outcome of a positive belief as the expression of a sincere and humane, sometimes despondent, resignation" (Roy Pascal).

Raabe displayed enough intellectual keenness in grasping the moral dilemma posed by an increasingly complex world but he described it only too often with the limited range of a petit bourgeois who, while apprehending the slow destruction of all traditional values with great alarm, despaired of finding any meaning in life and history, and preferred to live his life out in a small town hidden away from everything which threatened to draw him into the maelstrom of time.

Raabe is said to have hardly left his study during the last decades of his life. This self-imposed isolation from the world did not prevent Raabe's imagination from exploring it, not however by observing its disturbingly new social trends but by delving into nooks and crannies, its attics and backrooms. There his heroes live in contrast to the world whose haste, hustle and lust for acquisitiveness they despise. They are always on the defensive. Those who are doomed and of evil disposition are the active characters of his novels who make all the worldly gains. Raabe never looks for the humane personalities among those who are successful but among those who are lonely or overlooked, among the oddities and eccentric fellows. Because there were strong didactic impulses at work in Raabe, he did not write art for art's sake but he was always out to drop hints how to master this so difficult life. Often he did so through his humour. It could be sentimental but it was mostly quizzical and occasionally acid and sharp. Therefore the emphasis of character as a stylistic device became more important to him than the progress of the story's action. It is this predilection for didactic digressions which has always blocked the way to Raabe and which has so much contributed to him being accounted a minor writer, just because he curiously failed to come to grips with his time.

An Austrian contemporary of Lenau who did not content himself with contemplating the tragi-comedy of the stupidity, wickedness, and intolerance of this transitional period passively was JOHANN NESTROY. This writer who is often called the "Viennese Aristophanes" proved himself to be blunter and more aggressive than Ferdinand Raimund, his predecessor, as entertainer of the Viennese people. Since Grimmelshausen Nestroy was probably the first German who consciously made the most of the various uses his command of language offered him to denounce the social conditions of his time. The magic comedy of the Viennese folk-plays which signified probably the end of the Baroque theatre, not yet nurtured upon literature but upon the immediacy of the scene, became a sarcastic, social satire with Nestroy who exposed Metternich's police system and castigated many contemporaries through his biting parodies.

Nestroy was one of the first advocates of a literary functionalism : life, after all, was only the result of his own shrewd and superior wit. The intellect became his sharpest rapier which could even allow the toleration of feelings and unreality for sheer strategical reasons. His antagonism to the world of the poet stands out when one calls to mind Nestroy's brilliant parodies of German literature. After Shakespeare he was one of the first authors in direct contact with the theatre, not only as a playwright but also as an actor in his own comedies and farces. Nestroy's themes originated entirely from the Viennese milieu from which he singled out the petty bourgeoisie which formed at the same time his audience. This down-grading of the social milieu marked a decisive event in the history of the German theatre : no longer was the audience obliged to gape at the actors on the stage, now it was sitting among them. Nestroy chose his heroes even from below the milieu of the petty bourgeoisie. For the greater part they are all poor and insignificant, and most of them unappreciated. Metternich's censors did not suspect them of political sedition, as the "juste milieu" of the ruling classes was not directly attacked, although Nestroy's wit attacked them in a cunning and devious way.

Nestroy, in his crafty fight against the prevailing conditions of his time, discovered meta-theatrical possibilities in the multifarious ways language could be used and abused. "Nestroy is the first German satirist, in whom the language wonders about things. He frees the language from its rigidity, and it yields him a new thought for every phrase" (Karl Kraus). The greatest possible satirical effect in Nestroy's comedies and farces was achieved within the narrowest confines. He used the simplest means of popular criticism and verbal turns, of lingual combinations and distortions, of deliberate slips of the tongue and of extemporisations. When the protagonist died this brilliant side of him perished too. Hence the typical construction of his plays barred Nestroy the way to fame, particularly his peculiar "lingua Austriaca" which he commanded with such a masterly skill.

At Christmas 1967 four plays by Nestroy were simultaneously given in Vienna's theatres. It was safe to assume then and now that hardly any other German theatre would still have a play by Nestroy in its repertoire. This "lingua Austriaca" of Nestroy which he turned into an undiluted theatrical language *"verhält sich, weil sie Ausdruck einer tiefpessimistischen Welt-und Seelenanalyse ist, zur alt-österreichischen Alltagssprache wie das Negativ zum Positiv"*.[14] In Vienna people are not inclined to overestimate themselves. This attitude is perfectly expressed in Nestroy's language : *"Ueberhaupt hat der Fortschritt das an sich, dass er viel grösser ausschaut, als er wirklich ist."*[(15)] This scepticism towards oneself had become one of those philosophies which corroded the former Austro-Hungarian monarchy. It is significantly rendered by Nestroy : *"Ich glaub' von jedem Menschen das Schlechteste, selbst von mir, und ich hab' mich selten getäuscht."*[(16)] The Latin *"homo sum"* Nestroy translated succinctly: *"Ich bin halt ein Viechskerl."*[(17)] One can only endorse Alfred Polgar's dictum who once said : Nestroy's works are the finest monument ever put up to a people's natural mother-wit.

Considerable surprise was expressed in many quarters in 1919 that the honour of a Nobel Prize in literature had fallen to CARL SPITTELER, a poet who was then little known outside Switzerland. Even twenty years before he was hardly known in the German-speaking parts of Switzerland although the poet began to write in the heyday of Gottfried Keller who had early recognised the "untimeliness of his fiction". This "untimeliness" which pursued Spitteler throughout his life contributed much to his still not being a recognised notability today. Spitteler was a lonely poet, an individualistic postscript to the romanticism of the nineteenth century. It was not his fault that he strayed into a century where he tried to play the part of a new Pastor Brand and to demonstrate the right of a genius to be true to itself, even at the risk of drifting into a state of anti-social anarchy. Not until Nietzsche who sensed a kindred spirit, tried to establish Spitteler as "the finest of German aesthetic writers" did the poet succeed in publishing anything of what he had written.

Nietzsche owed clearly not a little to Spitteler who was taught by Jacob Burckhardt while a school boy in Basel. There are many affinities betweeen Spitteler's *Prometheus und Epimetheus* and Nietzsche's *Thus Spake Zarathustra*. "While Nietzsche is the thinker who seeks artistic symbols for ideas, Spitteler is, in the first instance, the artist who visualises and creates."[18] And as Spitteler regarded himself as a seer and leader—in this interpretation of the poet's mission not much unlike the German poet Stefan George—he refused to display the least understanding for the great literary movements of his own time. He derided unceasingly "the fanaticism of Panrealism, or Naturalism as a monstrous stupidity and narrow-mindedness". The social protest of the Naturalist pedants, their attempt "to increase the red corpuscles through burning questions, red flags and murderous strike actions" appeared to Spitteler only as a sort of mental and spiritual leukaemia. He openly mocked at those who tried "to exorcise the poetic diabetes through sweat and filth, dialectics and dynamite". He was considered to be disagreeable and troublesome, and the world learned to treat Spitteler as an outsider.

The epic was the congenial form of expression for Spitteler which enabled him to escape into realms of dream-like fantasies not unlike those quaint speculations of Jean Paul. But the difference between Jean Paul and Carl Spitteler displayed itself in the mere fact that the Swiss poet nurtured a very conscious "Weltanschauung", a pessimistic philosophy of a sad and ever declining world, as conveyed to him by the idols of his youth Schopenhauer and Burckhardt. Spitteler, as an acolyte of a religion without substance did not even believe in his own gods! He was consumed with an egotism which never met with satisfaction. He could tell the world much that was right but little that was true and lasting.

One is therefore somewhat puzzled to read that his main work, the epic poem *Olympischer Frühling,* was once considered to be the "Divine Comedy" of this century. In hindsight his novel *Imago* (1906) appears to be far more significant, as it turned out to be the first exemplary psycho-analytical description of the subconscious stirrings of the soul. While Jean Paul was able to permit his imagination to soar into the unlimited realms of imagination, Spitteler, very much contre-coeur, descended into the uncharted depths of experiences which he as little fathomed as Jean Paul could gauge the dimensions of his own rich fantasy. Carl Spitteler was a living anachronism in a time which permanently savoured a growing interest in experiencing the bed-rock of life, not in the mirror of a distorted imagination but rather as a hard fact of immediate, realistic experience.

NOTES AND TRANSLATIONS

1. viz. *Times Literary Supplement,* October 11, 1963.

2. Stefan George called Jean Paul "a father of impressionist art" in 1894.

3. viz. essay "Blick auf Jean Paul" (1913) in *Hugo von Hofmannsthal's Collected Works,* vol. Prose III (S. Fischer Verlag, 1952).

4. "A walking doom in a dressing-gown."

5. viz. essays "Jean Paul oder die Verlassenheit des Genius" and "Jean Paul in Frankreich" in Robert Minder's *Dichter in der Gesellschaft* (Insel Verlag, 1966).

6. viz. Roy Pascal, *The German Novel,* pp. 31, 298 (Manchester University Press, 1956).

7. viz. *Times Literary Supplement,* June 1, 1967.

8. Ibid.

9. "The world of positivism and naturalism, the phantom of a world becoming impenetrable, begins to dawn in all complexity through Hoffmann for the first time." viz. Paul Fechter *Geschichte der deutschen Literatur,* vol. I, p. 188 (Sigbert Mohn Verlag, 1960).

10. viz. Benno von Wiese, *Die deutsche Tragödie von Lessing bis Hebbel,* vol. II, pp. 237–308 (Hoffman & Campe, 1948).

11. viz Martin Esslin, *The Theatre of the Absurd,* p. 243 (Eyre & Spottiswoode, 1961).

12. I swear the beautiful oath, ever to be faithful
   to the Sublime Law, and will, devoted to
   the service and full of sacerdotal feelings,
   administer your noble office of a prophet
   August von Platen: *Die Morgenklage*

13. "Time may attack a poet's spiritual values, may age his ideas, but his art, the magic of mood, the gracefulness of his characters survive ... There are hours when men need the comfort of simplicity, peace, loyalty, perseverance, and of quietness, when art replaces prayers. Then such pious, heart-felt books are gladly welcome and smile consolation. Adalbert Stifter belongs to these guileless poets. Out of his simple heart, out of a narrow life in a poor country he has given us what will prove important and lasting." viz. *Gesammelte Werke,* p. XXIII (Weichert Verlag, 1899).

14. "this 'lingua Austriaca' is to the every-day language of old Austria as the negative to the positive because it reflects a deeply pessimistic analysis of world and soul." Otto Basil in *Nestroy,* p. 17 (Rowohl Verlag, 1967).

15. "Moreover this can be said about progress that it looks much bigger than it is in reality."

16. "I believe the worst of every man, including myself, and I have rarely been mistaken."

17. "I am just a scoundrel."

18. viz. *The Contemporary Review,* vol. CXIX, pp. 74–75.

Jean Paul

Jean Paul

by J. W. SMEED

Johann Paul Friedrich (he himself was to change the "Johann" into "Jean" out of admiration for Rousseau) was born in Wunsiedel in Upper Franconia on March 21, 1763, and spent his early years in small towns in that rather remote corner of Germany. His father, at Jean Paul's birth, schoolmaster and organist in Wunsiedel and later a clergyman, died in 1779, leaving the family in poverty. Years later, Jean Paul was to describe his environment in this early period of his life as a "spiritual Sahara Desert". However, from the age of thirteen onwards, he was able to borrow books from the friendly pastor of a neighbouring village, who possessed a large library. The young Jean Paul was an avid reader and came to know something at least about a startling variety of subjects, although his knowledge was haphazard and piecemeal. Between 1781 and 1784 he studied theology at the University of Leipzig, but not with any great application. By the time that poverty compelled him to discontinue his studies, he had anyway already made up his mind that he wanted to be an author, and in the following years supported himself with a number of jobs as private tutor in order to be able to write in his spare time.

On his mother's death in 1797, Jean Paul left the small town of Hof where the family had lived since 1779. In 1801, he married Karoline Mayer and three years later settled in Bayreuth, where he was to spend the rest of his life, and where most of his mature work was written. Jean Paul's last years were embittered by the suicide of his son Max in 1821, and he himself died on November 14, 1825.

I N his day one of the most idolised writers in Germany, and after his death one of the most imitated, Jean Paul has remained comparatively unknown in England, apart from a brief vogue in the nineteenth century, following Carlyle's attempts to popularise him here. The reasons are not far to seek : many of his best works are very long, they are all stylistically difficult and demand some patience and perseverance from the reader. But the rewards are correspondingly great. Jean Paul's output is very large : it includes six long novels, many shorter narrative works, comic character-studies and idylls, satires, visionary pieces, collections of aphorisms, and writings on aesthetics, politics and education. It is obviously not possible to give even a brief account of all these here, but I

31

have tried to discuss works which are representative of the various aspects of his creative writing. If I have given most space to his humorous works, this is because I think that they wear better than the sentimental ones.

Jean Paul's earliest published works were two collections of satires, *Grönländische Prozesse* (1783) and *Auswahl aus des Teufels Papieren* (1789). Both subject matter and method are borrowed from the English satirists of the eighteenth century, so that we find Jean Paul writing in a curiously unconvincing and artificial way, often about matters outside his experience. Studying Swift and Pope and their German imitators, he had come to believe that the art of satire consisted of developing and varying a theme by means of metaphors, witty analogies and the like. The more difficult and abstruse the comparisons and conceits, he felt, the better. No one would read these satires for pleasure nowadays; their importance lies in the fact that they helped to establish Jean Paul's characteristic wayward manner.

In the early 1790s, however, the sentimental side of Jean Paul's character asserted itself, and he wrote the two novels which first made him famous, the unfinished *Unsichtbare Loge* (1791–2) and *Hesperus* (1795). The key to an understanding of these novels is, I believe, to be found in an essay included as a digression (*Extrablatt*) in *Die unsichtbare Loge*. Entitled "Von hohen Menschen", this essay sets forth a totally unworldly ideal of personality and behaviour. *Der hohe Mensch* is characterised by "die Erhebung und der Unförmlichkeit zwischen unserem Herzen und unserem Orte über die Erde, das Gefühl der Geringfügigkeit alles irdischen Tuns ... den Wunsch des Todes und den Blick über die Wolken".[1]

Possessed by an ideal of transcendental perfection, he holds the pursuit of worldly success or satisfaction in contempt. Both *Die unsichbare Loge* and *Hesperus* present groups of "hohe Menschen", who are set off against more worldly characters. Ecstatic or elegiac scenes between the "hohe Menschen" contrast with the satirical treatment of courtiers and mercantile philistines. But it was, needless to say, neither these satirical elements nor the fantastic and complex plots of the two novels which made Jean Paul popular, but rather the scenes of idealised love and friendship between "hohe Menschen". Often such scenes involved music, which was for Jean Paul, as for the Romantics after him, the most intense and the purest of the arts and the one best able to give expression to man's spiritual yearnings. It is always the most "romantic" instruments that figure, flutes and horns, violas d'amore, glass-harmonicas and Aeolian harps. ... *Hesperus,* particularly, strikes the modern reader as almost morbidly sentimental and obsessed with death. The motto to the first volume gives the burden of the whole work : "Die Erde ist das Sackgäßchen in der großen Stadt Gottes ... wahrhaftig, sie ist fast gar nichts."[2]

The works of the middle period (*Siebenkäs*, 1796–97; *Titan*, 1800–3; *Flegeljahre*, 1804–5) curb both the luxuriant figurative style of the early satires and the excessive sentimentality of the novels just discussed.

Siebenkäs is the story of a lawyer, married to Lenette and living in poverty in the small town of *Kuhschnappel*. Lenette is completely bound by the values of her middle-class background. Respectability, social conformity and the need to keep up appearances "matter". She is in fact a living example of what Hebbel was later to declare to be the ruling characteristic of the middle classes : "Gebundenheit in der Einseitigkeit".[3] She cannot understand her husband's indifference to money, his careless attitude towards conventional standards or his devotion to an inner life of the imagination. Siebenkäs has in fact much of Jean Paul in him : the heightened sensibility, the wild and extravagant humour, the creative impulse. When he is planning to write a book, his creative exultation almost bursts the walls of their narrow home. At the same time, increasing poverty forces them to pawn various belongings, and this is a source of agony to Lenette in her struggle to keep up appearances. So the two gradually drift apart. *Siebenkäs* is Jean Paul's most realistic novel; one which, in its portrayal of the German *bourgeoisie,* anticipates the work of the nineteenth century novelists in many respects.

Titan is Jean Paul's *Entwicklungsroman,* his attempt to show an ideal of "harmonious" personality (in the Greek sense) and to demonstrate that the sublimity of the "hohe Menschen" was compatible with practical aptitude. As in all such novels, the ideal is contrasted with the less balanced attitudes towards life, manifested by a number of characters with whom the hero, Albano, comes into contact, and who influence his development—usually by virtue of being warning examples. Through them we can learn a great deal about Jean Paul's attitude towards various trends in the Germany of his day. In the figure of Gaspard he attacks the aristocratic coldness and the over-emphasis on purely aesthetic values which, as he thought, characterised Weimar Classicism. In Schoppe, he expresses his antagonism to the Idealist philosophy of Fichte and to Romantic subjectivity in general. Fichte's philosophy said—or seemed to say— that the world of objects exists only by virtue of being posited by the Ego. Schoppe studies Fichte and gradually comes to feel himself to be living in a world of shadows, surrounded only by the projections of his own consciousness :

> Gern sei er vor dem Spiegel gesessen und habe sich in ein langes Gespräch mit sich eingelassen; zuweilen hab' er in die *camera obscura* gesehen, dann schnell wieder in die Gegend, um beide fenden regen Bilder der *camera* würden von der äußern Welt zu vergleichen, und habe unoptisch genug behauptet, die lau-vergrößert, aber täuschend nachgeäfft.[4]

He ends in madness—the madness of extreme subjectivity which, Jean Paul held, was one of the trends which threatened balance and sanity in his age. Another aspect of Romantic subjectivity is attacked through the figure of Roquairol, described by Jean Paul as "Kind und Opfer des Jahrhunderts".[5] Jean Paul felt that the cult of feeling was a disease of the day, that young men ran through the gamut of emotional experiences at too early an age, so that the sensibilities became jaded and the search for new experiences ever more frantic. All this applies to Roquairol : emotionally precocious, he deliberately whips up his feelings, anticipating events in his imagination, so that actual events disappoint him and ever-stronger emotional stimuli become necessary. At the same time, since this cult of the feelings is so deliberate and conscious, Roquairol is a witness to his own emotions and thus robs them of all spontaneity and immediacy. Jean Paul expresses all this symbolically by describing Roquairol's life as a play, and Roquairol himself as an actor playing a part. This part culminates in suicide : while acting in a play which deals with his own situation, Roquairol shoots himself.

Thus *Titan* already shows the extent to which Jean Paul was out of tune with his age. In his later years, he grew disillusioned and apathetic. His marriage had become progressively more jogtrot, he felt increasingly out of touch with new trends in German literature and thought and began to doubt the value of his own work. One finds frequent evidence of this growing resignation in the years from 1806 on :

> 1806 : "... da das Beste von mir vollendet ist : so kann mir's gleichgültig sein, was ich noch auf der Erde zu tun haben soll."

> 1815 : "Ich denke eigentlich jetzo nicht an den Tod, ich bin schon gestorben."

> 1816 : "Meine innigsten Freuden und Leiden hab' ich jetzo nur in den Träumen."[6]

To this period belongs a group of remarkable comic novels, all of which joke bravely about this disillusionment (*Schmelzle*, 1807 *Doktor Katzenbergers Badereise*, 1809; *Fibel*, 112; *Der Komet*, 1812–22).

The wittiest and the most famous of these comic novels is *Doktor Katzenbergers Badereise*. The plot is, by Jean Paul's standards, simple, resting on the sort of mistaken identity which has furnished writers with comic situations through the ages. The celebrated poet and dramatist Theudobach (whose real name is Nieß) is travelling to the spa of Maulbronn to give a public reading from his works. He shares a coach with Katzenberger and the doctor's daughter, Theoda, who has written to him in admiration of his works; he has hopes of a romance. He travels under his real name, representing himself as a friend of the author Theudobach and promising himself a dramatic and emotionally titillating scene when he finally reveals his true identity to Theoda. But in Maulbronn there is another Theudobach, an army officer, and also an author (he has written on mathematics and fortifications). Never having heard of Theudobach the poet, he denounces poor Nieß as an impostor. Theoda, who feels that she has been cheated by her poet-hero—although in fact she has only been deluded by her own romantic daydreams—turns her back on Nieß and falls in love with the officer instead. Nieß has certain characteristics which were quite foreign to Jean Paul's nature : an egregious vanity and a romantic admiration for a misty Teutonic past (the title of his main work is : *Ritter einer größeren Zeit*). But in one way he reflects an important truth about Jean Paul himself. Theoda's expectations concerning Theudobach as a person are, of course, based on his works, and Nieß' physical appearance and his behaviour by no means meet these expectations. Some visitors to Bayreuth recorded their disappointment on finding that the author of *Hesperus* and *Titan* put them in mind more of a brewer or an innkeeper than of an intense and enthusiastic novelist. In fact, a few years after the publication of *Katzenberger*, the Theoda–Theudobach comedy was played out in real life, but with a tragic ending. In 1813, Jean Paul received four passionate love letters from Marianne Lux, a girl twenty four years his junior. His attempts to calm her and to persuade her that his only possible attitude towards her was one of fatherly affection were unsuccessful, and Marianne committed suicide in May 1814. One result of Jean Paul's setting up lofty ideals of friendship and love, as in *Hesperus*, was that his readers tended to demand similar emotional responses from him, expecting reality to live up to the ideals of fiction and the man to the author. How do you picture Theudobach to yourself? asks Nieß, still sheltering behind his anonymity, and Theoda replies

naively : "Wie die edleren Geschöpfe dieses Schöpfers selber."[7] The
discomfiture of Nieß can thus be taken as a wry admission of the
extent to which real life lags behind the ideal. But romantic idealism
is still more devastatingly attacked through the figure of Doctor
Katzenberger himself.

Katzenberger is Jean Paul's most brilliant character-study, representing the *reductio ad absurdum* of the scientific attitude. Everything is regarded by him purely from the scientific—usually the
medical—point of view. Science is his way of life, his obsession. His
interest in monsters and abortions is so intense that he almost regrets
that his daughter was born normal! Even aesthetic experiences are
evaluated according to ruthlessly utilitarian and physiological con-
siderations : comedy is to be preferred to tragedy because laughter
is more beneficial to health than is sorrow.[8] Traditional romantic
clichés are quickly disposed of :

> "Bei der Trennung von Ihrer Geliebten mag Ihnen doch im
> Mondscheine das Herz schwer geworden sein?" sagte der Edel-
> mann. "Zwei Pfund—also halb so schwer als meine Haut—ist
> meines wie Ihres bei Mond—und bei Sonnenlicht schwer,"
> versetzte der Doktor.[9]

Yet it would be wrong to regard Katzenberger solely as a grotesque character-study of a fanatical man of science. Behind the caricature there is a serious point which Jean Paul is concerned to
make. This becomes clear during Katzenberger's passionate defence
of his favourite study, that of abortions and monsters :

> Gerade die Weise, wie die Natur zufällige Durchkreuzungen und
> Aufgaben . . . doch organisch aufzulösen weiß, dies belehrt. Sagen
> Sie mir nicht, daß Mißgeburten nicht bestehen, als widernatür-
> lich; jede mußte einmal natürlich sein, sonst hätte sie nicht bis
> zum Leben und Erscheinen bestanden. . . . Alles Leben, auch nur
> *einer* Minute, hat ewige Gesetzte hinter sich . . .[10]

The study of the "eternal laws" which govern organic life is a
religion for Katzenberger :

> Die Wissenschaft ist etwas so Großes als die Religion—für jene
> sollte man ebensogut Mut und Blut daransetzen als für
> diese . . .[11]

Thus it is not wholly parodistic when Jean Paul applies the word
"feurig" to Katzenberger's medical tirades; the implication is that
the poets and tragedians have no monopoly of ardent feelings. In
passages such as the two just quoted, we suddenly realise that this

preposterous figure is also a personification of the purest and most intense intellectual curiosity. Thus *Doktor Katzenbergers Badereise* represents the most drastic inversion of the *Hesperus*-world which it would be possible to imagine : poetic idealism withers in the climate of Katzenberger's utilitarian objectivity, and the poet is jilted in favour of the mathematician!

Jean Paul's style is unmistakable. Let us listen to him for a moment on this very point concerning the abandonment of youthful idealism :

> Die Menschen, nämlich die edleren unter ihnen, haben wie bisher fortgefahren, sich von den Insekten zu unterscheiden, welche in der jungen Zeit als Raupen nur rohes Kraut genießen, sich an Blumen aber erst entpuppt in älterer als Schmetterlinge hängen, indem ungekehrt solche Menschen schon in der Jugend nach den süssen Blumen der sittlichen Ideale durstig fliegen, und erst nach der Entpuppung im gesetzten Alter auf den Krautblättern der etwas unsittlichen Gemeinheit kriechen und kauen.[12]

From Sterne he had learnt to prefer a meandering and digressive way of telling a story to any sort of straight and direct narrative. He plays games with the reader, teases him. He plays too with language itself, inventing new words and compounds, often in comic analogy to existing words : *Zweisiedler, Spätstück* (= "spätes Frühstück"), *Unrechtsgelehrte, Unheilkünstler.* He composes in figures of speech ("Noch kein Autor hat so oft 'wie' oder 'gleich' hingeschrieben als ich.").[13] From being a deliberately cultivated manner in the earliest works, this figurative style became natural to Jean Paul; he thought, wrote and talked in figures of speech. His pages are full of witty analogies and allusions from his encyclopedic reading. Relationships are discovered between apparently quite *un*related sets of objects or phenomena :

> Das Haus von Schleunes war ein offner Buchladen, dessen Werke (die Töchter) man da lesen, aber nicht nach Hause nehmen konnte. Obgleich die fünf andern Töchter in fünf Privatbibliotheken als Weiber standen, ... so waren doch in diesem Töchter-Handelhaus noch drei Freiexemplare für gute Freunde feil.[14]

Schiller had an interesting comment to make on Jean Paul after meeting him in Jena in 1796 :

> Ich habe ihn ziemlich gefunden, wie ich ihn erwartete; fremd wie einer, der aus dem Mond gefallen ist, voll guten Willens und

herzlich geneigt, die Dinge außer sich zu sehen, nur nicht mit dem Organ, Womit man sieht.[15]

Jean Paul looks at the world with tremendous eagerness, as if constantly fascinated and elated by what he finds, but he does indeed see it as if he were from another planet and had different organs of perception, ignoring the obvious links and causal relationships that the rest of us would see, and instead bringing the most disparaging things together (through metaphor, allusion, etc.), rearranging the objects of our familiar world into new patterns which shock us out of acceptance and force us to re-examine each thing or event in the light of the comparisons, implicit or explicit, which Jean Paul makes. "Das ist große Kunst: da ist nichts selbstverständlich",[16] we might be tempted to say, borrowing from Brecht.

Jean Paul hoards up all the potentially comic or incongruous data which come his way. Life, he seems to say, is so funny that one hardly needs to invent. When Katzenberger is provoked to reminisce about a youthful romance, his tale reaches its climax with:

> Sie antwortete gerührt: wird Er immer so an mich denken, Amandus? Ich versetzte wild: Beim Henker! an uns beide; wohin ich künftig auch verschlagen und verfahren werde, und in welchen fernen Fluß und Bach ich auch einst schauen werde— es sei in die Schweina in Meiningen—oder in die Besau und die Gesau im Henneberg—oder in die wilde Sau in Böhmen—oder in die Wampfe in Lüneberg—oder in den Lumpelbach in Salzburg— oder in die Sterzel in Tirol—oder in die Kratza oder in den Galgenbach in der Oberpfalz—in welchen Bach ich, schwör' ich dir, künftig schauen werde, stets werd' ich darin mein Gesicht erblicken und dadurch auf deines kommen, das so oft an meinem gewesen, Suse.[17]

The comic effect depends of course on the list of rivers and streams, every name a studied affront to his listener's romantic expectations. But the point I wish to make here is that Jean Paul did not have to invent any one of these names; he was able to find the raw material for this particular comic scene in a popular geographical compilation of the day (J. E. Fabri's *Geographie für alle Stände*, 1786). This is not of course to say that Jean Paul is not a highly imaginative writer, merely to suggest that his imaginative activity most commonly consists of presenting things from the world around him in fresh combinations. The preference is always for the out-of-the-way, the truth-is-stranger-than-fiction type of fact. It is typical that, in the short comic novel *Schmelzle,* the *sole* piece of information concerning canaries is that they could be trained to fire off tiny cannons, and that the *sole* reference to hamsters is to their ferocity in (allegedly) threatening even horses when provoked. It may be noted here that popular and semipopular works on natural history, geography, travel, biography etc. in the eighteenth century were full of such odd titbits of information. It is as if, in the century of Rationalism, men, having thrown out the supernatural, needed to seek imaginative satisfaction in the "strange-but-true" type of fact or anecdote.

Yet to concentrate on the comic and fantastic elements in Jean Paul's style is to tell only half the story. His works contain some of the most highly-charged passages of rhythmic prose in German literature. The mood may be ecstatic or elegiac. Such passages are commonest in the early novels, where, as already mentioned, friendship and love had been treated in near-mystical terms.

> Aus welcher unsichtbaren Hand, dacht' er schauernd, gehen diese Töne, die von Engeln abzugleiten scheinen, wenn sie über die zweite Welt fliegen, von vereinigten Seelen, wenn eine zu große Wonne sich zum Seufzer ausatmet und der Seufzer sich in verwehtes Getön zerlegt? Es ist ihm zu vergeben, daß er an einem solchen Tage, der seine Seele in immer größere Erschütterungen stezte, in diesem Schauder der Nacht, unter diesem melodischen Trauerbaum, an diesem Allerheiligsten des unsichtbaren Emanuels, daß er endlich glaubte, dieser sei an diesem Abend aus dem Leben geflohen, und seine Seele voll Liebe fliege noch in diesen Echos um ihn und sehne sich nach der ersten und letzten Umarmung.[18]

This, oversentimental as it seems to modern taste, is what aroused the enthusiasm of Jean Paul's readers in the 1790s.

In fact the two contrasting styles, the comic and the ecstatic, reflect the contrasting sides of Jean Paul's character. Seldom can a writer have been so obsessed with the dualism of thought and feeling, soul and body, temporal and eternal. ... As has been mentioned, the early novels depend on such contrasts for their very construction. Work after work explores various manifestations of the dualism which, for Jean Paul, characterised mortal life. Many of his most typical and recurring images reflect this obsession. Earthly life is represented as a masked ball, a slave-ship, a "Plato's cave". Human activities are likened to children's games, and man's emergence after death into the *zweite Welt* to the emergence of a butterfly from the chrysalis. Music images, and motifs based on the contrast of light and darkness abound, with all their traditional meta-physical or even mystical associations. This dualistic interpretation of the world affects Jean Paul's characterisation quite radically. Man can turn his back on the world (as do the "hohe Menschen") or he can pursue worldly ends, extinguishing the divine spark within himself. (A few of his characters, however, have a naïve innocence and contentment which make them unaware of any conflict between the real and ideal; these can find happiness in a limited sphere, without even knowing that it *is* limited : this point is made in Jean Paul's most famous idyll, *Leben des vergnügten Schulmeisterlein Maria Wutz.*) A burlesque account of the warring elements in man's nature is to be found in the short satire "Die Doppeltgänger" (in the comic appendix to *Titan.*) This satire deals with a pair of Siamese twins. One, Peter, is conscientious, methodical, but philistine; the other, Seraph, is "ein Tragikus, Lyrikus, Fagotist, Epigrammatist und Genie wie nur wenige".[19] The conflicting demands made by the practical and the poetic sides of man's nature are comically resolved here : each of the twins "rules" on alternate days.

The same idea is worked out more elaborately in the unfinished novel, *Die Flegeljahre.* Walt, the hero, is left a large fortune on condition that he carry out a number of tasks and activities which had formed part of the legator's own early experiences. These are a curious lot : Walt must spend a day tuning pianos, a month as a gardener, three months as a notary, and so on. The intention of the legator, Van der Kabel, in setting Walt to re-enact these experiences is clear enough : Walt is described in the will as an unpractical and idealistic poet, and to fulfil the conditions of the legacy will—or ought to—enable him the better to cope with the practical demands of life. He has a twin brother, Vult, as far as character is concerned, is his opposite, realistic and satirical where Walt is dreamy and trusting. He endeavours throughout to open Walt's eyes to realities, to assist him in his tasks and to protect him against the cupitity and treachery of his fellow-men. But in vain; Vult's insights into the shady aspects of human nature seem merely cynical and unjust to Walt (O Gott, Vult! ... kann der Sterbliche so hart richten?"),[20] and Vult bitterly concedes failure : "dem redlichen, nicht ganz viehdummen Bruder glaubt der Poet weniger als weichem Diebsgesindel ..."[21] The word "weich" is important : Walt's feelings have been played upon and, against this, Vult's reasoned arguments are powerless. So, through the figures of Walt and Vult, Jean Paul has given form to contrasting aspects of human nature. It is significant that the work is unfinished, and that

Walt shows little sign of having learnt much from experience. Indeed, the novel breaks off at a moment where Vult has clearly given his brother up as a hopeless case. The tensions between the two sets of impulses in man are irresolvable : this seems to be the message of the *Flegeljahre*. It is clear that this novel, and even "Die Doppeltgänger", owe much of their force to the fact that Jean Paul is satirising himself; he too was made up of such irreconcilable contrasts. He despised the world as a gross insult to our idealistic yearnings for transcendental perfection—and yet settled in Bayreuth because of the beer ! It is amusing to note that, at a festive meal in Heidelberg in 1817 in Jean Paul's honour, the professors' wives were treated not to a learned or poetic discourse, but to a panegyric on sauerkraut. Jean Paul was Peter *and* Seraph, Walt *and* Vult. As many critics have pointed out, if he had been able to resolve the contradictions within himself, he might have led a happier life—but he could not have written the *Flegeljahre*.

The conflicts within man are, for Jean Paul, ultimately metaphysical in nature; they are due to "die Unförmlichkeit zwischen unserem Herzen und unserem Orte". (Walt acts as he does because he still expects reality to conform to the ideal; Vult acts as *he* does because he knows that it won't.) The only thing which can reconcile us to the failings of life on earth is humour : "Der Humor . . . vernichtet . . . das Endliche durch den Kontrast mit der Idee."[22] That is to say : humour makes finite existence bearable by showing its infinite distance from transcendental perfection as something comic. (This view of humour was later taken up by Heine, and in this country by Coleridge, of course, who paraphrases Jean Paul on humour more than once.) There are many characters in Jean Paul's novels who illustrate this attitude, who reject human dignities and pretensions as ridiculous and mock them through words and actions. The world is a madhouse, says Siebenkäs to Lenette, in the course of one of his tirades against conspicuous consumption :

> Du sitzest hinter deinem Nähkissen und kannst nicht sehen, daß die Menschen toll sind und schon Kaffee, Tee und Schokolade aus besondern Tassen, Früchte, Salate und Heringe aus eignen Tellern, und Hasen, Fische und Vögel aus eignen Schüsseln ver-speisen—Sie werden aber künftig, sag' ich dir, noch toller werden und in den Fabriken so viele Fruchtschalen bestellen, als in den Gärten Obstarten abfallen . . .[23]

—the point being that the difference between the highest and the lowest, the richest and the poorest, the most pretentious and the least, is reduced to vanishing point as soon as we compare *any* aspect of reality, *any* human achievement, dignity or possession, with the ideal. Or here is Vult on philistine attitudes towards music :

> Denn wie besonders Musik entheiligt wird . . . das höre! Tafelmusik lass' ich noch gelten . . .; von verfluchten verruchten Hofkonzerten . . . red' ich gar nicht vor Grimm . .; aber das ist Jammer, daß ich in Konzertsälen, wo doch jeder bezahlt, mit solchem Rechte erwarte, er werde für sein Geld etwas empfinden wollen; allein ganz umsonst. Sondern damit das Klingen aufhöre ein paarmal und endlich ganz,—deswegen geht der Narr hinein. Hebt noch etwas den Spießbürger empor am Ohr, so ists zwei—, höchstens dreierlei : (1) wenn aus einem halbtoten Pianissimo plötzlich ein Fortissimo wie ein Rebhuhn aufknattert, (2) wenn einer, besonders mit dem Geigenbogen, auf dem höchsten Seile der höchsten Töne lange tanzt und rutscht und nun kopfunter in die tiefsten herunterklatscht, (3) wenn gar beides vorfällt. In solchen Punkten ist der Bürger seiner nicht mehr mächtig, sondern schwitzt vor Lob.[24]

Vult, incensed and embittered by this prostitution of what for him is the highest of the arts, seeks both revenge and refuge in mockery.

But Jean Paul's concept of *Humor* is best illustrated by his last two novels, *Fibel* and *Der Komet*. The idea for *Fibel* was suggested to Jean Paul by an ABC-book with crude rhymes accompanied by equally crude woodcuts. Why not write an imaginary and satirical biography of the author? We read of Fibel's childhood and of his desire to be a writer. He attains fame through his ABC-book and is easily persuaded by a friend that he is a great author. But in old age he realises his folly and vanity, and retires from the world to live as a hermit : "Es ist mir jetzo vieles auf der Erde gleichgültig, ausgenommen der Himmel darüber . . ."[25]

The hero of *Der Komet*, Nikolaus Marggraf, is brought up as the son of a chemist, but, when he presently learns that he is in fact the illegitimate son of a prince, he sets out to seek his real father. He takes to using the Royal We, raises his friends to positions of high-sounding dignity, and aspires to a form of life appropriate to his new station. But all he achieves is a grotesque travesty of princely splendour. Thus the humour of these two works does indeed "annihilate" finite pretensions. For in them Jean-Paul suggests, if only obliquely, that the proudest achievements of the human spirit are, *sub specie aeternitatis*, no more significant than a ridiculous book of rhymes for children, and that worldly pomp is fundamentally as irrelevant to man's true nature and destiny as is Nikolaus' would-be splendour to *his* real nature. If this is so, if nothing in mortal life is other than paltry and ridiculous when compared with the ideal, the only thing left to do is to laugh.

Jean Paul is a writer of extremes. His most grotesque fancies can make the modern Theatre of the Absurd seem tame, his play with narrative form makes even Sterne seem almost straightforward. His books contain a gallery of eccentrics, comparable with those to be met with in the pages of Peacock or Dickens. (Keller and Raabe are both indebted to him, but their invention is a good deal less exuberant.) Various attempts have been made to hit on a formula which would give some idea of Jean Paul's manner. Goethe labelled his genius "oriental", measuring it against the restraint and formalism of the classical ideal. Many critics have implied something similar by applying the word "baroque" to him, and in fact the profusion of decorative detail, the artificial conceits, the apparent desire to accommodate the whole of knowledge and experience between the covers of a single work, and to show possible links between any and all phenomena and concepts—all this does show an affinity with the Baroque writers, especially in Germany. More recently, Wolfdietrich Rasch has compared Jean Paul to a one-man band.

As for Jean Paul's influence : virtually all aspects of his work have been imitated at some time or another, especially during the first half of the nineteenth century, when writer after writer fell under his spell. In my opinion, it is the comic Jean Paul who has had the most lasting influence and who is likely to find most readers today. But Jean Paul's Dreams, too, have aroused great interest in a century which has seen the systematic investigation of the human unconscious and the vogue of Surrealism ... These Dreams are attempts to express in visionary form Jean Paul's central metaphysical preoccupations : the desire for mystical union with God, the nature of the afterlife, the struggle between doubt and faith.[26] Like the mystics, Jean Paul often resorts to paradox to express the ultimate and inexpressible. Here (from the last chapter of the *Flegeljahre*) is his variation on the ancient mystical idea that everything finite is merely the echo of an inaudible (divine) tone :

> ... vernimm das alte Widerhallen; noch kein Wesen hat den Ton gehört, den es nachspricht. Wenn aber einst der Widerhall aufhört, so ist die Zeit vorbei, und die Ewigkeit kommt

zurück und bringt den Ton; sobald alles sehr still ist, so werd'
ich die drei Stummen hören, ja den Urstummen, der das älteste
Märchen sich selber erzählt . . .[27]

—Realities incomprehensible to man are expressed in terms of
tones inaudible to human ears. The silence which so often settles
over the mystic's attempt to describe his most ineffable experiences,
and the witty chatter through which Vult and Schoppe try to keep
their *Weltschmerz* at bay : these are the extremes between which
Jean Paul's writings move.

TRANSLATIONS

1. Elevation above the earth, a conviction of the triviality of all earthly
activities and of the lack of accord between our heart and our station . . .
a wish for death and a glance that ranges above the clouds (*Sämtliche
Werke* (SW), ii, 209 f.).
2. Earth is the *cul de sac* in God's great city . . . in truth, it is almost
nothing.
3. Being shackled by narrowness of outlook.
4. He used to like sitting in front of the mirror and having long conversations with himself; sometimes he would look into the *camera
obscura* and then quickly at his surroundings again to compare the two,
and maintained in defiance of optics that the external world enlarged
the moving pictures of the *camera*, but distorted them (SW. ix, 322).
5. Child of the century, and its victim.
6. i: As my best achievements are behind me, it is a matter of indifference to me what I still have to do on earth.
ii: I do not think of death now; I am already dead.
iii: My most fervent joys and sorrows come now only in dreams.
(Wahrheit, ii, 136, 138).
7. Like the nobler creations of this creator himself (SW. xiii, 113).
8. SW. xiii, 206 f.
9. "When you parted from your beloved, was not your heart heavy in
the moonlight?" asked the nobleman. "Two pounds—that is, half as
heavy as my skin—is the weight of my heart and yours in moonlight or
sunlight," replied the doctor. (SW. xiii, 108).
10. It is precisely the way in which nature always finally manages
to find an organic solution to every biological abnormality or problem
which is instructive. Don't tell me that monsters do not survive because
they are unnatural. Each must have been natural once, or it would not
have survived up to the moment when it appeared alive . . . All life, if
only of a moment's duration, has eternal laws behind it (SW. xiii, 117).

11. Science is every bit as great as religion—and one should be just as ready to stake body and soul on it (SW. xiii, 283).

12. Men—of the nobler sort, that is—continue as before to differ from the insects which as caterpillars in their early life feed on raw cabbage leaves and only later, when they have turned into butterflies, alight to feed on flowers; for on the contrary such men fly thirstily after the sweet flowers of moral ideals while still young, and only when they emerge into old age do they crawl about on, and feed off, the cabbage leaves of ordinary life—which is not specially moral (SW. xvii, 429).

13. Never has an author written "as" or "like" as often as I have.

14. Schleunes' house was a bookshop, where one could read the works (the daughters), but not take them home. Although the five other daughters stood as wives in five private libraries, there were still in this daughter-trading-house three copies going cheap for good friends (SW. iii, 323).

15. I found him more or less as I expected: as strange as a visitor from the moon, full of good will and eager and ready to look at things around him, but not with the organ with which people usually look at things (letter to Goethe, 28/6/1796).

16. That is great art; there nothing is self-evident.

17. She replied with emotion: "Will you always think of me like this, Amandus?" I answered wildly: "Yes, by the devil! of both of us; wherever life may cast me about and convey me in the future, and in whatever distant river or stream I may happen to look, whether it is the Schweina in Meiningen . . . (the list of comic names follows) . . . whatever stream I may look into in the future, I swear to you that I will always see my face reflected there and thereby come to think of yours, which has so often been pressed against mine, Suse" (SW. xiii, 97).

18. From what invisible hand, he wondered with a shudder, do these notes proceed, which seem to glide down from angels as they fly across the other world, from united souls, when too great an ecstacy breathes itself out in a sigh and the sigh melts into scattered notes of music? He may be forgiven if, on a day which had transported his soul into ever more violent emotions, in this night of awe, under this melodious weeping willow, at this most holy spot of the invisible Emanuel, he finally came to believe that Emanuel had parted life on this very evening and that his soul, filled with love, was flying around him in these echoes, yearning for the first and last embrace (SW. iii, 197 f).

19. A tragedian, lyric poet, bassoonist, writer of epigrams and a genius rivalled by few (SW. viii, 246).

20. Oh Heavens, Vult! can mortal man judge so harshly?

21. The poet believes his honest and not altogether stupid brother less than a sentimental band of thieves (SW. x, 375).

22. Humour annihilates the finite through the contrast with the Idea (SW. xi, 112).

23. You sit behind your sewing-cushion and cannot see that men are mad, and already drink coffee, tea and chocolate out of special cups,

fruit, salad and herrings off particular plates, and hares, fish and poultry from particular dishes. But in the future, I tell you, they will become even madder, and will order as many different kinds of fruit dishes from the factory as there are kinds of fruit falling off the trees in the orchard (SW. vi, 160).

24. For listen how music in particular is profaned! Table-music I will allow; accursed, infamous concerts at court I will pass over altogether out of sheer rage; but it is a crying shame that—in concert halls, where everyone has paid to come in after all, and I expect with some justification that he will want to feel some emotion for his money—my hopes are all in vain. All the fool wants is for the music to stop a few times, and for it finally to stop altogether. And if there is anything which makes the philistine prick up his ears, it is two things or at the most three. (1) When from a half-extinct pianissimo a fortissimo clatters up like a partridge, (2) when a player, especially on the violin, dances and slips about for a long time on the tightrope of the highest string and then tumbles head over heels onto the lowest notes, (3) when both things happen at once. In moments like this, the honest citizen is no longer in command of his emotions, but sweats in admiration (SW. x, 182 f).

25. Now much on earth is indifferent to me, apart from the heavens above it (SW. xiii, 508).

26. Cf. J. W. Smeed, *Jean Paul's Dreams*, O.U.P., 1966.

27. Listen to the ancient echo; no being has ever heard the tone which it repeats. But when the echo ceases, time is past, and eternity returns and brings the tone with it. As soon as everything is very still, I shall hear the three silent ones, even the original silent one who recounts to himself the oldest tale of all ... (SW. x, 477. For a detailed interpretation of this passage, see *Jean Paul's Dreams*, pp. 98 f).

BIBLIOGRAPHY

Works: The critical edition of Jean Paul's works is: *Sämtliche Werke*, Historisch-kritische Ausgabe, hrsg. von der Preußischen Akademie der Wissenschaften ... Hrsg. E. Berend ... Weimar, 1927 ff.

1. Abteilung: Zu Lebzeiten des Dichters erschienene Werke.
2. Abteilung: Nachlaß.
3. Abteilung: Briefe.

Quoted as *SW*. All quotations are from the "1. Abteilung", and have been slightly modernised.

Bibliography: E. Berend, *Jean-Paul-Bibliographie*, neu bearbeitet und ergänzt von J. Krogoll, Stuttgart, 1963.

Secondary Literature

H. Alker, *Jean Paul: Wandel seines Bildes in der Kritik* (Diss.), Wien, 1946.

J. Alt, *Jean Paul,* Munich, 1925.

H. Bach, *Jean Paul's Hesperus* (= "Palästra" 166, 1929).

J. Czerny, *Stern, Hippel und Jean Paul,* Berlin, 1904.

B. Emrich, *Jean Pauls Wirkung im Biedermeier* (Diss.) Tübingen, 1949.

E. Förster (ed.), *Denkwürdigkeiten aus dem Leben von Jean Paul Friedrich Richter,* Munich, 1863 (4 vols.).

W. Harich, *Jean Paul,* Leipzig, 1925.

W. Hoppe, *Das Verhältnis Jean Pauls zur Philosophie seiner Zeit* (in *Neue Jahrbücher f.d. klass. Altertum, Geschichte, und die Literatur, und f. Pädagogik,* 4 Jg., 1901).

M. Kommerell, *Jean Paul,* Frankfurt a/M, 1933.

W. Krauss, *Das Doppelgängermotiv in der Romantik* (= *Germanische Studien* 99, 1930).

H. Meyer, *Der Sonderling in der deutschen Dichtung,* Munich, 1963.

C. Otto and E. Förster (ed.), *Wahrheit aus Jean Pauls Leben,* Breslau, 1826–33 (8 Heftlein). Quoted as *Wahrheit.*

W. Rasch, *Die Erzählweise Jean Pauls,* Munich, 1961.

R. Rohde, *Jean Pauls Titan* (= "Palästra" 105, 1920).

F. J. Schneider, *Jean Pauls Altersdichtung,* Berlin, 1901.

Clemens Brentano

Clemens Brentano

by IAN HILTON

Clemens Brentano was born on September 9, 1778, in Ehrenbreitstein and was one of a large family. He studied in Halle and Jena, where he completed his first major work *Godwi* (1801). Together with Arnim and Görres he founded the so-called Heidelberg school of Romantics, and with Arnim was responsible for *Des Knaben Wunderhorn* (1806–8). At this time too he started composing his *Märchen*. The subsequent years were rather unsettled and he travelled widely, to Berlin, Prague, Vienna, Munich, etc. About 1816 a spiritual crisis induced a fervent return to the Catholic Church, and he spent years at the bedside of the stigmatised nun Katherina Emmerich, whose visions he duly recorded. He died on July 28, 1842, in Aschaffenburg.

> "Selig, wer ohne Sinne
> Schwebt, wie ein Geist auf dem Wasser,
>
> . . . .
>
> So auch der Sänger."[1]

> "Wir hatten nichts genährt als die
> Phantasie, und sie hatte uns teils
> wieder aufgefressen."[2]

IN an age of fascinating personalities Clemens Brentano was one of the more colourful figures to burst forth upon the rapidly changing European scene at the start of the nineteenth century. Through friendship and marriage he was connected with leading figures of the day in many walks of life. His mother was the Maximiliane Laroche who had attracted the young Goethe on his return from Wetzlar in 1772 and through family connections Clemens too came within the orbit of the poet prince and the world of Wieland. As friends he counted Arnim and Savigny (these as brothers-in-law too), Schinkel, Görres, the brothers Grimm, Eichendorff; he was in the same club as Kleist, Adam Müller, Fouqué; was tolerated, even if not fully accepted in the literary circle of the Schlegels and Tieck; met Beethoven and Wordsworth. Today, a century and a quarter later, Brentano is remembered primarily for his co-compilation of *Des Knaben Wunderhorn,* some lyric verse and a few tales (the most familiar introduction for students to Brentano being *via Geschiohte vom braven Kasperl und dem schönen Annerl*).

Between son and father, an Italian merchant who had settled in Frankfurt, a certain tension existed because of the latter's attitude towards the mother, to whom Clemens felt very close. Both parents died before he was twenty, the death of his mother leaving him in despair. The need for understanding in the light of these circumstances—the search for love and security of the kind associated with the family unit—was Brentano's life-long problem. It helps to explain his ultimately unsatisfactory relationships with various women including Sophie Mereau (who was ideally to act as *virgo, sponsa* and *mater*) on the one hand and his reliance, on the other, on stronger, independent men like Arnim and Savigny. But friendship was not sufficient for Brentano, to be tolerated (as in the Schlegel circle) far from adequate.

> "Ich habe viele gute Freunde (he wrote to Antonie Brentano), aber sie sind es nur wegen meines äussern Wesens, ins Innere kann die Freundschaft niemals blicken, da reicht nur die Liebe hin, ohne zu verwunden."[3]

And love on his uncompromising terms Brentano was never really to find. His own subjectivism merely heightened the complexity and anguish of his search. "Dieser unversöhnliche Kampf mit dem eigenen Dämon war die eigentliche Geschichte seines Lebens und Dichtens," Eichendorff was to recall[4] and his picture of Brentano as a volatile, erratic and capricious man is well known and borne out by the opinions of others who came across him. Thus, Henry Crabb Robinson, who first met Brentano in 1801, described him as

> "a man of rather soft and engaging appearance and manneri and very agreeable when he pleased, but was intensely self-willed. His habits were those of an idle man indulging his own wayward fancies, constantly joking, punning and playing on the lute. He was not malignant, but utterly regardless of the feelings of others."[5]

Indeed, he was no respecter of persons, even friends, which alienated some. Fools he did not suffer gladly or silently, and his attitude to the philistine is manifested—almost *ad nauseam*—in such satires as *Der Philister vor, in und nach der Geschichte*.

Brentano grew up in an age of political uncertainty and unrest following the French Revolution. His time at Heidelberg, Berlin and Vienna undoubtedly awakened his patriotic consciousness. In Berlin he joined the *Christliche-Deutsche Tischgesellschaft*, founded by Arnim and Adam Müller in 1811, a time when, Crabb Robinson records, "the people of Germany are still inveterate against the French. In Berlin the popular feeling was strong and decided".[6] But though he expressed envy of Arnim and his activities,[7] he himself hesitated to actively participate in the subsequent Napoleonic Wars apart from writing some patriotic verse (*e.g.* Soldatenlied") and *Festspiele*. Equally not for Brentano was the routine of commercial life which could have frustrated his powers of inventiveness—already evident from an early age. His reaction to everyday life comes out in his artistic yearnings. In 1804 he lamented to Arnim[8] that he had not composed a line for a year and talks of his "poetischen Tod"—and that but a bare twelve month after his marriage to Sophie Mereau, a marriage which he avowed at the time, would, far from imposing limitations upon him, free him and bring order to his life of discontent.

By the turn of the century Brentano was already a poet and writer—though his poetry was not widely known before the 1852 edition, indeed much of his work remaining unpublished during his lifetime. The "irregular ballads and songs inserted in a very irregular novel entitled *Godwi*[9] provide an indication of Brentano's poetic talent. *Godwi, oder das steinerne Bild der Mutter*, written in 1798–1800 and published in 1801, was a product of his Jena period —as was his first publication *Gustav Wasa* (1800), a satire full of literary polemic directed against Kotzebue and others, and showing the influence of Tieck (as Dorothea Schlegel for one was quick to point out). Brentano's time as a student at Jena, then the intellectual and literary centre in Germany, brought him into contact with Fichte, Tieck and the Schlegels, and *Godwi* was clearly a product of that age and environment. The autobiographical elements in the novel—Friedrich Schlegel criticised him for writing so subjectively—are manifest in the partial self-mirrorings in the characters of Maria (Brentano's early works were in fact written under that pseudonym), Godwi and Römer, and in the memory of his own parents in the character drawings of the Firmenti; Brentano's own childhood is recalled in the inserted "Szene aus meinen Kinderjahren" and his love of the Rhine remembered in the depiction of that area as a setting in the story. The work reflects certain affinities with Goethe's *Wilhelm Meister* (*inter alia* in the character sketches, where, for example, Eusebio is a likeness to Mignon, Werdo to the Harper, etc.), with Friedrich Schlegel's *Lucinde* and Tieck's novels. *Godwi* is the account of a young man's variegated experiences of life and reactions to Nature, Art and Love, in language which, sometimes ecstatic, always appeals to the senses and emotions. Godwi is driven by an inner urge and is ever restless. Not for him the "Zweck des Daseins, des Nützlichseins". He writes to Röhmer :

"Mit deinem Zweck hat es wenig auf sich, durchlaufe dein System, du kömmst nicht weiter, du stehst im Zirkel, und zwar in dem kleinsten—Arbeit um Geld, Geld um Brot, Brot um Nahrung, Nahrung um Stärke zur Arbeit."[10]

and advocates :

"Glück und Genuss ist der Zweck unsers Lebens und muss in uns selbst liegen . . . Leben heisst Fühlen und Fühlenmachen, dass man dasei, durch Genuss, den man nimmt und mit sich wiedergebt."[11]

Brentano was clearly aware of the *credo* of the older Romantics. His own use of the sonnet form, for instance, reflects A. W. Schlegel's advocacy of the sonnet. And even if he did find the philosophical ideas of Fichte hard going and the theorisings of the Schlegels not in strict accord with his own temperament, he nevertheless had views on aesthetic ideals which find expression in the novel :

"Alles, was zwischen unserm Auge und einem entfernten zu Sehenden als Mittler steht, uns den entfernten Gegenstand nähert, ihm aber zugleich etwas von dem Seinigen mitgiebt, ist romantisch."[12]

"Das Romantische ist also ein Perspectiv oder vielmehr die Farbe des Glases und die Bestimmung des Gegenstandes durch die Form des Glases."[13]

"Das Romantische selbst ist eine Übersetzung."[14]

There are thoughts on Time, which for Brentano meant a fleeting moment or sequence of unconnected moments which were self-sufficient, and on Form :

"Die Gestalt selbst dürfe keine Gestalt haben, sondern sei nur das bestimmte Aufhören eines aus einem Punkte nach allen Seiten gleichmässig hervordringenden Gedankens. Er sei nun ein Gedachtes in Stein, Ton, Farbe, Wort oder Gedanken."[15]

The last sentence, incidentally, provides an excellent indication of Brentano's own attitude to synaesthesia, which in fact was to figure prominently in his work.[16]

Brentano described *Godwi* as "ein verwilderter Roman" on the title page and indeed it is a novel in which the imagination runs riot and causes the work of art to seem to take on an existence independent of its creator. And this impression is heightened in the sequence in the second part of the novel where Maria sees a statue in Godwi's garden apparently coming to life as the sun rises :

"Vor mir war das Bild gleichsam geboren. Ich sah es in der Nacht wie in Liebe und Traum, im Mondlichte wie mit dem Begehren, erschaffen zu werden, in des Morgens Dämmerung wie in der Ahndung des Künstlers, mehr und mehr in den Begriff tretend, und ich stand vor ihm und sah, wie es hervordrang mehr und mehr in die Wirklichkeit, und endlich zum vollendeten Werke ward im Glanze der Sonne, getrennt von dem Schöpfer, der nur ein Gebärer ist, für sich selbst, mit allen Rechten seiner Gattung."[17]

But the hand of the artist remains very much in evidence in the writing of *Godwi*. And this is perhaps most readily observable in the frequent use of romantic irony, which is the means of deliberately destroying illusion and restoring a note of objectivity to the proceedings. The complex structure of the novel itself reflects this very process. Maria is the supposed editor of the first part of the novel which comprises correspondence between various characters, and himself a character and narrator in the second part. Illness causes the fragmentary continuation of the story—partly by his own hand, partly by his friend Godwi. The novel concludes with the death of Maria and some parodistic poetic epitaphs. The manipulations and interferences of the author (Brentano) in his various guises—e.g., the sequence in the second part of the novel where Maria and Godwi go out into the garden ("Dies ist der Teich, in den ich Seite 146 im ersten Band falle"[18]) to discuss the writing of the book :

"... Sie muten, mir doch nicht zu, dass ich Thuen Otilien hätte zum Weibe geben sollen?" "Nein, soviel nicht—aber ich hätte mich wenigstens umbringen müssen, weil sie mich nicht nehmen wollte oder konnte—einen anderen Ausweg wüsste ich nicht—ihr untreu werden?—das ganze Publikum hätte auf mich geschimpft..."[19]

—display at one and the same time an involvement and a distancing, fantasy and reflection.

The poetic insertions in the novel are several and include some of Brentano's best known verse. Poems such as "Lore Lay" and

"Ein Fischer sass im Kahne" (just like the setting of the Rhine in
the story) deliberately recall and help to revive the past and traditional poetry. Both the above are written in the old *Volkslied* and
ballad convention and comprise four line stanzas with simple
sentences and rhythmic pattern to achieve the musical effect. Their
theme is of love enchantment and yearning. In "Lore Lay"—one
is inevitably reminded of Heine's later treatment of the same theme
—the witch hates the sensual magic spell of her own beauty and
longs for death. The mock artlessness of the old convention where
the poet recounts a tale already told is attempted, but one cannot
ignore in the poem the subjective element and the concluding
ironic touch :

> "Wer hat dies Lied gesungen?
> Ein Schiffer auf dem Rhein,
> Und immer hats geklungen
> Von dem Dreiritterstein :
> > Lore Lay
> > Lore Lay
> > Lore Lay
> Als wären es meiner drei."[20]

"Sprich aus der Ferne" is a clearly more elaborate poem and is a
lyrical dialogue of the soul and night. The balancing of the inner
and outer worlds is reflected in the short and long lines respectively and the rhythm of the poem is correspondingly adjusted.
The effects of synaesthesia help toward fusion :

> "Wenn des Mondes still lindernde Tränen
> Lösen der Nächte verborgenes Weh,
> Dann wehet Friede. In goldenen Kähnen
> Schiffen die Geister im himmlischen See.
>
> > Glänzender Lieder
> > Klingender Lauf
> > Ringelt sich nieder,
> > Wallet hinauf."[21]

The symbolic poem "Wenn der Sturm das Meer umschlinget" also
contains elaborate antithetical pairings with its themes of love and
longing, day and night, life and death, time present and infinity.

The restlessness of Godwi mirrored the unsettled wanderings of
Brentano himself. Like the hero of his fairy tales, he was out to
seek his poetic fortune in the world of art. By 1804 he was in
Heidelberg, where Arnim subsequently met him and joined forces.

Romantically evocative Heidelberg was destined to take over from Jena as the centre of romantic thought and activity, was the centre for the so-called Heidelberg Romantics with Arnim and Brentano in the van. At this time a definite change of mental attitude was beginning to take place in Germany. The rise of Napoleon and the accompanying low ebb of German fortunes (culminating in the Prussian defeat in the Battle of Jena, 1806) stimulated fervent feelings of patriotism and a corresponding rejection of the age of Classicism and the concepts of the French Revolution. Instead one looked back to the glorious German past of the Middle Ages and beyond, which meant in turn a revival of folk-songs and legends. It is against this background that the particular contribution of Brentano must be viewed in his celebrated co-compilation with Arnim of *Des Knaben Wunderhorn,* an anthology of folk-songs which caught the popular imagination. Undoubtedly *Des Knaben Wunderhorn* is a spiritual legacy to the collection—a quarter of a century earlier—of Herder (who had died in 1803), though the Arnim-Brentano anthology is German-based as against Herder's more international collection. The work was published in three volumes from 1806–8. The first volume was dedicated to Goethe, who was favourably disposed towards it in his review. The romantic belief in the *Volksseele* played its part here too as in the wider field of literature (and other spheres of life: Savigny Brentano's brother-in-law and Professor at Berlin University—propounded his own theory of law to the effect that the historical folkspirit should determine the constitution and the laws).[22] But the poems themselves were not drawn from the "people" as such, so much as from a variety of literary sources and from different centuries including the seventeenth. Arnim and Brentano were, however, at such pains to recapture the artlessness of the *Volkslied* that they even indulged consciously in artistic licence, correcting and improving the poems where it was felt necessary. Görres for one considered them, nevertheless, to be a faithful mirror of the people, and whatever the shortcomings of the anthology, its appearance was greeted with enthusiasm. Certainly it was to inspire and stimulate a wealth of subsequent lyric poetry from Eichendorff to Uhland, Mörike to Heine.

The effect achieved by Arnim and Brentano with *Des Knaben Wunderhorn* on the people under the spell of "medieval" poetry, the brothers Grimm were to emulate with their collection of *Kinder- und Hausmärchen* volumes. Brentano himself had been contemplating collecting *Märchen* for publication[23] as well as writing them. The *Märchen* was by that time an already fashionable literary form. Novalis had had firm views on its importance for the Romantics, but of more practical benefit for Brentano were Tieck's evocative tales. As it turned out, the *Märchen* perhaps proved to be the most suitable mode of expression and outlet for Brentano's imaginative mind and temperament. Story-telling and the writing of tales attracted Brentano throughout his productive years. In 1805 he had written to Arnim about the idea of "die italienischen Kindermärchen für deutsche Kinder zu bearbeiten",[24] and from about 1809 on he was engaged in Berlin and in the loneliness of Bukovan on the reworking of some German tales, about which he wrote in a letter to Reimar in 1816.[25]

More often than not his tales were adaptations of old traditional folklore themes, upon which he allowed his powerful imagination free rein. He turned to the past in the hope perhaps that it might prove a move towards a more acceptable form of reality, certainly a move at any rate away from the great gulf that existed in his own life of unhappiness and unfulfilment. He planned a cycle of medieval tales, but as was to happen at other times his ambitious plans were not realised. In fact only one tale which was to have been the framework for several Old German Tales was commenced and that remained a fragment. *Aus der Chronika eines fahrenden Schülers*—published in 1818, though he had been toying with the project since 1802[26]—conjures up the mock medieval world and atmosphere in the tale of the pious and naive young wandering scholar who reflects upon childhood, nature, religion and art. The story may well reveal an affinity with the Tieck/Wackenroder *Herzensergiessungen eines kunstliebenden Klosterbruders,* but at the same time it does provide an insight once more into Brentano's own make-up and being, whether it be in the interpolated lyrics— the seemingly artless (yet really very sophisticated) *Volkslied* style of "Es sang vor langen Jahren", with its theme of longing and love and an intricate scheme of internal rhymes and partly repeated lines, or the devotional "baroque" poem "Hör, liebe Seel! Wer rufet dir?" that recalls Brentano's predilection for Friedrich von Spee and seventeenth-century poetry; or the passionate yet sincere note contained in the passage on Gothic art inspired by the Strasbourg Minster (one is reminded, of course, of Goethe's words on the same subject in *Von deutscher Baukunst*). What one does not find here, however, is Brentano's natural gaiety and rich fantasy which is manifest in his *Märchen* proper.

The so-called Italian group of tales was based primarily on the *Pentamerone* of the Neapolitan baroque poet Basile, and mostly dates from 1805–11. The framework-tale is *Liebseelchen,* where

Prince Röhropp arranges for the telling of a cycle of tales to divert a magic spinning doll. Brentano is clearly four square behind the Prince when the latter talks of the art of the story-teller :

> ". . . nichts ziert einen erfahrnen Menschen so sehr, als wenn er schöne Geschichten zu erzählen weiss, Geschichten, bei deren Anhörung der Weber sein Schiff, der Advokat seine Feder, der Apotheker seinen Mörser, der Scherenschleifer sein Rad und Kinder ihr Butterbrot ruhen lassen, um besser zuhören zu können."(27)

The tales that are then told are basically conventional with stock situations and themes. *Myrtenfräulein*, for example, tells of the love of a prince for a myrtle maiden who grew from a myrtle cutting planted in a china tub. Rosenblättchen in the tale of that name, likewise born of a plant cutting, marries a fine prince in the end, despite the wicked step-mother. In *Witzenspitzel* the smart lad kills the giant and his wife, and is rewarded with the hand of the king's daughter in marriage. *Baron von Hüpfenstich* is the tale of a king and a flea who becomes the king's favourite and eventually marries his daughter. The traditional and familiar theme of the magic ring, which fulfils all wishes of whoever wears it, is seen to good effect in the story of *Schulmeister Klopstock und seine fünf Söhne*, where the youngest son rescues the princess from the giant and wins her hand, and, of course, in *Gockel und Hinkel*—perhaps the best of these tales—where Gackeleia marries Kronovus and becomes queen of Gelnhausen.

The reader of these tales immediately enters into the familiar fairy-tale world of castles and woods and nearby towns, a world peopled by kings, princess, princesses and simple folk, giants, witches, fairies and animals of all description; a world in which the hero, off to make his fortune, wins through in the end despite the evil machinations of people, witches or giants. The style of story-telling is conventional too, in accordance with the *Volksmärchen* tradition : "Once upon a time there was a king, schoolmaster, etc. . . ."; "In a big dark forest in Germany there lived a little old man and his name was Gockel . . .", the stories start, and continue in a direct, straightforward manner, scene after scene, deed upon deed, the sequences being linked more often than not by "und", "aber", "da". And there is the conventional happy ending : "And then they were married, and Witzenspitzel and the princess lived in the giant's castle, where they are to this day"; ". . . and they came to Besserdich and have ruled there well to this day" (from *Fanferlieschen*).

But on top of this the hand of Brentano is unmistakably to be observed, so that the *Volksmärchen* does in fact become a *Kunstmärchen*, a sophisticated version of the original nursery tale. The element of inventiveness and lightheartedness is in evidence from the start of these Italian tales, but more noticeably so in the somewhat later and more freely adapted stories of *Schulmeister Klopfstock* (written about 1812, though not published until 1846–47) and *Gockel und Hinkel* (written about 1815–16, but published in 1838), and, of course, in his *Rheinmärchen*. For example, in his predilection for names that will characterise his humans and animals : Witzenspitzel for the bright lad, Hecheltonie, Haspelrosa, Kunkelriecke ... etc., for the spinnerwoman, Hüpfenstich for the flea, Lämmerfrass for the wolf, Honigbart for the bear. To this can be added Brentano's delight in the involved extension of motifs and in elaborate punning, which produce almost endless variations. In *Myrtenfräulein* Prince Wetschwuth (after our own Wedgwood) lived in the "porcelain capital"; there is an extended sequence of "black" humour in *Fanferlieschen,* where the subjects are to hold a memorial service for their dead king.[28] There is the rose motif in *Rosenblättchen,* and the bell motif in *Schulmeister Klopfstock,* where King Pumpan of Glockotonia gives his daughter Pimperlein in marriage to the youngest son of the schoolmaster, Trilltrall.[29] In *Gockel und Hinkel* (whose daughter is Gackeleia) there is an elaborate egg motif : The king of Gelnhausen, Eifrassius and queen Eilegia live in their castle Eierburg (made of egg shells) and celebrate the great festival of the Order of the Easter Egg.[30] The possibilities are virtually without limit.

The humorous piling up of things, whether it be of motifs already observed in *Gockel und Hinkel* and the above-mentioned celebrations at Glockotonia, or the enumeration of the items on the food list for the Mouse king,[31] of the members of Gockel's household,[32] of the animals attending the service in memory of King Laudamus[33] etc., can reach the proportions of baroque conceit, as, for example, in Prince Röhropp's address to the spinnerwomen in *Liebseelchen.*[34] Brentano clearly took joy in playing with words, and interest in their musicality, to the extent that on occasions he would almost seem to be preoccupied with the sound of things as against the story as such.

Ironic sallies also reveal the hand of Brentano behind the mock artlessness of the tales. The building up of atmosphere and colour is knocked down with one blow, as in the prime example in *Baron von Hüpfenstich* of the description of castle Knochenruh :

"Es war nicht ohne Kunst gebaut. Lauter Totenbeine und Totenköpfe, die standen oben herum, und weil die Haare noch auf ihnen waren, spielten diese recht schön im Wind und sausten. Es war gar nicht so übel ausgedacht . . . Siehe, alle die Knochen . . . mit welchem Geschmack sind sie geordnet! Ist das nicht modisch? Ist das nicht gothisch?[(35)]

The overall impression, though, is of rich fantasy and lighthearted-ness, perhaps best characterised—even allowing for the inherent irony—in the conclusion to *Gockel und Hinkel,* where Gackeleia, now the queen of Gelnhausen, wishes for the transformation of the events of the tale into a *Märchen* after the manner of Tieck's "reversible world".

As mentioned, the *Rheinmärchen* are more freely constructed than the Italian stories, certainly the earlier and shorter ones. As for the Italian tales, so too here was a cycle envisaged, but the grandiose project was not fully realised. What exists is the frame-work tale, and within this framework tale three other stories. Here Brentano's historical consciousness is revealed in his feeling for the German past of "Berg und Burg". His sources for these tales are basically German legends. The framework-tale of *Müller Radlauf,* for example, is a very free—and elaborate—adaptation of the Bishop Hatto legend and the Pied Piper of Hameln, and describes the adventures of the simple miller Radlauf who wins for himself the hand of the inevitably beautiful princess Ameleya and becomes king. But in the very telling of the tale the story-teller's artistry emerges to make the story a sophisticated version of a folktale. Artistry is displayed in the interweaving of stories, *Märchen* within *Märchen,* for Radlauf can only win his bride Ameleya (and the children of Mainz too) back from the fortunately friendly Father Rhine (whither they had all previously been enticed by Prince Mauseohr from Trier) by the telling of so many tales, one for each person. So Radlauf wins back his princess by relating the fate of his ancestors and his journey to the Black Forest (*Das Märchen von dem Hause Starenberg*); Frau Marzibille gains her daughter Ameleychen by telling the tale of *Murmeltier*; and Schneiderlein Meckerling gets back his son Garnwichserchen with the telling of *Schneider Siebentot.*

Brentano may well give the appearance of following the tradition of the *Volksmärchen* thematically and stylistically. The reader remembers the simple evocation of mood—through visual, but more likely musical imagery—in nature, whether it be the Black Forest or the world beneath the surface of the Rhine; the conventional use of numbers like three or seven or their multiples (the three wishes of the magic ring, Frau Lore Lay with her seven daughters, Frau Mondenschein with her seven, etc.). Nevertheless Brentano's penchant for elaboration constantly breaks through, the involved intricacies seeming to lure him like the Lore Lay herself. The use of numbers becomes an exact process of calculation and itemising in *Schneider Siebentot*,[36] the variations of themes endless—e.g. the variations of the mouse/rat theme in the framework tale of *Müller Radlauf*, and word plays on occasions such that Brentano would once again seem to be won over to sounds for their own sake—as in the song of the bird in *Das Märchen von dem Hause Starenberg*.[37]

Once again too romantic irony is present, as for example in the incident in the tale of *Müller Radlauf*, where Brentano makes himself and Arnim appear as two boys in a boat on the Rhine. And satire—which was to be found in the Italian tale of *Dilldapp*—is also encountered in these *Rheinmärchen*, be it orientated literary-wise as in *Murmeltier*, where it is directed against Voss (for long the adversary of the Heidelberg Romantics; he had been very critical of the "tampering" with the songs in *Des Knaben Wunderhorn*) and Campe (the self-styled purifier of the German language)[38] or of a political and social nature as in the framework tale of *Müller Radlauf*.[39]

Fundamentally Brentano had no desire to teach or preach deeper meanings in his tales, as did, say Novalis. However sophisticated his versions may be, they are still based on the traditional themes of Cinderella, Bluebeards, the Sleeping Beauty, etc., familiar as ever to generation after generation of children. The fairy tale may be casually dismissed by people as a bit of make-believe and not taken very seriously, just as Brentano himself was not taken very seriously by many (Tieck for one thought him and his sister Bettina histrionic and insincere) and considered the child who never grew up. And one can point to the end of *Gockel und Hinkel* where all present, including the story-teller, are transformed into children. But the poet consciously becomes a child and part of that world of make-believe, which, however, is not all that fanciful and far-fetched. The poet enters the alogical dream world of the fairy tale, yet sometimes the dream comes true, as Radlauf himself experienced. So the poet's tales become suitable for children of all ages, for they can have a certain relevance to life in that they go back to the origin of things and provide a link with nature and truth. Writing at a time of political upheavals, when he might well ask what was logical and real, Brentano attempted through his tales to catch a glimpse of the real world. Man is safe so long as he trusts in nature and animals, which can guide and assist him. In *Rosenblättchen,* for example, the duke is prevented from returning home after a visit to the fair by a terrible storm. He then remembers that he has forgotten to purchase the promised articles for Rosenblättchen. He returns and buys them and discovers he can get home safely without further ado. The contact between humans and animals is very close. Mice traditionally help people (as seen in *Gockel und Hinkel,* for example), and birds are the conventional intermediaries between heaven and earth—in addition to their being favoured by Brentano for their musical qualities! Gockel, Hinkel, Gackeleia, etc., have animal names; the flea becomes Baron von Hüpfenstich and the fish are changed into princes.

Die mehreren Wehmüller und die ungarischen Nationalgesichter date from the time of Brentano's stay at the family estate at Bukovan in Bohemia and were published in 1817. The setting and the local colouring in the use of dialect reflect in part his stay there. The familiar pattern is followed of having a framework tale within which other tales are related. The celebrated portrait-painter Wehmüller has to tarry at the Hungarian-Croatian border because of the threat of plague. The time is whiled away in telling tales. *Das Pickenick des Katers Mores* related by the Croatian noblemen is a tale—based on a theme from folklore—of witches changing into cats; this is followed by the Frenchman Devillier's humorous tale on the same theme, *Erzählung von den Hexen auf dem Auster-felsen*; the last tale is a comic account of a demon huntsman, told by the Venetian Baciochi (*Erzählung vom wilden Jäger*). The framework tale then takes over as the travel ban is lifted. The mystery of Wehmüller's two doubles who seemed to have been following him everywhere (with all the attendant romantic irony in the *Doppelgänger* treatment) is finally resolved in humorous fashion. The one turns out to be a rival painter Froschauer, the other is his wife Tonerl who had dressed in her husband's clothes for supposed reasons of safety when she set out to meet him. The stories are a mixture of the grotesque and the rib-tickling humorous, with the merry, lighthearted note predominating. The cycle ends with the assurance by the author that he will tell more of the tales that had been promised for the entertainment of the assembled company (but which are now not really required since the ban on travelling has been lifted), as the fancy takes him.

One of the poems, *"Weltlich Recht"*, contained in the anthology *Des Knaben Wunderhorn* and a couple of tales apparently told him by Luise Hensel's mother would seem to form the basis for

Brentano's tale of fate, *Geschichte vom braven Kasperl und dem schönen Annerl* (1817) with its theme of unhappy love brought about by an exaggerated sense of honour. Kasperl is the proud soldier returning home to discover that his father is a thief, and commits suicide as he cannot bear the disgrace. Annerl, who has left the security of the Rosenhof in search of greater honour out of love for Kasperl, is seduced and kills the resulting child. The young innocents in an evil world are driven with tragic inevitability to their doom. The old woman who relates the tale to the narrator is trying to gain a reprieve for Annerl who is due to be executed in the morning. A reprieve is granted, but it arrives too late to save Annerl. By the grim hand of fate—or the long arm of coincidence —Grossinger is both the seducer and the bearer of the reprieve. The atmosphere of predestined doom is heightened, for example, by the apron motif and the executioner's sword rattling in its case when Annerl was present, and by the story of the French non-commissioned officer. This last episode plus the parallel situation of the Duke seducing the sister of Grossinger are illustrations of Brentano's liking for variations on a theme as witnessed in the *Märchen*. But what one does not find here as against the *Märchen* is the element of humour. What is impressive, however, is the contrast throughout of the mock-artlessness of the old woman's tale as she unfolds it on the one hand, and, on the other, the sense of urgency which becomes the more real as time passes, but of which the old lady seems unaware—a contrast which builds up to the tense climax. Alongside the familiar romantic elements of superstition, the liking for the dream, the mill setting, the "Volk" element in the old woman telling her tale, more realistic features creep into the story than have been noticed hitherto. The remote setting of "Berg und Burg" has given way to that of a town and its citizens at the time of the Wars of Liberation. The realistic element is seen to very good effect in the fine perspective at the end of the story of the narrator, who was not such a good rider and had fallen behind, observing Grossinger in the distance trying to shout the news of the reprieve, only for his voice to be drowned in the noise of the gunfire of practising artillery, whilst the sun glitters on the sword raised and ready to descend on Annerl.

The time Brentano spent on the Bukovan estate was an extremely productive literary period for him. Besides the *Wehmüller* sequence of stories, he was actively engaged upon verse and drama. With the dramatic element ever evident in his own human relationships, it is perhaps natural that he should turn to the theatre. Indeed he was a theatre critic for a short time and had connections with the theatre people of Berlin, Vienna and Prague. But just as his own life was unbounded, so too was his drama unchecked, with little ability or regard shown for construction. What one perhaps remembers in his grandiose-conceived theatrical endeavours which were never successful is the musical expression. Already in 1801 he had written *Ponce de Leon* (published in 1804). This was nominally his entry (there were twelve others) in response to a competition organised by Goethe and Schiller in an attempt to raise the standard of comedy in the German theatre. Significantly no prize was awarded. Goethe in a letter to Brentano in response to a plea for the play's return[40] refers to its "guten Humor und angenehme Lieder". Certainly the lyric insertions constitute the best feature, along with some verbal witticisms. Heine thought that it bustled along in the most delightful confusion, and Crabb Robinson saw in it nothing but light wit. The romantic setting is Spain and the play is full of complex intrigues and confusions over identities that are stretched to the limit until all ends well with no fewer than five marriages being arranged to sort out the confusion. Brentano later revised the play for presentation on the stage and in fact it had under the title *Valeria oder Vaterlist* its first performance on February 18, 1814, in the Hoftheater in Vienna. It proved also to be its last performance. One can understand Brentano's mood and feelings as expressed in his letter to Arnim on April 5 of that year.

Stemming from his time at Bukovan is *Aloys und Imelde*, Trauerspiel in fünf Akten, a long play occupying some two hundred pages of text in the Hanser edition. Brentano himself thought highly of the piece.[41] It appears that he lent the original manuscript to a friend, Varnhagen, who confiscated it for alleged insulting remarks by Brentano about Rahel Robert, the celebrated Jewish literary salon hostess in Berlin. Brentano only received this manuscript back in 1814. In the meantime he had rewritten two acts but subsequently—and perhaps characteristically—dropped it. The work remained unpublished until 1912 after both manuscripts had come into the possession of the Königliche Bibliothek in Berlin. Brentano depicts the unhappy love story of Aloys and Imelde against an eighteenth century backcloth after the time of the Camisard revolt of the Huguenots. The problems facing the couple prove too powerful and both die in the end. Aloys kills himself, believing Imelde to have died in a fire. She, however, was rescued and commits suicide over his corpse. It is really a fate drama. Just as Kasperl and Annerl had to succumb in the hard and wicked world, so too do these go inexorably to their predestined doom, and this process is intensified by the recurrent poem "O Zorn, du

Abgrund des Verderbens Wo ist, O Liebe, deine Tiefe", which
runs like a leitmotif through the play and reminds one of the force
of the song on the Day of Judgment in *Geschichte vom braven
Kasperl und dem schönen Annerl*. But there is a singular lack of
real dramatic conflict and the construction is too loose with the
many digressions, including a play within a play sequence in
Tieckian and Shakespearian style. The imitative nature of the piece
is further emphasised in the creation of a secret society à la *Wilhelm
Meister*, so dear to the Romantics. The play once again leans
heavily on complications and misunderstandings and the character
drawings are not always well defined, so that the main characters
suffer at the hands of the host of subsidiary ones. Brentano's extravagant verbal caprices are once more in evidence. *Die Gründung
Prags*, ein historisch-romantisches Drama, is a product too of that
interlude at Bukovan, where Brentano also took time off to pay
visits to Prague. An even longer play (some three hundred pages in
the Hanser edition), it is a tragedy in rhyming iambic pentameters
on the theme of the mythical founding of Prague by Libussa. For
his sources Brentano basically turned to old Slavonic mythology
and obtained material for his plot with the assistance of Dobrovsky
and the Prague poet Meinert. There are no fewer than five versions of this vast and complicated undertaking which was published
in 1815 after the initial concept in 1812. It constituted Brentano's
most ambitious project and originally was intended clearly as an
opera on the lines of Werner's *Wanda, Königin der Sarmaten, eine
romantische Tragödie mit Gesang* (1810), which he admired. Unfortunately the additional length of Brentano's play only meant even
less dramatic unity and emphasis, and Brentano would have done
well to follow more closely Werner's example in the matter of the
actual construction of the piece. Despite the dramatic potential in
the main theme of the clash of paganism and christianity, the play
is not rich in action and there are so many other diverse elements,
complications and multiplications of predestined fate, that the
whole is virtually a shapeless mass. One critic has described it as a
"megalithic document of failure".[42] Certainly one cannot but help
recall a better dramatic effort on the same theme by Grillparzer,
who knew of Brentano's play and from 1819 planned his own
version.

By the age of thirty-eight Brentano had reached a crisis, an
emotionally and spiritually lonely man. His tortured emotional life
gave him no peace nor the promise of better things in his personal
relations with people, notwithstanding his meeting with Luise
Hensel whom he met in 1816 and who was to exert a profound

influence over him in the following years. He wrote to her of his "innere Doppeltätigkeit"(43) and of the uselessness of his life :

"Vergeblich!—Kennst Due dies schreckliche Wort? Es ist die Überschrift meines ganzen Lebens."(44)

He had already expressed his doubts as to his validity as an artist to Wilhelm Grimm :

"Meine dichterischen Bestrebungen habe ich geendet, sie haben zu sehr mit dem falschen Wege meiner Natur zusammengehangen; es ist mir alles misslungen . . ."(45)

As he had not enjoyed a balanced relationship with the world "where men sit and hear each other groan", Brentano had first turned to the world of nature in his *Märchen*. But the world he encountered there proved unable to produce the final and lasting answer to his problems. As an alternative refuge he now turned to the Catholic Church into which he had been born, but to which he now returned with an ever increasing fervour over the remaining years. In pursuance of this religious zeal he went to the bedside of the stigmatised nun Katherina Emmerich and for years duly recorded her religious visions until her death in 1824. The result was fourteen volumes of manuscript upon which he later worked and in 1833 the first edition was published of *Das bittere Leiden unseres Herrn Jesu Christi*. Its appearance aroused interest out of curiosity to the extent that a second edition of two thousand copies was ordered the next year. Certainly after 1817 Brentano withdrew increasingly from the world and his religious fervour is such that in 1819 he wrote to his brother Christian :

"Ich habe alle meine theologischen Bücher abgesondert und verpacke sie, die anderen gebe ich mit allem zum Verkauf."(46)

In 1837, when he met Crabb Robinson and Wordsworth by chance in Munich, Crabb Robinson recorded :

"Brentano was in his way courteous in French, though he rattled about religion in a way that could but half amuse and half disgust Wordsworth. For Brentano is a strange mixture of drollery and assumed earnestness in religious matters that amounts to fanaticism."(47)

Brentano's own journeyings in the last years too tended to be spiritual adventures rather than worldly ones. His attitude to his own pre-conversion writings was very definite also. In 1827 he called his *Märchen* "das unnütze Zeug",(48) and a year earlier had rejected his *Romanzen vom Rosenkranz* in far more denunciatory terms. [49]

Romanzen vom Rosenkranz is another incomplete project. It was commenced in 1803 and continued sporadically until 1812 when he broke off after completing twenty out of the planned twenty-four cantos. The work itself, however, was not published until 1852. The overall plan for the work—though in fact it was not carried out in full—Brentano outlined in a letter to the artist Philipp Otto Runge[50]. It was to be an apocryphal religious poem on the theme of the origin of "Rosenkranzandacht", into which was to be woven an extravaganza of other themes and motifs. The necessary act of atonement was to be achieved by three virgin sisters, who underwent a fantastic series of adventures where they were exposed to evil, before they were able to win through in the end and break the chain of inherited guilt—and all this against the medieval Italian background of Bologna in the thirteenth century! Brentano had wished Runge to draw marginal sketches for his book and the relevant letter reveals broadly enough his liking for word and idea associations :

> "Das Ganze selbst möchte sich einer Folge mit Arabesken da verflochtener Gemälde vergleichen, wo die Gestalt unausprechlich ist, und wo das Symbol eintritt, wo die Gestalt blüht oder tönt."[51]

The lyrical epic poem is truly rich in fantasy, and the flower symbolism provides the fullest example : Each of the three sisters is called a rose (Rosarosa, Rosadora, Rosablanka) and each has a rose-like birth mark; their mother is Rosatrista... etc. Many more intricate elaborations of the rose motif follow, reminding the reader very strongly of the procedure already observed in the *Märchen*. The short trochaic lines with their assonance or rhyme do allow Brentano to display his musicality to good effect once more in the poem.

The climaxes in Brentano's life produced some good work. This religious crisis was no exception. *"Frühlingsschrei eines Knechtes aus der Tiefe"*, one of his best ever poems, emerged about 1816 (*Geschichte vom braven Kasperl und dem schönen Annerl*, recognised as one of Brentano's best stories, stems from that time too). This religious poem expresses the poet's remorse in simple four-line rhyming verses. The baroque parallels and antitheses of thought and phrase serve to deepen the note of sincerity. Baroque in its richness of vocabulary and thought is "Erntelied", another fine poem from this later phase; its theme is of the harvest and death and it shows clearly Brentano's affinity with seventeenth century poets like Friedrich von Spee.

Indeed, it is as a poet that Brentano should be remembered. The lyrical element permeated his whole life and work, not just in the narrower field of poetry itself but also in his *Märchen*, even in his ill-fated dramas, and in his letters. Some of his poems have been set to music by such composers as Mendelssohn, Schumann and Brahms, but his verse of course with its rhythm and colour produces its own musicality. And this is true whether one considers a poem by Brentano in the mock artless style of the *Volkslied* or an unmistakably baroque tinged poem. Both in their respective ways are emotional confessions. "Der Spinnerin Lied" from *Aus der Chronika eines fahrenden Schülers*, for example, would seem to be an artless poem of simple four line rhyming stanzas on the theme of the lonely spinner in the moonlight dreaming of past happiness and present sorrow, in other words the conventional theme of love and longing :

> Es sang vor langen Jahren
> Wohl auch die Nachtigall,
> Das war wohl süsser Schall,
> Da wir zusammen waren.

> Ich sing und kann nicht weinen,
> Und spinne so allein
> Den Faden klar und rein,
> Solang der Mond wird scheinen.

> Da wir zusammen waren,
> Da sang die Nachtigall,
> Nun mahnet mich ihr Schall,
> Dass du von mir gefahren.

> So oft der Mond mag scheinen,
> Gedenk ich dein allein,
> Mein Herz ist klar und rein,
> Gott wolle uns vereinen.

> Seit du von mir gefahren,
> Singt stets die Nachtigall,
> Ich denk bei ihrem Schall,
> Wie wir zusammen waren.

Gott woll uns vereinen,
Hier spinn' ich so allein,
Der Mond scheint klar und rein,
Ich sing und möchte weinen.[52]

The language is simple and limited, the syntax likewise. But the poem becomes sophisticated in the way that Brentano imbues it with his feeling for rhythm in the application of internal rhyme and recurrent or partly recurrent lines.

Unmistakably Brentano appeals to the eye and the ear, to feeling not the intellect in his evocative poems as he conjures up the past and the future and depicts the world of nature, the stars, the moon, the night. The short poem *Abendständchen* expresses his liking for the effects of synaesthesia exquisitely; where visual and tonal elements fuse in the "sounds drifting golden downward" and the "light of the sounds" glancing up to the poet :

Hör! es klagt die Flöte wieder,
Und die kühlen Brunnen rauschen,
Golden wehn die Töne nieder—
Stille, stille, lass uns lauschen!

Holdes Bitten, mild Verlangen,
Wie es süss zum Herzen spricht!
Durch die Nacht, die mich umfangen,
Blickt zu mir der Töne Licht.[53]

Brentano would seem to qualify as the quintessential Romantic, the wanderer in search of his goal yet destined never to happily reach it in his lifetime. He is the paradoxical figure of a man whose very nature was antithetical to order,[54] yet who acknowledged the need for order; a man who poked fun at the philistine and reacted so positively to everyday life, yet was conscious of his own failings and aware of the bourgeois concept of duty and responsibility—as reflected perhaps in the occasion of his moral attitude towards his sister Bettina,[55] to whom he was very attached and who retained a spark of Promethean fire throughout her life. And hard though he tried to lose himself in the dreamlike alogical world of his *Märchen*, that world never fully measured up to his demands and he could not bring himself to take the final step. Brentano is the Romantic artist with a bad conscience—with one foot kept firmly on the ground and one eye set objectively. And the realism is observable not just in his own writings on occasion (as in *Geschichte vom braven Kasperl und dem schönen Annerl*) but also is his being a keen collector of books, and perhaps more strikingly in his other literary capacity as editor—in addition to *Des Knaben Wunderhorn* he brought out a new edition of Friedrich von Spee's *Trutznach-tigall* and Jörg Wickram's *Der Goldfaden*—and in his more minor role of translator from Italian, Spanish and French.

This poet of the mixed blood and the two cultural heritages of the Mediterranean and the North was destined to be a solitary figure, "living, yet partly living". One recalls that Brentano had met through the *Christlich-deutsche Tischgesellschaft* another tragic and lone figure in German literature, Kleist. And one of the poets Brentano admired was Hölderlin—equally tragic and lone.

In other ways too the enigma that is Brentano remains. Not only was he himself unwilling for much of his work to be published during his lifetime, but, it seems, so too were his literary executors. Some manuscripts have appeared for the first time in recent years. The short story *Der arme Raimondin* was first published in 1944; the first complete publication of the novellistic fragment *Der schiffbrüchige Galeerensklave* occurred in 1949.

NOTES AND TRANSLATIONS

1. "Blessed is he who drifts like a spirit over the water ... so too the poet." From Brentano's poem "Nachklänge Beethovenscher Musik". The poet had been much moved on hearing some of Beethoven's music.

2. "We had nurtured nothing but fantasy, and that had partly consumed us again." Letter to Sophie von Schweitzer, April 1842.

3. "I have many good friends, but they are such only because of my outer being, friendship can never glance within to the very heart, only love can do that without hurting it." Letter to Antonie Brentano, 1799? Cf. too ch. 4 of the second part of *Godwi*.

4. In *Erlebtes:* "Halle und Heidelberg". "This irreconcilable struggle with his own demon was the real story of his life and work."

5. As quoted in H. Marquardt: *Henry Crabb Robinson und seine deutschen Freunde*, Göttingen, 1964, Vol. I, p. 60.

6. H. Marquardt, op. cit., Vol. II, p. 24.

7. Letter to Arnim, July 5, 1813.

8. Letter to Arnim, October 3, 1804.

9. Crabb Robinson; as quoted in H. Marquardt, op. cit., Vol. I, p. 37.

10. "There is little of significance in your purpose in life, if it were to run through your system, you won't get any further. You are standing in a circle—and that the smallest, too—work for money, money for bread, bread for nourishment, nourishment to provide the strength to work" (Clemens Brentano: *Werke* (Hanser Verlag), Vol. II. p. 41).

11. "Happiness and enjoyment is the aim of our life and it must lie within ourselves . . . Life means feeling, and making it felt that one exists, through enjoyment, which one takes and gives with oneself" (Brentano, op. cit.).

12. "Everything that stands between our eye and a distant visible object as an intermediary and brings us closer to the distant object, but also contributes something of its own, is romantic" (Brentano, op. cit., p. 258).

13. "The romantic is then a telescope, or rather the colour of the glass, and the definition of the object by the form of the glass" (op. cit., p. 259).

14. "The romantic is translation" (op. cit., p. 262).

15. "Form itself should have no form but it should just be the definite cessation of a thought which is pressing forth equally in all directions— whether it be something that has been thought in stone, sound, colour, words or thoughts" (op. cit., p. 259).

16. Cf. the fountain incident at the start of ch. 9 of *Godwi* Pt. I— "here is sound, colour and form combined (in the fountain with light playing on it) in a strange confusion".

17. "Before me was the statue as if just born. I saw it in the night as if in love and dream, in the moonlight as if with the desire to be created, in the morning twilight as if in the premonition of the artist, more and more shaping as a concept. And I stood before it and saw how it forced itself more and more into reality, and finally grew into a completed work of art in the rays of the sun, separated from the creator who only gives it birth, as something in itself, with all its inherent rights" (op. cit., p. 294).

18. "This is the pond in which I fall on page 146 in the first volume" (op. cit., p. 307).

19. "You don't imagine that I should have let you marry Ottilie?—No, not really—but I should have had to kill myself because she would not have me—I couldn't think of another way out—be unfaithful to her?— the whole reading public would have been cross with me . . ." (op. cit., p. 307).

20. "Who has sung this song? A sailor on the Rhine, and always there has echoed from the rock of the three knights: Lore Lay, Lore Lay, Lore Lay, as if there were three of me" (op. cit., p. 429).

21. "When the moon's quietly soothing tears dissolve the night's secret pains, then peace wafts by. In golden boats the spirits sail on the heavenly waters. The tinkling course of shining songs curls downwards, floats up" (op. cit., p. 156).

22. In his *Vom Beruf unserer Zeit für Gesetzgebung und Rechtswissenschaft* (1815).

23. Letter to Wilhelm Grimm, July 2, 1809.

24. "working on some italian tales for german children". Letter to Arnim, December 23, 1805.

25. Letter to Reimer, February 26, 1816.

26. The manuscript of the original story was discovered in the early 1920s in a Trappist monastery in Alsace. Prior to that one had had to rely on a copy by an unknown hand.

27. "Nothing sets off a man of the world as much as his ability to tell fine stories, stories which in the telling will cause the weaver to leave his shuttle, the advocate his pen, the apothecary his mortar, the knife-grinder his wheel and children their bread and butter" (op. cit., Vol. III, p. 314).

28. Op. cit., p. 387–8.

29. Op. cit., p. 482.

30. Op. cit., p. 527.

31. Op. cit., p. 563.

32. Op. cit., p. 526.

33. Op. cit., p. 388.

34. Op. cit., p. 313.

35. "It was ingeniously built. Nothing but dead men's bones and skulls, which were placed all round on top, and because the hair was still on them, it blew nicely in the wind and made sighing noises. It was not a bad scheme at all ... look, how all these bones have been tastefully arranged! Isn't that stylish? Isn't that gothic?" (op. cit., p. 360).

36. Op. cit., p. 290.

37. Op. cit., p. 141.

38. Op. cit., p. 244.

39. Op. cit., p. 72.

40. Letter of October 16, 1802.

41. Letter to Meline Brentano, December 8, 1812.

42. R. Tymms: *German Romantic Literature* (London, 1955), p. 247.

43. Letter of December 1816.

44. "Useless!—Do you know this terrible word? It's the heading to my whole life" (letter of December 1816).

45. "I have finished my poetic endeavours. They have hung too closely to the false way of my nature. Everything has turned out badly for me ..." (letter of February 15, 1815).

46. "I have set aside all my theological books and am packing them, the others, I am giving with all the rest to sell" (letter of April 3, 1819).

47. H. Marquardt: op. cit., Vol. II, p. 382.

48. In a letter to Böhmer, February 16, 1827.

49. In a letter to Böhmer, July 3, 1826.

50. In a letter, March 18, 1810.

51. "The whole should be like a sequence of paintings interwoven with arabesques, where the form is inexpressible, and where the symbol occurs, where the form flowers or resounds" (letter of January 21, 1810).

52. "Many years ago the nightingale did sing, and a sweet noise it was, when we were together. I sing and cannot weep, and spin so alone the thread clear and pure, so long as the moon does shine. Then we were together, then the nightingale did sing, now its sound reminds me that you have left me. Whenever the moon does shine, I think of you alone, my heart is clear and pure, would that God would unite us. Since you have left me, the nightingale sings constantly, and when it makes its sounds I think of when we were together. Would that God would join

us, I spin here so alone, the moon shines clear and pure, I sing and should like to weep."

53. "Listen! The sounds of the flute and the cool rippling fountains, they float down golden—quiet, quiet, let us listen. Gentle entreaties, mild demands, how sweetly the heart is addressed! Through the night which surrounds me the light of these sounds glances up to me."

54. Letter to Arnim, October 12, 1803.

55. Letter, May 1802.

SELECT BIBLIOGRAPHY

C. Brentano: *Werke*, edited by M. Preitz, 3 vols., Leipzig and Vienna, 1914.

C. Brentano: *Werke*, edited by F. Kemp, 3 vols., Munich (Hanser Verlag) 1963 ff.

C. Brentano: *Gedichte, Erzählungen, Briefe*, edited by H. M. Enzensberger. Fischer Bücherie, Frankfurt, 1958.

C. Brentano: *Briefe*, edited by F. Seebass, 2 vols., Nürnberg, 1951.

M. E. Atkinson: *Brentano, Geschichte vom braven Kasperl und dem schönen Annerl* (together with *Tieck, Der blonde Eckbert*), Blackwell Texts, Oxford, 1952.

H. M. Enzensberger: *Brentanos Poetik*, Hanser Verlag, Munich, 1961.

R. Guignard: *Chronologie des Poésies de Cl. Brentano*, Paris, 1933.

F. Gundolf: *Romantiker*, Berlin, 1930

W. Hoffmann: *Clemens Brentano*, Francke Verlag, Berne, 1966.

R. Huch: *Die Romantik*, Leipzig, 1931.

H. Levin-Derwein: *Die Geschwister Brentano in Dokumenten ihres Lebens*, Berlin, 1927.

I. Seidel: *Clemens Brentano*, Stuttgart, 1948.

R. Tymms: *German Romantic Literature*, Methuen, London, 1955.

M. Jahlmann: *Das Märchen und die Moderne*, Stuttgart, 1961.

E. T. A. Hoffmann

E. T. A. Hoffmann

by JOHN REDDICK

Hoffmann was born in Königsberg (East Prussia) in 1776. His dissolute advocate father having abandoned his neurotic mother and their two surviving children in 1779, he spent a mean, lonely childhood with an unmarried uncle and his sister. After schooling and law studies in Königsberg (1782–95), he became a civil servant. Outside his conscientious professional work, he energetically cultivated his talents of music and drawing; only later, in Plock (1802–4), did he begin to try his hand—unsuccessfully—at writing. Posted in 1804 to Warsaw, the "Paris of Poland", he soon became a public figure as, among other things, a conductor of large scale orchestral concerts, which included compositions of his own. Napoleon's defeat of Prussia in 1806 cut this existence short, for Hoffmann lost his job in the general dissolution of the civil service. After destitute and most difficult months, he managed to find a new job as musical director of the theatre and opera house in Bamberg, where he and his Polish wife moved in September 1808, and where he took on every task as the need arose, from composing to set-building and scene-shifting. His income was poor and sporadic, and he had to give music lessons to the scions of the wealthy. His passionate involvement in one of these pupils, Julia Marc, became one of the most determinant experiences in his life. He quit Bamberg in April 1813, and spent over a year of poverty, sickness and war in Leipzig and Dresden; but he also began at last to make writing his central means of expression. Thanks to Hippel, his oldest friend and a man of large influence, he regained a civil service post in 1814 at the Berlin "Kammergericht", and therewith found a stable existence again at last. Outside his job, in which he was hardworking and punctilious, he became a notable figure in Berlin's lively salon and café life, and also soon made a name for himself as an author. He protested publicly against State machinations aimed at suppressing social unrest and, after ridiculing the Head of Police in *Meister Floh*, came into serious conflict with the authorities. In spring, 1822, a fatal paralytic illness befell him and, after continuing to dictate stories to the last, he died on June 25, 1822.

"Was soll aus der Kunst werden
in dieser rauhen, stürmischen Zeit?"
Hoffmann, II, 267[1]

THERE is perhaps no other author in modern German literature whose writings have provoked such a startling divergence of critical opinion, or inspired such a confusion of myths and falsehoods, as E. T. A. Hoffmann. His literary worth?—"Dies ungesunde Gemisch", says Goedeke's "Grundriß der deutschen Dichtung,[2] and for Josef Nadler : "Hoffmann schreibt unnachahmlich schlecht"[3]; for Hans Mayer, on the other hand : "Er hat ein großes Werk hinterlassen."[4] And his meaning?—In Rosteutscher's view "Hoffmanns Seelendrama (. . .) spielt sich ab auf dem Hintergrunde *kosmischer Mythologie*",[5] whereas in the eyes of Georg Lukács Hoffmann is "ein wirklich großer *Realist*";[6] and there are, besides, almost as many other interpretations as there are interpreters. But the importance of these divergences is not what they tell us about the contrary attitudes of critics : it is the fact that they reflect a profound multivalence in Hoffmann's work itself, a multivalence that characterises it in almost all its parts; in the words given to Medardus in "Die Elixiere des Teufels" : "Ich bin das, was ich scheine, und scheine das nicht, was ich bin."[7] Accordingly, the reader can hope to find no one universal pattern in Hoffmann that will account for everything : the labyrinth ultimately always proves too large.

All the same, though, it does seem possible to isolate certain recurrent patterns and modes in the stories, and to identify certain persistent, formative pre-occupations, in accordance with the narrator's remark, towards the beginning of Johannes Kreisler's "fragmentarische Biographie", that the reader may in the end perhaps "meinen, daß, trotz des Anscheins der Abgerissenheit, doch ein fester durchlaufender Faden alle Teile zusammenhalte."[8] Hoffmann may well have been reflecting his own conception of his art when, in the same work, he figured Meister Abraham and his paper-cutting :

> "Meister Abraham verstand sich darauf, Kartonblätter so zuzuschneiden, daß, fand man auch aus dem Gewirre durchschnittner Flecke nicht das mindeste deutlich heraus, doch, hielt man ein Licht hinter das Blatt, in den auf die Wand geworfenen Schatten sich die seltsamsten Gestalten in allerlei Gruppen bildeten.[8a]"

Before we can look for these significant patterns, however, we must recognise some of the cardboard components in Hoffmann's world for what they are. It is no coincidence that "Celionati", one of Hoffmann's fictive characters who most fascinatingly reflects him *qua* creator, is repeatedly described as a "Charlatan" (III, 17, 56, 100, 102, 111, 124; cf. Alpanus, II, 160!) or that Meister Abraham, a similar figure is referred to as a "Taschenspieler" :[9] Hoffmann is undoubtedly a charlatan himself in certain respects, a purveyor of false contrivances. One level at which this applies is that of *plot,* for Hoffmann is sometimes quite happy to contrive ramshackle, disjointed intrigues, blatantly unmotivated entrances and exits, transparently stagey setpieces of moonlight witchery, dark intrigue, cloaks and daggers etc.—what in fact Hoffmann himself styled "ein ganzes Arsenal von Ungereimtheiten und Spukereien".[10] Another level at which Hoffmann can ring false is notoriously that of language. This is particularly true when he writes within particular "genres" such as the Idyllic (e.g. "nature", "beautiful girls", "domestic bliss") or the Tragick; but it is also often true when he is trying to convey ordinary human emotion—as August Langen remarked : even in Kreisler's most passionate utterances in *Kater Murr* the words are "nur Klischee".[11] Summarily speaking, the reader finds that Hoffman's style almost always tips over into derivative mediocrity when the author attempts to don cothurns and "play it straight". Significantly, it is precisely this pattern that is dwelt on in *Prinzessin Brambilla,* the work in which Hoffmann plays most fascinatingly on the question of the artist and his true mode of "delivery" : so long as the actor Giglio Fava remains committed to tragedy, his existence is one of blindness and false postures; it is only when he experiences the validity of the *ironic* mode of the commedia dell'arte that he becomes genuine at last. This is most profoundly true of Hoffmann himself : he is only fully genuine, and therewith fully effective and luminous, when he manipulates his created world as a detached *ironist.*

If this contention is a valid one, then it renders dubious one of the most inveterate and cherished of Hoffmann interpretations, whereby he is held to be essentially a "metaphysicist" and "myth-creator" in the best Romantic tradition (an interpretation that is epitomised by the title of one recent book : *E. T. A. Hoffmann's Other World. The Romantic Author and His "New Mythology"*).[12] So tenacious and insidious is this view that a variant form of it has even turned up in a Marxist critique, for H. G. Werner finds that "Hoffmann [. . .] deutete die Triebkräfte menschlichen Tuns und gessellschaftlichen Geschehens im metaphysischen Sinne".[13] This kind of view does seem to me to be a radical misconception.[14] However much Hoffmann was influenced by such as Novalis, G. H. Schubert, Schelling, Fichte, and however many of their notions may have found their way into the "décor" of his writings, there is little evidence that either his generative "Hauptidee",[15] or the actual "durchlaufender Faden" of his work, are in any meaningful way Romantic or metaphysical. The relatively early *Der Dichter und der Komponist* (1813) is a fascinating document in this respect. It would seem at first sight a Programme of Romantic Intent:

—Der Dichter rüste sich zum kühnen Fluge in das ferne Reich der Romantik; [...] so [...] daß man, wie in einem beseligenden Traume, selbst dem dürftigen, alltäglichen Leben entrückt, in den Blumengängen des romantischen Landes wandelt [...].[16]

This very possibly is what Hoffmann did indeed long for in a part of his soul, with that same longing that made him always want to be a composer far more ardently than a writer. But it was incongruent with his actual talents—and the true bent of these is clearly intimated later on in this very same text, when Hoffman turns to a discussion of "Opera buffa"!—the operatic mode derived from that same "commedia dell'arte" in which, at the other end of his creative life (1820), he has Giglio Fava find his true being: "Hier ist es nun das Fantastische, ... das *keck ins Alltagsleben* hineinfährt und alles *zu oberst und unterst dreht*" (etc.).[17]

But if Hoffman's "Hauptidee" is not to create transcendental myths, but to contrive situations in which everyday reality is turned topsy-turvy, what then is the purpose and method of this process? There is one particular metaphor that Hoffman repeatedly uses which symbolises it most effectively: that of the *mirror*. The notion is programmatically stated in the early "Berganza" (1813):

Der Blick des wahren Dichters durchschaut die menschliche Natur in ihrer innersten Tiefe und herrscht über ihre Erscheinungen, indem er ihre mannigfaltigste Strahlenbrechung in seinem Geiste wie in einem Prisma auffaßt und reflektiert.[17a]

And at the other end of Hoffmann's creative span as a writer, we find him propounding the very same notion in a written defence of *Meister Floh* when he was threatened with indictment over the Knarrpanti episode: he justified the story as the "Geburt eines humoristischen Schriftstellers, der die Gebilde des wirklichen Lebens nur in der Abstraktion des Humors wie in einem Spiegel auffassend reflectiert".[18] These words uncannily anticipate the famous defence of *Le Rouge et le Noir* by Hoffmann's fellow-ironist, Stendhal, eight years later:

Eh, monsieur, un roman est un miroir qui se promène sur une grande route. [...] Et l'homme qui porte le miroir dans sa hotte sera par vous accusé d'être immoral! Son miroir montre la fange, et vous accusez le miroir ! Accusez bien plutôt le grand chemin où est le bourbier, et plus encore l'inspecteur des routes qui laisse l'eau croupir et le bourbier se former.[19]

An ironical reflecting of the given social reality, then, is one function of Hoffmann's creative mirror. But it has another function, more persistent and much more profound : it reflects an *outward visible image* of the *otherwise secret inner being* of individual characters, that is to say of the fictive people whom Hoffman invents as representatives, perhaps, of that given reality. Once again, *Prinzessin Brambilla* explicitly illuminates the process, for the mirror-like waters in the "Urdargarten" allegory are

nichts anders, als was wir Deutschen Humor nennen, die wunderbare, aus der tiefsten Anschauung der Natur geborne Kraft des Gedankens, seinen *eignen ironischen Doppeltgänger* zu machen, an dessen seltsamlichen Faxen er die seinigen und—ich will das freche Wort beibehalten—die Faxen des ganzen Seins hienieden erkennt und sich daran ergetzt—[20]

In this particular case, the confrontation with the "ironischen Doppeltgänger" that manifests inward being is blithe and beneficial : "Doch wie sie sich in dem See erblickten, da *erkannten* sie sich erst, schauten einander an, brachen in ein Lachen aus" (Hoffmann's italics).[21] But there is also an opposite pole to this, whereby the ironic mirror reveals an inward being of desperate brokenness and distortion. In *Kater Murr*, Hoffmann creates a sharp paradigm of this kind of process : after having already established a mirror relationship between Kreisler and the mad, savage artist, Leonard Ettlinger (cf. especially III, 262, 269), Hoffmann suddenly confronts the hero with his seemingly corporeal "Ebenbild, sein eignes Ich, das neben ihm daherschritt"[22]—Kreisler's normal ironic defences prove useless : he is "vom tiefsten Entsetzen erfaßt, [. . .] zum Tode erbleicht",[23] and even his most essential power of music is frozen : "erstarrt ist mein Gesang, denn der Ich hat seine weiße kalte Totenhand auf meine Brust gelegt".[24] It is only then that Kreisler and the reader discover the "Mechanik" (III, 272) behind the apparition, the actual mechanical device, i.e. the "Hohlspiegel" that Meister Abraham has set up outside his door. Hoffmann has Kreisler complain that it was just a "Fopperei",[25] a meaningless trick ("Kunststückchen")—but the retort that is put in Abraham's mouth (III, 271-72) is crucial, for it indicates that fundamental principal behind Hoffman's mirror process : that it is *not* gratuitous

trickery, but a device for bringing out into the open that otherwise secret inner being, the "geheimnisvollen Organism".

If this analysis is founded, then clearly there is no substance in
the hoary claim that Hoffmann subscribed essentially to a metaphysical rationale of existence. Undeniably, the "décor", the "super-
structure" of his writing, is heavy with portentous invocations of
Dark Fate, antagonistic forces and the like, but this arguably is
automatic writing, with Hoffman happily tapping "das ganze
Reservoir deutscher Schauerromantik".[26]—And whenever he is
being truly himself, i.e. an ironist, he guys it, as repeatedly in
Brambilla, or as in *Klein Zaches* : "... ein dunkles Verhängnis reißt
mich fort!" exclaims Balthasar; "—'Ha-ha,'—lachte Fabian hell
auf, 'ha ha ha—wie fein—wie poetisch, wie mystisch! ...' "[27] In
his "Hauptidee", Hoffmann surely is fundamentally an *empiricist*,
with the generative if implicit premise that the nature of society
with its inhabitants derives from a logic of their own, however
obscure, and with the further, explicit premise that this nature, if
not the labyrinthine logic behind it, may be demonstrated via his
mirror.

The phrase "society with its inhabitants" is a deliberate one :
Hoffmann never illuminates society through its institutions as such,
but exclusively through its inhabitants and their attitudes. One
might even adduce it as part of Hoffmann's "Hauptidee" that
much his greatest concern is with *people*; as he has the narrator
suggest in *Brambilla* : isn't it "das eigne Innere der auftretenden
Gestalten" which is "der rechte Schauplatz"[29] of a story? What
specifically interests him is the relationship of people (*a*) to themselves, and (*b*) to other people—and therewith to "society" and to
"existence". This produces a wide span of dramatic personae whose
fictive existences range from the "largely private" to the "totally
public", but who mostly oscillate, with characteristic ambivalence,
between the two. At the one end we might locate, say, Giglio Fava,
whose story only contingently involves society; at the other, Fürst
Irenäus, perhaps, or Fürst Paphnutius.

When we take a closer look at those figures whom Hoffmann
created as representative of *society*, we soon find that their identifying characteristic, in one or another form, is *ungenuineness*; that
is to say : they have no personal, organic Self, but possess an identity only in terms of their society; they are in fact prisoners of what
Sartre was later to define as "mauvaise foi". This phenomenon is
projected in numberless forms. A remark in *Kater Murr* is typical :

"der Hof verwirft überhaupt, jedes tiefere Gefühl als unstatthaft
[...] und gemein", and : "Die Fürstin hatte sonst Gemüt und
Herz, aber das seltsam halb lächerliche, halb widrige Ungeheuer,
Etiquette genannt, hatte sich auf ihre Brust gelegt wie ein bedroh-
licher Alp".[30] The same notion occurs with the poodle Ponto, in a
section that pivots on "sozialen Umgan(g)" and "Individualität"[31] :
he is said to have once had a "Kern des Guten" but "der fond, in
dem den Kern des Guten steckt, liegt so tief, und über ihm hat sich
so viel Unrat eines ausgelassenen Lebens gesammelt, daß er im
Keime ersticken muß".[32]

Where his acquaintance Kater Murr falsifies his "ehrliche natürliche Natur"[33] largely through his complacent vanity and philistinism, Ponto the poodle is created as representative of a different,
more calculated falseness : the principle of deliberate social pretence for the sake of utterly selfish betterment, for Ponto's "welt-
kluges Benehmen",[34] like those other con-men's Tartuffe and
Krull, has its basis entirely in "der foppenden Benutzung der Tor-
heit anderer".[35] Ponto also voices another associated motif that
is central to Hoffman, when he reports his uncle's emphatic
assertion that Murr's "Stand" and "niedere Abkunft" as a mere cat
make it unthinkable that he should ever attend a "Pudel-
assemblee".[36] For this motif of "rank" and "class" is one that
Kammergerichtsrat Hoffmann continually plays on as a token of
the social order : there are very few figures in all his writing who
are not created in terms of some kind of rank or status : "der
Student" Anselmus and "Archivarius" Lindhorst, Zaches as "Minister", "Serapion" as a former "Graf", "Rätin" Benzon, "Ritter"
Gluck—a full list would be immense. Characteristically, the motif
is given its most trenchant form with Kreisler : once his uncle had
become a "Geheimer Legationsrat", he was revered by all as having
achieved "das höchste Ziel alles menschlichen Strebens"[37]—and in
turn the young Kreisler himself (like his creator in real life!) was
misled into following the same "schiefe Richtung des Weges", thus
denying the "wahre einzige Tendenz meines Lebens".[38] We shall
come back to this decisive event later on.

One of Hoffmann's most persistent metaphors for "ungenuineness" is significantly the "mechanical". Thus for instance an ironical
passage in the Kreisleriana claims that music's true function is to
relax a man so that he may return refreshed "zu dem eigentlichen
Zweck seines Daseins [...], d.h. ein tüchtiges Kammrad in der
Walkmühle des Staats sein".[39] "Kater Murr" similarly speaks in
terms of the "Hofmaschine"[40] and the "Räderwerk der Staats-
maschine",[41] and Irenäus' father is said to have had no inward

being but a "hölzerne(s) Gestell"[42] instead, whilst Irenäus himself
registers the virulent psychological turmoil in Hedwiga as simply a
"Schaden" in a "Räderwerk [...], das sonst niemals stockte".[43]
This metaphor, together with its associate one of "puppets" (cf.
for instance III, 158 and 188) is, of course, one that countless other
writers of the period found it apt to use as well, from, say, Lenz
through "Bonaventura", Kleist and Tieck to Büchner (to name
only a few!). But it also ties up with a timeless fascination of ironic,
comic writers for *robot-like rigidity* in human behaviour, as
exploited most classically by Molière. Repeatedly in Hoffmann we
find an ironic illumination of cerebral "plans" and "schemes" that
are fatuous and false in direct proportion to their blind inflexibility :
Fürst Paphnutius' comic decree "daß von Stund an die Aufklärung
eingeführt sei";[44] Knarrpanti's absurd systematic investigation into
a nonexistent crime; Leuwenhoek's regressive and futile attempts
to bend Dortje and the fleas to his own rigid purpose; Irenäus'
systematic pretence that Sieghartshof is a genuine court and he
himself a ruler in the true image of Frederick the Great;[45] Zaches'
rigid conviction of his own cleverness (—"Adieu, Mütterchen, klug
bin ich genug")[46]—whereupon he falls flat on his face time after
time until—Prime Minister now!—he finally meets his Maker in
the chamber pot; Theodor's deliberate prosecution of his "romantische, ja wohl ritterliche Liebe"[47] for Seraphine : Euphemie's and
Medardus' designs for ruling over "die läppische Puppenwelt, wie
sie sich um uns dreht"[48]—yet their pretensions are "nur das
krampfhafte Winden des gefesselten Raubtiers im Käfig!";[49] the
false Rätin Benzon, typically, is full of "Entwürfe" and "Pläne",[50]
and exclaims to Meister Abraham : "Laßt uns zusammen diesen
kleinen Hof beherrschen, der in der Tat des Gängelbandes
bedarf".[51] Hoffmann reflects this basic pattern time without number, and it is worth noting that, however pessimistic he undoubtedly
was about the viability within society of "true being", he almost
without exception has his exponents of "false being" come a cropper
in the end, just as Molière has his Tartuffe fail at the last for all
his pernicious interim success. (Rätin Benzon might appear to con-
trovert this, in that she has seemingly succeeded at the book's close
in her plan for arranging a marriage between Julia and the cretin-
ous Prince Ignaz : but the decisive thing here is that this is the
close only of an unfinished fragment, not of a completed book.)

It comes as no surprise to find that Hoffmann reflects this pattern of falseness and of antagonism to individuality as having been
in turn falsely legitimised by being rationalised into a formal moral
code. We have already seen, for instance, how the Court of

Irenäus condemned genuine emotion as "unstatthaft und gemein". Rätin Benzon, the most cold-hearted[52] and self-aggrandising[53] exponent of the social order in all Hoffmann, is cast as the typical advocate of this code when he has her argue "daß es ein gefährliches Spiel ist, sich über jene [konventionellen] Verhältnisse erheben und dem Weltgeist näher treten zu wollen in der Mystifikation des eignen Seins";[54] elsewhere, too, she is made the apostle of "alle konventionellen Verhältnisse" and the enemy of individuality (e.g. III, 182, 329). This woman claims to be a defender of "alles, was durch die richtige Ansicht des wirklichen Lebens bedingt und als unsere Zufriedenheit begründend anerkannt wird".[55]—but what a fraud this is! For in her secret past there was a "strafbare Schande"[56] and a total failure of her life, such that "Verzweiflung"[57] consumed her, leaving only "dead ashes",[58] and her present fervid "morality" is a false thing, a "künstliches Gebäude"[59] thrown up on a "Grundstein, den ein Blitzstrahl zermalmte".[60]

We move here into one of the most crucial areas that Hoffmann probes and mirrors : the obscure background from which the falseness and dissonances of society derive. And instead of metaphysical notions, we repeatedly find him positing an empirical causation, namely *some form of severe dislocation* within or amongst those social creatures that are humans. A programmatic passage in *Kater Murr* on the upbringing of children is revelationary, a passage put in the mouth of that pedagogic pillar of society, Professor Lothario :

> Der Professor war für die offene Gewalt, da die Gestaltung der Dinge zum äußern Wohl es fordere, daß jeder Mensch, alles Widerstrebens unerachtet, so zeitig als möglich in die Form gepreßt werde, wie sie durch dar Verhältnis aller einzelnen Teile zum Ganzen bedingt werde, da sonst sogleich eine verderbliche Monstruosität entstehe, die allerlei Unheil verursachen könne.[61]

This undoubtedly reflects the theory and practice in society as Hoffmann saw it—witness for instance the lament against schools where the children are "nach bestimmter Norm zugesschnitten" "ohne Rücksicht auf ihre Individualität".[62] But in fact it is precisely such practices which, far from preventing "Monstruosität", actually encourage it, as Hoffmann suggests via Meister Abraham's retort that the same principle applies with the young as with "Partiell-Wahnsinnigen",[63] namely that "der offne Widerstand immer wahnsinniger mache, wogegen die selbst errungene Erkenntnis des Irrtums radikal heile".[64] This helps to mark out what is perhaps the most fundamental polarity of all in Hoffmann's world : at one end, monstrous, sterile, false patterns of existence, with constraint, dislocation, conflict as their cause; on the other, a fruitful wholeness and sanity, with genuine, personal awareness as its base. And it is important to note that a distribution chart of Hoffmann's characters would show them more heavily clustered towards the former pole.

There are two works which manifest the opposite poles with especial clarity, respectively : *Die Elixiere des Teufels* and *Prinzessin Brambilla*. In the one : a constant dislocated gyration; in the other : a steady progression from total falseness through divided identity to total integrity and genuineness. And in these stories Hoffmann incorporated two passages which are as it were in parallel but in contrary motion, and which are astonishing revelations of the conceptions informing the works. Let us juxtapose them. First the one from the "Elixiere", put in the mouth of that strange and delightful luminary, Schönfeld, alias Belcampo :

> "was haben Sie denn nun davon! ich meine von der besonderen Geistesfunktion, die man Bewußtsein nennt und die nichts anders ist als die verfluchte Tätigkeit eines verdammten Toreinnehmers —Akziseoffizianten—Oberkontrollassistenten, der sein heilloses Comptoir im Oberstübchen aufgeschlagen hat und zu aller Ware, die hinauswill, sagt : 'Hei .. hei ... die Ausfuhr ist verboten ... im Lande, im Lande bleibt's'. Die schönsten Juwelen werden wie schnöde Saatkörner in die Erde gesteckt, und was emporschießt, sind höchstens Runkelrüben, aus denen die Praxis mit tausend Zentner schwerem Gewicht eine Viertelunze übelschmeckenden Zucker preßt . . ."[65]

And the passage in *Brambilla*, spoken by the narrator (in the same paragraph that suggests that "das eigne Innere der auftretenden Gestalten" is the proper sphere of writing) :

> —wie so tot, so bettelarm, so maulwurfsblind wär' unser Leben, hätte der Weltgeist uns Söldlinge der Natur nicht ausgestattet mit jener unversieglichen Diamantgrube in unserm Innern, aus der uns in Schimmer und Glanz daa wunderbare Reich aufstrahlt, das unser Eigentum geworden! Hochbegabt die, die sich dieses Eigentums recht bewußt! Noch hochbegabter und selig zu preisen die, die ihres innern Perus Edelsteine nicht allein zu erschauen, sondern auch heraufzubringen, zu schleifen und ihnen prächtigeres Feuer zu entlocken verstehen.[66]

In both passages, then, an inward potential of "jewels" is predicated. But in the one case this potential is distorted and deformed by the severe constraints of private "Bewußtsein" and public "Praxis"; whilst in the other it is presented as capable of the most genuine realisation and enhancement.

The lines via Belcampo are surely most remarkable; for they prefigure with uncanny accuracy the modern rationale of psychology. No surprise then that Freud saw fit to write a study of *Der Sandmann*! And again here : what price metaphysics in the face of these few lines! How fascinating, too, to see that Hoffmann's mirror reflects these distorted growths and their noxious effluvium principally in terms of a sex-guilt-power syndrome—and "syndrome" is a deliberate word : "Krankheit"[67] is one of the most persistent of all Hoffmann's motifs, and is central even to *Prinzessin Brambilla*.[68]

Hoffmann's very first presentation of Medardus, the hero of the "Elixiere", is in terms of a dislocation in his past, for the opening words of the novel are : "Nie hat mir meine Mutter gesagt, in welchen Verhältnissen mein Vater in der Welt lebte";[69] (and this echoes the very first depiction, at the beginning of the *Kreisleriana*, of Hoffmann's greatest figure, Johannes Kreisler : "Wo ist er her?— Niemand weiß es!—Wer waren seine Eltern?—Es ist unbekannt!"[70]). The second sentence then goes on to adumbrate the book's seminal pattern of degeneration : Medardus' father was himself enmeshed in "Frevel" and "Todsünde";[71] and his child was made aware of it, though subconsciously, via the "Erzählungen und einzelnen Äußerungen meiner Mutter über ihr früheres Leben, die mir erst später verständlich worden".[72] This last point is a critical one : however much the narrator-hero may gesture ("nach meiner aus Romanen und Komödien gezogenen Theorie"!)[73] in terms of a "böses Verhängnis",[74] etc., the generative conception of the book is *not* fatalistic, but predicates "Bewußtsein" as a decisive factor : the pristine potential of each man is a store of *jewels*, in Hoffmann's view, and the nature of that potential when realised depends on the individual's particular "awareness" of existence. It is Belcampo, again, who is given to imply, in a startling phrase, that he "existier(t) [...] überhaupt nur durch (s)ein eignes Bewußtsein".[75]

In the slightly later story, *Der Sandmann*, Hoffmann has Klara (perhaps the only really convincing, full-blooded woman character in his works) elaborate this notion with great lucidity in her fictive letter to Nathanael : "alles Entsetzliche und Schreckliche, wovon du sprichst, [ging] nur in Deinem Innern vor [...], die wahre (—n.b.!) wirkliche Außenwelt aber [hatte] daran wohl wenig teil [...]".[76] Coppelius as a "dunkle Macht" [77] is a "projection" on Nathanael's

part: "es ist das Phantom unseres eigenen Ichs, dessen innige
Verwandtschaft und dessen tiefe Einwirkung auf unser Gemüt uns
in die Hölle wirft oder in den Himmel verzückt".[78] (—The famous
lament of Rimbaud's, sixty years later, at once comes to mind:
"Je me crois en enfer, donc j'y suis".) And with this seeming
"devilish force" : "Solange du an ihn glaubst, *ist* er auch und wirkt,
nur dein Glaube ist seine Macht".[79] Klara herself is depicted as
having an inward "wholeness" such that she can recognise what is
true and fruitful ("festen, durch das heitre Leben gestärkten Sinn";
"erkennen", II, 17)—and how characteristic of Hoffmann that this
"genuine" figure, like Giglio Fava at the end of "Brambilla", should
have *humour* and *ironic detachment* as a predominant trait : "Sei
heiter—heiter!—Ich habe mir vorgenommen, bei Dir zu erscheinen
wie Dein Schutzgeist und den häßlichen Coppola [...] mit lautem
Lachen fortzubannen".[80] With Nathanael, however, the distortion
is irremediable : his reading of existence, while illusive in terms of
Klara's "wahre, wirkliche Außenwelt", none the less constitutes *his*
true though distorted identity. He appears to recover after the
affair of the duel (II, 26), but relapses and ends up in a lunatic
asylum (p. 36); again he seems to recover, thanks to the benign
and rich atmosphere of Klara's family: "—Jede Spur des Wahnsinns
war verschwunden, bald erkräftigte sich Nathanael in der sorglichen
Pflege der Mutter, der Geliebten, der Freunde."[81]; there is even
the image that Hoffmann recurrently uses to symbolise "fulfilment" : the "Gütchen in einer angenehmen Gegend".[82] But the
monstrous reality finally breaks through the façade with catas-
trophic force, and in an upsurge of sexuality and violence,
Nathanael tries to murder Klara and then kills himself.

This is the end-point—but what of the origins? How did
Nathanael's "jewels" degenerate into monstrousness? It is characteristic of Hoffmann's conceptions that the Nathanael fiction very
strongly figures this degenerative phase; and characteristic, too, that
this phase consists of a pattern of severe trauma in childhood : the
boy's violent fantasies, stimulated by the old nanny's gruesome tale
(II, 8 f.), and his experience of gross physical violence and dislocation with Coppelius—an experience that is "false" by Klara's
criterion, but desperately "real" by his, to the extent even of
physical sickness for several weeks. The figuration of Aurelie in the
Elixiere is likewise exemplary in this respect. As with Nathanael,
Hoffmann uses the fiction of an adult writing a letter that uncovers
her traumatic past, and the key metaphor is typical: *"Ich muß
zurückgehen in meine frühe Kinderzeit, [...] denn schon damals*

wurde der Keim in mein Innres gelegt, der so lange Zeit hindurch verderblich fortwucherte[83] (my italics). With Aurelie as with Nathanael, there is the motif of a parent furtively involved with someone "devilish", but here it is compounded by sexuality (Aurelie's mother's incestuous love for Francesko). And Aurelie's resultant fixation is also sexual! Francesko's portrait marks her awareness even as a very young child (I, 466), becomes vivid again in puberty (467–8), and becomes corporeal to her fantasy during adolescence (468), such that she becomes ill with a "fantastische Liebe zu einem Wesen, das nur in mir lebte".[84] Just as Nathanael projected his morbid fear of the "Sandmann" on to Coppelius, so Hoffmann has Aurelie project her morbid passion for the animated portrait on to Medardus (469 f.)—thus enmeshing in *his* misshapen pattern of existence. The most significant factor with Aurelie, however, is that her sexuality is not only warped in its fantasy objects : it is also an acutely divisive force within her once it is compounded by a sense of *guilt* : "Nun erst wußte ich, daß es frevelhafte Liebe gebe, mein Abscheu dagegen kämpfte mit dem Gefühl, das meine Brust erfüllte".[85] And with Aurelie, as with Nathanael, Hoffmann reflects the syndrome of distortion and alienation in terms of physical illness (477).

With this compound of dynamic guilt, sexuality and conflict, we have in fact the key generative pattern of the book, the gyrations of Medardus and his adjuncts being cast almost exclusively in terms of it, and of its concomitant phenomena : violence and the compulsive urge to possess and dominate. Significantly enough, we find the same pattern generating a major part of Hoffman's other novel as well : Hektor and Hedwiga in "Kater Murr" might be characters transposed directly from the one novel to the other, and Hoffmann endows Hedwiga with a "psycho-biography" that very closely echoes Aurelie's, and which has in addition the "Sandmann" motif of a childhood trauma of physical violence (III, 260 f.);— as Kreisler is given to say to Ettlinger, the perpetrator of that violence : "Wisse [...], daß die Wunde, die du dem armen Kinde [...] beibrachtest, noch immer nicht recht geheilt ist, so daß sie vor Schmerz manchmal allerlei Faxen macht".[86] It is not only in the two novels and *"Der Sandmann"*, however, that this pattern of violent sexuality is generative : we find it at the heart of many stories, and one of the most savage and bitter scenes in all Hoffmann's writing characteristically arises from it, i.e. the lines where Berganza sees the drunken, lascivious Monsieur George stagger into the bridal chamber of his "keuschen, engelreinen Braut" and set about mauling her with his "rohen Fäusten".[87] This passage is

particularly important since it reflects clearly (perhaps too clearly)
the origins of the pattern in Hoffman's own life : the desperate,
traumatic failure of his love for Julia Marc on her marriage to the
crude and vulgar business-man, Georg Gröpel. (*Berganza* was
written in February–April, 1813, only a few months after Julia's
wedding.)

It is notable that this motif of impurity and sexuality not only
determines the personae of Hektor and Hedwiga in the much
later *Kater Murr*, but also plays a large part in Hoffman's figuration of the Kreisler-Julia Benzon relationship;—the prefigurative
and in a sense ominous first words that Julia ever hears Kreisler say
are " 'Wieder verfehlt—*keine Reinheit*—[. . .]' ".[88] Indeed the
tension between "purity" and "corruptness" is nowhere sharper than
in this relationship. For the most part, Julia is conceived like Klara
in that she has a genuine, fruitful being; indeed she is figured as
an embodiment of "pureness" in an almost emblematic, medieval
way : her "Seele" is "wie [. . .] ei(n) klare(r) reine(r) Spiegel";[89]
there is in her "ein reiner kindlicher frommer Sinn";[90] she has no
"lüsternen Vorwitz";[91] and hence "hat der finstre Höllenegeist
der Sünde keine Macht über dich".[92] But with all this, she is still
figured as having within her a severe threat of degeneration. With
the introduction of Hektor, Hoffmann re-creates yet again his
Gröpel-Julia Marc situation; and Julia Benzon is not proof against
his influence : he provokes a poisonous fascination in her (III, 295),
her dreams centre on him in a topos experience of sexuality and
violence (296), and ultimately she yields to him in the flesh and is
stopped by Kreisler just as she is going off with him to a fisher-
man's hut (310). In "Der Sandmann", Hoffmann had Klara also
yield to the poisonous influence of Nathanael, but then recover her
"wholeness" thanks to her proper awareness, her "festen Sinn" (II,
15–16)—and this is precisely the pattern with Julia : she, too,
recognises that the threat is a function of her own being : " 'Barm-
herziger Himmel [. . .] schütze mich nur vor mir selber !' "[93] and,
in terms of the cardinal "Sandmann" principle that "nur dein
Glaube ist seine Macht", Hoffmann has her recognise destructive
passion for what it is and resolve to "fest [. . .] halten an dem
Glauben, daß [dies Gemüt] ewig rein, ewig davon frei bleiben
wird".[94] But of course we do not know how Hoffmann envisaged
the final outcome with Julia, for the novel was never completed !
Was it perhaps partly because he was too ambivalent in his own
mind about the inner reality of Julia Marc/Julia Benzon that he
left his greatest work hanging in mid-air?

*   *   *

"Inner reality"? We are back here with the fundamental notion of Hoffmann using his mirror to manifest the real inward being of his characters. And we find of course that he figures the "Monstruosität" theme in the various stories precisely in terms of this notion;—we have in fact already looked at a paradigmatic instance : Kreisler's arresting confrontation with a normally latent part of his being, thanks to Meister Abraham's "Hohlspiegel". What is chiefly involved here is another and critical elaboration of Hoffmann's constant pre-occupation with "genuineness", and we may isolate it as a motif of *"personal identity"*. Given the psychological rationale evinced above, such a motif comes as no surprise : since genuine identity, in the etymological sense of "oneness" and "wholeness", is achieved only by those who can realise their jewelled potential in full, then all the others, with their more or less warped and alienated potential, must inevitably be more or less severely divided within themselves;—in Hoffman's constant image : "zerrissen". In this light, we can elaborate on our earlier contention : we can say that Hoffmann's concern with "true inward being", his concern with people's relationships with (*a*) themselves, and (*b*) other people, is figured exclusively in terms of the notion of "identity". Is there a fruitful identity between a man's image of himself, and his actual inward reality? Is there a fruitful identity between a man's genuine reality and the reality of his environment? It is these questions that are the source of artistic tension in almost every story that Hoffmann ever wrote.

The figure of Medardus in the *Elixiere* is again exemplary of the one pole :

Ich bin das, was ich scheine, und scheine das nicht, was ich bin, mir selbst ein unerklärrich Rätsel, bin ich entzweit mit meinem Ich![95]

And : "ich konnte mich selbst nicht wiederfinden";[96] and : "Mein eignes Ich [. . .] schwamm ohne Halt";[97] and again, programmatically : "Mit meinem Selbst mehr als jemals entzweit, wurde ich mir selbst zweideutig".[98] His awareness of himself is totally fragmented ("Mein Ich [war] hundertfach zerteilt"),[99] and Hoffmann gives this effective shape through the virtuoso use of a "rôle" motif : Medardus dons a multitude of different clothes and assumes a multitude of different "identities"—but feels himself in real possession of none of them for very long. His every sense of stability is illusive, whether it be in the "Handelsstadt", in the Court or on return to the monastery. The one bitter constant of his existence is the irremediable syndrome of lust-violence-guilt. And it is this that gives rise to a motif which, together with that of "rôles", is the paramount structure of the book : the motif of "Doppelgänger". The reader is faced with a haunting, most remarkable situation : in this book the fiction of "real people" has gone almost completely by the board. The Prior, the Fürst, the Doctor and other auxiliaries may be fictively "real". But Viktorin? the mad, savage "monk"? Hermogen? Aurelie? the Maler? Each of these seems to have a "reality" only as a "projection" of Medardus' distorted "Bewußtsein". Even the queen on a playing card can become "Aurelie" so corporeally to him that he feels guilty of raping her (I, 402; and cf. supra : her reverse projection of her own fantasy passion on to him!). Is Viktorin truly a figment of Medardus' mind when he topples over the cliff (319)?—for in "Viktorin's" own story, as related through the Prior, it was the other way around : Medardus was "Mein Ich", "das Ich meiner Gedanken".[100] Medardus' own double explicitly exists "nur in meiner Fantasie."[101] And it is characteristically the "mad" Belcampo who is given to say of the "Maler" : "da er eine *bloße Idee* ist, muß er getötet werden können durch eine Idee".[102] Most importantly, too : the supposed "elixir" of the title functions only by autosuggestion : in the objective opinion of the young Count and his companion who are deliberately introduced into the story, the stuff is no more nor less than excellent wine (307).

The structure of the novel as a whole is so arranged that even the reader experiences its multivalence at every turn. With its leitmotifs, its multiple-mirror-image characters, its narrations of single events from multiple standpoints, it achieves the sometimes astonishing effect of imposing on the reader the spectacle of an indeterminate number of figures scurrying vainly through an indeterminate mirror-lined labyrinth. And one passage, the assessment of the situation by the Prior towards the novel's end (539 ff.), is so created that it conveys a dislocated sense of "reality" that one might normally think was the invention of Kafka. True : the novel ends limply and has a hundred gross faults; but it has at least as many virtues.

At the opposite pole from Medardus, of course, we find Giglio Fava. He, too, has a severe crisis of identity, coming into physical conflict with himself (III, 60), and being characterised in terms of the same topoi of "illness" and "madness" as Medardus and many others (cf. especially III, 108 f.!). But : unlike Medardus or Nathanael, Giglio's "jewelled potential" is not distorted or deformed but simply dormant and hidden; thanks to the mirror of irony and humour, he perceives his true being, "kills" his false self in a comic duel, and thus attains to a genuine "identity" and integrity as a "mit sich einiger Mensch" (to quote *Das Majorat*).[103] In *Meister Floh*, too, the pattern is fundamentally the same : Peregrinus Tyß likewise achieves a genuine wholeness, his inward truth being "unselfish emotion and love" in place of Giglio's "irony". And Giglio and Peregrinus alike grow into a rich organic relationship with their surroundings—the "wahre, wirkliche Außenwelt", as Hoffman had Klara describe it.

Medardus and Giglio Fava, then, mark the opposite limits in Hoffman's figurations of the "identity" motif in respect of "people's relationships with themselves", and almost every central character in his stories can be located somewhere on the scale. Towards the one pole : perhaps Nathanael Spikher (*Die Abenteuer der Sylvesternacht*), Cardillac (*Das Fräulein von Scuderi*; this of course is the most famous tale of Hoffmann's, and Cardillac is the obvious model for Stevenson's *Dr. Jekyll and Mr. Hyde*), Elis Fröbom (*Die Bergwerke zu Falun*); somewhere in the middle : figures like Marie (*Nußknacker und Mausekönig*), Julia Benzon, and Theodor (*Das Majorat*); and towards the other pole : Anselmus (*Der goldne Topf*), Balthasar (*Klein Zaches*), Ännchen and Amandus (*Die Königsbraut*) and, of course, Peregrinus Tyß in *Meister Floh*.

On this particular scale of the motif of "personal" identity, the distribution of characters is clearly fairly even. How then is the earlier assertion justified that Hoffmann's figures cluster more towards the pole of dislocation than the pole of integrity? This soon becomes evident when we illuminate that other motif of "identity between people and their surroundings". And it likewise becomes rapidly evident that we are concerned here with probably the most central and certainly the most plangent themes of all Hoffmann's writing. It is characteristically Johannes Kreisler—Hoffmann's greatest creation—in whom the fundamental dislocated pattern is most grievously manifest. In Meister Abraham's emblematic words to Rätin Benzon and her like :

"was habt ihr alle gegen diesen Johannes, was hat er euch Böses getan, daß ihr ihm keine Freistatt, kein Plätzchen gönnt auf dieser Erde? [. . .]"[104]

Kreisler is radically a "Fremdlin(g) in der Welt",[105] and his total eccentricity vis-à-vis society is manifest even in his name (—a name that is typically an alias, his original name having long since been

estranged from him, III, 182); as Hoffmann has him say to Rätin
Benzon :

> "[. . .] Sie können nicht wegkommen von dem Worte Kreis, und
> der Himmel gebe, daß Sie denn gleich an die wunderbaren
> Kreise denken mögen, in denen sich unser ganzes Sein bewegt
> und aus denen wir nicht herauskommen können, wir mögen es
> anstellen, wie wir wollen. *In diesen Kreisen kreiselt sich der
> Kreisler* [. . .]"[106] (my italics).

With Kreisler and his analogues throughout the works, we find
precisely the same topoi as with the Medardus-category of "individuals divided within themselves" : recurrent emblematic passages of
"madness", "sickness", "trauma", "dungeon", "unfulfilment",
"conflict", "violence", "alienation", "flight", "itinerancy", "isolation", "abnormal clothing", "desert", "alcohol" "rôle-playing",
etc.[107] But these topoi have of course a quite different function
with Kreisler and company : they are normally indicators, not of
dislocation and "Monstruosität" *within* the character, but of a more
or less radical dislocation between the character and his environment. To put it more sharply : whereas the topos of "madness"
(much the most persistent single one in Hoffmann) is with
Nathanael or Medardus, and in a transient sense with Giglio Fava,
a reflection of *their* inward falsity and distortion, it is with Kreisler,
Gluck, "Serapion", a reflection of the non-identity between their
inward *genuineness* and that falsity in society which we have
previously evinced. With Kreisler, Hoffmann characteristically
extends the pattern right into his childhood : we have seen how
his family, in its false aspirations and norms, blinded him to his
true potential, "die wahre einzige Tendenz meines Lebens", and
misled him into taking up a legal career, until—too late!—he
realised what had happened : " '[. . .] der Gedanke eines ganzen
verlornen Lebens [erfaßte] mich mit trostlosem Weh [. . .], als ich
mich in Ketten geschlagen sah, die mir unzerbrechlich
dünkten !' "[108] (This same externally-induced alienation from oneself is similarly figured in the novel in Meister Abraham (III, 350 f.).

This process with Kreisler is, of course, a direct reflection of
Hoffmann's own family experience, but it is worth noting that he
does not conceive it as something unusual : it is explicitly described
as "der gewöhnlichste Lauf der Dinge";[109] and we have already
seen the distorted origins and effects of society's repressive principles of education as voiced through Professor Lothario. Few
indeed are the people who, once exposed to society, to "die Praxis"
with its "tausend Zentner schwerem Gewicht" (to re-quote the

critical Belcampo passage), can keep any kind of mine-shaft open to that pristine jewelled potential which Hoffmann optimistically posits (in this respect he is of course an heir of the Enlightenment and of Classical humanism . . .). It is as a result of this that we find a notion in Hoffmann that clearly prefigures Stendhal's "Happy Few" : a kind of scattered fraternity of kindred spirits— "verwandte Geister" in Hoffmann's recurrent phrase—who know to some greater or lesser extent what "genuineness" means. The cardinal question remains, though : how far, and in what way, can a member of this vulnerable fraternity enter into a viable relationship with his environment?

The pattern is revealing with the heroes of the *Topf, Zaches, Die Königsbraut* and *Meister Floh* (the stories being all styled "Märchen"). All the protagonists are figured as indeed achieving an integrated relationship with their environment after having once realised their own true Self. But to what degree is this environment "social"? With Anselmus and Serpentina in the *Topf* : not at all. They are projected as achieving that rarest of things in Hoffmann : sexual fulfilment (I, 203 : Inbrunst des glühendsten Verlangens", "Fest der Liebe"[110] etc.), and as taking up residence on a grandiose "Rittergut". But where is this comfortable estate? Not in the Dresden of the story, nor anywhere in empirical reality —but instead in a mythical "Atlantis". How "real", too, *is* their alleged "Leben in der Poesie"?[111] It is explicitly a "Vision" of the fictive narrator's in his miserable, very real garret (203). Is it not perhaps just a "Phantom [seines] eigenen Ichs", to re-quote Klara's phrase? Hoffmann himself, in a letter to his publisher Kunz, said the story was characterised by *"durchgehaltene Ironie"* (my italics),[112] and far from being the "Romantic myth-making" that so many have taken it for,[113] it precisely anticipates the structure of the "Elixiere" in being a hall of mirrors in which ambivalence is ultimately the only reality.[114]

The position in *Zaches* and *Die Königsbraut* is much more straightforward : Balthasar and Candida, and Amandus and Ännchen, are relatively unironically portrayed in their achievement of emblematic "domestic bliss". But their environment is scarcely more "real" or "social" than Anselmus' Atlantis : Balthasar and his wife end up in a magical country estate (II, 189) in a tiny and imaginary principality (II, 124 f.), while Amandus and Ännchen have their fictive existence in an equally tiny and imaginary country village.

The setting of Peregrinus Tyß' ultimate genuine love in *Meister*

Floh, on the other hand, is more "real", and in this the story runs parallel to the slightly earlier Brambilla: the loves and marriages of Peregrinus and Giglio are located exclusively within *towns,* and within real towns: Frankfurt and Rome. Though "real", however, their setting is still figured as a domestic and circumscribed one, with no kind of involvement in the larger public reality of society in general. And significantly enough, we find this to be invariably the case wherever Hoffmann depicts a "Happy Few" persona as being integrated with his environment. Kreisler himself exemplifies this: he is shown at one stage in *Kater Murr* as feeling entirely at one with existence, as thinking that he has at last found an "Ankerplatz";[115] but the setting for this is a country abbey—and even this becomes an extension of the normal social order, in that the Abbot is in league with Rätin Benzon, while Cyprianus is an agent of the Pope. The situation is even sharper with "Serapion": he is richly integrated with his environment, but not only is his sylvan hermit's existence quite separate from the normal social order—his conception of it is also entirely imaginary, and Hoffman adumbrates a significant, typical background of "trauma", "flight from society" and "lunatic asylum" (II, 218, 224).

With *Serapion* and his previous "normal" identity as Graf P., the full pattern of the motif becomes clear: while a "genuine" individual may conceivably integrate with his empirical environment at a private domestic level, like Peregrinus Tyß, there is no chance at all, in Hoffmann's view, of his identifying with the larger, public reality. He will always be an alien, a "Fremdling in der Welt", because of the irretrievable discrepancy between his "genuineness" and society's gross falsity, the "Mißverhältnis des innern Gefühls mit der Gestaltung des Lebens".[116] In the epigraphic words of the early "Kreisleriana":

> eine verhängnisvolle schwere Zeit hat den Menschen mit eiserner Faust ergriffen, und der Schmerz preßt ihm Laute aus, die ihm sonst fremd waren.[117]

Did Hoffmann see any solution? Did he see any means whereby the "genuine" could ease their grievous position in an alien society? One pat answer lay ready to hand: to escape; to evaporate into incorporeal dream and fantasy and so waft through the bars of the cage and out into the insubstantial air:

> Doch sind es lediglich die Träume, in denen uns recht die Schmetterlingsflügel wachsen, so daß wir, dem engsten festesten

Kerker zu entfliehen, uns bunt und glänzend in die hohen, in die höchsten Lüfte zu erheben vermögen.[118]

It is this kind of response to reality that Hoffmann figured in personae such as Anselmus and *Serapion*—and in Kreisler, too, in the form of his theme of "artistic love", thereby there is no external physical object, but instead an inward idol, born of his own creative being (III, 262 f.). But this easy escapist response clearly did not satisfy Hoffmann as genuine. The real question was not "how to opt out", but : how to stay firmly *within* the given social reality, however alien, and establish some kind of viable relationship to it. And when we survey those "genuine" figures in the stories who are imperilled by society in its falseness, we repeatedly find that Hoffmann's solution to the problem is a defensive stance of *ironic insight and detachment*. The theme is already present even in the opening paragraphs of his first published work : a "skurriles Lächeln" plays around "Gluck's" mouth—and vies with the 'tiefen, melancholischen Ernst, der auf der Stirn ruhts";[119] Rat Krespel's response to the death of Antonie is to laugh loudly and sing a gay song (II, 239); Berganza, Belcampo and Kreisler all go in for the comic stage (I, 110; I, 520; I, 238); Bastianello, alias Celionati, is given to believe that "die höchste Tragik" can be created on the stage by "eine besondere Art des Spaßes",[120] and Giglio Fava discovers his true being in the commedia dell'arte.

It is, of course, Kreisler in whom this motif of ironic detachment is most emphatically figured. In the characteristic phrase prefacing the second set of *Kreisleriana* : "So wurde oft sein höchster Schmerz auf eine schauerliche Weise skurril".[121] He is supremely one of those whose stance of "Humour" is born "aus der tieferen Anschauung des Lebens in all seinen Bedingnissen, aus dem Kampf der feindlichsten Prinzipe",[122] and it is thanks to this stance, thanks to the protective comic mask pressed close to his face, that, far from evaporating into the nether air, he can walk in amongst the "ungenuine" masses and positively "sich einbürgern in die seltsame Welt".[123] The alternatives are clear : the richly genuine can either try to involve themselves emotionally in society, try to attain their true goals through the corrupt social reality—and become inevitably an eternal "Fremdling in der Welt"; or they can maintain a safe emotional detachment behind a Harlequin's mask, and so acquire at least a kind of citizenship, however much of a pale and fragile surrogate that may be.

It is here that our survey of E. T. A. Hoffmann comes full circle.

For this ironical stance is one that characterises not only Kreisler, Giglio Fava, Celionati, Belcampo, Klara and a host of others amongst his fictive personae : it is also Hoffmann's own most luminous and characteristic stance, his own vibrant "Hauptidee", as the beginning of the essay tried to show. And it is not a meaningful tautology to assess Hoffmann in terms of his own polarity of "genuine"–"false", and to say that it is only as a mirror-wielding Ironist that he is properly genuine and effective? to say that he is in principle always a false posturer when he quits this ironic mode? —If this is valid, it is easy to see that E. T. A. Hoffmann's main and true position in the European literary tradition is *not* that of "Romanticist" or "myth-creator", *not* that of "Realist", *not* that of "purveyor of the dark side of existence", but that of being an heir to the aristocratic line of such as Rabelais, Grimmelshausen, Reuter, Lesage, Sterne, Smollett; and more significantly : a most remarkable forebear of such as Heine, Stendhal, Fontane, Gide, Thomas Mann, Kafka, Grass. And whatever else he may contingently be, E. T. A. Hoffmann is a great Ironist.

NOTES

1. All page references are to the Insel "Volksausgabe": *E. T. A. Hoffmann: Werke*, Frankfurt-am-Main, 1967.

2. VIII, § 234, p. 473 : "this unhealthy mish-mash".

3. *Literaturgeschichte der deutschen Stämme und Landschaften*; Regensburg, 1924; IV, p. 109. "Hoffman writes incomparably badly."

4. "Die Wirklichkeit E. T. A. Hoffmanns"; this penetrating essay is reprinted in the Insel *Hoffmann* (*v.* bibliography); IV, 501 : "He left behind a great body of work".

5. *Das ästhetische Idol*, p. 124 (*v.* bibliography). "Hoffmann's spiritual drama is enacted against a background of cosmic mythology." (My italics.)

6. Georg Lukács, *Skizze einer Geschichte der deutschen Literatur*; Berlin, 1953; p. 57 "a truly great realist". (My italics.)

7. I, 332, "I am what I seem and seem not what I am."

8. III, 167, "be of the opinion that, despite the appearance of fragmentariness, a strong and constant thread does after all bind together all the various parts".

8a. III, 201, "Master Abraham had a way of cutting sheets of cardboard in such a way that although you could at first make nothing of the confusion of cut-about patches, you only had to hold a light behind the sheet for all kinds of groups of the strangest figures to form in the shadows cast on the wall."

9. III, 160, 278, "conjuror".

10. III, 7, "a whole arsenal of nonsense and spookeries".

11. In *Deutsche Philologie in Aufriß,* ed. W. Stammler, 2nd edn., I, Column 1245, "nothing but clichés".

12. *V.* bibliography.

13. *E. T. A. Hoffmann,* p. 83 (*v.* bibliography).

14. Cf. Heine's famous judgment: "Hoffmann war als Dichter viel bedeutender als Novalis. Denn letzterer mit seinen idealischen Gebilden schwebt immer in der blauen Luft, während Hoffmann [...] sich doch immer an der irdischen Realität festklammert" (*Werke,* ed. Elster, V, 301). Cf. also the same differentiation in the present day by Hans Mayer, IV, 491, 493.

15. III, 7, "governing notion".

16. II, 256, "—May the poet gather himself for bold flight to the distant Realm of Romanticism; such that the reader, as in a blessed dream, is removed from drab every-day existence and wanders in the flowery ways of the romantic land".

17. II, 262, "here, on the other hand, it is the fantastical which enters boldly into everyday life and turns everything topsy-turvy".

17a. I, 119, "The gaze of the true poet sees into human nature in its innermost depths, and rules over its manifestations by gathering up their most manifold refraction in his mind as in a prism, and reflecting them".

18. IV, 507, "offspring of a humoristical author who simply gathers up the shapes and forms of real life in the abstraction of humour as in a mirror, and reflects them".

19. *Le Rouge et le Noir,* Paris, Garnier, 1960, p. 357. "Well, my good man, a novel is a mirror which moves along a highway. And you accuse the man who carries the mirror in his basket of being immoral! His mirror reflects the mire, and you accuse the mirror! You should instead accuse the highway where the slough is, and even more the Inspector of Roads who allows the water to stand and the sloughs to form."

20. III, 56, "nothing other than what we Germans call 'humour', that wondrous power of a man's mind, born of the deepest insight into nature, to create its own ironical double, in whose strange buffoonery he recognises and enjoys the spectacle of his own and also—I allow myself the impertinent phrase—the spectacle of the buffoonery of all existence here on earth—".

21. III, 121, "Yet as they saw themselves in the lake, they *became aware* of themselves for the first time, looked at one another, and broke out laughing".

22. III, 270, "image, his own ego, striding along beside him".

23. Ibid., "gripped by the deepest horror, pale as death".

24. Ibid., "my song is frozen, for my other me has laid its white cold hand upon my breast".

25. III, 271, "bit of dupery".

26. Hans Mayer, IV, 482, "the whole reservoir of German 'penny dreadful' Romanticism".

27. II, 136, "a dark force is tearing me away", " 'Ha ha' came Fabian's ringing laugh, 'ha ha ha—how fine—how poetic, how mystical' ".

29. III, 58, "the real inward being of the figures of the piece", "the proper field of action".

30. III, 323–4, "the Court rejects every deeper feeling of whatever kind as vulgar and inadmissible", "the Princess had once had emotions and a heart, but that strange, half laughable, half repulsive monster called Etiquette had laid itself on her breast like a menacing elf".

31. III, 435, "social commerce", "individuality".

32. Ibid., "the hole in which that seed of goodness hides lies so deep down, and is covered by so many vile accretions of a dissolute life, that it must inevitably be stifled in the bud".

33. III, 197, "honest natural nature".

34. III, 231, "urbane behaviour".

35. Ibid., "the duping use of others' foolishness".

36. III, 233, "class", "inferior origins", "poodles' congress".

37. III, 214, "the highest goal of all human striving".

38. Ibid., "crooked bent of the road", "one true direction of my life".

39. I, 31, "to the proper purpose of his existence, i.e. to be an industrious cog in the pounding mill of the state".

40. III, 162, "machine of Court".

41. III, 158, "cogs of the state machine".

42. III, 159, "framework of wood".

43. III, 469, "a piece of clockwork that never stopped before".

44. II, 126, "that from this very hour the Enlightenment be established".

45. This general set-up of Hoffmann's involving the "Sieghartshof" must surely have been a model for Stendhal's *La Chartreuse de Parme,* the similarities being too remarkable for chance. Balzac certainly seems to have thought so (cf. Teichmann, *La Fortune d'Hoffmann en France* (*v.* bibliography), p. 182).

46. II, 172, "Bye bye, little mother, I'm clever enough now".

47. II, 55, "romantic, nay chivalric love".

48. I, 341, "this petty world of puppets that turns around us".

49. I, 348, "nothing but the twisting and turning of the fettered beast of prey in his cage". Cf. 443, Medardus to himself: "wahnwitziger Tor, wo sind nun deine hochfliegenden Pläne [. . .]".

50. III, 333, "schemes", "plans".

51. III, 334, "Let us rule this tiny court together, which is truly in need of a leading-string".

52. Cf. III, 327, 331, 332.

53. Cf. III, 327, 462.

54. III, 331, "that it is a dangerous game to want to raise oneself above those circumstances of conventional life and get closer to the 'World Spirit' in a sham mystique of one's own existence".

55. III, 329, "everything that derives from the right and proper view of real life and which is recognised as the basis of our contentment".

56. III, 333, "a vile and punishable deed".

57. III, 332, "despair".

58. Ibid.

59. Ibid., "artificial edifice".

60. Ibid., "foundation-stone already crumbled by a stroke of lightning".

61. III, 384, "The Professor was in favour of open force, as the ordering of things to the public good demanded that every individual should, regardless of any attempts at resistance, be squeezed as early as possible into that mould which is determined by the relationship of constituent parts to the whole, since a corruptive monstrousness would otherwise arise which would wreak all manner of ruinous damage".

62. III, 210, "according to a predetermined norm", without regard to their individuality". Cf. also 192, and especially 473!

63. III, 384, "the partially mad".

64. Ibid., "open resistance always made them even madder, whereas a genuine, personal recognition of error was radically healing".

65. I, 488, "what do you get from it then! I mean from that particular function of the mind which we term awareness and which is nothing other than the accursed activity of a damned customs official who has set up his unholy counter in the nut and says of all the goods that want to leave: 'Hey . . . hey . . . it's forbidden for that to leave the country, it stays here, right here.' The most beautiful jewels are stuck into the earth like base seeds, and what grows out of them are at best beetroots, from which reality, with its ten-ton weight, squeezes a fraction of an ounce of evil-tasting sugar . . ."

66. III, 58-9, "—how dead, how miserably poor, how molishly blind our life would be if the Spirit of the World had not endowed us creatures of Nature with that inexhaustible mine of diamonds within us from which the Wonderful Realm, become now our possession, shines up at us in sparkling light! Highly gifted are they who are properly aware of this possession! Even more highly gifted and to be called blessed are they who know not only how to gaze at the jewels of their inner Peru, but also how to bring them out and how to cut them and entice from them a grander and fierier sparkle."

67. "sickness".

68. Cf. III, 109 ff.

69. I, 283, "Never did my mother tell me in what circumstances of life my father lived".

70. I, 20, "Where did he come from?—Nobody knows!—Who were his parents?—That is unknown!"

71. Loc. cit., "outrage", "mortal sin".

72. Ibid., "tales and various remarks of my mother about her earlier life, which I have only since understood".

73. I, 399, "according to my theory as derived from novels and plays".

74. "evil fate".

75. I, 485, "exists exclusively through his own awareness".

76. II, 15, "everything terrible and frightful of which you speak

happened only within your own mind, the genuine and real outside world very likely had little part in it".

77. II, 16, "dark power".

78. II, 17, "It is the phantom of our ego, whose intense kinship with us and profound effect on our emotions either casts us into hell or raises us in ecstasy to heaven".

79. II, 23, "So long as you believe in him, he *is,* and is effective, your belief is his only power".

80. II, 17, "Be gay—be gay!—I have decided to appear to you in the form of your guardian angel and to chase ugly old Coppola away with peals of laughter".

81. II, 38, "—Every trace of his madness had disappeared, Nathanael soon regained his strength under the attentive care of his beloved, her mother, his friends".

82. Ibid., "small estate in a pleasant setting". Cf. also the last paragraph of this same story. And cf. similar patterns in e.g. *Topf, Zaches, Das Fräulein von Scuderi, Brambilla, Meister Floh.* The image is ironised, though, in *Murr*: III, 156, 176, 303–4.

83. I, 465, "—I must take you back to my early childhood, for it was then already that the seed was laid down within me which grew so rankly and poisonously throughout so many years".

84. I, 469, "fantastic love for a being who existed only within my mind".

85. Ibid., "It was only now that I realised that there was such a thing as outrageous passion, and my repulsion against it struggled with the emotion that filled my breast."

86. III, 269, "Know that the wound which you inflicted on the poor child has still not properly healed, so that in her pain she sometimes gets up to the oddest tricks."

87. I, 108, "chaste, angelic-pure bride", "crude fists".

88. III, 168, "Missed it again—*no purity*—" (my italics).

89. III, 388, "soul", "like a clear pure mirror".

90. III, 389, "a pure childlike pious spirit".

91. Ibid., "lustful forwardness".

92. III, 467, "the dark hellish spirit of sin has no power over you".

93. III, 469, "Merciful Heaven, protect me, I pray you, from myself!"

94. III, 390, "hold fast to the conviction that this spirit of mine will remain ever pure, ever free from it".

95. I, 332, "I am what I seem, and seem not what I am; an unaccountable riddle even to myself, I am divided utterly against my ego".

96. Ibid., "could find myself no more".

97. I, 331, "my own ego floated without anything to hold on to".

98. I, 389, "More than ever divided against myself, I became even in my own eyes ambiguous".

99. I, 479, "my ego was split in a hundred pieces".

100. I, 545, "my ego", "the ego of my thoughts".

101. I, 457, "only in my imagination".

102. I, 371, "since he is a mere idea, it must be possible to kill him with an idea".

103. II, 72, "a person at one with himself".

104. II, 330, "What do you all have against this poor Johannes, what wrong has he done you that you allow him no refuge, no small place of his own on earth?"

105. III, 372, "stranger in the world".

106. III, 183, "You can't get away from the word Circle, and may Heaven grant that your mind turn at once to those wondrous circles within which our existence moves and from which we cannot escape, no matter what tricks we try. In these circles Kreisler spins".

107. It is Helmut Müller who has established this notion of "topoi" in respect of Hoffmann. V. bibliography.

108. III, 214–15, "the thought of a whole lost existence gripped me with disconsolate woe when I saw myself fettered in chains that seemed to me unbreakable!"

109. III, 213, "the very commonest run of things".

110. "fervour of the most glowing desire", "glorious celebration of love".

111. I, 204, "existence in the realm of poetry".

112. "constantly maintained irony".

113. Cf. most recently, K. Negus's book (v. bibliography).

114. Similarly, it radically puts into practice the principle of "illusion-breaking" propounded in the more or less contemporaneous and most fascinating document: "Der vollkommene Maschinist" (v. I, 53 ff.).

115. III, 349, "anchorage".

116. III, 389, "disproportion between inward feelings and the shapes and forms of actual existence". Cf. Goethe's famous alleged description of "Tasso" in terms of "die Disproportion des Talents mit dem Leben"!

117. I, 51, "a fateful oppressive age has gripped man with an iron fist, and the pain of it forces sounds from him that were ever alien to him before".

118. III, 264, "Yet it is only in dreams that our butterfly wings properly grow, such that we are able to escape even the most narrow and solid dungeon and fly up in many and brightly hues into the high, the highest regions of the air".

119. I, 10, "comic smile", "deep melancholic seriousness that lay on his forehead".

120. III, 66, "the most intense tragedy", "an especial kind of humour".

121. I, 233, "Thus in a horrible way his deepest suffering often turned into comedy".

122. III, 226, "of a profounder insight into life with all its restrictions, of struggle with the most antagonistic forces". The same explicit notion occurs elsewhere too; cf. III, 330–31; especially: III, 56.

123. III, 473, "establish a firm place in that peculiar world".

SELECT BIBLIOGRAPHY

I

Standard critical editions:
Sämtliche Werke, ed. Carl Georg von Maassen (vols. 1–4, 6–10; left incomplete), München, Müller, 1908–1928.
Werke, ed. Georg Ellinger (15 vols.), Berlin, Bong [1912].

Some current editions:
Poetische Werke, ed. K. Kanzog (12 vols.), Berlin, de Gruyter, 1957–62.
Sämtliche Werke, ed. W. Müller-Seidel, Fr. Schnapp, W. Kron, W. Segebrecht (5 vols.), München, Winkler, 1960–65. (Also published privately through the "Wissenschaftliche Buchgesellschaft", Darmstadt, 1967.)
Briefwechsel, ed. H. von Müller, Fr. Schanapp, Vol. I, München, Winkler, 1967.

II

Some studies of Hoffmann:
Ellinger, G. *E.T.A.H. Sein Leben und seine Werke*, Hamburg, Voß, 1894.
Sucher, P. *Les Sources du Merveilleux chez E.T.A.H.*, Paris, Alcan, 1912.
Harich, W., *E.T.A.H. Das Leben eines Künstlers*, Berlin, Reiß [1920].
Bergengruen, W. *E.T.A.H.*, Stuttgart, Cotta, 1939. New edition: Zürich, Arche, 1960.
Schenck, E. v., *E.T.A.H. Ein Kampf um das Bild des Menschen*, Berlin, Die Runde, 1939.
Korff, H. A., in: *Geist der Goethe-Zeit*, second, revised edition, Leipzig, Koehler & Amelang, 1953. Vol. 4, pp. 543–639.
Meyer, Herman, in: *Der Typus des Sonderlings in der deutschen Literatur*, Amsterdam, 1943; new edition: München, Hanser, 1963, pp. 100–135.
Ricci, J. F.-A., *E.T.A.H. L'homme et l'oeuvre*, Paris, 1947.
Hewett-Thayer, H. W., *Hoffmann: Author of the Tales*, Princetown, Univ. Press, 1948.
Rosteutscher, J., in: *Das ästhetische Idol*, Bern, Francke, 1956.
Mayer, Hans, *Die Wirklichkeit E.T.A. Hoffmanns*, in: *E.T.A.H. Poetische Werke*; Berlin, Aufbau, 1958, vol. I. Also in: Mayer, H. *Von Lessing bis Thomas Mann*, Pfullingen, 1958. Also in the Insel edition used in the above essay, vol. 4.
Teichmann, E., *La Fortune d'Hoffmann en France*, Geneva, Droz, 1961.
Werner, H.-G., *E.T.A.H. Darstellung und Deutung der Wirklichkeit im dichterischen Werk*, Weimar, Arion, 1962.
Thalmann, M., in: *Das Märchen ünd die Moderne*, Stuttgart, Kohlhammer, 1961.

—— In: *Romantik und Manierismus*, Stuttgart, Kohlhammer, 1963.

Müller, H., *Untersuchungen zum Problem der Formelhaftigkeit bei bei E.T.A.H.*, Berne, Haupt, 1964.

Negus, K., *E.T.A.H. Hoffmann's Other World*, Philadelphia, Univ. of Pennsylvania Press, 1965.

Voerster, J., *160 Jahre E.T.A.H.-Forschung 1805–1965*, Stuttgart, Eggert, 1967.

Christian Dietrich Grabbe

Christian Dietrich Grabbe

by K. F. JAY

Grabbe was born in Detmold in 1801, the only child of a minor official of humble origins, and of a peasant mother. The father administered the local prison and it was in this limiting environment that the boy grew up. A precocious intelligence enabled him to enter the local grammar school, and the savings of his parents made it possible for him to matriculate in the law faculty of Leipzig in 1820. What sparse information we have of his schooldays sounds ominous: he appears a solitary one, uncomfortable and gauche in the company of social superiors, performing drinking feats in order to show off, and one desirous of passing for an original genius. These traits grew apace in Leipzig where the frequentation of low haunts as well as some literary efforts soon superseded serious legal studies. It was here that Grabbe most likely contracted the disease which was to contribute to his early physical decline. In 1822 Grabbe, now penniless, appeared in Berlin where his studies remained stagnant but where his connection with progressive literary circles stimulated his dramatic ideas. His passport to acceptance was the manuscript of his first tragedy, the origins of which lie in his six-form days at Detmold. The *Herzog Theodor von Gothland* is by all standards an astounding tour-de-force. He sent it in September 1822 to Ludwig Tieck, and commentators have justly dwelt upon Tieck's warnings and on the deep abyss of desperation which this extraordinary work revealed. Without resources and defeated in an ill-starred attempt to embark upon a stage career, the prodigal returned to the paternal home in Detmold, where after a short period of recuperation he passed the legal examination in 1824 and set up as an advocate. Remaining the "odd-man-out" of Detmold society, he managed nevertheless to establish a reputation as a reliable jurist and after a few years secured an official appointment in addition to his legal practice. Throughout this period he wrote plays and some literary criticism. In 1833 he married a lady ten years his senior who belonged to the "society" of the tiny principality; this union was as ill-conceived as can be imagined, leading to interminable irritations and becoming at least partly responsible for Grabbe's deterioration. Neglect of his professional duties, combined with heavy drinking and declining health, led to his resignation from office and in 1834 to his departure from Detmold. He went first to Frankfurt and later to Dusseldorf, where Karl Immermann supported him, but material and social success and recognition escaped him. Mortally ill and virtually a beggar he returned to Detmold where he died in 1836: the somewhat sordid and unremarkable life of an unheroic and unattractive man.

I

"Weil es verderben soll, is das
Erschaffene erschaffen."[1]

CONSIDERING the short span of his creative life and his
debilities, Grabbe's output of important works is appreciable.
He left some major dramas such as *Gothland, Don Juan
und Faust*, two Hohenstaufen plays, *Napoleon, Hannibal* and *Die
Hermannsschlacht*, an interesting fragment *Marius und Sulla*, the
comedy *Scherz, Satire, Ironie und tiefere Bedeutung*,[2] several
minor plays and some critical essays.

The discussion of Grabbe's position in literature, of his dramatic
work and the views expressed in it started already in his lifetime
and has never ceased since. Though standards and methods of
literary critique have changed, opinions remain as sharply divided
as they were 140 years ago, varying from acknowledgment to scorn-
ful condemnation.

Grabbe was first and foremost a dramatist. The state of German
drama in the twenties of the nineteenth century was truly depressing. The recurrent course in the history of German drama had been
its dependence on foreign models, from which it managed to free
itself only occasionally. Before Lessing, dramatic writing frequently
amounted to little more than an imitation of the strict classicism of
Corneille, Racine and Voltaire, but without the genius of the great
Frenchman; after Lessing came the fateful discovery of the genius of
William Shakespeare which stimulated not only the excesses of the
Sturm und Drang poets,[3] but also Goethe's *Goetz von Berlichingen*
and Schiller's *Die Räuber*. While Goethe and Schiller soon struck
out on lines of their own, yet another influence made itself felt in the
shape of the *Schicksalsdramen*,[4] based vaguely on a misinterpreta-
tion of classical Greek ideas, represented on a higher level by
Schiller's *Die Braut von Messina*,[5] on a lower by the output of
Adolph Muellner and Zacharias Werner. Finally, at the time of
Grabbe's birth, Romanticism began to invade the stage, already
foreshadowed by the lyrical sections of Goethe's *Egmont*, reinforced by Schiller's unfortunate *Die Jungfrau von Orleans*,[6] and
taking its strength from foreign models, in particular from the
work of Walter Scott. In the background of these divers currents
hovered Nordic patterns, stressed by Herder, but of much longer
standing.

It is upon this confusing scene that Grabbe enters, and it can
therefore hardly surprise us that his first tragedy *Gothland* com-

bines features of Shakespeare, Schiller, Klinger and Muellner in a
pseudo-Nordic setting. The story is that of a high-minded aristocrat,
who enticed by his arch enemy—significantly a Negro!—commits
fratricide and thereafter embarks upon a career of mounting crime
and spiritual self-destruction on an unprecedented scale : Macbeth,
Richard the Third, Tamburlaine the Great and Karl Moor, all in
one. While the dramatic sequence is often unskilled and motivation
not always convincing, this is nevertheless a work of extraordinary
and dynamic strength, reminiscent of the best Sturm und Drang
creations, but profounder, and touching continuously upon the
fundamental issues of human existence, dealing not only with the
relationships of man to man, but also of man to fate and exploring
the nature of Good and Evil. It is, at the same time, a witness to
deep-seated inner conflicts in the adolescent author. Gothland's
downfall, while appearing to have been brought about by the evil
machinations of a foe and the hostility of a fundamentally malicious
universe, are shown to be lastly due to flaws in his character.
Ludwig Tieck, then at the height of his fame, spotlighted Grabbe's
psychological state when in a famous reply he stated : "I have
encountered passages, which might be called great, verse that is
illumined by true poetic force; moreover, the play is so little
maudlin, vague and imitative, as to present itself as terrifyingly
original, revelling as it is in horror, cruelty and cynicism, that
thereby it not only treats in an ironic spirit all other gentle sentiments, but at the same time destroys the spirit and essential life of
the play, including its inherent cynicism ... If, moreover, you are
still young ... then I am apprehensive on your behalf; for if you
have already lost genuine poetic optimism and vitality, where are
you going to find bread during your wanderings through the desert?
I would then warn you not to follow these destructive paths of
life. ..." A truly prophetic statement!

Several basic characteristics of Grabbe's approach and themes
manifest themselves already in his first play : he is fascinated by the
"uomo singolare", the outstanding man; the conviction that however great a man, he will be laid low by the gods, by fate or his
lesser fellowmen and that the hallmark of genius is ultimate doom;
that man's intentions may be of the best but that while "he carries
eagles in his head, his feet are stuck in the mire"; and consequently,
the uselessness of pursuing any aims, good or evil, as all endeavour
terminates in a great void, the Nihil, in which even death and
extinction are a matter of complete indifference to the victim.
"This was the first drama of almost total nihilism, written with the
pathos of the romantic period" (L. von Wiese). In the shallow

depression of the twenties, it justly created a sensation, and Grabbe's associates in Berlin, among others Heinrich Heine, acclaimed it as a work of genius.

Grabbe's next dramatic attempt, probably designed to curry favour with the powerful Tieck, an attempt to create a romantic comedy under the title of *Scherz, Satire, Ironie und tiefere Bedeutung* [2] must be deemed a failure. Grabbe lacked a genuine sense of humour and the lightness of touch required. He succeeds better with his satirical allusions, but his development as a satirist had to wait until much later.

Grabbe called his second play a "comedy", yet the long title indicates that he aimed higher. Comedy is a perfectly legitimate vehicle for a message and for criticism of society, but it has to be "comedy", that is an appeal to sympathetic participation evocable through amusement. Molière's message is unmistakable, but even his worst characters retain a modicum of human dignity and are thus pitiable and redeemable.

Grabbe's comedy is comic only in the sense of a vulgar Punch and Judy show, in which despicable puppets hit one another and a devil performs tricks. The true comedian is in sympathy with his characters while Grabbe despises them. With the exception of the colourless heroine Liddy and her noble uncle, too noble to be true, each character is worm-eaten, as it were. Not even the devil is a dignified fiend, but a rather poor specimen; the poet is a despicable versifier, the schoolmaster a drunken and scheming impostor, Gottliebchen the most boorish of all boors, and Mollfels one who drags his nobler feelings for his beloved into the gutter in his bibulous state.

The play represents, in comic disguise, yet another version of a theme, already expressed in much better shape in *Gothland* : nihilism and the negation of purpose. Grabbe was aware of this when in a letter to his publisher Kettembeil (June 1, 1827) he stated that the play was founded on the same basic views as his *Gothland*. The "tiefere Bedeutung" is expressed by the devil : "Die Welt ist ein mittelmaessiges Lustspiel, das ein unbaertiger, gelb-schnabliger Engel, der noch in der Prima sitzt, waehrend seiner Schulferein zusammengeschmiert hat".[6a] A poet who holds such convictions cannot be a comedian. Nor does "Ironie and "Satire" come off better. It was not until Grabbe had been hammered by suffering that he developed a more compassionate attitude.

It was in Leipzig and Berlin that the poet discovered his penchant for history. Much ink has been spilled by commentators over the question whether Grabbe was or should have been an historian and whether he pinpointed nodal periods and interpreted historical situations more precisely than his dramatic contemporaries or the professional historians. It is quite true that he allowed himself less liberties with historical facts than Schiller, and anachronisms are rare. But lastly Grabbe was not an historian but a playwright, and like his great French contemporary Alexandre Dumas père, he used the elements offered by history simply as raw material for plots, altering chronology and sequence. His first historical project is the fragment *Marius und Sulla*. Though never completed, the poet has left fairly comprehensive notes about his intentions. The drama is set in one of the critical stages of Roman history, when the old order is breaking and ambitious men are fishing in troubled waters. Significantly the figure of the great dictator Sulla is cast in the mould of Gothland, except that he manages to control men and circumstances and is a cold-blooded rationalist tyrant. Emerging as victor, he finds himself master of the world, "the globe like a cringing slave lies beneath his feet". Surveying his triumph the thought invades his mind that all he has achieved is useless to him, that he needs none of the power to be himself—and he resigns. Once more, a hero fails, not because outside powers have laid him low, but in the moment of victory he despises the spoils.

Painfully aware of the mediocrity of the patriotic and historical plays of his day, Grabbe now embarked upon the task of presenting the German nation with a series of six to eight major historical spectacles. The inspiration is not far to seek; Shakespeare had given to his native country a dramatised past, Schiller had approached the same problem obliquely and with barely veiled allusions in *Wilhelm Tell*, Kleist had tried to perform a similar task with his *Die Hermannsschlacht*, while lesser authors had also produced strings of plays, including the Hohenstaufen period. Having read Raumer's monumental history of the Hohenstaufen, Grabbe had ready-made material. The first play, which he calls a tragedy, is his *Kaiser[7] Friedrich Barbarossa*, largely a colourful pageant, romantic in tone, interspersed with anachronist compliments for contemporary dynasties, the Hohenzollern and the Wittelsbach, putting on show as many personalities and celebrities as possible, including Richard Coeur de Lion, the poet Ofterdingen and many others. But through a back door as it were, at least one tragic situation and one tragic hero creep in, in the shape of the conflict between the Emperor and Duke Henry the Lion, and in the misfortunes and discomfiture of the latter. Henry is another edition of the "great man", driven by a dark fate to destroy his friendship with Barbarossa and to gamble away his power and his lands. In the second play of the series, *Kaiser*[7] *Heinrich der Sechste*, more powerful and less diffuse than the previous one, the author seems to have abandoned the original idea of presenting a popular spectacle to the German nation. The figure of the outstanding son of the great Barbarossa takes possession of the poet and he becomes preoccupied with a new type of titanic personality, political man. Heinrich's meteoric progress, his Macchiavellian amorality in politics, his faithlessness and ruthlessness, his general "beyond good and evil" attitudes, reinforced by symbolic actions such as the climbing of Mount Etna—the continuous growth of power, are watched by the spectator with baited breath—what will come next? To what further heights can this mortal rise? And then suddenly, the titan is felled by Death. The stupendous contrast between extreme ambition and mundane glory on the one and the lightning realisation of the impermanence of human achievement—climax and anticlimax—make this scene on Mount Etna one of the most tragically impressive in the history not only of German tragedy. The rising crescendo, climbing from step to step, higher and higher, is suddenly silenced; comparisons with the most dramatic passages in the tone poems of Tchaikovsky and Richard Strauss obtrude.

Grabbe never completed the Hohenstaufen cycle. After having already virtually abandoned his original design in the second play, he had become attracted by the figure of Napoleon, and determined to come to grips with a contemporary problem. The great usurper had died only recently, and speculation about the reasons for his rise and ultimate failure was current. Walter Scott's voluminous biography was avidly read, and in Paris Alexandre Dumas wrote a spectacle in which the emperor's career from Toulon to St. Helena was pictured in a number of loosely connected scenes. Grabbe's *Napoleon oder die hundert Tage*[8] represents a new departure in the poet's development : his hero is almost what we would call in modern parlance a "non-hero", part of a more important historical setting, a mere link in the flow of events. What he says and does on the stage is less important than the image he has created and is still creating in the minds of his supporters and his opponents. It is the people, French or Prussian, that acts rather than the hero. *Napoleon* is a strangely diffuse work, no longer a stage play in the accepted sense of the word, an epic dramatisation in prose on the lines of Thomas Hardy's *The Dynasts*. Were it written today we would accept it as a scenario for a film, as it anticipates film techniques.

Grabbe's last historic work, *Die Hermannsschlacht*, produced under conditions of extreme mental and physical anguish, goes even further along these lines. Generally condemned as a stage play, it assumes a new importance if seen as a film script. The latter drama lays no claim to being a tragedy, and it is equally difficult to see Grabbe's Napoleon as a tragic hero. Napoleon lacks tragic insight or tragic guilt feelings, despite the fact that everything points to the single truth that he is discarded and defeated because he has outlived his historic usefulness, that the "Weltgeist"[9] has moved on and that consequently Bonaparte has become an anachronism.

This leaves us with *Hannibal*, by the present writer and some critics considered Grabbe's maturest and greatest tragedy, completed after *Napoleon*. It was designed as the personal tragedy of a very great man, set against the historical background of the tremendous struggle between the Roman and the Carthaginian nations. This awesome and deeply moving work gives us an idea of what Grabbe might have become had not physical illness and dark forces within prematurely destroyed him. The new hero is intensely human, he does not speak in hyperboles, he is a man and not a "superman". His aims are not excessive, nor is he ambitious for himself. His stature both as a feeling human being, a patriot and a leading military and political figure is expressed with great economy of words and reflected in the hatred of his enemies and the loyalty of his followers. The play, starting at the moment of Hannibal's greatest triumph, the victory at Cannae, weaves a tragic pattern of a continuous descent from step to step, from setback to setback, from the loss of his brother's relieving army to the evacuation of the Italic base, from the defeat at Zama to humiliating exile and lonely self-destruction in Asia Minor. The action has the compelling and metallic quality of Greek drama, with the exception that it is not the envy of Fate that brings the great Carthaginian down, but his own identification with a task, which, in view of the weakness and treachery of his own people, was, probably from the very beginning, unattainable of achievement. It is the meanness of the human environment which causes his ultimate destruction. This great man indulges in no self-pity, but is capable of viewing his destiny philosophically. He is wedded to a chosen cause and goes down with stoical resignation : "Long stormed the gales until at last the frost arrived and the waves stood still !"

This is perhaps the apposite place for some remarks about Grabbe's essay "Ueber die Shakespearo-Manie".[10] This has been very widely condemned as an iconoclastic and heretical upstart's outburst against the greatest dramatic poet of all times, motivated solely by sensation-mongering and jealousy. In fact, closer study reveals that it is nothing of the sort, but rather, as Grabbe himself states in the preface, an attempt to delineate the future of German drama. Grabbe saw clearly that Shakespeare was not the only available model, and he made a plea for a new originality, which could be attained only by gaining freedom from the hold Shakespeare had on German authors. As a counter-weight he recommended the study of Aeschylus and Sophocles, and surprisingly rendered justice to the great French classicist tradition. "Despotism is unbearable in art, as it is in life", and Germany stood in need of her own national drama. The tone of the essay is provocative—manifestoes of this type invariably are, and so is Victor Hugo's famous preface to "Cromwell" but the theme was one of vital importance at a time when the translations of Schlegel and Tieck were rapidly turning the Englishman Shakespeare into a German author. Grabbe was not only the sole man of letters sounding this warning, but in his own work attempted to break new ground. If he failed in this, his was a noble failure.

Quite apart from his early plays and his historical drama stands *Don Juan und Faust*, Grabbe's only excursion into metaphysical tragedy. It goes beyond the limits of a brief essay to add to the ever-growing commentary, both in German, French and English, on the history of these literary prototypes which Grabbe daringly confronted and combined in one action. Yet next to Marlowe's *Doctor Faustus* and possibly Goethe's *Faust*—Part I, Grabbe's creation is probably the dramatically and intellectually most satisfactory rendering of the combined themes, granting also the tremendous difficulty facing the author when confronting two dramatic prototypes of almost universal significance, figures which had appeared in innumerable shapes on the contemporary stage. There is none of the shallowness of Klingemann's Faust, nor the extensive fantasies of a Klinger or the proliferation of the deserted maiden Gretchen and her middle-class sufferings. Plainly the poet's concern is with two opposing life principles. Grabbe avoided Byron's mistake, whose *Manfred* offers almost nothing but meditative recitation, and created a central plot : the conflict between the sanguine southern hedonist Don Juan and the nordic polymath Faust, who clash over the possession of a beautiful woman. Most of the traditional trimmings of the two themes are employed, though Grabbe's Faust figure is nearer to Byron's Manfred than to Goethe's Faust, the disappointed savant, sells himself to the Devil and embarks upon a career of power and pleasure, while the poet skilfully indicates the ferment and chaos which the impossibility of transforming a reflective sage into a sensuous lover causes : the intellectual concept of the senses leads to shipwreck. Grabbe paints a marvellous picture of a possessed megalomaniac, describes the pathology of a self-destroyer, of a hero who utterly defeated descends to hell, but promises us a continued fight in the hereunder. To have been able to create a Faust, almost totally different from existing models, alone is an appreciable achievement. Yet Faust remains unconvincing both as a sage and as a lover, and this was doubtlessly the poet's intention; Faust cannot evoke compassion in his boundless and remote megalomania. By contrast, the figure of Don Juan is one of Grabbe's most attractive creations. It is as if Grabbe, the ugly little man with the domed brow of the thinker and the weak chin, the one whom life was in the process of defeating, the shy one and the failure with women, had projected his wish dreams upon the greatest of all lovers and sensualists, Don Juan, the man of action for action's sake, the enemy of metaphysical reflection, the gambler at high stakes, the hero who has "neither in front of him nor behind him a luminous realm of values". Don Juan is the author of his own ethics, and his amorality is a deliberate choice. Yet this hero too fails, as his philosophical opponent Faust does. Both are chaotically active, only to face nothingness. As Santayana said : "absolute will is a great dupe ... the will is absolute neither in the individual nor in humanity". Both metaphysical striving and materialist insatiability lead to the ultimate limbo.

II

What is Grabbe's place in the development of German Drama? We have seen that he strikes a new and independent line in which he tries to break with a past he condemns and that he sets his face against the conventions of the sterile age into which he was born. His work, however faulty in parts, *forms the vital link between the German classics and Kleist on the one hand and Friedrich Hebbel on the other*. It is immaterial that Grabbe was not alone in his efforts and that Georg Büchner, much better known outside Germany, pursued similar objectives. Because a fervent conviction propelled him, his dramas are still discussed, praised or condemned, while the plays of his contemporaries, so well received in their day, now hardly figure in the histories of German literature.

An innovation which Grabbe introduced was the active use of the masses. The common people, either in the shape and disguise of the chorus in classical tragedy, or as Shakespearean citizens and market folk, had always appeared on the stage, but it was Grabbe who gave them a permanent place in the rôle of active participants —a development also promoted by Büchner. After somewhat hesitant and tentative beginnings in the fragment *Marius und Sulla* and in *Barbarossa*, the masses exert full impact upon the action of the drama in *Napoleon, Hannibal* and *Die Hermannsschlacht*, where the poet, without abandoning his interest in the destiny of the great titular heroes, clearly places the great men into the dimensions of time and space as represented by common people. The application of this new discovery is pushed to extremes in *Napoleon*, and quite deliberately; Grabbe said in a letter : "Napoleon is not a major task. He is a fellow whom his egotism drove to an exploitation of his age—apart from selfish aims, he did not, being a Corsican and only half-French, know what his aims were; he was smaller than the Revolution itself." Grabbe, who wrote his *Napoleon* in the year of revolutions, 1830, saw the new dynamic of the masses, which by other dramatists had been used for diversionary scenes or as a sounding board only. Grabbe explored and learned to understand the cross-fertilisation of leader and crowd perfectly. The seemingly inert mass is a potentially explosive force, which can be electrified into action by a man who understands the signs of the times. This man may be a common agitator such as Saturninus (*Marius und Sulla*) and Jouve (*Napoleon*), or a more titanic figure. Without mobilising the human substratum the hero cannot act. Nobody is a leader who has no masses to lead and opportunities for leadership arise almost accidentally from the course of history. Grabbe poured scorn upon the writers of his day who appeared to be oblivious of the omens of a new age. "The world events which are now breaking upon us like melting glaciers . . . will be useful to us in so far as they will drown with their thunder the reedy whisperings of a Raupach, the coquettish trills of a Sonntag, the critiques of every shop assistant . . . Gravity will prevail . . . ." Grabbe prophetically anticipated the age when the masses would play their part in political history, and certainly in *Napoleon* and *Die Hermannsschlacht* action depends not so much on the will of the great hero than upon the interplay of hero and multitudes—a situation characteristic of the modern era. Of less importance, but nevertheless significant, is Grabbe's mastery of battle scenes. With bold strokes this little civilian grasped the essentials of campaigns and engagements, and went successfully far beyond the token battles of past plays.

Grabbe's overall importance as a dramatic force is therefore undeniable, but his evaluation in purely poetical terms poses a much more difficult question. Taking his verse first : his lines do not appear to come easily to him. Much is sheer Shakespearean and Schillerian imitation or strongly reminiscent of the winged

trochaic rhythm of the fate dramatists. Certainly in his early plays
bombast and ranting declamation are frequently found. Moreover,
Grabbe's lack of refined culture and variance of eroticism prevented
him from presenting satisfactory love scenes. Here his verse is
reminiscent of a bad libretto. And yet, when his own psychological
problems invade action or characters, some truly good and deeply
expressed lines make their appearance. He fails in an epic description of Nature; his paean to the Alps in *Don Juan und Faust* is but
a faint reflection of Byron's majestic lines in *Manfred*, but he does
succeed if, as in an El Greco, nature becomes intimately linked with
the soul of his hero, when the external scene becomes expressive
and reflexive of interior states. This identification of two worlds,
the inner and the outer, appears already in his first drama *Gothland*; when the hero receives the news of his beloved brother
Manfred's death, he approaches the window :

> "Sieh, es ist Herbst, und an
> Der Gelbsucht krankt die sterbende Natur;
> Auf öden Feldern heult der rauhe Nord;
> Laut rauscht das falbe Laub—es winselt nach
> Vergänglichkeit!—Erstorben ist der Lenz
> Und seine grüne Blätterpracht verwelkte—"[11]

But lastly it is prose and not verse that is Grabbe's true medium,
and one wonders how much bombast and forced rhetoric could
have been avoided, had Grabbe adopted prose earlier than he did.
A letter to Immermann in December 1834 proves that the poet had
come to this conclusion himself : "You are absolutely right as regards the verse in *Hannibal*, it is a mongrel, and I shall break it like
new rough cobblestones and turn it into prose. Thereby my mind
obtains fuller scope . . .". From now on every remark, every word
are in place, the speeches are relatively short and the heroic declar-
ations cease. Some literary historians have repeatedly asserted that
Grabbe's creative life was one of continuous decline, but the very
success of the contraction both of action and word in his late
Hannibal shows tremendous progress, all the more remarkable in
one already marked by death. A random passage from *Hannibal*
proves our point. The passage chosen represents the moment when
Hannibal, whose last hopes are pinned on the arrival of Hasdrubal
and his reinforcements, is cruelly apprised by the enemy of his
brother's death and defeat.

> Hannibal : "Ich fühle mich zu wohl und fürchte fast, es steht
> mir ein Unheil bevor."

Ein als karthagischer Krieger verkleiderter Römer (der unter
dem Mantel ein Paket zu halten scheint, tritt an Hannibals Seite;
für sich) :
"Es steht neben dir !"
Hannibal : "Mein Glück wäre vollendet, säh' ich des Bruders
teures Haupt."
Der Römer (wirft ihm den Kopf Hasdrubals vor die Füsse):
"Hier ist es !"
Hannibal : "Gut ! das Schauspiel endet, wie es muss ! Mit einem
Theaterstreich !"[12]

The tragic irony of the scene and the hero's stoic reaction are the
hallmark of effective tragedy.

Apart from this rapid growth of concision, Grabbe develops in
his last great drama a new and detached view of disaster. Nothing
can alter Hannibal's equanimity. The new attitude of the hero is
poignantly brought out in his confrontation with the miserable
petty king Prusias who has offered the hapless refugee his hospi-
tality. Patiently Hannibal listens to the king's ridiculous patter and
replies in a humorous vein. Was Grabbe by now capable of laughing at his own misfortunes? To sum up : not only do we find in
Grabbe a continuous development of dramatic expression, culminating in the excellent prose of *Hannibal*, but we also find a refinement of the very experience of disaster. Grabbe has become superior
to the bombastic self-pitying hero. Grabbe's growing maturity of
the conception of historical key figures no longer permits him to
cast them in the mould of supermen. One of the criticisms levelled
against Grabbe is that he uses a heavy-handed sledge hammer
approach. This may be valid for his earlier work, but the very fact
that in his last plays he shows definite satirical gifts disproves the
accusation. Both in *Napoleon* and in *Hannibal* satire is skilfully
used to deepen the characterisation of persons and periods. In-
stances of this are the masterly scenes depicting the fossil atmosphere at the restored Bourbon court and the conversations between
Hannibal and King Prusias. There is an admirable lightness of
touch.

III

Did Grabbe present to us a coherent view of life, and if so, did
this influence German thought? We can state at once that it was not
Grabbe's intention to propound metaphysics, for his entire attitude
was averse to deeper philosophical speculation; it may even be
assumed that he was unfamiliar with the new stirrings in German

philosophy, nor even fully acquainted with Hegel, though some of Hegel's vocabulary is found here and there. Grabbe felt the strong urge of personal expression, and, having discovered his medium, namely drama, he presented a drama of action. There is nothing of Immermann's sensitive reflection, as offered in "Merlin", none of Byron's philosophising poems. The ontological propositions made by Duke Gothland and his enemy Berdoa, namely that man is a playball of fate and marked out for destruction, are stereotypes, found in the literature of all peoples and all ages, the Greeks, the Book of Job, Goethe, Byron, Shelley, and, of course, on a much lower plane in the German fate drama. Yet even as stereotypes, some of Grabbe's lines ring true and must be reflections of his state of mind :

> "Zerstörend, unerbitterlich, Tod
> Und Leben, Glück und Unglück an-
> Einander kettend, herrscht
> Mit alles niederdrückender Gewalt
> Das ungeheure Schicksal über unseren Häuptern."[13]

> "Allmächtige Bosheit also ist es, die
> Den Weltkreis lenkt und ihn zerstört"[14]

> "Weil es verderben soll, ist das Erschaffene
> Erschaffen."[1]
>
> (quotations from Gothland)

Grabbe was later to move from this position and to assume complete indifference on the part of the higher powers.

Grabbe's threefold purpose in writing plays was to gain recognition in a society in which he felt himself to be an an outsider, secondly to achieve a materialisation in dramatic characters of the chaotic urges in inhibitions from which he suffered; in the third place, to convey his vision of drama. It is impossible to escape the conviction that much that is found in Grabbe's heroes is Grabbe himself. There is much more of our poet in Gothland, Don Juan, Heinrich VI and Hannibal, than there is a Schiller in Karl Moor and other early heroes. Whether or not non-identification and distance or identification and proximity are the elements determining or contributing to the shaping of dramatic character, is one of the controversial questions of dramatic analysis. It would plainly be ludicrous to see Shakespeare in all his figures : Hamlet, Titus Andronicus, Richard III and Othello; yet the Olympian remoteness and detachment of a Shakespeare is not given to all. Goethe can clearly be seen in the characters of Weislingen (Goetz), Clavigo,

Egmont and Fernando (Stella). It would therefore be dangerous to turn down the possibility of a personal identification of poet and character. Our knowledge of Grabbe's psychological difficulties, the tragic compound of genius and sordidness, the "de profundis" atmosphere surrounding much of his life, the sinking into despair and material misery—all these factors make it almost certain that we can find much of Grabbe in his dramatic characters. "All his suffering, his own acrimony about the course of events, his own immeasurable scorn for the teeming mediocrity . . . are laid squarely upon the shoulders of Hannibal" (S. Wukadinowic). Grabbe says in a letter : "This play, like a worm, gnaws my heart and the more I approach its end, the more does the theme move me. The last scenes agitate me more than any other of my plays. They tear me and I often flee them like a child."

This is one of the factors making his tragedies, certainly the later ones, so profoundly moving—as documents of confession and suffering. The almost superhuman qualities of some of the heroes are the wishdreams of a soul aware of its debilities, of a psyche that "carried eagles in the head but whose feet stuck in the mire". Lastly, Grabbe succeeds in creating an acceptable character only when a positive identification, either as projection or direct, is discernible. Wherever this is missing, characters lack life or are drawn faultily. Because of Grabbe's ignorance of the nobler side of eroticism and of "ladies", practically all his heroines remain puppet-like, reciting stock phrases. Nor does he succeed with "normal" and balanced characters, such as the Emperor Barbarossa. His vision was too introspective to enable him to encompass character traits other than his own. The many letters which have survived do not help us much, as Grabbe invariably tried to impress the recipients with his originality at the expense of truth—even where his own work was in question.

Granted then that our poet did not intend to propound metaphysical tenets, does any coherent view of an ontological and ethical nature emerge from his characters? The attitude of some of his heroes would perhaps be defined more aptly as "Weltschmerz"[15] than as philosophical. If we accept W. Rose's (*From Goethe to Byron*) definition that "Weltschmerz is the psychic state which ensues when there is a sharp contrast between a man's ideal and his material environment, and his temperament is such as to eliminate the possibility of any sort of reconciliation between the two", then this label may fit some of Grabbe's heroes. The "Weltschmerzlers"[16] sad musings and sentiments do not necessarily add up to a coherent system of thought.

The basic view of the world which emerges from an examination of the characters is deeply pessimistic. As in Georg Büchner, man is born to failure. The dice are heavily loaded against him by the very system or organisation of the universe, both in its material and in its human aspects. Whether you decide to become a villain (Gothland), a superman (Faust), sensualist materialist (Don Juan), a super-ruler (Heinrich VI), an adventurer and opportunist (Napoleon) or a selfless and unambitious idealist (Hannibal)—ultimately you perish. Caught in the universal toils it seems to be immaterial whether you have objectively incurred guilt or feel subjectively that your ruin is due to misdeeds or flaws in your moral being. In fact, few of Grabbe's heroes are aware of subjective guilt at all or cherish notions of atonement. In the earlier plays the senselessness of action is contrasted with the urge to action. We are destined to a life of chaotic striving only to rush blindly into the appalling disaster of utter failure. A more mature thought occurs in *Hannibal*, a stoic attitude. The evil forces are silent or neutral, and only the trough of mediocrity of his fellow-men engulfs the hero. All these characters are lonely figures, all stand out among the lesser men, all have made Jean-Paul Sartre's "choice", the "pour-soi" and face the "dreadful freedom", and like Sartre's patterns they are in eternal conflict with all others—"Hell is other people!"

We do, however, not wish to give the impression that Grabbe's approach to the problem of human life was identical with the modern ideas of Existentialism. It is true that Existentialism can be interpreted as a reaction against the facile system-building and unjustified optimism of conservative philosophy. It does not set out to construct laws applicable to all men and valid for all time. It concentrates on the importance and the condition of a unique figure, the individual, set into an alien environment, both physical and human. It leaves it to the individual to find his own solution in this journey from Nihil to Nihil. Life thus has basically no meaning of an objective nature, but must be given a subjective meaning by each man. Man's life then is parenthetical, moving between the poles of birth and death. The adoption of a meaning is an act of deliberate choice, and it is immaterial whether man opts for "good" or "evil". Man therefore is an atomised individualist.

Much of this does remind us of Grabbe's heroes—with one all-important difference : Grabbe's figures feel no responsibility whatever, while Existentialism stipulates a definite responsibility once the fatal "choice" is made by man. Already Kierkegaard postulated that the subjective position, the way of life adopted, carried a heavy burden of responsibility. None of the heroes, with the possible exception of Hannibal, show responsibility to themselves, nor do they feel any obligation towards God : they live in a world without God and "have to support their existence without objective meaning" (B. von Wiese).

The heroes move in chaotic activism and perpetual motion; *they resemble an automatic train running along a track which suddenly ceases, because a saboteur has removed the rails.* Sometimes there is not even a collision—and without this the drama defeats itself. There is no doubt in our mind that this hopeless sense of life, which admits of no consolation whatever, was born of the turmoil and torment of Grabbe's mind and psyche. He felt titanic gifts and experienced failure, without realising that the latter were largely the result of his genetic make-up and his inability to overcome the demons which tore him to pieces. Grabbe was deracinated, and his view of man and his actions is prophetic of the so-called "modern age". The era of the super-monster, foreshadowed by a raving Gothland and a cold-blooded tyrant Sulla, did, indeed, come, and it is probably no accident that the Nazis praised the poet as the originator of the "Führerdramen".[17]

And yet, we must not exaggerate Grabbe's pre-occupation with "supermen". Nietzsche (*Der Wille zur Macht*)[18] lists as the qualities of the superman the following : logical singleness of purpose, leading to indifference to the opinions of others; the use of others according to the superman's own ethical norms; scepticism as regards all accepted beliefs; the use of the masses as a mirror in which the superman's powerful drives are reflected. A closer inspection of Grabbe's great men reveals that only Faust qualifies as a Nietzschean "superman".

Nobody can deny Grabbe's feeling for and preoccupation with history. Did he hold any views about the meaning of history? After all, his was the age of Herder, Friedrich von Schlegel and Hegel. Moreover the romantic school idealised the past. Grabbe, however, refuses speculation as to a moral meaning of history. He cannot recognise any ethical or other order in the course of events. His answer appears already in "Gothland" :

> "Der Mensch erklärt das Gute sich hinein,
> Wenn er die Weltgeschichte liest, weil er,
> Zu feig ist, ihre krause Wahrheit kühn
> Sich selber zu gesteh'n."[19]

As Friedrich Sengle has underlined (*Das deutsche Geschichts-*

drama),[20] to Grabbe history was a naked struggle of physical forces, "an ocean aimlessly moving to and fro, wind and weather, which only now and then combine to offer the sublime spectacle of a storm".

Grabbe left no school and no literary heirs. He seems to have been a "dead man" before he disappeared from the scene. Some few critical and biographical contributions were made after his death by his friend Eduard Duller, but literary critique and the stage managers forgot him. Hebbel's scathing remarks and Wilhelm Scherer's popular *Literaturgeschichte*[21] and its unfair condemnation of Grabbe discouraged research and reappraisal. There is no trace of an influence on either Schopenhauer or Nietzsche. Grabbe's merits as a pioneer were overshadowed by Georg Büchner's work. Grabbe's tragedy of isolation and frustration thus continued even after his death.

> "Durch die Mitwelt geht,
> Einsam mit flammender Stirne der Poet;
> Das Mal der Dichtung ist ein Kainstempel!"[22]
> (Ferdinand Freiligrath, on hearing of Grabbe's death)

TRANSLATIONS

1. Because 'tis destined to decay, creation is created!
2. "Jest, satire, irony and deeper meaning."
3. Storm and Stress.
4. Dramas of Fate.
5. *The Bride of Messina.*
6. *The Maid of Orleans.*
6a. "The world is a mediocre comedy, written by a beardless fledgling angel in the sixth form between terms."
7. Emperor.
8. *Napoleon and the Hundred Days.*
9. Spirit of the age.
10. *On the Shakespeare Mania.*
11. "Lo, it is autumn and from
    Jaundice suffers dying nature;
    Savage northwind howls in stubble fields;
    Loud rustle fallow leaves—they
    Whimper for corruption—and Spring has died
    And sere is all its green and leafy splendour!"
12. *Hannibal:* "I feel so well that I almost fear impending disaster."
    A Roman, disguised as a Carthaginian soldier (who under his

cloak appears to carry a parcel), takes his place beside Hannibal; aside: "It is already upon you!"

Hannibal: "Complete would be my happiness, saw I but the brother's beloved head!"

The Roman (casting Hasdrubal's head in front of his feet): "Here it is!"

Hannibal: "Excellent! The play is ending as it has to—with a stage trick!"

13. "Destructive and relentlessly, Death
and Life, Bliss and Unhappiness
Chaining to one another, gigantic Fate
Rules with almighty force
Above our heads."

14. "Omnipotent spite it is
That steers the world and wrecks it."

15. Melancholic weariness of the world around one.

16. Those holding the view of no. 15.

17. Leader dramas.

18. *Will to Power.*

19. "Man, when reading universal history, interpolates the principle of goodness, because he is too craven to confess to himself its wayward reality."

20. *The German Historical Drama.*

21. *History of Literature.*

22. "Amongst his contemporaries walks
Solitary and with flaming brow, the poet.
The sign of poetry is the mark of Cain."

BIOGRAPHICAL NOTE

Editions

S. Wukadinowic: *Grabbes Werke* (Berlin, 1912). This is the best and most comprehensive edition, including Grabbe's letters.)

A. Franz and P. Zaunert: *Grabbes Werke* (Liepzig and Vienna, 1910).

P. Friedrich: *Grabbes Werke* (Weimar, 1923).

H. Stresau, *Christian Dietrich Grabbe—Dramatische Dichtungen* (Berlin, 1944).

B. Von Weise: *Christian Dietrich Grabbe—Auswahl* (Stuttgart, 1943).

Biographical and critical works

A. Bergmann: *Christian Dietrich Grabbe—Chronik seines Lebens* (Detmold, 1954).

K. F. Jay, *A Re-examination of Grabbe's Tragic Heroes* (Southampton, 1957).

O. Nieten: *Christian Dietrich Grabbe—Sein Leben und seine Werke* (Leipzig, 1908).

F. J. Schneider: *Christian Dietrich Grabbes Persoenlichkeit und Werk* (Munich, 1934).

Aspects of Grabbe's works are discussed in the follgwing:

E. M. Butler: *The Fortunes of Faust* (Cambridge, 1952).

F. Sengle: *Das Deutsche Geschichtsdrama* (Stuttgart, 1952).

B. v. Wiese: *Die Deutsche Tragoedie von Lessing bis Hebbel* (Hamburg, (1952, 2nd edn).

August von Platen

August von Platen

by W. D. WILLIAMS

Graf August von Platen-Hallermünde, to give him his full name, was born at Ansbach in 1796. His father was a retired Hanoverian officer, employed as head-forester, and the family therefore moved very definitely in upper-class circles. His childhood was happy if somewhat lonely and he was turning out little plays for family festivities at the age of seven. Then to the cadet-school at Munich and thence to the royal page-school, the best opening for any career. Here he formed a friendship with the Crown Prince Ludwig which was later to stand him in good stead. He was writing lyrics and planning epics and tragedies and studying foreign languages. In 1813 his hatred of Napoleon took him into the army, he served in a long and comfortable campaign in the Rhineland and Eastern France. His regiment was not at Waterloo and Platen found the barrack life a good opportunity for study. He was finding himself more and more out of sympathy with the prevailing literary fashions, and was experimenting with every possible variety of verse forms, planning various epics and a novel. In 1818 he obtained permission to enter a University and chose to go to Erlangen, attracted by Schelling's lectures, which impressed and influenced him greatly. He studied hard—forestry, science, history, aesthetics, philosophy and above all languages. He met Jean Paul, Rückert, Goethe, A. W. Schlegel, Arndt—and realised he must break away from all of them. His works of this time includes his first book of poems (*Ghaselen,* 1821), and his fairy-play *Der gläserne Pantoffel* (1824). In 1824 he paid his first visit to Venice, which he liked so much that he overstayed his leave—he was still an army officer—and was arrested on his return. But Prince Ludwig succeeded to the throne in 1825 and immediately granted him indefinite leave. *Sonette aus Venedig,* 1824, conveys his feeling for that city, and his two plays *Die verhängnisvolle Gabel* (1826) and *Der romantische Ödipus* (1829) effectively satirise much of the literary fashion of the day. In 1826 he finally left Germany and spent the rest of his life wandering through Italy, never settling down, moving continually from place to place, striking up passing acquaintanceship with various Germans, such as the Byronic figure of the Swabian poet Wilhelm Waiblinger, who died in Naples in 1830. He obtained a salary finally from Ludwig of Bavaria, but returned only twice on short visits to his homeland. His health was failing, he became more and more egotistic and misanthropic, and finally in 1835, in Sicily, he took continual overdoses of medicine against cholera and died at Syracuse.

PLATEN is one of those poets who tend to be dismissed as cold and without feeling, showing immense technical virtuosity in the cultivation of purely formal values uninspired by the impulse of passion and imagination. His name, indeed, has sometimes been used as a sort of catchword to indicate the extremely empty and unfeeling playing with words, the cultivation of verse-forms in the spirit of dexterity and virtuosity unaccompanied by the urge to communicate feeling, which is the very antithesis of poetry. The same sort of charge is frequently brought against, for instance, the "parnassien" poets in France, against the later Munich poets at the end of the nineteenth century in Germany, and against such a writer as C. F. Meyer, who has only in quite recent times received his due. In Platen's case, such a view cannot survive a full knowledge of his work, though a slight acquaintanceship with it may seem superficially to confirm it. The older critics have not always helped by tending to treat of Platen and Rückert together, as though they were strictly comparable. The formal justification of this is not hard to find, since the two men were contemporaries, they were both great scholars, masters of many languages, they both imitated foreign forms, particularly the Persian verse-forms which we shall consider later, and they both show an immense technical virtuosity and ingenuity in handling the most complicated metres and rhyme-schemes. But beyond this the comparison breaks down. Rückert, despite his large output of verse, and the esteem in which he was held in his lifetime, and despite the daring experiments which he carried out, was a great scholar and critic, a cultured man and connoisseur rather than a poet of the first rank. Whereas Platen, with his equally eclectic culture and even greater command of language—he was at home in about a dozen—shows throughout essentially a poet's response to experience, and though much of his work may be called "artificial", yet succeeds eventually in convincing us of the genuineness of his poetic accomplishment.

It is fair to say, at the start, that his creative impulse is essentially the product of a conflict with life as he knew it, rather than an expression of the fullness and abundance of life. He is fundamentally a "sentimentalisch" poet, not a "naiv" one, to use Schiller's famous distinction. And this conflict takes basically two forms. The first is a personal matter, the fact that his homosexual nature made personal relationships for him a matter of continual pain and disillusionment. We shall have more to say of this later. And the second is his violent sense of estrangement from the prevailing fashions, intellectual and literary, in the Germany of his day. It was this which involved him, for instance, in his violent

dispute with Heine, and which led to his abandonment of his
homeland to settle in Italy for the last ten years of his short life.

This estrangement from the literary fashions of his time is of
course a necessary result of his most uneasy and ambivalent
relationship with the general Romantic climate in which his
generation grew up. Throughout his life, his work shows quite
plainly how deeply it is rooted in the fundamentally Romantic
pre-suppositions of the time, and yet its life-blood is a continual
attempt to reject and pour scorn upon just those pre-suppositions.
We shall see this clearly in his plays, but it is no less apparent in
a great proportion of his poetry.

There is a further point, perhaps less important than these two
factors, but which nevertheless must not be under-estimated. It
can be seen very clearly if we mentally compare Platen with his
almost exact contemporary Heine. Turning from the Rhineland
Jew to the aristocrat from Bavaria is like entering a different world.
By birth, upbringing and temperament no two men could be more
unlike. Heine came of a poor family, Platen's home was reasonably
prosperous, Heine experienced from the beginning the hardships
and disappointments which coloured his whole life, Platen was
brought up in comfort, given the best possible schooling, and in
his youth at least knew no physical hardship. And, much more
important, Heine was tortured always by the haunting doubt of
the ultimate value and significance of art, Platen was convinced
throughout that only art possessed any ultimate significance. Platen's
whole upbringing made it inevitable that spiritually he should
belong to a much older generation than Heine. His was the world,
in his boyhood and youth at least, of the emancipated eighteenth
century court, with its leisure, its delicate if a little artificial
sensibility, its precise code of manners, its strict hierarchy, its complete serenity and certainty that its way of life was good. Heine's
boyhood was passed in the nineteenth century, the century of bustle
and turmoil, of commercial competition, of ill-mannered pushing
and grabbing, of frenzied questioning of the whole basis upon
which such elegant and aristocratic societies as that of the Platens
was built up. This point is not without significance when we come
to see that Platen's development led him from an early romanticism
back to a type of poetry, and that his best, which in truth has
important elements in it which can be called classical.

His life has been abundantly documented by the two-volume biography of Schlösser, about twelve hundred large pages, and
equipped with indices and liberal notes. The book is authoritative
though cumbersome, based on Platen's diaries, which only

appeared at the beginning of this century, and tells the tale, in the most exhaustive detail, of his repeated attempts to come to terms not only with his own personal fate but also with the literary and intellectual climate into which he was born.

It is apparent that his early verses—nature poetry, patriotic verses, a very little love-poetry—consist mainly of an experimental playing with all possible varieties of subject and form. As early as 1816 he had tried his hand at a fate-tragedy, following the prevailing fashion, and he had plans for various epics and a novel before he went to the University. But in the course of his studies, during which his originally fervent protestantism had merged into a high but somewhat shapeless deism and concentrated more and more on an ethical direction, his studies in oriental culture led him to concentrate on Persian verse-forms, particularly the "ghasel". In this he is, of course, following in the footsteps of Goethe—whose *Westöstliche Divan* appeared in 1819, and Rückert among others, and simply exploiting a contemporary fashion. His first collection of verses, the *Ghaselen* of 1821, was well received, and was followed by other collections in the next few years.

Most of these poems are directly inspired by Platen's experience with personal relationships, and many generalise his reaction to his often extreme suffering into a broadly stoic fatalism or into a cultivation of the beautiful as a refuge from the storms of life. The first attitude is expressed in this poem :

Hab' ich doch Verlust in Allem, was ich je gewann, ertragen;
Aber, glaubet mir, das Leben läßt sich dann und wann
    ertragen !
Zwar der ganze Druck des Leidens riß mich oft schon halb zu
    Boden,
Doch ich hab' ihn immer wieder, wenn ich mich besann,
    ertragen :
Mir geziemt der volle Becher, mir der volle Klang der Lauten,
Denn den vollen Schmerz des Lebens hab' ich als ein Mann
    ertragen !
Trennungsqual, verschmähte Liebe, Freundes Haß und
    Widersacher
Hab' ich, und was sonst der Faden des Geschicks mir spann,
    ertragen;
Doch nun fühl' ich, wie auf Fitt'gen, bis zum Himmel mich
    gehoben,
Denn es lehrte mich das Leben, daß man Alles kann ertragen !
Und es öffnet gegen Alle sich das Herz in reiner Liebe,

Und ich will so gern mit Allen dieses Lebens Bann ertragen :
Schließt den Kreis und leert die Flaschen, diese Sommernächte
   feiernd,
Schlimm're Zeiten werden kommen, die wir auch sodann
   ertragen.

(Neue Ghaselen XVI)

The second, which on the whole is more common at this time,
finds moving expression in a number of poems of which this one
is typical :

Er, dessen Sinn durch Schönes nicht anzufachen ist,
Er ist's, für den die Erde der Hölle Rachen ist.
Die Schönheit als das Leben beseelt den Leib der Zeit,
Der ohne sie ein Haufen von toten Sachen ist.
Wer, ohne sie, noch möchte bestehn in einer Welt,
Die, wenn auch reich an Schätzen, es auch an Drachen ist.
O selig, wer im Herzen ein schönes Bild erkor,
Bei dem es süß zu schlummern und süß zu wachen ist!
In dessen Augen Seele, in dessen Gliedern Maß,
Und dessen Träne lieblich wie dessen Lachen ist!
Mir bleibt das Schöne ferne, der ich es stets besang,
Sprich, Weiser, was in Fällen, wie der, zu machen ist?
Es steuert nach dem Hafen des Glücks mein Herz umsonst,
Das auf dem Meer der Liebe der kleinste Nachen ist!

(Neue Ghaseln XLIX)

It is plain that his predilection for the Persian form with its recurring rhyme and strict pattern of alternations, was for him not
simply an imitation of the fashion set by Goethe and others, but
responded very much to a need of his own being, which demanded
that his emotional overflowing be continually shaped within a rigid
form, or else it might risk running away into total chaos. His desire,
here and elsewhere, is to chisel out statuesque and immobile verses,
entirely unsensuous, sometimes a thought too philosophical, but
hard and clear and balanced. He follows romanticism, of course, in
the cultivation of oriental forms and qualities, while protesting viol-
ently all the time against the whole romantic cast of mind. This is
true in general throughout his life, and not simply in respect of
formal matters like the choice of verse-forms. He is fundamentally a
Romantic, however much he denies it, he is of the Byronic school
of homeless wanderers, unhappy and unfulfilled, who see a perfection always on the horizon; his passionless objectivity, his extreme
cultivation of formal values, is a cloak thrown over his natively

romantic sensibility, indeed it is more, it is a necessary protection for himself against the continual threat of disintegration. It is this which had led to the charge that his poetry is false and his work a piece of large-scale pretence. Things are in reality a great deal deeper than this. His sensibility could be described as essentially feminine, and we can see how in his poetry he endows his work with an exaggerated masculinity in compensation. But in his life this led to extreme misery, as a consequence of his homosexual inclinations. Inevitably we find him, over and over again, cultivating friendships which at a certain point are suddenly broken off because of the too ardent expression of his love. And continually therefore he is disappointed, frustrated, and sometimes embittered. In his diary in 1819 he notes :

> Je souffre cruellement et plus que je n'ai mérité. Oh pourquoi! pourquoi la Providence m'a ainsi formé. Pourquoi m'est-il impossible d'aimer les femmes, pourquoi faut-il nourrir des inclinations funestes, qui ne seront jamais permises, qui ne seront jamais mutuelles? Quelle impossibilité terrible, et quel sort qui m'attend.

Here is one of the deepest roots of his poetic manner. His suffering convinced him that art and life are two antagonistic entities, that beauty is a pale goddess, a "belle dame sans merci", who lives remote and must be wooed far from ordinary existence. The ideal of art is therefore rooted not in life but in its opposite. So we have the poet setting himself to banish from his work the impulses of human life and to cultivate the pure patterns. His native feeling, his peculiar version of the romantic searching and yearning, does, of course, come out strongly sometimes, as in this well-known poem of 1820 :

> Wie rafft' ich mich auf in der Nacht, in der Nacht,
> Und fühlte mich fürder gezogen,
> Die Gassen verließ ich, vom Wächter bewacht,
> Durchwandelte sacht
> In der Nacht, in der Nacht,
> Das Tor mit dem gotischen Bogen.

> Der Mühlbach rauschte durch felsigen Schacht,
> Ich lehnte mich über die Brücke,
> Tief unter mir nahm ich der Wogen in Acht,
> Die wallten so sacht
> In der Nacht, in der Nacht,
> Doch wallte nicht Eine zurücke.

Es drehte sich oben, unzählig entfacht,
Melodischer Wandel der Sterne,
Mit ihnen der Mond in beruhigter Pracht,
Sie funkelten sacht
In der Nacht, in der Nacht,
Durch täuschend entlegene Ferne.

Ich blickte hinauf in der Nacht, in der Nacht,
Ich blickte hinunter aufs Neue :
O wehe, wie hast du die Tage verbracht!
Nun stille du sacht
In der Nacht, in der Nacht,
Im pochenden Herzen die Reue!
(*Romanzen und Jugendlieder* XXXIV)

This is justly considered one of his most successful pieces. It is, of course, a great deal simpler than is his wont, it operates with much of what one might call the standard Romantic images and has a most characteristic incantatory quality which is rare in Platen. But there is even here an uneasy tension between what is said and what one feels might be said, what is, so to speak, lying in wait to be said. Longfellow translated the poem and gave it the title "Remorse", which is not inappropriate, though it rather coarsens the impact of the original delicate expression.

After his first visit to Venice in 1824 and the unfortunate period of arrest on his return, Platen has clearly found himself as a poet, and his work becomes increasingly original. He cultivates the Persian forms even more assiduously, especially the Ghasel, and some of his can be said to rival Goethe's famous *In tausend Formen*. The rhyme in this form, which must be established in the first couplet and thereafter recur every alternate line, is expected to be of at least two syllables, and is frequently as many as six, so it is plain that enormous ingenuity is needed to handle the form successfully. These are poems on love's pains and joys, on the delights of wine, on friendship, on the calm peace of one's house and of rest, each one like a glittering jewel, with no relevance to anything outside itself. To say they are entirely objective is not only quite untrue, but also quite misses the point. Platen is attempting to create an impression of balance and pattern which always lay before him as an ideal, of means suited to ends, of a perfect union of object and expression. He prefaces his first collection of Ghaselen with four lines (themselves a Ghasel) in defence of this principle :

Im Wasser wogt die Lilie, die blanke, hin und her,
Doch irrst du, Freund, sobald du sagst, sie schwanke hin
    und her !
Es wurzelt ja so fest ihr Fuß im tiefen Meeresgrund
Ihr Haupt nur wiegt ein lieblicher Gedanke hin und her !

(Ghaselen. epigraph)

This is his claim—that the perfection of each of these pieces is
not an arbitrary harmony, a plaything of fancy, but is rooted deep
in the "Meeresgrund" of human aspiration and in the urge to
perceive and create beauty. This is an explicit onslaught against
romanticism, and also, of course, against the opposite doctrine, the
view of the writers of Jung-Deutschland that art must touch reality
at all points, that we must be reminded always of the connection
between the beauty we contemplate and the struggle of our daily
lives. This is dangerous doctrine indeed, and Platen was right to
deny it, though this was one of the things which brought down
upon him the wrath of Heine, as we shall see. Nor, of course, are
things quite as clear-cut as his practice here would indicate. In
much of his work, especially in his plays, there is a decided streak
of social as well as literary satire, and in his *Polenlieder* and
other political poems written near the end of his life he shows
a marked power in invective. Nevertheless in these oriental forms,
and in some of the sonnets which he cultivated so assiduously, there
is continually a danger that his control is clamped on so hard as
to strangle the emotional life of the poem, and reduce the whole
to an exercise in formal ingenuity, of "l'art pour l'art"; this again,
of course, has tended to invite the charge of artificiality.

At the same time he is assiduously cultivating the sonnet form,
exploring the avenues opened up by Schlegel, Rückert, Petrarch
and Shakespeare, all of whom are consciously taken as models.
Again it is surely the strict control which the form enforces which
attracts him to it, and which enables him to give satisfying and
impressive expression in these poems to feelings and yearnings that
threaten always otherwise to dribble away into self-pity and complaint. The *Venezianische Sonette,* the first fruits of his visit to
Venice in 1824, appeared in the same year, though he had to
have the book printed at his own expense. These have been called
the most perfect sonnets in German. This is a typical one :

Wie lieblich ist's, wenn sich der Tag verkühlet,
Hinaus zu sehn, wo Schiff und Gondel schweben,
Wenn die Lagune, ruhig, spiegeleben,
In sich verfließt, Venedig sanft umspühlet !

In's Innre wieder dann gezogen fühlet
Das Auge sich, wo nach den Wolken streben
Palast und Kirche, wo ein lautes Leben
Auf allen Stufen des Rialto wühlet.

Ein frohes Völkchen lieber Müßiggänger,
Es schwärmt umher, es läßt durch nichts sich stören,
Und stört auch niemals einen Grillenfänger.

Des Abends sammelt sich's zu ganzen Chören,
Denn auf dem Markusplatze will's den Sänger
Und den Erzähler auf der Riva hören.

(Sonette, Venedig XX)

In the fourteen sonnets on Venice, Platen expresses his love for the
city in a series of impressions of statuesque and rigid perfection.
The poems have the measured dignity of Venice itself, the strictly-
proportioned but ornate and grandiose palaces mirrored in the
still reflections of the canals, and bathed in the brilliant Italian
sun. These too are chiselled poems, immobile and unsensuous, made
of marble, so to speak, like the city they glorify, undisturbed by
the rush and clangour of events, beyond the reach of ephemeral
quarrels and petty trivialities. Some of George's poems are comparable to Platen's in this respect, but very few others. Platen
celebrates essentially the beauty of the city, often enshrined for
him in the works of the classical painters and sculptors or in the
façades of the palaces. And he is aware of the decay which is
everywhere apparent, in this ripeness, in this blessed balance of a
fine civilisation, built by a proud people for whom artistic production is as natural as the growth of a flower. In a sonnet which
begins by describing quite simply Titian's picture of St. John in
the wilderness, the sestet runs :

Wer kann sich weg von diesem Bilde kehren,
Und möchte nicht, mit brünstigen Gebärden,
Den Gott im Busen Tizians verehren?

O goldne Zeit, die nicht mehr ist im Werden,
Als noch die Kunst vermocht die Welt zu lehren,
Und nur das Schöne heilig war auf Erden!

(Sonette, Venedig XXVIII)

These lines express a great deal of the feeling Platen has for the
place of art in life, and indicate the roots of his disillusionment

with his own time and especially with his own country. He makes
an entry in his diary a week after writing this particular sonnet :

> "Mein französischer Begleiter ist auch der Meinung, daß die
> Poesie immer mehr ins Sinken gerät und immer mehr ein
> Gegenstand des Luxus, anstatt eine Sache des Volkes wird.
> Darum geschehe es denn auch, daß den neueren Dichtern die
> Poesie gar nicht mehr genügen wolle. Die Welt sei ernster
> geworden und Poesie habe aufgehört, das intellektuelle Leben
> des Volkes zu sein."

(Tagebuch, Sept. 24, 1824)

But although there is an undertone of complaint all through, the
general burden of these sonnets is of celebration and thankfulness
for the survival of so much beauty.[1] The shimmering radiance, the
peaceful nobility, the colour and grace and effortless ease of a great
civilisation is conveyed without the theatricality that one detects for
instance in Nietzsche's famous poem on Venice. Perhaps the last
of the cycle expresses the dominant mood as well as any :

> Wenn tiefe Schwermut meine Seele wieget,
> Mag's um die Buden am Rialto flittern :
> Um nicht den Geist im Tande zu zersplittern,
> Such' ich die Stille, die den Tag besieget.

> Dann blick' ich oft, an Brücken angeschmieget,
> In öde Wellen, die nur leise zittern,
> Wo über Mauern, welche halb verwittern,
> Ein wilder Lorbeerbusch die Zweige bieget.

> Und wann ich, stehend auf versteinten Pfählen,
> Den Blick hinaus in's dunkle Meer verliere,
> Dem fürder keine Dogen sich vermählen :

> Dann stört mich kaum im schweigenden Reviere,
> Herschallend aus entlegenen Kanälen,
> Von Zeit zu Zeit ein Ruf der Gondoliere.

(Sonette, Venedig XXXI)

The impact of Venice on him has indeed wrought a great transformation. Whether it was the new leisure which he now enjoyed,
or the clearness and brilliance of the air in this kind climate, or
the revelations which the great pictures of the Renaissance artists
were to him, as they were later to another fugitive from the North,
the Swiss poet Conrad Ferdinand Meyer, or, most likely, a com-

bination of these, there is henceforward in his work a sustained
and often successful effort to transmute his experience, his bitter
experience, of life, into poetic form, which gives much of his poetry
from now on an unmistakeably classical air and classical significance. Goethe makes his Tasso say near the end of his play :

> Und wenn der Mensch in seiner Qual verstummt,
> Gab mir ein Gott zu sagen, wie ich leide.
>
> (*Tasso* V 5)

The lines could well apply to Platen, who admired Tasso so much,
and is now deriving fresh strength and certitude from breathing
the air of Tasso's country. In his work now is no longer just wish-
fulfilment and fantasy, or confession and lamentation, but a calm,
sane and enormously tireless forming and shaping of the artistic
vision. If his art is a mask, a compensation-mechanism for his
frustrated life, this is no longer relevant. All art, after all, is that
in some degree. His apprenticeship is now served and his artistic
conscience is a delicate instrument which rarely lets him down.

Many of his sonnets are, of course, not on Venice at all. Many
are still concerned with the agony of love, the frustration of his
personal life. There is a whole cycle, for instance, of twenty sonnets,
which the editor of the collected works, Max Koch, suggests might
be called *Sonnets to Jonathan,* addressed to Platen's Erlangen
friend Karl Theodor German.[2] These are full of the vicissitudes
of a love-relationship, with reproaches alternating with tenderness,
self-criticism with adoration, hope with despair. This one is
typical :

> Wenn ich so viele Kälte dir verzeihe,
> Geschieht's, indem ich bei mir selber sage :
> Er weiß ja nicht, wie sehr ich meiner Tage
> Zufriedenheit an seinen Namen reihe!
>
> Er weiß ja nicht, wie sehr ich ihm verleihe,
> Was Liebevolles ich im Herzen trage,
> Was gerne teilt des Lebens Lust und Plage,
> Ja, was dem Leben gibt die höchste Weihe!
>
> Du weißt es nicht, und soll ich dir's beschwören?
> Oh nein! ich wage kaum, mit dir zu sprechen,
> Um nicht den Traum, der mich beglückte, zu stören.

Wie sehr mich Schönheit auch und Reiz bestechen,
So fürcht' ich doch, sie könnten mich betören,
Es könnte doch an Liebe dir gebrechen!

(*Sonette,* Erste Sammlung L)

But at times the note struck is much more ominous, as in this famous sonnet :

O süßer Tod, der alle Menschen schrecket,
Von mir empfingst du lauter Huldingungen :
Wie hab' ich brünstig oft nach dir gerungen,
Nach deinem Schlummer, welchen nichts erwecket!

Ihr Schläfer ihr, von Erde zugedecket,
Von ew'gen Wiegenliedern eingesungen,
Habt ihr den Kelch des Lebens froh geschwungen,
Den mir allein vielleicht wie Galle schmecket?

Auch euch, befürcht' ich, hat die Welt betöret,
Vereitelt wurden eure besten Taten,
Und eure liebsten Hoffnungen zerstöret.

Drum selig Alle, die den Tod erbaten,
Ihr Sehnen ward gestillt, ihr Flehn erhöret,
Denn jedes Herz zerhackt zuletzt ein Spaten.

(*Sonette,* Erste Sammlung LVII)

These poems, and many more, show how tender and noble is Platen's feeling, far removed from the squalid nastiness of which he was accused by Heine.[3]

It is time we considered Platen's plays, which, although today valued more as indications of the literary fashions of his time than as artistic creations in their own right, were during his life the subject of violent controversy and contributed not a little to the unhappiness of his relations with his own country. It is certain that from an early age he viewed himself as destined to make an important contribution to the theatre, and fragments and short pieces pour from his pen from 1817 onwards. The first collected volume of plays appeared in 1824, consisting of *Der gläserne Pantoffel* and a couple of much smaller pieces. Platen's version of the Cinderella story, with an admixture of the theme of the Sleeping Beauty, is based naturally on Perrault and written in an entirely light-hearted and entertaining vein. It is remarkable, like all his dramatic work, for the extraordinary dexterity of the author's manipulation of a widc variety of verse-forms, including sonnet, ballad, and terza rima. The second volume of plays, published in 1828, was a much more substantial production, containing three full-length works. *Der Schatz des Rhampsinit*, a pleasant comedy from an anecdote of Herodotus concerning mistaken identities in love-affairs, shows a great deal of wit and a skilful touch, and is also noteworthy for its use of the Ghasel-form and again of inserted sonnets. *Der Turm mit Sieben Pforten* is a rather feeble little piece about the rescue of a Neapolitan girl from the wicked Dey of Tunis, while the third play *Treue um Treue* is a dramatisation of the story of Aucassin and Nicolette, with interspersed songs and much use of Ghasel-verses. None of these can be said to be of much account today. It is the plays after 1825 which can still be read with pleasure and are still sometimes performed, particularly *Die verhängnisvolle Gabel* (1826) and *Der romantische Ödipus* (1829). And it is these two plays which brought down upon Platen the bitter hatred of Heine and other contemporary writers in Germany. Platen's satire of the fashionable fate-tragedy is, it must straightway be admitted, both extremely clever and extremely malicious. He has by now made a most conscientious and painstaking study of the ancient Greek theatre, and especially of Aristophanes, whose influence is apparent throughout the play. Indeed, a number of Platen's essays make it clear that he sees his rôle in the theatre of his time as similar to Aristophanes'. He is to lay bare the foibles and falsities of his age and by merciless satire to castigate and thus correct them. In *Die verhängnisvolle Gabel*, therefore, we find him using trimeter and tetrameter and many other artificial verse-forms with something of the effect of Aristophanes. His wit is frequently entertaining, often wounding, and sometimes in faulty taste, as when a character says :

> "Dass nenn ich Freundschaft, welche bis zum Nabel geht,
> Allein der Blick der Liebe sinkt veschämt herab."

He satirises not only the immediate targets (Müller, for instance, and other writers of fate-tragedies), but also many other manifestations of contemporary culture, from school-learning to the cult of Robinson Crusoe, Kotzebue and Rossini. He has a ghost in the approved fashion, but this one is a figure of fun; and the deadly fate-ridden weapon is here a fork, with which the murderer finally kills himself. There is an aristocratic sensibility at work here, an intellectual snobbery, which is not always very engaging. It is all very well to maintain that :

"Die Kunst ist keine Dienerin der Menge"

but there is a sneering note in these lines :

> Und schwierig ist's, mit Würde sich zu fassen,
> Auf einen Stuhl, den Schiller leer gelassen.

Nevertheless the piece is entertaining still, and it is unfair to dismiss it as simply a relic of bygone controversies.

The other play *Der romantische Ödipus* is very much bound up with the contemporary literary situation, with a character Nimmermann, a satirical caricature of Platen's hated contemporary Immermann, who sets out to rewrite the story of Oedipus so as to improve on Sophocles' version. The middle three of the five acts present the "improved" version, while the first and last acts constitute the frame, with a character called Verstand (an exile!) coming in at the end to make a violent denunciation of Nimmermann's puffed-up pride. The whole forms a lively and witty piece, but a great deal of the point is lost without a fairly detailed knowledge of the literary scene of the time.

It was this play which provoked Heine's onslaught, since Heine is himself also a target for Platen's satire. In *Die Bäder von Lucca* Heine replied in the most vicious and spiteful attack ever made by one German writer on another. He poured scorn on Platen's works, and descended to the most outrageous attack on his homosexuality, implying that his life was a succession of unprincipled acts of self-indulgence. He attacked, of course, his aristocratic birth and his cultivation of exotic and artificial metres and accused him basically of betraying life by shirking its problems, running away from it into a barren formalism. It is this latter charge which has to a large degree conditioned Platen's reputation, and it is plain from our consideration of his work so far that there is some ground for it, though not to anything like the extent that is commonly believed.

It was in 1825, just before his final break with Germany and self-exile to Italy, that Platen composed what is probably his best-known poem, and certainly one of those which show his powers at their best, the strangely haunting *Tristan* :

> Wer die Schönheit angeschaut mit Augen,
> Ist dem Tode schon anheimgegeben,
> Wird für keinen Dienst auf Erden taugen,
> Und doch wird er vor dem Tode beben,
> Wer die Schönheit angeschaut mit Augen !

Ewig währt für ihn der Schmerz der Liebe,
Denn ein Tor nur kann auf Erden hoffen,
Zu genügen einem solchen Triebe :
Wen der Pfeil des Schönen je getroffen,
Ewig währt für ihn der Schmerz der Liebe !

Ach, er möchte wie ein Quell versiechen,
Jedem Hauch der Luft ein Gift entsaugen
Und den Tod aus jeder Blume riechen :
Wer die Schönheit angeschaut mit Augen,
Ach, er möchte wie ein Quell versiechen !

(Romanzen und Jugendlieder, XXXIX)

How wrong Platen could sometimes be about his work is shown by the terms of the letter which he sent to his friend Fugger on January 13, enclosing this poem. He says :

"Ich füge dir hier ein Lied bei, das aber wahrscheinlich nicht komponierbar sein wird. Es gehört zu einem künftigen Drama, 'Tristan und Isolde'. Ich traue mir wenig lyrisches Talent zu. Meine Sachen sind unglaublich schwerfällig : *Gesang*."

Or rather, his is partly right and partly totally wrong. Thomas Mann's famous essay on Platen,[4] with whom he is conscious of a great deal of fellow-feeling, singles out this poem for special attention, seeing in it the very epitome of Platen's highest and most successful endeavour. He praises Platen's classical qualities, his restraint and control, and quotes this poem as an example of them, but not without emphasising the precarious nature of the balance that is here maintained. He sees Platen as a sort of combination of Tristan, the knight whose search for love is also an encounter with death, and Don Quixote, whose impulse to love is closely allied to self-betrayal and a desperate self-illusion.

It is plain that this poem of 1825 expresses intuitions and intimate experiences close to Platen's heart. Curiously, in this very year Goethe delivered himself to Eckermann of an oft-quoted judgement on Platen : "Es ist nicht zu leugnen, er besitzt manche glänzende Eigenschaften : allein ihm fehlt—die Liebe." One can see the grounds for Goethe's opinion, but must in all fairness reject it, and this *Tristan*-poem indicates clearly and movingly the extraordinarily honest appraisal Platen makes of his fundamental sensibility. We have said that he totally rejected much of the Romantic tradition of which he was heir, and we have seen his savage onslaught on many of its qualities. But at the very bottom of his soul the basic Romantic identification of Beauty with Death is deeply etched. It is this which lies at the root of all Romantic agony, it is this which the tears of the poets from Leopardi to Baudelaire and the Symbolists ultimately lament. It is this which Schiller again and again can find inescapably welded to his fine and noble idealism. To some extent all art is a lament for the imperfections of life and by implication therefore an impulse towards death, but the essential sign-manual of the Romantics is their conscious cultivation of this, and the exaltation of the yearning it entails into a divine radiance. It is possible, of course, to say that when such poets as Novalis speak of the desire for death or the welcoming of death they do not mean death at all, but eternity or some similar apotheosis. We need not take all this literally, but we must beware of not taking it literally enough. The poets call it death, and here Platen does the same. It has much of the quality of death—and the assertion of the instinct towards death (with which after all Freud has argued that we are all endowed) is very much aligned with the creativity of art. So at least the general Romantic doctrine holds, and there are good grounds for believing that to a degree all artistic creation pre-supposes something of the sort. Certainly Platen shows himself here as thoroughly Romantic in essence, however much many of the contemporary manifestations of the fashion enraged and disillusioned him.

The point is worth lingering on, since it is an indication of an important affinity between Platen and Heine. Both are examples of what may be called the back-lash of Romanticism. Both of them combine the spiritual basis of Romantics with an acute awareness of the poverty of the Romantic tradition as manifested in contemporary literature. In Heine this leads to the well-known intellectuality and irony which is the mainspring of all his work. In Platen the same fundamental discord issues in the persistent and valiant cult of the unromantic qualities, so that his poetry is sometimes damped and overlaid by striving for effects which are alien to it. But in his best work he does succeed for an instant in overcoming the limitations his experience of life imposes, and we see a fine sensibility joined to extreme technical mastery, the poetry a total fitting of expression to emotion.

During the years in Italy, Platen continued to compose many sonnets and also turned his hand more and more to the use of ancient metres, pouring forth a great number of odes, hymns, epigrams, eclogues and idylls. Many of these were on public events, or celebrated particular buildings or places, but frequently a personal note breaks through. Usually he rigorously follows a chosen

Greek metre, and he undertakes considerable study of the practice of the Greek Poets, but on occasion he invents a metre of his own, as in this short ode, inspired by a beautiful artist's model, in January, 1827.

Wenn du, Natur, eine Gestalt bilden willst,
Vor den Augen der Welt, wie viel du vermagst, darzutun,
Ja, dann trage der Liebling
Deiner unendlichen Milde Spur.

Alles an ihm werde sofort Ebenmaß,
Wie ein prangender Lenz, von Blüten geschwellt, jedes Glied;
Huldreich alle Geberden,
Alle Bewegungen sanft und leicht.

Aber in sein Schwärmergesicht prägest du
Den lebendigen Geist, und jene, wiewohl fröhliche,
Doch kaltblütige Gleichmut,
Wiegend in Ruhe Begier und Kraft.

(Oden VIII)

The most pessimistic side of Platen's feeling is given memorable expression in the ode *Der bessere Teil* of October 1830 which begins with the lines :

Jung und harmlos ist die Natur, der Mensch nur
Altert, Schuld aufhäufend umher und Elend;
Drum verhieß ihm auch die gerechte Vorsicht
Tod und Erlösung.

Stets von heut auf morgen vertagt die Hoffnung
Ihr Phantom. Auswandert der Mensch in fremden
Himmelsstrich; doch tauscht er indes die Not nur
Gegen die Not aus!

and ends on this note :

Tätigkeit löst Rätsel und baut der Menschheit
Schönstes Werk; doch schmähe sie drum ein stilles,
Sanftes Herz nicht, weil es erwählt den bessern
Teil, wie Maria!

(Oden XXVII)

This intense cultivation of classical forms, especially the highly complicated Pindaric metres, is a further testimony to the essential need of Platen's spirit to impose the most burdensome shackles upon himself in order to control and give form and shape to his natural emotional impulses. Nietzsche somewhere argues that the essential symbol of artistic excellence is not simply that the artist dance, but that he dance *in chains*. The image exactly describes Platen's endeavour, and one can see this urge to strictness and tightness of form playing a part in his poetic practice which is if anything increasing during his years in Italy. He throws his net ever wider, experimenting continually in every possible form and handling them all with a great deal of skill.

In his early days he had tried his hand at the ballad, and in his last years he cultivates this form with a large amount of diligence and some success, taking as his subjects historical anecdotes, many of them from Gibbon's *Decline and Fall*, which he is reading at this time with avidity. Most are perhaps little more than dramatised history, though one, *Luca Signorelli*, written in 1830 and based on an anecdote told by Vasari, has earned some admiration. It is from this time too, from the year 1831, that the *Polenlieder* date, Platen's one serious venture into sustained political polemic, in this case focused on the plight of the oppressed Poles in their struggle for freedom. The poems are thoroughly admirable in tone, but do not achieve a very high degree of power, perhaps because invective is not, and by his nature cannot be, a comfortable mode for Platen to adopt.

But he does not cease to cultivate the forms he had begun with, particularly the *Ghasel*, and on occasion he manages to express a wealth of lyrical feeling in this form. A good example of a late Ghasel, written in 1832 and placed at the beginning of the collection *Ghaselen Letzte Sammlung* which was published in 1834, is the following :

> Farbenstäubchen auf der Schwinge
> Sommerlicher Schmetterlinge,
> Flüchtig sind sie, sind vergänglich
> Wie die Gaben, die ich bringe,
> Wie die Kränze, die ich flechte,
> Wie die Lieder, die ich singe :
> Schnell vorüber schweben alle,
> Ihre Dauer ist geringe,
> Wie ein Schaum auf schwanker Welle,
> Wie ein Hauch auf blanker Klinge,
> Nicht Unsterblichkeit verlang'ich,
> Sterben ist das Los der Dinge :

Meine Töne sind zerbrechlich
Wie das Glas, an das ich klinge.
(*Ghaselen*. Letzte Sammlung I)

The poem is, in its way, as typical of one side of Platen's sensibility as *Tristan* is of another. Indeed one may say that between the two poles represented by these poems Platen's poetic work continually moves.

We have paid little attention to his epic poetry, though it should not be forgotten that throughout his writing life he was composing longer narrative poems, the best known of which, and the most successful, is *Die Abbassiden*, composed between January 1829 and December 1830. It runs to eighty pages, and tells an Eastern fairy-tale in easy and smoothly-running five-beat blank verses. There is a great deal of charm about the work. Most of his plans for epics remained unfinished, and one might perhaps agree that the reason for this lay closely connected with the fundamental nature of his poetic gift. The form which truly brings out his strength is any short but rigidly controlled one, or, if he attempts a freer more purely lyrical outpouring, then it must be made to obey some simply engineered patterning, perhaps by the use of a refrain or the repetition of lines, as in *Tristan*. Without such "chains" Platen's talent all too often issues in low-tension expression and a somewhat turgid emotionalism.

The more we encounter his work, the more it is borne in upon us that his sensibility is certainly not cold and formalistic, that he is not guilty of Goethe's charge of lacking love. He continued to write some of his best work in the form of the sonnet and the sonnets of his later years are among his best. This one for instance :

Es sei gesegnet, wer die Welt verachtet,
Denn falscher ist sie, als es Worte malen :
Sie sammelt grausam unsern Schmerz in Schalen,
Und reicht zum Trunk sie, wenn wir halb verschmachtet.

Mir, den als Werkzeug immer sie betrachtet,
Mir preßt Gesang sie aus mit tausend Qualen,
Läßt ihn vielleicht durch ferne Zeiten strahlen
Ich aber werd' als Opfertier geschlachtet.

O ihr, die ihr beneidetet mein Leben,
Und meinen glücklichen Beruf erhobet,
Wie könnt in Irrtum ihr so lange schweben?

Hätt' ich nicht jedes Gift der Welt erprobet,
Nie hätt' ich ganz dem Himmel mich ergeben,
Und nie vollendet, was ihr liebt und lobet.
                    (*Sonette*, Erste Sammlung XLVII)

Or this one, with which he closes his *Sonette, Erste Sammlung* :

Es sehnt sich ewig dieser Geist in's Weite,
Und möchte fürder, immer fürder streben :
Nie könnt' ich lang' an einer Scholle kleben,
Und hatt' ein Eden ich an jeder Seite.

Mein Geist, bewegt von innerlichem Streite,
Empfand so sehr in diesem kurzen Leben,
Wie leicht es ist, die Heimat aufzugeben,
Allein wie schwer, zu finden eine zweite.

Doch wer aus voller Seele haßt das Schlechte,
Auch aus der Heimat wird es ihn verjagen,
Wenn dort verehrt es wird vom Volk der Knechte.

Weit klüger ist's, dem Vaterland entsagen,
Als unter einem kindischen Geschlechte
Das Joch des blinden Pöbelhasses tragen.
                    (*Sonette*, Erste Sammlung LXII)

In all his lyrical work, and in these later poems perhaps even more than earlier, he expresses a passive resignation that may on occasion seem despondent and maudlin. But never is this expressed for its own sake, always he is attempting to throw all that is frustrated and unsatisfied in his life—his impulse to love and fellowship and joy which is continually so brutally thwarted—into the service of the austere and greedy mistress who is his art. Perhaps this poem, which was written at Palermo on October 11, 1835, seven weeks before his death, may be allowed to sum up, in its bitter but good humoured simplicity, the basic posture of his spirit.

Du bleibst dir selbst in jeder Pein,
Ob Alle dich verließen,
Und Luft und Sonne bleiben dein :
Wer ganz mit seinem Schmerz allein,
Der lernt den Schmerz genießen
                    (*Ges. Werke*, Vol. XII. Nachträge 7)

NOTES

1. Ernst Bertram in his Nietzsche-book, describing Venice, speaks of its "Zweideutigkeit ... aus äusserste Todesnähe und letzter Lebenssüsse gemischt" (p. 266) and sees here the attraction the city exerts on all "double-natures", like Platen or Meyer or Nietzsche.

2. He is simply following the suggestion of Platen himself who uses the name "Jonathan" as a cloak for the real name.

3. The sort of experience which was all too common throughout Platen's life is described many times in his diaries. The following extract, for April 5, 1823, recounts the end of his relationship with Knöbel.

"Ich habe heute das Fürchterlichste meines Lebens erfahren. Knöbel, gegen den ich, ich darf wohl sagen, die reinste, die innigste Liebe empfand, sagte mir heute mit wenigen dürren Worten, dass ich ihm lästig sei, dass ich ihm meine Freundschaft habe aufdringen wollen, dass ich jedoch meine Rechnung ohne den Wirt gemacht habe, dass er nicht die mindeste Neigung für mich empfände, und dass ich ihn sobald als möglich verlassen solle. Ja, dies waren vielleicht noch seine mildesten Ausdrücke. Ich sage nichts über das Nähere; denn was wäre hier noch zu sagen, nachdem dieses gesagt ist? Genug, dass ich den Tod in der Seele trage.... Es ist nicht Knöbels Verlust allein, es ist die ungeheure Gewissheit, dass mich die Natur bestimmt hat, ewig unglückselig zu sein."

4. In "Adel des Geistes", now reprinted in *Ges. Werke Band IX*.

BIOGRAPHICAL NOTE

August Graf von Platen, *Sämtliche Werke in 12 Bände*, Historischkritische Ausgabe, ed. Koch und Petzet, Leipzig 1909. (Still the best edition.)
Die Tagebücher des Grafen August von Platen, ed. Laubmann und Scheffler, 2 vols., Stuttgart, 1896, 1900. (An abridged edition, ed. Petzet, appeared in München, 1905.)
Briefwechsel des Grafen August von Platen, ed. Scheffler und Bornstein, 3 vols., 1911, 1914, 1921.
The fullest account of Platen's life and works is given by Rudolf Schlösser, *August Graf von Platen*, 2 vols., München, 1910.

Specialised studies of Platen include the following:

Will Schiller: *Platen und George*. Erlangen 1930.
Karl Stiegelmann: *Platens Ästhetik*. München 1925.
Vojtech Jirát: *Platens Stil*. Prague 1933.

The following include some account of Platen's poetry:

A. Closs, *The Genius of the German Lyric*, London, 1938.
Emil Ermattinger, *Die deutsche Lyrik seit Herder*, 3 vols., Leipzig, 1925.
Johannes Klein, *Geschichte der deutschen Lyrik*, Wiesbaden, 1957.
P. Witkop, *Die deutschen Lyriker*, 2 vols., Leipzig, 1921, 1925.
S. S. Prawer, *German Lyric Poetry*, London, 1952.

Nikolaus Lenau

Nikolaus Lenau

by MICHAEL BUTLER

Lenau (pseudonym of Nikolaus Franz Niembsch, Edler von Strehlenau) was born on August 18, 1802, at Csatád in Hungary. His childhood and youth were characterised by poverty and confusion. His father, a dissolute and inveterate gambler, died when the boy was barely five, his mother, a fiery passionate woman, lavished all her frustrated love on her only son whom with the help of her two daughters she spoilt extravagantly. A nomadic existence—worsened by his mother's equally unsuccessful second marriage—introduced the impressionable youth to the beauties of the Hungarian countryside but did nothing to counter his innate restlessness exemplified by his constant vacillations at university between philosophy, law, agriculture and medicine, none of which he ever studied to a conclusion. How far Lenau's later melancholy and pessimism were due to an "erbliche Belastung"[1] and how far the product of experience is ultimately impossible to determine accurately. But it is clear that such an upbringing was bound to have a pronounced influence on a nervous system as hypersensitive as Lenau's.

His restlessness drove him from Hungary to Stuttgart, and from there to the United States. But only after a short stay he leased his American possessions and returned to Germany, disappointed and tired of America. Lenau's disturbed mind was incurably at odds with the world. Finally an unhappy love affair with a married woman drove him insane. In 1847 Lenau was transferred to the asylum at Oberdöbling, near Vienna, where he died, a tragic human vegetable, on August 22, 1850.

IN the autumn of 1836 Nikolaus Lenau wrote to Sophie von Löwenthal: "Mein Fehler ist, daß ich die Sphäre der Poesie und die Sphäre des wirklichen Lebens nicht auseinanderhalte, sondern beide sich durchkreuzen lasse" (IV 27).[2] The remark shows not only the poet's perception of his own problem but also his unwillingness to control its fatal implications. For Lenau's energy was consumed by an obsessive struggle between painful experience and its poetic expression, between an unsympathetic reality and his ideals, which left no room for compromise, no time for a rational demarcation between life and art. At the same time, he was continually aware of the poetic possibilities of this dichotomy and thus fell victim to a basic passivity which enabled him to analyse through his poetry his problems and sensibility with a

ruthless egocentricity. Analysis, however, was not a cure, and it is
doubtful whether Lenau by temperament was ever seriously interested in a cure which might also have damaged the main-spring of
his art. By the time he had found his own voice as a poet, the
relationship between passive suffering and poetry had taken on the
dimension of an infernal dialectic. Shortly before he left for
America, he wrote to his friend Karl Mayer : "Ich will mich
selber ans Kreuz schlagen, wenn's nur ein gutes Gedicht gibt"
(III 142).[3] That this was not a pose, a fashionable piece of Byron-
ism, his tragic mental collapse and early death stand as adequate
testimony.

Lenau's earliest poems were written not under the influence of
Goethe, whose astonishing range cramped the style of many of his
younger contemporaries, nor of the Romantics but of Klopstock
(whose popularity had proved especially lasting in Vienna where
Lenau began his studies) and the humbler poets of the Göttinger
Hainbund. The elegiac odes of Hölty, in particular, with his
presentiment of death, attracted Lenau's admiration, and so did
the melancholy nature poetry of Matthisson whose knowledge and
love of mountains he shared. A precocious world-weariness, stemming from an even earlier Baroque tradition, is also noticeable in
these youthful, imitative poems :

> Eitles Trachten, eitles Ringen
> Frißt dein bißchen Leben auf,
> Bis die Abendglocken klingen,
> Still dann steht der tolle Lauf. (I 133)[4]

Quickly, however, Lenau began to move away from formal experi-
mentation and literary models and reveal an intense musicality of
language and a concreteness of image which on the one hand
relates him to the achievements of the Romantics, and on the other
to the coming age of realism. The rhythmical quality of *Die
Werbung*, for example, is an instance of Lenau's pronounced musical gift—he was a brilliant exponent of both guitar and violin—and
his ability to create the exciting atmosphere of a Hussar recruiting,
whilst in *Die Heideschenke* the poet sets human figures—shepherds,
robbers, gipsies—against their natural background of the rolling
Hungarian steppe with a sharpness of detail that contrasts with the
Romantics' preference for allusiveness and imprecision.

This process of maturation was accelerated by two events which
determined more than anything else the course of Lenau's life and
the content of his poetry : the collapse of an erotic ideal in his love
for Berta Hauer and that of his religious faith on the death of his

mother from cancer. These experiences brought him face to face with the problem of *pain*, physical and metaphysical. It is at this point that life and art coalesced as Lenau chose the latter as the only way of finding an explanation and compensation.

The affair with Berta Hauer began in 1823 when Lenau was twenty-one and she fifteen. The three years the idyll lasted were probably the happiest of the poet's life. During this time, however, he was busy creating a private vision of ideal womanhood and by persisting in seeing Berta as its incarnation, he gradually lost touch with the reality that had given the relationship its validity. Shortly after the birth of a daughter, Adelaide, the dream was over. Whether one accepts the view of Berta's moral turpitude or sees the end of the affair as a natural disintegration that the poet's pride could not accept, having staked so much, is finally irrelevant. For Lenau *believed* Berta was deceiving him, doubted even whether the child was his. The bitterness of this disillusionment never left him—in fact, it prevented him from ever reaching fulfilment with another woman. The great passion of his manhood is, significantly, for a married woman, unobtainable from the outset : Sophie Löwenthal.

As a schoolboy Lenau had been subject to religious doubt. An uncle had introduced him to the free-thinking of Voltaire, and his study of philosophy, however superficial at the time, contributed to his general unease. But it was the loss of his mother in 1829 that turned intellectual scepticism into existential uncertainty. With the collapse of these two ideals of erotic love and religious faith, the poles of Lenau's "Weltschmerz" are defined. The rest of his life and work is basically a series of desperate oscillations between sensuality and asceticism, monotheism and pantheism, determinism and nihilism in a search for self-justification in an indifferent and rapidly changing world. The resultant dissonance makes Lenau one of the clearest and most fascinating representatives of his time.

Lenau's "Weltschmerz" is both egocentric and self-conscious. However, the political reaction of Metternich's system with its brutal censorship and stifling provincialism also contributed its measure. A sense and need of freedom—however personally conceived and interpreted—was a permanent feature of Lenau's character, and in the artificial stagnation of the Vormärz with its conformity and lack of creative outlets he saw his own rootlessness amply confirmed. A frequent patron of Neuner's famous "Silbernes Kaffeehaus" in Vienna, Lenau came into contact with all the leading liberal minds of the capital, including Franz Grillparzer and Anastasius Grün, and he shared their political views as well as their feeling of impotence. The crushing of the Polish Revolt in 1830 was greeted with widespread dismay among these man and their South German contemporaries—Uhland, Schwab, Kerner among others—and Lenau's defiant *Polenlieder*, if somewhat conventional and sentimental in retrospect (the exception is the powerfully evocative *Die Nächtliche Fahrt*), take their place with Platen's as an expression of that "Europamüdigkeit"[5] prevalent among many intellectuals after the defeat of their hopes after 1815. Significantly, however, neither Platen nor Lenau saw any opportunity for action close at home, unlike the genuine revolutionary Georg Büchner, and Lenau's "engagement" in particular lacked the unifying central principle which a well-defined patriotism or political programme might have given him. Nevertheless, a passion for freedom and hatred of tyranny remained with him all his life and find their strongest echo in *Die Albigenser*.

The poetry of this first phase—up to the poet's departure for Swabia in 1831—contains in embryo all the main themes of his later work : love, nature, faith, freedom—all seen in the shifting light of transience and regret. The love poems centre mainly on Berta and are dominated by the bitterness of that experience. *Die Waldkapelle* is the most interesting in that it relates—an uncanny prophecy—loss of faith and insanity to the central figure's betrayed love. Significantly, the madman continues to blaspheme and haunt the chapel, scene of his former happiness. Like Lenau himself, he cannot effect a radical break with past suffering and succumbs to self-laceration. Amongst the early *Heidebilder, Himmelstrauer* stands out for its evocation of the peculiar atmosphere of the Hungarian heathland and for the remarkable combination of poetic mood and neatly observed natural phenomena. The same skill is apparent in the ten poems of the cycle *Wanderung im Gebirge,* inspired by Lenau's frequent visits to the mountains of Steiermark and the Salzkammergut. The long, allegorical poem *Glauben. Wissen. Handeln* draws together several of these early themes. Here the poet looks back elegiacally on his lost youth and tells how he forsook Paradise with Life, his "holde Braut", to search for the tree of knowledge whose fruit proved in the end unobtainable. The pain of this realisation and the impossibility of regaining Paradise make him turn to political action for companionship. But this is seen as a senseless struggle for a dead patriotic ideal : Germania has long since joined the shades of Greece and Rome. The poem anticipates in many ways the crisis of *Faust* without betraying anything of that work's depth or lyrical beauty.

*   *   *

The decision to leave the cramping atmosphere of Austria was made easier for Lenau by a modest legacy from his Grandmother. Arriving in Stuttgart in 1831 he quickly won the admiration and affection of Gustav Schwab and other poets of the "Schwäbische Dichterschule". Through the former the first contact to the publisher Cotta was made, and the appearance a year later of his first collection of poems laid the foundations for his fame. Throughout the happiness and recognition of these days, however—Lenau was welcomed everywhere as an exotic Byron figure—the old melancholy was never far away. Perversely, he saw this happiness as a warning, a lull before the inevitable storm, and the meeting with Lotte Gmelin and his love for her provoked only a terrible conflict in his mind. In a letter to Justinus Kerner he revealed his sense of impotence and inner discord which were the chief reasons for his renunciation of Lotte : "O Kerner! Kerner! ich bin kein Aszet; aber ich möchte gerne im Grabe liegen. Helfen Sie mir von dieser Schwermut, die sich nicht wegscherzen, nicht wegpredigen, nicht wegfluchen läßt!" (III 97).[6] He had arrived in Stuttgart with his themes and attitude to life already solidified. There was to be no change of direction, as he indicated to Karl Meyer : "Mein innerstes Wesen ist Trauer, und meine Liebe schmerzliches Entsagen" (III 10).[7] The product of the Lotte experience was the *Schilflieder*.

The cycle forms an isolated and untypical moment of peace in the poet's emotional life. The *Schilflieder* with their preference for evening, moonlight, the creation of an undefinable "Stimmung" are deeply Romantic but far from "epigonenhaft". The impressionistic technique, the symbolism and the intense musicality of the structure are Lenau's own hallmark. The group of five poems are arranged in rhythmic and tonal balance and stand out for their perfection of form, the fusion of word and idea. The basic elements—the moonlight filtering through the darkening reeds on to the still water of the pond—are subtly transformed into melancholy symbols of renounced love. Storms, experienced empathetically as a release from tension, are followed by a gentle, sad resignation as Nature echoes and responds to the poet's mood :

> Auf dem Teich, dem regungslosen,
> Weilt des Mondes holder Glanz,
> Flechtend seine bleichen Rosen
> In des Schilfes grünen Kranz.
>
> Hirsche wandeln dort am Hügel,
> Blicken in die Nacht empor;

Manchmal regt sich das Geflügel
Träumerisch im tiefen Rohr.

Weinend muß mein Blick sich senken;
Durch die tiefste Seele geht
Mir ein süßes Deingedenken
Wie ein stilles Nachtgebet. (I 20.)[8]

Lenau's departure for America in the summer of 1832 was
prompted by two main reasons. On the one hand he was attracted
by the economic prospects of establishing a regular income through
the purchase and renting of land, on the other he shared the
romantic vision of the New World, endemic in contemporary
European literature, as a land of promise and stupendous natural
phenomena : "Ich brauche Amerika zu meiner Ausbildung. Dort
will ich meine Phantasie in die Schule—die Urwälder—schicken"
(III 142).[9] This conscious search for external stimuli to poetic
creation was symptomatic of the poet's ingrained passivity. The
question of political disillusionment which helped to increase German emigration tenfold in the decade 1830–40, and which Lenau
touched on in the "Polish" poem *Der Maskenball*, appeared in the
end to play a subordinate rôle. In fact, typically, the letters up to
his departure began to show an increasing scepticism about the
whole adventure, which took on all the features of a convulsive
flight from reality.

The American experience proved, indeed, a disaster. The strain
of the two sea-crossings, privations and self-neglect, led to a serious
deterioration in his already fragile health. Above all, total intellectual isolation helped to disrupt the relationship with Nature he had
seemed to achieve in the *Schilflieder*. In the *Atlantica* poems Nature
is felt as hostile, heartless, at best indifferent. The sea is apostro-
phised as "der alte Mörder Ozean" as it snaps up in its greedy jaws
the unfortunate cabin boy (*Der Schiffsjunge*). The mood includes
spring which is also now divorced from man's fate (*Die Heidelberger
Ruine*) :

Mag der Hügel noch so grünen;
Was dort die Ruine spricht
Mit verstörtem Angesicht,
Kann er nimmer doch versühnen.

Mit gleichgültiger Gebärde
Spielt die Blum' in Farb' und Duft,

Wo an einer Menschengruft
Ihren Jubel treibt die Erde (I 98).[10]

The sense of communion that enabled the poet to conclude *Die Wurmlinger Kapelle* :

Hier ist all mein Erdenleid
Wie ein trüber Duft zerflossen;
Süße Todesmüdigkeit
Hält die Seele hier umschlossen (I 52).[11]

has disintegrated. Above all, the "Urwald" from which he had hoped so much is experienced as "grauenvoll"—a place where life and death are locked in a centuries old struggle (*Der Urwald*).

The intense subjectivity that made Lenau's relationship to Spinoza a permanently ambivalent one received still greater impetus during these lonely months in America, and even the two poems *Der Indianerzug* and *Die Drei Indianer* (written after his return) with an apparently objective theme—the dispossession and expulsion of the native Indians by the white man—are in fact vehicles for the expression of Lenau's own homelessness and sense of alienation. Lenau romanticises the Indians—as Chateaubriand did before him —with the result that the Indian Chief has all the unreality of Rousseau's noble savage. The same subjectivity is seen in *Ahasver, Der Ewige Jude,* but this time Lenau achieves a heightened pathos due to the symbolic quality already inherent in the theme. The Wandering Jew, like Faust and Don Juan, has made frequent appearances in German Literature, and Lenau's handling of the subject has all the immediacy of his own existential dilemma. *Ahasver* is the clearest example of Lenau's pessimistic fatalism in America. It is also the "Vorspiel" to *Faust*.

Goethe's death in 1832 and the astonishing appearance of the Second Part of *Faust* brought the legend into fresh prominence, and of all the many post-Goethean Fausts in the nineteenth century, Lenau's (published in 1836, revised 1840) is both the most fascinating and the most symptomatic of the period. Lenau consciously opposed Goethe's conciliatory optimism; his work is concerned not with the salvation of a "striving" Faust but with his irretrievable damnation. Thereby he returns the legend to the mediaeval tradition that produced Marlowe's "tragical history". But instead of recreating the religious certainties of mediaeval Catholicism, Lenau placed his Faust as the centre of a very modern crisis. Faust faces the Void : the absurdity of life without absolute values. God is

silent, human knowledge by definition inadequate. In this situation
Faust falls an easy victim to Mephistopheles who persuades him to
turn his back on Christ and seek the enlightenment he has been
denied via Revolt. Faust's boyhood friend, Isenberg, offers him the
vision of marriage and family as an antidote to metaphysical
despair—but he arrives too late.[12]

Having detached Faust from Christ, Mephistopheles isolates him
from Nature by plunging him into lust in order to intensify his
egocentricity. He combines the traditional Christian rôle as Tempter
with that of Faust's conscience. He shows him "truth" in the form
of the results of his actions and by simultaneously mocking his
remorse drives him deeper into the oblivion of sin. Faust's downward path is halted, however, for an agonising moment when he
meets Maria, the incarnation of ideal womanly beauty. Through
her he glimpses a chance of breaking out of the vicious pact with
the devil. But the escape route of love (Lenau will return to it in
Don Juan although from a different perspective) is brutally closed
by Faust's murder of his rival, Maria's fiancé. Thus by breaking the
Natural Law, Faust is cut off from Nature and completes the second
step towards damnation.

In the two important scenes, *Der Abendgang* and *Das Waldge-
spräch*—the latter added in 1840 but clarifying rather than disturbing the original concept—Mephistopheles underlines Man's divorce
from Nature. The Jews and Christians with their messianic illusions
have broken the pantheistic bond between Man and Nature exemplified in Greek and Hindu culture. Even the great Jew, Spinoza,
was unable to retrieve the old unity. Faust has reached the stage
whether neither Christ nor Nature—neither a transcendental nor an
immanent God—can satisfy his egocentric demands. One way Man
is the insignificant creature of an all-powerful God, the other a
mere means to Nature's own unfathomable ends. All too readily
Faust accepts Mephistopheles' tendentious exposition and the devil's
cunning alternative : the retreat into Self, the refuge of solipsism :

> Mein Faust, ich will dir einen Tempel bauen,
> Wo dein Gedanke ist als Gott zu schauen.
> Du sollst in eine Felsenhalle treten
> Und dort zu deinem eignen Wesen beten (II 86).[13]

Between these two key scenes is placed, in contrast, Faust's moving farewell to his mother's grave. The gentle flowing melody of
this scene, with its elegiac regret at the loss of innocence and the
frustrations of his mother's hopes for him, bring Faust, in fact, close
to a sense of reconciliation. But as in the Isenburg and Maria

episodes, Mephistopheles is quickly on hand. These are the moments, however, when Faust's humanity is seen most clearly and where his tragedy takes on universal appeal.

Before the descent into total despair, Faust faces one last encounter, one last alternative : the hedonist Görg. Against Faust's restless search for the Absolute and final arrogant claim of parity with God is placed the epicurean's contentment to trust to his senses and accept the world as it is. Since they have never revealed themselves to him, Görg ignores God and Nature equally, preferring an empirical materialism which rejects religious speculation (and by implication traditional German idealism) as a pernicious waste of energy. Görg embodies a healthy life-principle opposed to the negative influence of Mephistopheles ("Das Minuszeichen alles Guten") whose overtures he instinctively rebuffs. And yet, despite the attractive quality of the man—he is conceived in solid, non-romantic terms— his limitations in the end detract from his credibility. The fact remains that what has once been thought cannot be un-thought. Görg represents far too simple an answer to act as an effective counterweight either for Faust or for Lenau.

The consequences of Faust's hubris are clear : the retreat into Self produces a total disorientation. In a delirium of despair, Faust begins to see life, his own ego, Good and Evil, Mephistopheles himself, as fragments of a confused dream of God's. The contours of reality dissolve. Man's search for the Absolute is merely a sign of God's imminent awakening and is therefore free of any spiritual guilt. Renouncing the pact with the devil, Faust declares with tragic irony :

> Ich bin ein Traum mit Lust und Schuld und Schmerz,
> Und träume mir das Messer in das Herz! (II 123).[14]

Mephistopheles' triumphant return after Faust's suicide indicates an unexpected return to the concept of a personal God :

> Du warst von der Versöhnung nie so weit,
> Als da du wolltest mit der fieberheißen
> Verzweiflungsglut vertilgen allen Streit,
> Dich, Welt und Gott in eins zusammenschweißen.
> Da bist du in die Arme mir gesprungen,
> Nun hab' ich dich und halte dich umschlungen! (II 123).[15]

This together with the Monk in the scene *Die Verschreibung*, the only occasion when the voice of God is heard, was due largely to the influence of Sophie Löwenthal and is in strong contrast to the pessimistic nihilism in the development of Faust which mirrors so clearly Lenau's own search for a convincing "Weltanschauung". Yet there is in the poem a recurring theme of nostalgia for past innocence and the simplicities of childhood faith that helps to give this "surprising twist", as Lenau himself called it, an emotional if not a logical or artistic justification.

The structure of this predominantly lyrical poem is episodic— various scenes and groups of scenes could be transposed without difficulty. The two anti-Metternich scenes (*Die Lektion, Das Lied*) indeed, do not belong thematically in the composition at all, being straightforward political satire with no relevance to Faust's inner development. But despite this fluidity and lack of a well-defined shape or organised dramatic rhythm, the poem has great beauty. As a powerful expression of a desperate search for a hold in a world where all values and absolutes were in a state of confusing transition, Lenau's *Faust* is not only an impressive achievement but, together with *Don Juan*, the clearest example of "Weltschmerz" in German Literature.

Notwithstanding the great success of his first volume of poems (a second edition was quickly necessary) and the warm affection of his friends—especially the selfless, motherly Emilie von Reinbek in Stuttgart—Lenau's melancholia increased markedly during and after the composition of *Faust*. In September 1834 he wrote to his brother-in-law, Anton Schurz : "Die Hypochondrie schlägt bei mir immer tiefere Wurzeln. Es hilft alles nichts. Der gewisse innere Riß wird immer tiefer und weiter. Es hilfte alles nichts. Ich weiß, es liegt im Körper; aber—aber—" (II 287).[16] And in a letter to Emilie he betrays his typical confusion about the relationship of art to life : "Das beste Mittel ist, daß ich meine heftigen Gemütsbewegungen, von denen ich immer häufiger heimgesucht werde, in Gedichte entlade" (III 295).[17] In the same year Lenau met Sophie Löwenthal, the wife of Max Löwenthal, a high official in the Austrian Civil Service and an ambitious literary dilettante. It was to prove the most decisive encounter of his life. A light-hearted flirtation rapidly turned into a passion which racked the nerves of both for over ten years.

Sophie had much in common with Lenau. A sharp intellect and a delicate sensibility was combined with a vague feeling of having missed her way in life. But she, unlike Lenau, had children, a well-ordered domestic life and a central social position in Viennese society—none of which she ever had the slightest intention of sacrificing. On the other hand, she needed Lenau, and in this situation he was condemned to an impossible love. In the end it ruined his last chances of stability and happiness. His letters and work during this period reveal an increasing schizophrenia. One moment Sophie's beauty and influence over him were felt—recalling the Faust/Maria theme—as the proof of the existence of a personal, loving God, the next he wrote the beautifully moving sonnet *Der Seelenkranke* :

> Ich trag' im Herzen eine tiefe Wunde
> Und will sie stumm bis an mein Ende tragen;
> Ich fühl' ihr rastlos immer tiefres Nagen,
> Und wie das Leben bricht von Stund' zu Stunde (I 300).[18]

It is a pattern that repeats itself throughout the poet's life and makes impossible the marking of "stages" in his poetic development. His poems, including the longer "Versepen", are responses to temporary moods and situations and do not form links in a logical progression.

Sophie laid down the lines of their relationship in the formula "freudig kämpfen und entsagen".[19] This forced on Lenau an unnatural asceticism with the maximum of temptation which he could only maintain by a kind of hysteria. Although this helped to produce *Savonarola*, it was a frame of mind that could and did not last. But if the affair brought no fulfilment, it did produce a series of love letters that are the equal of any in the language : the *Tagebuchblätter*. Into these "love-notes", as opposed to the more formal correspondence with Sophie that her husband could share, Lenau poured all his frustrated emotions with a power and honesty that is quite remarkable. Of them he said himself : "Diese Zettel sind mir das liebste, was ich geschrieben habe. So unüberlegt sind mir dabei die Worte aus dem Herzen aufs Papier gesprungen, wie ein Vogel aus dem Nest fliegt. Wer mich kennen will, muß diese Zettel lesen" (IV 137f).[20] Indeed, in these "Zettel", some only a sentence or two long, Lenau lived out with unashamed recklessness the passion that was denied him in the flesh.

The 1830s in Europe brought an acceleration in the criticism of old traditions and patterns of thought. Institutionalised Christianity, in particular, came under fire. The Hegelian D. F. Strauß' *Leben Jesu* (1835) had tried to separate the historical figure of Christ from Christian myth; Heine was prophesying the end of Christianity itself and supporting a pagan emancipation of the senses, as were the writers of "Das Junge Deutschland". In the midst of this controversy, Lenau, inspired by his quasi-religious love for Sophie but more directly under the influence of the Danish Protestant theologian, Hans Martensen, whom he met in 1836, entered the lists against what he called scornfully the "Messiade des Fleisches".[21]

Martensen had drawn his attention to Rudelbach's recent Savonarola monograph (1835), and in 1837 Lenau published *Savonarola:
Ein Gedicht*. Conceived as the centre piece of a great epic trilogy,
Huss, Savonarola, Hutten, the fifteenth century Florentine monk
embodied Martensen's religious standpoint : "credo ut intellegam"
—faith is the prerequisite of knowledge, objective truth is only
obtainable through revelation. Encouraged also by the Munich
theosophist, Baader, Lenau naïvely hoped his undertaking might
begin a Renaissance of Christian principles.

Essentially, the poem is a Christian polemic against the sensual
Hellenism advocated principally by Heine. The conflict is fought
out in three major episodes : Savonarola's sermons against the
Pope's representative, Mariano, the monk's struggle for the soul of
the dying Lorenzo de Medici and the "conversion" scene in the
"Künstlerhain".

Savonarola's first sermon at Christmas, together with his dream
in prison shortly before his martyrdom, contains some of the loveliest lyrical passages in the work. In the sermon one can hear the
accents of Lenau's newly acquired religious certainty as the monk
condemns the worldly excesses of Rome. Mariano's reasoned reply
serves to underline the mystical asceticism of his opponent : Life is
short and meant to be enjoyed; God's love and pity are greater than
all human transgressions. In Savonarola's reply (*Die Antwort*) the
reader for the first time becomes aware of the deep ambiguity that
lies at the heart of the poem. For despite the vigour and expressive-
ness of the verse, Savonarola's fanaticism, his emphasis on "Schmerz
und Tod" and the suprarational approach to God—which apparently silences Mariano—are not convincing. Lenau himself was well
aware that Mariano's humanistic logic had proved more appealing
than Savonarola's lofty puritanism when he wrote to a friend : "Ich
wollte es nicht, aber der Dichter ist entschuldigt, denn er kann
seine innere Stimme nicht immer beherrschen" (IV 285).[22]

The ambiguity continues in the dramatic clash at the bedside of
the dying Lorenzo. Savonarola urges Lorenzo to repent for having
caused a "Weltdelirium" with his feverish dream of uniting Christianity with a pagan cult of beauty that has long since lost its
efficacy :

> Der Traum der Alten war verloren,
> Für sie so schön! für uns zu schal! (II 185).[23]

Yet there is a grandeur in Lorenzo's steadfast refusal to deny the
achievements of his life and in his humble desire for the monk's
final blessing. Savonarola's harsh withdrawal of this last comfort—

partly because of the addition of political undertones—does not attain the degree of self-evident righteousness that was clearly intended.

Similarly, in the famous "Künstlerhain" episode, the conversion of Leonardo and Michelangelo from antiquity to Christian themes (pointing to the Last Supper and the Pietà) is inadequately prepared and weakly motivated. The didactic purpose is all too plain. Furthermore, it is surprisingly the figure of Tubal the Jew that haunts the memory. Yet another addition to the long list of social outcasts in Lenau's poetry, Tubal is prominent not so much by his tenuous link with the poem as a whole but by the nature of his suffering. He contrasts sharply with the peculiarly colourless Savonarola (who only comes to life in the Lorenzo confrontation) and the cardboard figures of Leonardo and Michelangelo—and for a very good reason : however passionately Savonarola preaches a return to orthodoxy, it remains just as much a "Zukunftstraum" as Heine's vision of sensual emancipation; Tubal, on the other hand, represents reality :

> Ob auch der alte Jude rase;
> In seinen Reden, graus und wild,
> Auch im zerbrochenen Spiegelglase
> Zeigt sich von unserer Zeit das Bild (II 196).[24]

In fact, the melodramatic fashion of Tubal's conversion to Christ and death at the foot of a crucifix confirms that the inner discrepancy in *Savonarola* stems from the poet's own metaphysical uncertainty which not even the strict metrical unity nor the attempt at epic sweep could in the end disguise.

Savonarola represented Lenau's first major attempt to break out of the vicious circle of solipsism he had clearly delineated in *Faust* and tackle an objective social theme. It failed because Lenau never really regained the solid base of faith he needed. The resultant ambiguities and irony that are central to the poem foreshadow yet another compulsive change of viewpoint, and a long, monotonous poem composed at lengthy intervals, *Johannes Ziska: Bilder aus dem Hussitenkrieg* was all that was added to the projected triology.

Less than a year after the publication of *Savonarola* Lenau wrote to Martensen : "In Stunden düstern Affektes ist mir die Sache Gottes als eine unsichere ... erschienen" (IV 274).[25] He also reacted angrily to the criticism—particularly loud from the polemicists of the "Junge Deutchland"—that he had retreated into a reactionary mysticism. In this frame of mind Lenau turned to the thirteenth century crusade against the Albigensians which he characterised as "the Church's greatest tragedy".[26] For the first time in a longer work Lenau dispensed with a central character as focus and declared his "hero" to be "der Zweifel"—doubt which was to challenge all existent traditions and ways of thought in an effort to grasp at least negatively the sense of man's destiny. However, this plan was modified during the four years of its execution (1838–42). Ill-health and the worsening relationship with Sophie, who had promptly prevented the poet's half-hearted attempt to marry the famous opera singer, Karoline Unger, played their part, and it was only in 1840 that a serious study of Hegel gave the poem its final perspective.

As indicated by the poet's own description—"freie Dichtungen"—the composition has little organic unity but consists, in verse varying from the magnificent to the banal, of isolated impressions, lyrical interludes, horrific battle scenes, philosophical statements. The cramping four-line stanzas of *Savonarola* now open out into a variety of forms and metres which enable Lenau to take deeper breath for his ideas and avoid rhythmic monotony.

As in *Savonarola* Lenau uses a historical, religious subject to conduct a contemporary polemic. But the opening *Nachtgesang* marks the movement away from pious Christian hope in the next world, from the ascetic other-worldliness of Savonarola, towards a revolutionary desire to fight the forces of reaction here and now. The theme—the clash between the dogmatic authority of Pope Innocence III and the heretics of Provence (for the sake of economy and impact Lenau deliberately simplified the beliefs of the various heretical sects of Southern France into a basic manicheism)—is outlined in the section *Die Höhle*. Against the pale, ascetic Domenikus, founder of the Inquisition, is set the Albigensians' profession of free thought. The freeing of Man's mind from the tyranny of politico-religious dictatorship is seen as the essential preliminary to the thematically most important episode, *Das Gelage,* which significantly enough takes place in Paris. Amidst a throng of drinking, singing, arguing students the triumph of Hegel's "Weltgeist" is announced and applauded. The Trinity is explained in Hegelian terms as the progressive stages of human consciousness leading to the ultimate reign of the Spirit :

> Die neue Lehre soll die Welt besiegen !
> Der Geist ist Gott ! (II 382).[27]

Hegel's positivism, his view that everything in history must be "rational" since everything must lead inevitably to the final synthesis, produces Lenau's optimistic conclusion that "der Gedanke" will overcome the combined forces of princes, tyrants, popes. And with an admirable boldness in view of the censorship troubles he had already experienced over *Savonarola*, he draws his readers' attention to the contemporary meaning of his poem :

> Nicht meint das Lied auf Tote abzulenken
> Den Haß von solchen, die uns heute kränken . . .
> Den Albigensern folgen die Hussiten
> Und zahlen blutig heim, was jene litten;
> Nach Huß und Ziska kommen Luther, Hutten,
> Die dreißig Jahre, die Cevennenstreiter,
> Die Stürmer der Bastille, und so weiter (II 399f).[28]

However, long before Lenau reached this challenging *Schlussgesang* he had begun to feel the poem, with its incessant "Pfaffengreul", a burden. And this dissatisfaction is a symptom of a similar ambiguity of attitude that was noted in *Savonarola*. For despite the open avowal of Hegel, the poem does not, in fact, *demonstrate* a dialectical process. The Hegelian passages are instead abstract statements against which the horrors of battle, torture and massacre stand out in all too stark a reality. *Die Albigenser* falls thus into disparate parts, and like *Savonarola* convinces only the already converted.

Nevertheless, some of these parts are splendid poetry. The tragic figure of Alfar, the heretic leader, for instance, totally disillusioned by his suffering, parallels Tubal in the earlier work, but unlike Tubal he finds no release from the painful awareness of life's meaninglessness. He becomes the embodiment of nihilistic despair :

> Der Mensch mag glauben, zweifeln, wissen,
> Sein Leben ist vergällt, zerrissen (II 375).[29]

Lenau's gift for realistic description is also striking, and he achieves with neat economy a string of excellent portraits : Innocence III, Fulco, the troubadour turned religious fanatic (a warning to himself), Foix, the sensual nihilist who is the negative side of Görg in *Faust*. And the section, *Das Vogelnest*, forms a beautiful elegy on the nature of human folly. But these are isolated moments of success in a poem which all too frequently swings haphazardly from extreme to extreme. Doubt as a basis of enquiry becomes doubt as to the value of life at all :

Ist's nur ein Gotteskind, dem diese Welt
Als buntes Spielgerät zugefallen,
Das bald sich dran ergetzt, bald es zerschellt
Und seine Wünsche nur vermag zu lallen? (II 340)[30]

Both *Savonarola* and *Die Albingenser* were attempts to come to
grips objectively with the problems of his time, attempts to deny
his own deeply introspective nature. The tension that thus sprang
up between purpose and temperament radically damaged the
artistic equilibrium of both works.

During the last decade of his creative life, dominated by Sophie
Löwenthal, Lenau's poetry reached its clearest expression. The
nature and love poetry, with an important group of related sonnets,
reveal the same desperate search for an answer to nihilism which
runs through the "Versepen".

In 1834 Lenau published his only theoretical essay on nature
poetry in the form of a review. The weakness of the eighteenth
century poets, he declared—and the criticism was valid in general
for the work of the Swabian poets, too—lay in their practice of
simply enumerating natural phenomena or of seeking mere
parallels between human life and nature, whereas true nature
poetry must "die Natur und das Menschenleben in einem innigen
Kinflikt bringen, und aus diesem Konflikt ein drittes Organisch-
Lebendiges resultieren lassen, welches ein Symbol darstelle jener
höhern geistigen Einheit, worunter Natur und Menschenleben
begriffen sind" (VI 33).[31] Unfortunately, Lenau never developed
this vague theory with its echo of Jena romanticism, and indeed
frequently contradicted it in practice. He was at all times a conscientious craftsman, particularly as regards rhyme, (he also took
immense pains over the arrangement and proofs of his volumes)
but his thinking was too volatile to allow him to pursue the logical
development of theories. Yet the essay does point to Lenau's real
originality which lies not in any formal innovations—he remained
basically attached to inherited prosody—but in the uniquely powerful subjectivity with which he imbues all natural phenomena. The
heathland and the monotonous steppe of his Hungarian childhood,
the Austrian Alps and the sea, reed-banks and forest are in turn
incorporated into a rich "Seelenlandschaft" in which Lenau sought
to transcend his spiritual disharmony. Thus like the Romantics and

Goethe himself, Lenau gave to his relationship with Nature an essentially religious character, as the key poem *Das Kreuz* (1841) indicates :

> Ich seh ein Kreuz dort ohne Heiland ragen,
> Als hätte dieses kalte Herbstwetter,
> Das stürmend von den Bäumen weht die Blätter,
> Das Gottesbild von Stamme fortgetragen.
> Soll ich dafür den Gram, in tausend Zügen
> Rings ausgebreitet, in ein Bildnis kleiden?
> Soll die Natur ich und ihr Todesleiden
> Dort an des Kreuzes leere Stätte fügen? (I 221)[32]

But whereas Goethe came to a serene sense of the interdependence of all life, and Eichendorff, for instance, experienced Nature unproblematically as a confirmation of an unshaken religious faith, Lenau achieved only fleeting moments of peace and certainty— principally in the *Schilf-* and *Waldlieder*. In contrast to them stand the *Herbstlieder*—the attempt to find consolation in Nature on the basis of shared suffering. For suffering held for Lenau the possible key to the meaning of life, and this reveals his affinity with the late flowering of French Romanticism, with poets such as Nerval and Musset. (His lifelong reverence for Beethoven's music is due precisely to its effect of reconciling all painful dissonance : *Beethovens Büste*.) He takes autumn therefore as representing suffering Nature —Nature caught up in decay and death. Summer and winter by contrast play only a subordinate role in his nature poetry. It is true that there are a handful of poems of spring (*Liebesfeier,* for instance, or the lovely scene *Die Balze* in *Don Juan*) which go some way to revising the traditional image of Lenau as an incurable melancholic, but they are exceptions, as is—apart from its music— the famous *Bitte* which begins :

> Weil, auf mir, du dunkles Auge,
> Übe deine ganze Macht,
> Ernste, milde, träumerische,
> Unergründlich süße Nacht! (I 15)[33]

More typical is the final verse of *Herbstgefühl* with its wanderer-image so frequent in Lenau's poetry and so different from the "happy wanderers" of traditional German Romanticism :

> Ein trüber Wandrer findet hier Genossen;
> Es ist Natur, den auch die Freuden schwanden,

Mit seiner ganzen Schwermut einverstanden;
Er ist in ihre Klagen eingeschlossen. (I 281)[34]

Autumn is the end of a journey for Lenau. But ultimately the
negative quality of this pathos undermined its viability. The Lenau
"Ich" never really found a home in Nature—any more than it did
in Christianity—because the poet used natural phenomena—appre-
hended in unusually sharp, unromantic detail—as a reservoir of
convenient symbols whose content was arbitrarily defined by his
deeply subjective moods. Relatively thus destroyed their healing
power. Lenau's own honesty, in any case, constantly revealed this
discrepancy and prevented any romantic flight from reality :

Wenn alle Klagen einst in diesen Erdengründen,
Was jede heimlich meint, einander sich verstünden :

Dann wäre ja zurück das Paradies gewonnen,
In einem Freudenschrei das Klaggewirr zerronnen.

Trotz allem Freundeswort, und Mitgefühlsgebärden,
Bleibt jeder tiefe Schmerz ein Eremit auf Erden.

(I 316)[35]

Lacking any measure of the irony that enabled Heine, at least, to
disguise and combat the disruptive forces in *his* life, Lenau was
brought back again and again to the abyss of nihilism. He never
achieved the leap into the unknown which his contemporary, and
in some ways spiritual brother, Kierkegaard, insisted was the necessary next step after total despair. The love poetry and sonnets bear
this out only too clearly.

The poems Lenau grouped together as *Liebesklänge*—the
majority of which concern Sophie directly but all of which are
coloured by the relationship—are somewhat pale by the side of
the passion of the *Tagebuchblätter*, but they share the same tone.
Here, however, the pain of renunciation and the strain of secrecy
are to the fore. The rare moments of delight, for example *Liebes-
frühling*, are overshadowed by the impassable barriers to a fulfilled
love and Lenau's subsequent obsession with his own feelings : "Ich
bin ein Melancholiker; der Kompaß meiner Seele zittert immer
wieder zurück nach dem Schmerze des Lebens" (IV 28)[36]

During the nervous confusion of these years, it is fascinating to
see Lenau turning to the severe formal demands of the sonnet, as if
he were trying to defeat the growing chaos of his life by emphasising order in his art. But the content of these thirteen sonnets

reveal how far he was from a meaningful stability. Nostalgia for lost innocence (*Stimme des Kindes*) and the irreparable loss of his mother (*Der Seelenkranke*) expose him to the bitter irony of *Doppelheimweh*, where Man stands poised on the abyss longing for death yet clinging to life. The subsequent double sonnet *Einsamkeit* is Lenau's most unambiguous expression of despair in the face of a world without God, love or meaning. Nature is absorbed in her own decay; Man is alone, condemned to travel through a barren heathland to an unknown and unmarked destination :

> Der Wind ist fremd, du kannst ihn nicht umfassen,
> Der Stein ist tot, du wirst beim kalten, derben
> Umsonst um eine Trosteskunde werben,
> So fühlst du auch bei Rosen dich verlassen;
>
> Bald siehst du sie, dein ungewahr, erblassen,
> Beschäftigt nur mit ihrem eignen Sterben.
> Geh weiter : überall grüsst dich Verderben
> In der Geschöpfe langen dunklen Gassen;
>
> Siehst hier und dort sie aus den Hütten schauem,
> Dann schlagen sie vor dir die Fenster zu,
> Die Hütten stürzen, und du fühlst ein Grauen.
>
> Lieblos und ohne Gott ! der Weg ist schaurig,
> Der Zugwind in den Gassen kalt; und du?—
> Die ganze Welt ist zum Verzweifeln traurig. (I 305)[(37)]

The contrast to this desolation is found in the nine remarkable poems *Die Waldlieder,* the apogée of Lenau's nature poetry. Nature is no longer accused of heartlessness, as in the *Atlantica* poems; the poet is now filled with a sense of the harmony in all living things. The bird perched singing on a churchyard crucifix flies to the dark comfort of the forest, and the poet, too, leaves this symbol of suffering and returns to the bosom of Nature. Despite the devastations of storm and thunder, which appear to test his resolve, the poet is imbued with a feeling of serenity. Memories of the old melancholy and pain are reconciled by listening to the rejuvenating, secret voices of the forest. Nature is seen, in Hegelian terms, as "die schöne Braut" happily united with the Spirit, and the central figure of Merlin appears as the symbol of the poet's desire to join this union, Merlin who is privy to the deepest mysteries of life, who even knows the melodies locked in the breasts of sleeping birds. Sleep releases the poet from everyday cares and in his dreams he approaches himself these mysteries, the primaeval unity of Pan's world. "Vergänglichkeit", Lenau's life-long theme, is no longer felt as the cause of "melancholische Skepsis", to use his friend Gustav Pfizer's phrase, but as the manifestation of a pan-theistic cycle of death and re-birth. The Romantic yearning for a lost paradise, where the yearning becomes an end in itself, has been replaced in these poems by a confident note of acceptance, a Goethean certainty of belonging in the whole, which is strengthened by the realistic detail of the imagery and the rich variety of metre and versification. The final poem is the best of all Lenau's *Herbstlieder* :

Rings ein Verstummen, ein Entfärben;
Wie sanft den Wald die Lüfte streicheln,
Sein welkes Laub ihm abzuschmeicheln!
Ich liebe dieses milde Sterben.

Von hinnen geht die stille Reise,
Die Zeit der Liebe ist verklungen,
Die Vögel haben ausgesungen,
Und dürre Blätter sinken leise.

Die Vögel zogen nach dem Süden,
Aus dem Verfall des Laubes tauchen
Die Nester, die nicht Schutz mehr brauchen,
Die Blätter fallen stets, die müden.

In dieses Waldes leisem Rauschen
Ist mir, als hör' ich Kunde wehen,
Daß alles Sterben und Vergehen
Nur heimlichstill vergnügtes Tauschen. (I 455f)[38]

That the *Waldlieder* represented only a brief respite from the debilitating dualism of *Doppelheimweh* can be seen in the fact that Lenau was simultaneously working on a new subject—one that fascinated the nineteenth century mind : *Don Juan*. Into these "dramatische Szenen" (published posthumously in 1851) Lenau poured all the frustrated sensuality of his relationship with Sophie Löwenthal, condemning harshly the "monster Celibacy" and the whole concept of Biedermeier marriage. Just as he had turned his back on Goethe to secure his own re-interpretation of the Faust legend, so he reacted against the old Catholic tradition—especially familiar to his contemporaries since Mozart—or Don Juan, the remorseless but justly punished seducer. Lenau's *Don Juan,* indeed, is a close relative of his Faust (Lenau was not alone in sensing their inner kinship; in 1829 Grabbe had united them in an ambitious drama as rivals in love, and Kierkegaard's *Either/Or* of 1843 studied them together in the course of his analysis of Mozart.) But whereas Faust seeks for the ultimate meaning of life via his "Drang zur Erkenntnis" and kills himself in blind nihilistic despair, Don Juan stakes *his* life on sensuality and dies consciously and willingly in order to escape the overwhelming nausea of boredom that defeat generates. In this respect Don Juan is the profounder figure : Faust dies because he loses his mental balance when faced with the confusion of knowledge; Don Juan dies because he has seen through life and found Nothing.

Lenau's Don Juan demonstrates in his pursuit of sensual gratification another attempt to break out of the prison of Self and Time. (This, of course, is the link with *Savonarola* and *Die Albigenser*.) His progression from conquest to conquest constitutes a search for a partner who embodies perfectly the erotic female principle, whose possession would entail the simultaneous possession of *all* women— and by extension life. For life is "Ein restlos Drängen, Schaffen, Schwellen, Trachten/In allen Adern" (II 406)[39] sustained by the "God of procreation" who holds the world in a tireless erotic embrace. Thus in the oblivion of the sexual act Don Juan can feel himself literally absorbed into "God" as his "Hauch und seines Herzens Pochen" (II 407)[40]. Time in fact stops still. Yet from the start Don Juan senses the futility of his quest. He is condemned by the very transience of experience to a continual repetition, a continual "Sehnsucht" for the impossible "Ewig-Weibliche" that is the reverse of Goethe's intuition. For a moment, however, in the monologue on Anna, Don Juan does seem to glimpse his goal—the stilling of his passion, which significantly he associates with the nirvana of a "Liebestod" :

> Wenn ich den holden Leib umranke,
> Des Himmels Inbegriff und Schranke,
> Möchte ich vergötternd ihn verderben,
> Mit ihr in eins zusammensterben. (II 424)[41]

But Anna does not appear again in the poem. The dream vanishes and Don Juan is left, a prisoner of time, to continue his forlorn attempt to grasp eternity in a fleeting moment.

The theme of Man's essential aloneness, felt at its acutest in love, which runs throughout the work, creates a distinctively modern ambiance. The bitter-sweet scene between Don Juan and Clara (an echo of Karoline Unger) in which the impossibility of true communication between two human beings is acknowledged, can be compared with the opening scene of Büchner's *Dantons Tod*. Lenau's Don Juan has indeed much of the world-weariness of Büchner's Danton. A further fascinating variation on this theme is Don Juan's seduction of Isabella in the guise of her fiancée. The problem of identity and prejudice, the impossibility of seeing other people as they really are, which makes even marital sex a form of adultery, anticipates a quite twentieth century sensibility.

Don Juan's attempt to break out of his inner isolation through pleasure is the reverse of Faust's attempt to find truth by turning in on himself. However, the fatal characteristic of pleasure is its ephemeral nature, and Don Juan's foreknowledge that there is nothing after this world saps his strength until the way is open for the triumph of "Langeweile"—Ennui, the monster of Baudelaire's nightmare. Betrayed by his own life-force, Don Juan throws down his sword in a duel, in which he is clearly the master, and accepts death as the final absurdity :

> Mein Todfeind ist in meine Faust gegeben;
> Doch dies langweilt wie das ganze Leben. (II 448)[(42)]

Like *Faust,* Lenau's *Don Juan,* despite its dramatic moments, is essentially lyrical. In its present state there are obvious gaps and obscurities, but the outline of the composition and its ideas are clear. In one respect, at least, Lenau leaves no grounds for dissatisfaction : the lines of *Don Juan* contain some of the loveliest verse the poet ever wrote. In view of its rich musical texture, it is not surprising that Richard Strauß was inspired to create a symphonic poem from it. In the words of one eminent critic : "Lenau's *Don Juan* has still to meet his poetical peer in modern times outside Spain."[(43)]

In the last few years before his mental collapse, Lenau's physical condition grew steadily worse, particularly under the strain of constant travelling backwards and forwards between Southern Germany and Austria, much of which was not even necessary but a symptom of Lenau's need for external stimuli and change. A preliminary attempt in 1839–40 to start a new life with Karoline Unger had been easily blocked by Sophie. Four years later his engagement to Marie Behrends, also opposed by Sophie, was broken off at the onset of his breakdown. In July 1844 Lenau had written to Sophie : "Ich halte mich wirklich für ruiniert ... Es geht mit beschleunigter Geschwindigkeit holpernd and stürzend talab" (V 196f).[(44)] Indeed, a few months later, on October 22, the poet had to be conveyed to the asylum at Winnenthal where he dictated in a clear moment his last poem which opens:

's ist eitel nichts, wohin mein Aug' ich hefte!
Das Leben ist ein vielbesagtes Wandern,
Ein wüstes Jagen ist von dem zum andern,
Und unterwegs verlieren wir die Kräfte ... (I 536)[45]

It is revealing that the poem could have been written at any time in the previous fifteen years ...

Nikolaus Lenau is not a major figure in German Literature. His range, for all his ambition and occasional brilliance, is surprisingly narrow. But he is unjustly neglected—his *Faust* and *Don Juan*, in particular, deserve far more attention than they have received. Although he confused art with life so disastrously, he put an uncompromising honesty into his work which reveals a fascinating personality. He was an outsider in his life, a permanent guest in other people's houses, and an outsider in his poetry. Lenau does not fit neatly into any literary movement but is one of a group of highly gifted individuals who fell tragic victims of that widespread European phenomena which is known in Germany as "Weltschmerz".

TRANSLATIONS AND NOTES

References are to Eduard Castle's standard edition of Lenau's Works, Leipzig, 1910–23, 6 vols. Roman numbers refer to the volume, arabic to the page.

1. Hereditary taint.
2. My mistake is that I do not distinguish between the spheres of poetry and real life but allow them to intersect.
3. I will nail myself to the cross if only it will produce a good poem.
4. Vain striving, vain endeavour consume your short lift, until the evening bells sound and life's mad course is over.
5. Weariness of Europe.
6. O Kerner! Kerner! I am no ascetic; but I should like to be in my grave. Help me to get over this melancholy which won't be joked, preached or cursed away!
7. My innermost being is sorrow, and my love painful renunciation.
8. On the still pond the moon's lovely radiance lingers, weaving its pale roses in the reeds' green garland./ Deer wander on the hillside, gazing up into the night; sometimes the waterfowl dreamily stir in the depths of the reeds./ Weeping, I must lower my eyes; a sweet memory of you passes through the depths of my soul like a peaceful evening prayer.

9. I need America for my education. I will send my imagination to school there—to the primeval forest.

10. However green the hill grows, it can never make up for what this ruin tells with its stricken countenance./ Flowers with their colour and fragrance dance heedlessly where the earth exults before a human tomb.

11. Here all my earthly sorrow dissolves like a troubled haze; death's sweet weariness enfolds my soul.

12. This is a theme that haunted Lenau throughout his life and has its origins in the Berta crisis. Time and again Lenau relates human happiness to marriage and children and laments his ability to achieve even this minimum.

13. Faust, I will build you a temple where your Thought will be seen as God. You shall enter a hall of rock and pray to your own being.

14. I am a dream with lust and guilt and pain, and I dream the knife into my heart!

15. You were never so far from reconciliation as when, in the feverish heat of despair, you wanted to destroy all conflict, to weld together yourself, the world and God. It was then you sprang into my arms. I have you now and shall hold you fast.

16. Hypochondria is taking root deeper and deeper within me. Nothing can help me. That certain flaw within me is growing deeper and deeper, wider and wider. Nothing can help me. I know the cause is in my body; but—but—

17. The best method is for me to discharge into poems the violent emotions that are afflicting me ever more frequently.

18. I bear a deep wound in my heart and will bear it silently to the end of my days. I feel it relentlessly gnawing deeper and deeper and life disintegrating hour by hour.

19. Fight gladly and renounce.

20. Of all I have written I like these notes best. The words sprang so spontaneously from my heart on to the paper, like a bird flies from its nest. Whoever wants to know me must read these notes.

21. Messianic preaching of the flesh.

22. I did not wish it so, but the poet is excused, for he cannot always control his inner voice.

23. The Ancients' dream was lost, so beautiful for them! Too shallow for us!

24. However the old Jew may rave—terrible and wild of speech, the image of our time can be seen even in a shattered glass.

25. In hours of emotional depression God's cause seemed to me an uncertain one.

26. It is interesting to note that unlike Novalis and the Romantics Lenau did not subscribe to the cult of the Middle Ages. He saw instead a period of disunity and instability which coincided with his own experience.

27. The new teaching shall conquer the world! The Spirit is God!

28. The poem is not meant to divert attention to the dead or hate

from those who injure us today. . . . The Albigensians are followed by the Hussites who repay in blood the wrongs they suffered; after Huss and Ziska come Luther, Hutten, the Thirty Years' War, the fighters of the Cévennes, the stormers of the Bastille and so on.

29. Man may believe, doubt, know—but his life is soured, inwardly disrupted.

30. Has this world been given to some divine child as a colourful toy which one moment it delights in, the next smashes to pieces and who can only babble that it wants?

31. (Must) bring Nature and human life into an intimate conflict and produce out of this conflict a third living organism which should constitute a symbol of that higher spiritual unity in which human life and Nature are conceived.

32. Over there, I see a crucifix looming without a Saviour, as though this cold autumn weather, which sweeps the leaves stormily from the trees, had carried the divine image from its wooden stem./ Shall I replace it with an image of sorrow gathered from a thousand scattered features? Shall I attach Nature and her mortal suffering to that empty spot on the cross?

33. Stay over me, o dark eye of night; use all your power, grave, gentle, dreamy, unfathomably sweet night!

34. A gloomy wanderer finds companions here;—Nature, alike with vanished joys, harmonises with his melancholy; he is embraced in her lamentation.

35. If all earthly lamentation were one day to be in harmony, as each lamenter inwardly thinks, Paradise would be regained, the confused lamentation dissolve into a shout of joy.—But despite each friendly word and sympathetic gestures, all deep suffering on earth will remain isolated like a hermit.

36. I am a melancholic; the compass of my soul flickers back again and again to the pain in life.

37. The wind is a stranger, you cannot embrace it, the stone is dead, you will seek in vain a sign of consolation from its cold solidity. You feel yourself forsaken even amidst roses;/ Soon you will see them wither, oblivious of you, intent on their own decay. Pass on: dissolution greets you everywhere in the long, dark lanes of created beings./ Here and there you see them peering out of their cottages, then they slam the windows in your face, the cottages collapse, and you shudder./ Loveless and without God! The path you tread is horrible, the wind in the lanes draughty and cold; and you? The whole world is sad to the point of despair. (A brilliant analysis of the double sonnet has been made by Wolfdietrich Rasch: *Nikolaus Lenaus' Doppelsonnet "Einsamkeit"*, DVjs 1951, p. 214 ff. To this essay I am greatly indebted. It is reprinted in a shortened form in *Die Deutsche Lyrik*, Vol. II, ed. Benno von Wiese, Düsseldorf 1957, p. 150 ff.)

38. All around a growing silence, a loss of colour; how softly the breezes caress the forest to coax away its withered leaves! I love this

gentle dissolution./ The peaceful journey leads away from here, the time for love is past, the birds have sung their last melodies, and dry leaves sink lightly to the ground./ The birds have flown southwards, the nests, needing protection no longer, emerge from the decaying foliage, the tired leaves fall ceaselessly./ In the gentle rustling of this forest I seem to hear a wind-borne message that all death and decay is simply a hidden, peaceful and happy exchange.

39. A ceaseless pressure, creating, swelling, striving in every vein.

40. Breath and heart beat.

41. When I embrace her lovely body, the incarnation and boundaries of heaven, I want to worship and destroy it, to die as one with her.

42. My mortal enemy is in my power; but this wearies me like life itself.

43. E. M. Butler: *The Fortunes of Faust,* Cambridge, 1952, p. XIII.

44. I really think I am ruined . . . Life is going downhill, stumbling and falling, with increased speed.

45. Wherever I look, all is futility! Life is a much talked of journey, a confused rushing from one thing to another, and on the way we lose our strength . . .

BIBLIOGRAPHY

Nikolaus Lenau, *Sämtliche Werke und Briefe,* historical-critical edition by Eduard Castle, 6 vols., Leipzig, 1910–23.

Nikolaus Lenau, *Sämtliche Werke, Briefe,* ed. by Hermann Engelhard, Stuttgart, 1959.

Nikolaus Lenau, *Werke* Hoffmann und Campe, Hamburg, 1966. (Contains R. Schneider: *Der Katarakt.*)

Nikolaus Lenau and Sophie Löwenthal, *Briefe und Tagebücher,* ed. by F. Minckwitz, Weimar, 1963.

Bischoff, H., *Nikolaus Lenaus Lyrik, ihre Geschichte, Chronologie und Textkritik,* 2 vols. Berlin, 1920–21.

Castle, E., *Nikolaus Lenau,* Leipzig, 1902.

Castle, E., *Lenau und die Familie Löwenthal,* Leipzig, 1906.

Castle, E., *Lenaus Leben von Anton X. Schurz, erneut und erweitert,* I von. only, Vienna, 1913.

Errante, V., *Lenau, Geschichte eines Märtyrers der Poesie,* Mengen, 1948.

Martens, W., *Bild und Motiv im Weltschmerz, Studien zur Dichtung Lenaus,* Köln/Graz, 1957.

Turòczi-Trostler, J., *Lenau,* East Berlin, 1961.

Lenau Almanach, Vienna, 1959–1968.

Roustan, L., *Lenau et son temps,* Paris, 1898.

Schaerffenberg, M., *Nikolaus Lenaus Dichterwerk als Spiegel der Zeit,* Erlangen, 1935.

Adalbert Stifter

Adalbert Stifter

by KEITH SPALDING

Adalbert Stifter was born at Oberplan (Bohemia) in 1805. He was educated at the monastery school of Kremsmünster and then studied law at Vienna University. As a student and for a good many years beyond his University period he earned his living as a private tutor and a professional reader. Undecided whether to become a teacher or a landscape painter he was pushed by fortuitous circumstances into a literary career. In 1850 he accepted employment (as *Schulrat*) in the Ministry of Education and moved to Linz where he died in 1868.

WE owe it to Friedrich Hebbel whose ideas Adalbert Stifter rejected with every fibre of his being that we possess a clear credo in which Stifter sets out the aims of his writings. I am referring to the Preface to *Bunte Steine* (1853), in which he answered Hebbel and all his detractors. There he set up the signposts which mark the road he followed :

"Das Wehen der Luft, das Rieseln des Wassers, das Wachsen der Getreide, das Wogen des Meeres, das Grünen der Erde, das Glänzen des Himmels, das Schimmern der Gestirne halte ich für groß : das prächtig einherziehende Gewitter, den Blitz,, welcher Häuser spaltet, den Sturm, der die Brandung treibt, den feuerspeienden Berg, das Erdbeden, welches Länder verschüttet, halte ich nicht für größer als obige Erscheinungen, ja, ich halte sie für kleiner, weil sie nur Wirkungen viel höherer Gesetze sind. Sie kommen auf einzelnen Stellen vor und sind die Ergebnisse einseitiger Ursachen. Die Kraft, welche die Milch im Töpfchen der armen Frau emporschwellen und übergehen macht, ist es auch, die die Lava in dem feuerspeienden Berge emportreibt und auf den Flächen der Berge hinabgleiten läßt. Nur augenfälliger sind diese Erscheinungen und reißen den Blick des Unkundigen und Unaufmerksamen mehr an sich. ... So wie es in der äußeren Natur ist, so ist es auch in der inneren, in der des menschlichen Geschlechtes. Ein ganzes Leben voll Gerechtigkeit, Einfachheit, Bezwingung seiner selbst, Verstandesgemäßheit, Wirksamkeit in seinem Kreise, Bewunderung des Schönen, verbunden mit einem heiteren, gelassenen Sterben halt ich für groß : mächtige

Bewegungen des Gemütes, furchtbar einherrollenden Zorn, die Begier nach Rache, den entzündeten Geist, der nach Tätigkeit strebt, umreißt, ändert, zerstört und in der Erregung oft das eigene Leben hinwirft, halte ich nicht für größer, sondern für kleiner, da diese Dinge so gut nur Hervorbringungen einzelner und einseitiger Kräfte sind wie Stürme, feuerspeiende Berge, Erdbeben. Wir wollen das sanfte Gesetz zu erblicken suchen, wodurch das menschliche Geschlecht geleitet wird."[1]

The Preface has been reprinted so often—indeed no commentator on Stifter has ever felt able to circumvent it—that it need not be quoted in its entirety here. Its importance, however, is tremendous. When one holds it against Stifter's numerous essays[2] which deal with general subjects in a manner that is—on the whole—far from challenging, one is struck at once by the combination of passionate feeling and restrained formulation that characterizes every part of it.

Passion and restraint were indeed at war within Stifter. He was not by nature the Biedermeier type of bourgeois whom we meet in Spitzweg's paintings.[3] On the surface he might appear solid, integrated, contented and secure. He looked sedate and stolid enough, performed his official duties with utter conscientiousness, conducted himself as an exemplary husband and staunch friend, enjoyed good food and choice wines and collected cacti. With his abhorrence of violence, of excesses in thought or deed, of heterodoxy and anarchical sentiment he certainly lived what he depicted in his works as the good life and what he preached in the Preface to *Bunte Steine*.

Yet this seemingly calm outward appearance hid a restless inner life beset by anxieties, revolts and profound dissatisfaction. One cannot explain this dissatisfaction by pointing to his poor background, the political climate of Metternich's Austria or the hostility of contemporary writers who adhered to the liberal, emancipating, iconoclastic views of Young Germany. Such adverse factors merely added to dissatisfactions, inadequacies and despairs which lay much deeper. Hermann Bahr was the first literary critic to point to them :

"Wer sich ausgestoßen fühlt, wen das Leben ängstigt, wer keine Macht hat, es unmittelbar zu gestalten, der flieht in die Kunst wie in eine tiefe Höhle und gräbt sich ein."[4]

Over the last forty years different terms have been used by literary commentators to describe Stifter's feelings of isolation and inadequacy, and psychologists have dissected his mental make-up, calling him sometimes a "late developer", sometimes "permanently immature".[5] Such labels do not help; but many episodes lend substance to the view that Stifter never really mastered life.

The move from the simple village community in the Bohemian Forest where his father had earned a very moderate living as a small trader in flax and linen to one of the finest monastery schools in Austria, Kremsmünster, was the second shock to Stifter's sensitive nature—following closely on the first, his father's death in an accident, which had occurred when the boy was twelve. From a home in which simple affectionate women had taken care of him and a countryside little touched by Josephinian Enlightenment and cultural concerns Stifter was suddenly plunged into the rarified atmosphere of a school run by erudite monks, where he was taught by minds of great intellect and sophistication, swamped by knowledge and culture. Hardly had he found his feet in this new world and come to terms (of a kind) with the leaders of thought—both Classical and Romantic—who dominated cultured minds around 1820–30, when the next uprooting took place : the move from the rural cloistered Kremsmünster to the cosmopolitan and easy-going life of Vienna University. He appeared happy in the new surroundings, buoyed up by the writings of Jean Paul whom he adored, poor, but easily satisfied and earning enough through private lessons to suffer no real want, yet true enjoyment or life eluded him. The visits to his home between the University terms made him feel the widening gulf separating the village community he had sprung from and the ideal society of men that he dreamed of. There seemed to be no bridge between life as lived by the superstitiously religious, narrowly utilitarian, unimaginative folk at home and the life he believed in, which was patterned on ideas taken from Herder and Jean Paul. That he loved the people who led such dull and limited existences only increased his sense of isolation.

His studies, officially in the Faculty of Law, but in fact predominantly in the Faculty of Science,[6] absorbed him intellectually, but real solace came only through art. Landscape painting attracted him most, but increasingly he turned to writing—exuberant, romantic prose which owed much to Jean Paul, and poetry revealing an abundance of feeling, but little merit, immediacy or originality. Neither the prose writings nor the poems of those years rank as literature, and Stifter left them unfinished. Indeed, everything in his life at that stage was halfhearted, undefined, incomplete— juvenile in fact, and the constant urge to be with younger people (which never left him throughout his life) suited this indeterminate existence for the next ten years. During that time he fell in love with Fanny Greipl but could never convince her that he was willing to settle down to an orderly existence, he painted but could not decide to gain his livelihood through painting, he wrote but did not publish anything. He applied for posts but somehow managed to miss the vital interview or avoided taking the qualifying examination or fell ill at a critical moment. He was himself aware of his instability and confessed his inner loneliness in a letter (to Sigmund Freiherr von Handel, June 17, 1836):

> "O theurer, lieber Sigmund, ich fühle oft eine Einsamkeit, daß ich weinen möchte wie ein Kind, wenn ich nicht nebstbei doch ein so närrischer Teufel wäre, der flucht, wenn er weich wird, und kläglich schlechte Wize macht, wenn er gerne seiner Rührung Herr werden möchte . . ."[7]

The recipient of the letter might share and understand such emotionalism, but Fanny Greipl did not. When she learned that Stifter was also unfaithful, she broke off her engagement and Stifter felt once more tossed by an unkindly fate, baffled and insecure. Not that he yielded to pessimism—not yet. For the time being he lived a bohemian existence, disorganised rather than disorderly, teaching, painting, writing, willing to become a teacher of mathematics and physics should a suitable vacancy arise, finding happiness in the company of friends and pupils, but at the same time indulging in violent bouts of exuberance and dejection.

In this mood he fell in love with Amalie Mohaupt, partly out of spite because Fanny had rejected him. His statement to Fanny: "zeigen wollt" ich eurem Hause, daß ich doch ein schönes, wohlhabendes und edles Weib zu finden wußte[8] indicates how much his disappointment, his frantic attempts to assert himself against an indifferent world and his romantic lack of realism had impaired his judgment. Amalie was not *wohlhabend* but penniless; not *edel* but totally mundane, uneducated and unimaginative; besides, she was not his *Weib* in the sense in which the average reader would take the word. They lived together and there appears to have been a child which died after a few weeks, but with typical undecidedness and fear of committing himself Stifter did not marry Amalie until 1837, two years after the letter to Fanny had been written.

It was in these years of drifting that Stifter started to grope for clarity by writing his first completed prose works. It is significant that they were short—he was clearly quite unable at this stage to handle material that required extensive treatment—and equally significant that they were not primarily intended for publication. When the manuscript of his first Novelle was discovered by a pupil who saw it sticking out of Stifter's jacket pocket, he allowed himself

to be prevailed upon to have it published, and when an acquaintance a little later needed some material in a hurry, Stifter gave
him another work of his; but these publications of *Der Condor* and
Feldblumen were the work of chance. It is ironic that they brought
him immediate acclaim and thus settled the pattern of his entire
life from then onward. The would-be painter without a firm purpose was turned into a determined writer who wrestled with language with a thoroughness and dedication which had been entirely
alien to him until then.

Stifter himself, ever intent on nobly putting a fine gloss on his
entirely prosaic and disappointing marriage, maintained in the
years to come that his new life had really begun when he married
Amalie. This is totally untrue. His new life started when he fled to
literature and in creating his own kind of prose disciplined his own
existence.

Naturally he did not shake off his romantic enthusiasm and his
tendency towards extremes in feeling at once. *Der Condor* and
Feldblumen had been written under the influence of his erotic
failures, of his inability to win Fanny and his realisation that in
Amalie he had found an attractive body without a mind. In these
stories he had tried to justify himself, to salvage his self-esteem.
Significantly enough he never retouched these two works. He must
have seen that artistically they were inferior to what he could do
and that they reflected a state of mind which in calm recollection
he could not approve of. All the other stories created in the early
'forties were changed when he had come to realize that restraint
is better than extravagance, economy of words better than scintillating verbosity, intimation better than direct expression. It did not
take him long to discover the need to prune, tone-down and polish.
Within a few years his stylistic self-education was complete. To
name but one example : his *Abdias* of 1842 is essentially a Romantic
book, the version of 1845 by comparison is restrained, controlled,
terse and economical, a work of early Realism.[9]

As a creative artist Stifter underwent tremendous changes in
those years. The "late developer" had become a man. It had taken
him a long time to shake off his immaturity, his consciousness of
professional ineffectualness and personal inadequacy. Now, with
Fanny dismissed from his mind and Amalie established as an un-
recognizably idealized figure, he saw his work as an author as his
undoubted mission. He came to view the writer as a moral force,
himself as an instrument of the Spirit charged with the task of
spreading appreciation for moral values through his prose. It was
this conviction which drove him to labour more conscientiously—

re-writing the same passage again and again, chiselling, above all reducing every sentence to its absolute essentials.

Schiller, to whom one always turns when judging an artist who sets out to use his gifts towards the ethical improvement of mankind, charted the territory of the conscientious moralist writer :

> "Die moralischen Erscheinungen, Leidenschaften, Handlungen, Schicksale, deren Verhältnisse der Mensch im großen Laufe der Natur nicht immer verfolgen und übersehen kann, ordnet der Dichter nach künstlichen, d.i. er gibt ihnen künstlich Zusammenhang und Auflösung. Diese Handlung begleitet er mit Glückseligkeit, jene Leidenschaft läßt er zu diesen oder jenen Handlungen führen, dieses Schicksal spinnt er aus diesen Handlungen oder diesen Charakteren u.s.f. Der Mensch lernt nach und nach diese künstlichen Verhältnisse in den Lauf der Natur übertragen" (letter to Theodor Körner, 30 March 1789).[10]

This was exactly Stifter's aim, and the aim determined the choice of his subject matter as much as his style. He approached the content of stories as a teacher might—indeed, some critics have maintained (and in some parts of Stifter's works can demonstrate convincingly) that the pedagogue was stronger than the imaginative writer. He certainly limited his range by insisting that a moral purpose be reflected in all his writings. Hence the apparently unsophisticated story-content of his Novellen :

A man gives up the woman he loves for the sake of his mission as a writer. He achieves true happiness through resignation and through acceptance of the gifts bestowed on him by God (*Das Haidedorf*). An egotist striving for distinction and, considering himself superior to others, merely succeeds in becoming peculiar, indeed foolish. Hunting for the particular, he misses the essentials of life and ends in madness (*Die Narrenburg*). A man panders to his whims and loses all sense of values. He is rescued by contact with nature and a simple girl who between them open his eyes to the futility of his existence and guide him step by step towards understanding and happiness (*Der Waldsteig*). In such a summary fashion one could, if one wanted to, survey all six volumes of Stifter's *Studien*. The essentials in Stifter's world do not change. Circumstances and incidents provide variety. Yet even though one story may lead us to Africa and deal with non-Christian characters (*Abdias*), another may take us to the plains of Hungary among owners of vast estates (*Brigitta*) and a third may return to the problem of the artist's place in the world (*Zwei Schwestern*), the same fundamentals are preached : Man's moral task is to fit into God's creation. If he has the wisdom to accept the eternal values, to search for what is permanent, to live the good life, he will find happiness. Resignation will be required as an essential part of self-fulfilment, since he is not granted what he wants. Through willing acceptance of his duties as a moral being he realises himself. If, on the other hand, he makes demands on life which leave the needs of those around him out of account, he will end tragically.

However "simple" the story-content may be, Stifter's *Studien* as works of art are not simple. The events in the stories may be few and unsensational, but the conception of the personalities in them is subtle, marked by profound psychological insight, and their behaviour is far from conventional and predictable. He does not shirk complications in motivation, nor does he shrink from a frank examination of sexual desire. He does not avoid embarrassing situations out of prudery—the unexpected arrival of a sleepwalking girl in a man's bed (in *Drei Schmiede ihres Schicksals*) is treated in a delicate way, and where an inferior artist might have introduced a salacious note, Stifter resorts to very skilfully contrived humorous treatment. Indeed, it must be stressed that his desire to write as a responsible moralist does not make him consider the comic and the humorous as unworthy of his purpose. The gallery of Stifter's heroes and heroines thus contains a delightful collection of oddities, queer originals and foolish specimens whose foibles are very subtly and very humorously analyzed. It would also be wrong to dwell on the "simple" story and the plain message without stressing the skill with which simple events and insignificant objects in every story are invested with symbolic significance. Sentences which on the surface read like unassuming descriptions without any undertones or hints of a deeper significance, turn out to be the bearers of a symbolic load when pondered in the context of the whole tale. It is surprising when one considers Stifter's clear desire to write a moral tale and his magisterial approach to writing, how unobtrusive his art can be. As in the case of all the best prose writers one can enjoy each Novelle as a story *per se*, then peel off its outer layer of surface actions and discover underneath not only one further possible interpretation of the story but a variety of intimated routes towards the exploration of the seemingly simple narrative. A story such as *Abdias*, Stifter's first excursion into an exotic world, has been read with enjoyment for over a century as the thoughtful and interesting life-story of a Jew from his beginnings amid the rubble of a ruined town in the African desert through an era of adventures, wealth and power to his withdrawal into a remote corner of Austria. Yet even to-day a number of distinguished critics are putting forward new suggestions on how to interpret this story,[11] and the differences in their readings are such that we must marvel at the skill with which Stifter has suggested possible answers to the riddle of Abdias.

Simplicity in story-content and paucity of events go hand in hand with stylistic elaboration. Minute treatment of every element in his tales was dictated to him by his conviction that the important things of life are the unspectacular ones. If they were to be shown in their regular recurrence, their unchanging significance, then the writer had to take pains to go into every detail, make the regularity apparent by describing every phase and every aspect until the tangible object or the habitual activity has been made to take on an inner significance for the reader. Hence Stifter's long passages of unhurried descriptions of states, conditions, routine activities which tantalise the impatient reader. Stifter's prose, which wants to come to terms with reality and consciously avoids the rhetorical, the grand manner and the clever formulation, can only be appreciated fully by the reader who is content with each sentence as it comes, accepting it for its own sake and not looking upon it as a stepping-stone leading towards a climax or an unexpected turn of events. Indeed, Stifter would have considered himself a failure if the reader did experience surprise at the development of his characters. Life has its laws, and the incomprehensibly perverse in life is not fit subject-matter for the moralist writer. Stifter therefore described what stays within the law, the consistent flow of life, the meaningful routine, and since he confined himself to this unexciting side of life, he used every means at his disposal to give it literary significance.

He planned each sentence, weighed its parts and then arranged them in a balanced order. There might be two groups of two nouns each followed by an identical grouping furnished with an adjective each; the whole might then end in three verbs arranged in such a way as to produce a rhythmic ending, e.g. a dactyl followed by a spondee. The paragraph might then continue with a simple sentence (one noun with one weighty adjective and a simple verb), and this could be followed by a long period with three clauses—either of increasing weightiness and length or constructed in a descending order, terminating again with a rhythmic pattern. Every page, if subjected to minute analysis, shows results which are always equally striking: skilful numerical distribution of the parts of speech, measured cadences, subtle choice of epithets, intricate patterns of growing significance and increasing tension alternating with drawn-out periods suggesting hesitation or deliberation, leisurely

sentences giving an impression of the passage of time, clipped
staccato statements which with incisive terms throw sharp flashes
on the screen of the reader's imagination—they all appear in an
array of amazing variety on every page of the *Studien*.

This artistry was not imparted to him by some divine afflatus
which made him write unconsciously in such a structurally perfect
style. It was achieved by hard work, writing, re-writing, listening
to the periods, judging whether they were adequate, searching
patiently for the right word. This search for the really adequate
entailed also the removal of every simile that did not add to the
significance of the thing described, the deletion of every comparison or hyperbole that detracted from the proper appreciation of
the object. Foreign words were unnecessary, indeed a hindrance to
immediate perception of true meaning, so they had to go; simple
words—often homely terms with a regional flavour and therefore
certainly not the "best" words in a work of literature—took their
place.

Things had to speak for themselves. *"Die Dinge"* and *"was die
Dinge fordern"* occur again and again in Stifter's writings. This is
what distinguishes him from the later Realists who tended to see
things as symbols and therefore deprived them of part of their
reality as objects. Stifter does not want the things he describes to
"stand for", "to mirror", "to symbolize" or "to represent" anything
which lies beyond the things themselves. What is, is real, significant, intended. Every detail matters because it reveals Nature's purpose. We must penetrate to its essence, appreciate its value, see the
reason why it has the form we have before our eyes. It may not
have any special interesting features and may seem dull because it
belongs to the daily routine of our existence. All the more reason
then, Stifter maintains, to look closely at it. There is to him nothing
repulsive or unworthy in the regular, the periodically returning, the
seemingly monotonous. The really important facets of life are composed of regular and monotonous activities and events : sunrise and
sunset, sowing and reaping, work and rest. We must learn to look
closely at them, penetrate to their essence through loving appreciation—indeed, worship and love are the keys to understanding
as well as to the right way to live.

In this strain Stifter continued throughout the 'forties until the
moderate optimism underlying the faith he had cherished up till
then was destroyed by the Revolution of 1848. He had supported
moves towards the establishment of a constitutionally limited monarchy and had hoped that a better world would arise through the

granting of a more generous amount of freedom. The Revolution, when it came with violence, fanaticism and indeed civil war in some areas, disillusioned him completely. It became clear to him that an uneducated electorate was worse than a population without votes. Infuriated with the turn which things had taken, angry at his own opimism which now struck him as facile, he took the step he was to regret for the remainder of his life and accepted an appointment under the Ministry of Education. Based on Linz which now became his permanent home he inspected schools, supervised educational administration, rescued neglected works of art, wrote a text-book even, but the disappointments of office were greater than its joys. Worst of all, it limited the time he could devote to writing. Writing, however, mattered more to him now than ever before, because his urge to find solace in artistic creation was now reinforced by his almost missionary zeal to help in the education of mankind by depicting the right way to live.

That in this connection he should consider writing for and about children is not surprising. Schiller in a memorable passage near the beginning of his essay *Über naive und sentimentalische Dichtung* has made it plain why an idealist will always be attracted by the subject of children :

"Nicht weil wir von der Höhe unserer Kraft und Vollkommenheit auf das Kind herabsehen, sondern weil wir aus der Beschränktheit unsers Zustands, welche von der Bestimmung, die wir einmal erlangt haben, unzerstrennlich ist, zu der grenzenlosen Bestimmbarkeit in dem Kinde und zu seiner reinen Unschuld hinaufsehen, geraten wir in Rührung, und unser Gefühl in einem solchen Augenblick ist zu sichtbar mit einer gewissen Wehmut gemischt, als daß sich diese Quelle desselben verkennen ließe. In dem Kinde ist die Anlage und Bestimmung, in uns ist die Erfüllung dargestellt, welche immer unendlich weit hinter jener zurückbleibt. Das Kind ist uns daher eine Vergegenwärtigung des Ideals, nicht zwar des erfüllten, aber des aufgegebenen, und es ist also keinesweges die Vorstellung seiner Bedürftigkeit und Schranken, es ist ganz im Gegenteil die Vorstellung seiner reinen und freien Kraft, seiner Integritat, seiner Unendlichkeit, was uns rührt. Dem Menschen von Sittlichkeit und Empfindung wird ein Kind deswegen ein heiliger Gegenstand sein, ein Gegenstand nämlich, der durch die Größe einer Idee jede Größe der Erfahrung vernichtet; und der, was er auch in der Beurteilung des Verstandes verlieren mag, in der Beurteilung der Vernunft in reichem Maße gewinnt."[12]

Stifter can be assumed to have known the passage, and certainly the idea expressed by Schiller fitted his views, however unlikely Stifter himself was to formulate concepts with the clarity and penetration of which Schiller was capable. He certainly cared for children, understood them and could penetrate the world of their thoughts and emotions with uncanny insight.

All his spare moments now came to be devoted to what he called his *Kindergeschichten*; yet very soon it became obvious to him that the message he wanted to convey was not really comprehensible to children, because it was the same message which he had passed on in *Studien* (at least in their re-cast form as published between 1844 and 1850), except that it had acquired sterner undertones and reflected a deeper pessimism. Man had become more insecure, his destiny less predictable. His duties remained the same, but rewards and punishments were no longer so clearly recognizable as deserved or unavoidable as they had appeared before. By the time the collection was completed and furnished with the famous Preface, it presented a view of life which was beyond the understanding of children. *Kindergeschichten* became *Bunte Steine* (1853), Stifter's best-known creation, soon translated into other languages and seen by his contemporaries as the most mature product of the artist.

Apart from the sterner tone, *Bunte Steine* differs from *Studien* in several ways. The writer himself, who had been present as the narrator, occasionally offering a comment in *Studien*, has virtually disappeared in *Bunte Steine*. Besides, one new facet is added : stylization. Perhaps in an effort to be simple (which often strikes the reader as naive rather than simple),[13] and with the totally undisguised intention of presenting the permanent, the recurring and the essential, Stifter stylised his statements, repeated simple formulae, introduced leitmotifs, pruned statements and conversations until they appeared primitive and trite.[14] The effect of this is all the more striking because the reader soon discovers that all the stories move on two planes : the harmless, innocent, simple surface or foreground which contrasts with the dark, demonic, inscrutable forces whose presence in the background the reader cannot fail to perceive. Man lives his life as though he could control it, but the reader is made aware of the fact that we merely exist by God's grace.

Much has been written about Stifter's faith.[15] Attempts to claim him as a true Catholic or as an undoubted Humanist remain equally unconvincing. They treat Stifter as though he had arrived at profoundly intellectual, logically consistent articles of faith; yet if one thing is clear, it is this : Stifter's ratiocinative faculties were limited.

He never constructed a logical system of thought. On the subject of religion his pronouncements verge on the platitudinous : Religion and Art become identical when Art reaches its most advanced stage,[16] Art, Morality and Religion exist for their own sakes,[17] Religion is the supreme flowering of the human soul.[18] The power through which God expresses Himself in earthly phenomena is *das Göttliche*; hence Religion and Art are *göttlich*.[19] "*Wir heißen das Göttliche, in so ferne es sinnlich wahrnehmbar wird, auch das Schöne*".[20] The ideas behind a work of art, nature, the human form, the majesty of the moral law, the pre-destined path which the human race follows are all "divine".[21]

There is a vagueness about these statements, as about his remarks on evil and sin which inclines one to the belief that his convictions, however strongly held, were not based on careful reasoning and that the views he expressed merely reflected in most general terms what Kremsmünster had taught him on the basis of the prescribed handbooks.[22] There is no sign of a personal faith, of individual revelation or a direct relationship. There is never any mention of Christ by name; Christ appears only in allusions often as vague as those which refer to angels and to good spirits. Confessionalism is avoided in all his works, but this does not seem to betoken that he examined different approaches to religion and found them all wanting or all equally good. The tolerance advocated may be mere acceptance of the humanistic, enlightened teaching received at school,[23] reinforced because it happened to coincide with his abhorrence of fanaticism and violence in any area of human existence. There is no coherent philosophy behind it.

The same results can be obtained if one examines Stifter's political views. Conservative in essence but shot through with some liberal aspirations, patriotic but tempered with a pacifist cosmopolitanism, moderate in temper, humanitarian and enlightened with echoes from Herder and Humboldt—such are the general features, and appropriate quotations could be adduced for all of them. When examined closely, they turn out to be as vague, over-simplified, unoriginal and undistinguished as his religious pronouncements.[24] It was not in his nature to arrive at subtle distinctions, to set up logically unassailable systems, to reason brilliantly. Even in his scientific studies one does not come across original results or unusual insights but is struck by the collector's eagerness to string together facts and figures. There is no indication of a synoptic vision or the discovery of a unifying idea which characterized Goethe's scientific pursuits.

If Stifter can be seen as far from perceptive, original or strikingly independent in religious and political matters, it is not surprising that he should also fare badly when closely examined on the purely intellectual-linguistic level. Odd as it may seem, Stifter did not command a wide, varied or choice vocabulary. His grammatical knowledge was patchy, his syntax often far from faultless and his handling of different speech levels was poor to indifferent. The dialectal occasionally intrudes, colloquialisms stand out awkwardly and bookish words, often archaic even in Stifter's days, mar the simplicity of some sentences. In the last fifteen years of his life in particular he allowed ponderous compounds which belonged to civil service jargon (or reflect it in general structure) to intrude, and many of his own creations made up to avoid foreign terms are cumbersome inelegant failures. If his prose were to be judged simply from the technical-linguistic angle, Stifter would un-doubtedly have to be called an uneven stylist. Some critics have seized upon this eagerly and have drawn from it quite erroneous conclusions regarding the quality of Stifter's writings.

An introductory essay on an author cannot stray from its prin-cipal subject and therefore the question cannot be entered into whether a man can write unevenly and still be a great writer.[25] Suffice it to say that Stifter profoundly impressed such superb stylists as Nietzsche, Hofmannsthal and Thomas Mann, to name but three, as belonging to the greatest writers in the German lang-uage.

Stylistically, however, it was a mistake on Stifter's part when, in the last fifteen years of his life, he modelled himself increasingly on Goethe's style of the later decades, the *Altersstil*. Various factors pushed him in that direction : his growing aversion from the spirit of his era, the desire to turn to more comprehensive works in which he could paint a detailed ideal picture of the world, his turning-away from both Schiller and from Romanticism towards Classical concepts in life and art. A *Bildungsroman* in the manner of *Wilhelm Meister* appeared to him as the most suitable genre, and so his all-too-rare moments of leisure were devoted to *Der Nach-sommer*, the novel which was to alienate him from the general reading public for the next fifty years.

Der Nachsommer (1857) was bound to enrage the followers of Young Germany, but it was also certain to disappoint those readers who approved of the newly emerged Realist movement, for here Stifter depicted a world which one could not recognise as true; nor did it appear to delineate in minute realistic detail any society past or present. It was conceived as a novel, yet we gain no insight into psychological problems, are not introduced to fascinating characters, witness no important events. It is not even a "novel of development" in which the hero grows gropingly through trial and error into a personality. There is development, but only of a special kind, since the young characters Heinrich and Natalie will eventually be exactly like their old guides and teachers Risach and Mathilde : the experience leading them to the full realisation of their personalities will be based on living under the same code of laws as the older characters. Indeed the novel is an illustrated code of law setting out the guide-lines towards the perfect life. With infinite detail we are taken through the stages in which, in essence, the same territory is covered over which the reader had been taken in *Studien* and *Bunte Steine* : Man in his apprenticeship must begin with a study of nature in all its purposefulness, its inter-relations, its unending variety and its beauty. Only when he has grasped all these aspects and stands in awed worship before this manifestation of the divine, determined to fit into the plan that nature has mapped out for mankind, can the seeker proceed to the next stage of self-realisation. He must learn to recognise the divine as manifested in art. Advancing through craftsmanship and technical competence, followed by scientific or scholarly exploration, he will reach the highest stage which is Art—the divine in the garb of the beautiful. Creativity will follow, because true perception grants us insight. At that stage we are vouchsafed revelation and thus we approach the divine. Love will open our eyes, resignation will preserve our integrity. In this state of grace we appreciate the ordinary things of life and learn to cherish what is eternal. Routine is changed from something tedious into something sacred, it becomes a ritual. By filling our ordinary activities with meaning we make our lives meaningful, become personalities. Such attaining of meaningfulness can be expected to encompass wider and wider sections of humanity; gradually mankind will improve, rejecting violence, curbing passion, seeking harmony with nature, cherishing the beautiful. Thus by a utopian route Stifter returned to a kind of optimism, far removed from the lighthearted expectation of happiness for all mankind which had brightened the stages of his earlier career, but an optimistic affirmation all the same :

"Unsere Zeit ist ... eine Übergangszeit, nach welcher eine kommen wird, von der das griechische und römische Altertum weit wird übertroffen werden. Wird arbeiten an einem besonderen Gewichte der Weltuhr ... an den Naturwissenschaften. Wir können jetzt noch nicht ahnen, was die Pflege dieses Gewichtes für einen Einfluß haben wird auf die Umgestaltung der Welt und des Lebens. Wir haben zum Teile die Sätze dieser Wissenschaften noch als totes Eigentum in den Büchern oder Lehrzimmern, zum Teile haben wir sie erst auf die Gewerbe, auf den Handel, auf den Bau von Straßen und ähnlichen Dingen verwendet, wir stehen noch zu sehr in dem Brausen dieses Anfanges, um die Ergebnisse beurteilen zu können, ja wir stehen erst ganz am Anfange des Anfanges. Wie wird es sein, wenn wir mit der Schnelligkeit des Blitzes Nachrichten über die ganze Erde werden verbreiten können, wenn wir selber mit großer Geschwindigkeit und in kurzer Zeit an die verschiedensten Stellen der Erde werden gelangen, und wenn wir mit gleicher Schnelligkeit große Lasten werden befördern können? Werden die Güter der Erde da nicht durch die Möglichkeit des leichten Austauschens gemeinsam werden, daß allen alles zugänglich ist? Jetzt kann sich eine kleine Landstadt und ihre Umgebung mit dem, was sie hat, was sie ist, und was sie weiß, absperren : bald wird es aber nicht mehr so sein, sie wird in den allgemeinen Verkehr gerissen werden. Dann wird, um der Allberührung genügen zu können, das, was der Geringste wissen und können muß, um vieles größer sein als jetzt. Die Staten, die durch Entwicklung des Verstandes und durch Bildung sich dieses Wissen zuerst erwerben, werden an Reichtum, an Macht und Glanz vorausschreiten und die andern sogar in Frage stellen können. Welche Umgestaltungen wird aber erst auch der Geist in seinem ganzen Wesen erlangen? Diese Wirkung ist bei weitem die wichtigste. Der Kampf in dieser Richtung wird sich fortkämpfen, er ist entstanden, weil neue menschliche Verhältnisse eintraten, das Brausen, von welchem ich sprach, wird noch stärker werden, wie lange es dauern wird, welche Übel entstehen werden, vermag ich nicht zu sagen; aber es wird eine Abklärung folgen, die Übermacht des Stoffes wird vor dem Geiste, der endlich doch siegen wird, eine bloße Macht werden, die er gebraucht, und weil er einen neuen menschlichen Gewinn gemacht hat, wird eine Zeit der Größe kommen, die in der Geschichte noch nicht dagewesen ist. Ich glaube, daß so Stufen nach Stufen in Jahrtausenden erstiegen werden. Wie weit das geht, wie es werden, wie es enden wird, vermag in irdischer Verstand nicht zu ergründen. Nur das scheint mir sicher, andere Zeiten und andere Fassungen des Lebens werden kommen, wie sehr auch das, was dem Geiste und Körper des Menschen als letzter Grund innewohnt, beharren mag.[26]

Science as the new determinant of life, communication as the peacemaker, eventual victory of mind over matter—such were the

items salvaged from the debacle of 1848. Mankind took little notice
of them, and Hebbel offered the vacant crown of Poland to any
person capable of reading *Der Nachsommer* to the end.[27]

Stifter remained undeterred and started work on the next project.
This was to encompass a considerable period of Bohemian history,
and its first volume, *Witiko* (1865–67), dealt with events which fall
into the twelfth century. If it had been conceived as straightforward
history, it might well have been received more kindly by a generation fond of the works of Sir Walter Scott and Willibald Alexis.
Events in twelfth-century Bohemia were turbulent enough and their
story did not lack elements of grandeur. Stifter, however, wanted to
be "Homeric", totally unaware of how unsuitable Homer's style
was to the work he had in mind. Goethe could be "Homeric" in
Hermann und Dorothea, where he could use epic breadth and detailed description within an idyll; by writing in verse he could raise
the presentation of intrinsically prosaic objects and situations to a
level at which they become acceptable to the modern reader.
Stifter, writing in prose and deciding on an historical novel robbed
himself of the advantages Goethe had enjoyed. The adoption of an
Homeric style combined with his pedagogical impulse to preach
the gospel of the rule of law and of the victory of self-control over
passion made him create a quasi-idyllic historical novel of the
Middle Ages—a contradiction in terms. Whereas in *Der Nachsommer* the struggle for individual perfection had been presented
convincingly because it concerned four people living fairly secluded
lives, a similar striving in *Witiko* runs counter to the requirements
of an epic story purporting to deal with armies, pressure groups and
popular movements.

Some of the articles of Stifter's faith, such as respect for the individual, reverence for the private conscience, loving acceptance
of the positive sides of tradition and its expression through ceremonial could find a legitimate place in *Witiko* (and benevolent
critics have fastened on to them, forgetting the fact that Stifter had
had ample opportunity to present these articles of faith in stories
more suitable for them), but his attempt at distinguishing between
Tat and *Tätigkeit*, the former rejected as impulse-directed and
often harmful, the latter praised as the positive contribution by men
of worth towards the achievement of the good life, is entirely out of
place here, indeed his genius for the ordinary things of life totally
disqualified him as an historical novelist. The impression conveyed
in the novel that a simple upright man need only persevere in his
goodness, competence, piety and righteousness to achieve a position
of power in the land contradicts what the reader knows of media-

eval history, leaves the existence of evil and the vulnerability of
the good and the righteous out of account and therefore falsifies
history.

Even Stifter enthusiasts have to admit that his writings had by
that time reached a dangerous degree of stylisation. There is constant repetition of formulae, heavy accentuation of the ritualistic
aspect of mediaeval life, pruning of the narrative of all ornament,
hammering home of the ethical message in terms so simple as to
border on the banal. No writer in German of any significance
attempted anything like Stifter's style in *Witiko* until, some fifty
years later, the Expressionists hurled forth their convictions in
similarly contrived language.

Perhaps Stifter was reaching breaking-point. His health had
certainly deteriorated to such an extent that he was allowed to
retire from his official post.[28] The adoption of two girls had not
brought happiness, indeed the reverse—one had died of typhus, the
other committed suicide. Financial worries seemed to be eternally
with him, not because he had really insufficient means but because
he always lived beyond his income. Pathological fear could assail
him, and an outbreak of cholera in Linz made him flee to the
country for safety and at the same time put him on the rack with
shame for running away. He longed to be able to undertake
journeys to distant parts, but plans to find inspiration in this way
always miscarried either because there was no time or no money
or because he could not face a protracted separation from his wife
and his pets. Politically, Europe was moving in the wrong direction
and Bismarck, whom he detested, appeared to be gaining all his
objectives. The gap between reality and the world he believed in
and depicted in his works had widened so much that the stylisation
in *Witiko* (and remarks in some of his letters) can be seen as the
utterance of an obsessed man who shouts because nobody wants to
listen.

In 1868 illness gained the upper hand. Much of it may have
been a psychic malaise, the tortured mind attacking the body, but
in physical terms he suffered from chronic atrophy (some say
cancer) of the liver; the pain was excruciating, and his periods of
suffering became increasingly protracted. In the night of January
25/26, probably driven temporarily out of his mind by pain, he
cut his throat with a razor. The idea of suicide had always been
abhorrent to him, so much so that his strong denunciation of it
strikes the observer as significant. He hated it and he feared death
in a way that does not bear striking testimony to his Christian
faith. Yet it would be unprofitable to join the large group of writers

who have tried to "explain" his end. His achievements as a superb prose writer endure. His end merely illumines the ferocity of the struggle in which he was involved throughout his life.

It has become fashionable since the 'twenties to overpraise Stifter, and books calling him Goethe's equal and studies placing him on a par with Dante and Goethe[29] surely overstep the mark. On the other hand, even so perceptive a critic as Friedrich Gundolf totally underestimated and misjudged Stifter.[30] His reputation is not furthered by evaluations which deal in superlatives, and Stifter himself, a man of moderation, as he called himself,[31] would have felt uneasy when shown some of the panegyrics now in vogue. It is fairer to say that he was one of the great moralists of the nineteenth century and one of its best and most dedicated writers among the Realist group. As regards style, he was undoubtedly "das Genie des Gewöhnlichen"[32] and *"der deutsche Dichter der Nüance"*.[33]

NOTES AND TRANSLATIONS

1. The stirring of the air, the rippling of water, the growth of corn, the movement of the sea, the growing green of the earth, the brightness of the sky, the shining of the stars are what I consider great; the thunderstorm that approaches in splendour, the lightning which destroys houses, the tempest driving breakers before it, the volcano in eruption, the earthquake which overthrows entire countries, are for me not greater than the phenomena mentioned above. Indeed, I consider them smaller, because they are merely effects of much higher laws. They make their appearance in isolated places and are the results of special causes. The force which makes the milk in the saucepan of a poor woman rise up and overflow is the same as that which drives up the lava in the volcano and makes it spread down the slopes of the mountains. These phenomena are merely more apparent and attract more forcibly the attention of those who are uninformed and unobservant. . . . As it is in external nature, so it is also in inner nature, in that of the human species. A whole life devoted to justice, simplicity, self-discipline, reasonableness, activity within its own circle, admiration of beauty, completed by a serene and calm death is what I call great; powerful emotional disturbances, fearful outbreaks of anger, the lust for revenge, the excited mind which is eager for activity, tears down, changes, destroys and in its excitement often flings away life itself: these things I do not consider greater but smaller, as they are just as much the products of individual and special forces as tempests, volcanoes and earthquakes. We are concerned to discover the gentle law by which the human race is guided.

2. Published in three volumes under the title *Vermischte Schriften* in

Adalbert Stifters Sämmtliche Werke, edited by Gustav Wilhelm, vols. XIV, XV and XVI (Prag and Reichenberg, 1927, 1933 and 1935).

3. On Stifter's place within the *Biedermeier* see W. Bietak, *Das Lebensgefühl des "Biedermeier" in der österreichischen Dichtung*, Wien 1931.

4. "Whoever feels exiled, terrified by life, impotent to shape it directly, flees to art as into a deep cave and buries itself in it." Quoted from A. R. Hein, *Adalbert Stifter. Sein Leben und seine Werke* (reprint, Wien 1952) II, 245; cf. the different approach within the same context by F. Martini in his *Deutsche Literatur im bürgerlichen Realismus* (Stuttgart 1952), p. 500: *"Die Bezeugung einer inneren Harmonie des Daseins in dieser irdischen Welt ... war nicht nur eine Flucht der Schwäche in den Trost der Dichtung, nicht nur ein maskierendes Überdecken und Überformen der Daseinsnot, nicht nur ein stilisierender Ersatz des Ersehnten und Versagten ... sondern ein ... Bekenntnis und Glaubenszeugnis."* (The affirmation of an inner harmony in our existence on earth ... was not only a flight by weakness in the consolation of literary creation, not only an overlaying and transmutation intended to mask the anguish of life, not only a stylising substitute for things longed-for and denied ... but a ... confession of faith and a testimony.)

5. See particularly A. Winterstein, *Adalbert Stifter. Persönlichkeit und Werk. Eine tiefenpsychologische Studie*, 1946 and K. G. Fischer, *Adalbert Stifter. Psychologische Beiträge zur Biographie* (A.S.-Institut, vol. 10), Linz 1961.

6. For details see· M. Enzinger, *Adalbert Stifters Studienjahre 1818–1830*), Innsbruck 1950.

7. *Sämtliche Werke*, vol. 17, pp. 55–56.

8. Ibid., p. 36.

9. For a detailed stylistic comparison of the two versions see my annotated edition of *Abdias*, Manchester University Press, 1966.

10. Moral phenomena, passions, actions, destinies whose relationships man, looking at the vast course of nature, cannot always pursue and survey, are arranged in an orderly manner by the poet according to artificial relationships, i.e. he gives them inter-connexion and solution by artifice. He causes one particular action to be accompanied by happiness, he makes one particular passion lead to actions of one kind or another, he spins that particular fate out of certain actions or out of certain characters, etc. Gradually man learns to transfer these artificial relationships into the course of nature.

11. For different interpretations of *Abdias* see the works by J. Bindtner, J. Müller, K. Steffen, O. Stoessl, W. Silz, E. Lunding and J. P. Stern listed in the bibliography and the *Nachwort* by P. Requadt to the Reclam edition of the story.

12. We are moved in the presence of childhood, but it is not because from the height of our strength and perfection we look down upon it; it is, on the contrary, because, from our limitation—which is inseparable from the height of our strength and perfection we look down upon it; it determinableness and pure innocence of the child, and our feelings in

such a moment are too obviously mixed with a certain sadness for us to mistake their source. In the child predisposition and determinate state are represented, in us the fulfilment, and the latter is always infinitely inferior to the former. The child is therefore for us an image of the ideal—not of the ideal fulfilled but of the ideal enjoined, and it is therefore not at all the notion of its indigence and limitations, but on the contrary the notion of its pure and free power, its integrity and its infiniteness that moves us. To a man of morality and feeling a child will therefore be a sacred object, that is to say an object which through the magnitude of an idea sets at nought all greatness of experience, and which in spite of all it may lose in the judgment of the understanding, is richly compensated before the judgment of reason.

13. Stifter would not have objected to being called naïve or to have his works described as such. He expressed his views on the subject in *Der Nachsommer*, book 3, chapter 2 (p. 503 of the Bong edition): *"der Künstler macht sein Werk, wie die Blume blüht, wenn sie auch in der Wüste ist und nie ein Auge auf sie fällt. Der wahre Künstler stellt sich die Frage gar nicht, ob sein Werk verstanden werden wird oder nicht ... Es sind dies die Größten, welche ihrem Volke vorangehen und auf einer Höhe der Gefühle und Gedanken stehen, zu der sie ihre Welt erst durch ihre Werke führen müssen. Nach Jahrzehenten denkt und fühlt man wie jene Künstler, und man begreift nicht, wie sie konnten mißverstanden werden. Aber man hat durch diese Künstler erst so denken und fühlen gelernt. Daher die Erscheinung, daß gerade die größten Menschen die naivsten sind."* (The artist creates his work as the flower puts forth a blossom; it blossoms even if it is in the desert and no eyes will ever notice it. The true artist does not put the question in his mind whether his work will be understood or not.... Those are the greatest personalities who walk ahead of their peoples and stand on a pinnacle of feelings and thoughts towards which they must guide the world with the help of their works. After decades one thinks and feels just as those artists did, and one does not comprehend how they could have been misunderstood. But it is only through these artists that one has learned to think and feel in this way. This explains the phenomenon that it is exactly the greatest men who are also the most naïve.)

14. Stifter not only rejected effects (what he called *das Schillernde* (the scintillating, sparkling, dazzling), but he also expressly refused to propound specific doctrines or show a commitment to a special cause: *"der echte Künstler hat nie Tendenzen, außer die, ein Schönes zu bringen"* (the genuine artist never shows any bias except one: to present something that is beautiful) (S.W., vol. 16, p. 309).

15. See particularly the works by A. G. Müller, K. Steffen, H. Augustin and J. Müller listed in the Bibliography.

16. S.W., vol. 18, p. 141.

17. S.W., vol. 16, p. 317.

18. S.W., vol. 19, p. 94.

19. S.W., vol. 22, p. 203.

20. We also call the Divine, in so far as it becomes perceptible through our senses, the Beautiful; S.W., vol. 16, p. 382.

21. Cf. S.W. vol. 14, pp. 220, 218, 230, vol. 16, p. 122 and vol. 21, p. 32.

22. A full catalogue of the books used at Kremsmünster has been compiled by Moriz Enzinger in *Adalbert Stifters Studienjahre* (1818–1830), Innsbruck, 1950.

23. For details see K. J. Hahn, *A. Stifter. Religiöses Bewußtsein und dichterisches Werk*, Hall, 1938.

24. Details in G. Wilhelm, *Adalbert Stifter als politischer Schriftsteller* (*Österreichische Rundschau*, vol. 60), Wien 1919 and my (unpublished) dissertation *A.S.'s Attitude towards the State*, Birmingham, 1938.

25. For Stifter the question has been discussed in detail by Richard von Schaukal in *A.S. Beiträge zu seiner Würdigung*, Augsburg, 1926.

26. Our age . . . is a period of transition after which one will come which will far surpass Greek and Roman antiquity. We are labouring at a special weight on the cosmic clock . . . at the natural sciences. We cannot guess yet what influence the care devoted to that weight will have on the transformation of the world and of life. Partly we treat the statements of these sciences merely as dead possessions in books and lecture rooms, partly we have only applied them to trade, to commerce, to the building of roads and such like; we are still too deafened by the roar of the beginning to be able to arrive at judgments concerning the results, indeed we are still at the very beginning of the beginning. What will life be like when we shall be able to spread news over the earth with the speed of lightning. when we ourselves will reach the most widely scattered places of the earth at great speed and within a short space of time, and when with equal speed we shall be capable of transporting large loads? Will the goods of this earth through the possibility of easy exchange not become common to all so that everything will be accessible to everybody? At present any small country town with its surroundings can seclude itself with everything it has, everything it represents and everything it knows; soon this will no longer be the case, it will be swept into the general traffic. Then, in an effort to be equal to this universal contact, the amount that even the lowliest must know and be able to do will be much more extensive than now. The states which through the development of understanding and through education are the first to acquire this knowledge will lead in wealth, in power and splendour and will even endanger the existence of the others. What transformations, however, will the human spirit undergo in its entire structure? This effect will be the most important one by far. The struggle in this direction will continue to be fought; it started because new human conditions arose; the roar which I mentioned before will become louder; for how much longer it will go on, what evils will emerge—that I am unable to say; but a process of clarification will follow, the overpowering weight of matter faced by the spirit will make use of, and because it will have gained a new human enrichment, a time of greatness will come the like of which has not existed

before. I believe that in this way step after step will be climbed in the course of millenia. How far this will go, what shape it will take, how it will end—all this human reason cannot fathom. Only this one thing seems clear to me: that other times and other ways of living will come, however much that which is inherent in the spirit and body of man as its basis will persist. (*Der Nachsommer*, book 2, chapter 4, pp. 431–2 in the Bong edition.)

27. Hebbel, *Sämtliche Werke* (edit. Werner) XII, 184 (1904): *"Wir glauben Nichts zu riskiren, wenn wir Demjenigen, der beweisen kann, daß er sie* (i.e. *die drei Bände) ausgelesen hat, ohne als Kunstrichter dazu verpflichtet zu sein, die Krone von Polen versprechen."* This is on a par with his attack on Stifter's preoccupation with the ordinary things of life (ibid., p. 193): *". . . daß . . . Stifter einen "Nachsommer" schrieb, bei dem er offenbar Adam und Eve als Leser voraussetzte, weil nur diese mit den Dingen unbekannt sein können, die er breit und weitläufig beschreibt"* (we feel sure that we risk nothing if we promise the crown of Poland to that person who can prove that he has read these three volumes to the end without having been obliged to do as an art critic, and: . . . that . . . Stifter wrote such a book as *Der Nachsommer*, for which he obviously thought of Adam and Eve as his readers since only these two can be unaware of the things which he describes with such breadth and in such detail).

28. Note, however, his outcry in a letter: *"ich gebe den Schmerz nicht her, weil ich sonst auch das Göttliche hergeben müßte"* (I will not part with suffering because in that case I would also have to part with the divine). On the problem of *Schmerz* in Stifter's philosophy see the remarks in S. Gröble, *Schuld und Sühne im Werk Adalbert Stifters,* Bern, 1965.

29. e.g. H. Augustin in his book *Dante-Goethe-Stifter. Das fromme Weltbild des Dichters,* Basel, 1944.

30. In his book *Adalbert Stifter,* Halle, 1933.

31. S.W., vol. 17, p. 284 (to Heckenast, May 25, 1848): *"ich bin ein Mann des Maßes"* (and on several other occasions).

32. The genius of the ordinary; cf. J. Kühn, *Die Kunst Adalbert Stifters,* Berlin 1943 (but used by so many other critics that authorship of the phrase cannot be attributed to Kühn with certainty).

33. *The* German writer of the nuance; the phrase is J. Nadler's (in *Preußische Jahrbücher* 1922, p. 156).

BIBLIOGRAPHY

Adalbert Stifter, *Sämmtliche Werke,* Prag 1901–1927, then Reichenberg, 1927 ff.

Stifters Werke. Auswahl in sieben Teilen (edit. G. Wilhelm), Bong Edition, n.d.

Adalbert Stifter, *Witiko,* Insel Verlag Leipzig, n.d.

Adalbert Stifter, *Erzählungen in der Urfassung* (edit. M. Stefl), Augsburg, 1952.

A. R. Hein, *A.S.*, Prag 1904 (reprint: Wien, 1952).
W. Kosch, *A.S. und die Romantik*, Leipzig, 1905 (3rd edition Nymwegen, 1946).
E. Bertram, *Studien zu Stifters Novellentechnik*, Dortmund, 1907.
—— *Georg. Chr. Lichtenberg—A.S.*, Bonn, 1919.
H. Bahr, *A.S. Eine Entdeckung*, Zürich, 1919.
—— *Sendung des Künstlers*, Leipzig, 1923.
G. Müller, *A.S., der Dichter der Spätromantik* (Jahrbuch des Verbandes katholischer Akademiker), Augsburg, 1924.
R. v. Schaukal, *Stifters Stil* (Jahrbuch deutscher Bibliophilen 10/11), 1924.
O. Stoessl, *A.S.*, Stuttgart, 1925.
A. v. Grolman, *A. Stifters Romane*, Halle, 1926.
D. Sieber, *Stifter "Nachsommer"* (Jenaer Germanistische Forschungen, 10), Jena, 1927.
J. Bindtner, *A.S.*, Wien, 1928.
O. Pouzar, *Ideen und Probleme in Stifters Dichtungen* (Prager deutsche Studien, 43), Reichenberg, 1928.
J. Nadler, *Stifters Witiko* (Sudetendeutsche Sammlung, 6), Kassel, 1928.
G. Weydt, *Naturschilderung bei A. v. Droste-Hülshoff und A.S.* (Germanische Studien, 95), Berlin, 1930.
A. G. Müller, *Weltanschauung und Pädagogik Stifters*, Bonn, 1930.
W. Bietak, *Das Lebensgefühl des "Biedermeier" in der österreichischen Dichtung*, Wien, 1931.
K. Steffen, *Stifter und der Aufbau seiner Weltanschauung* (Wege zur Dichtung, 10), Horgen-Zürich, 1931.
F. Gundolf, *A.S.*, Halle, 1933.
W. Kohlschmidt, *Leven und Tod in Stifters Studien* (Dichtung und Volkstum, 36), 1935.
U. Roedl, *A.S.*, Berlin, 1936.
M. Mell, *A.S.*, Leipzig, 1939.
A. Märkisch, *Das Problem des Schicksals bei Stifter* (Germanische Studien, 233), Berlin, 1941.
E. Staiger, *Stifter als Dichter der Ehrfurcht*, Zürich, 1943.
J. Kühn, *Die Kunst Adalbert Stifters*, Berlin, 1943.
H. Augustin, *Dante-Goethe-Stifter: Das fromme Weltbild des Dichters*, Basel, 1944.
E. Lunding, *A.S.*, Copenhagen, 1946.
A. Winterstein, *A.S. Persönlichkeit und Werk. Eine tiefenpsychologische Studie*, Wien, 1946.
E. A. Blackall, *A.S. A critical study*, Cambridge, 1948.
W. Hausenstein, *A.S. und unsere Zeit*, München, 1948.
M. Ludwig, *Stifter als Realist* (Basler Studien zur deutschen Sprache und Literatur, 7), Basel, 1948.

C. Hohoff, *A.S. Seine dichterischen Mittel und die Prosa des 19. Jahrhunderts*, Düsseldorf, 1949.

M. Enzinger, *Adalbert Stifters Studienjahre*, Innsbruck, 1950.

H. Kunisch, *A.S. Mensch und Wirklichkeit. Studien zu seinem klassischen Stil*, Berlin, 1950.

P. Requadt, *Das Sinnbild der Rosen in Stifters Dichtung*, Wiesbaden, 1952.

A. v. Grolman, *Vom Kleinod in allen Zeiten*, Hamburg, 1952.

W. Silz, *Realism and Reality*, Chapel Hill, 1954.

F. J. Stopp, *The Symbolism of Stifter's Kalkstein* (German Life and Letters, January 1954), Oxford, 1954.

—— *Die Symbolik in Stiftens Bunten Steinen* (Deutsche Vierteljahrsschrift 1954), Stuttgart, 1954.

J. Müller, *Das Weltbild Adalbert Stifters* (Vierteljahrsschrift des A.S.-Instituts des Landes Ober-Österreich, vol. 4, Folge 3 u. 4), Linz, 1955.

K. Steffen, *A.S. Deutungen*, Basel, 1955.

O. Jungmair, *Adalbert Stifters Linzer Jahre*, Graz, 1958.

K. G. Fischer, *A.S. Psychologische Beiträge zur Biographie*, Linz, 1961.

J. P. Stern, *Re-Interpretations*, London, 1964.

Eduard Mörike

Eduard Morike

by MARTIN LINDSAY

Eduard Mörike was born on September 8, 1806, in Ludwigsburg, Württemberg. He was the son of a doctor who died early. After having received his formal education at the famous Evangelische Stift in Urach Mörike completed his studies of theology at the university of Tübingen. In 1834 he became vicar of Cleversulzbach where he remained until 1843, probably spending here his happiest years. Hardly forty years old he retired because of ill-health. In 1851 he married Margarete von Speeth, the daughter of a Catholic officer. His marriage was not well received by his family and friends. In order to earn a living Mörike accepted an offer in 1851 to teach literature at the Katharinenstift in Stuttgart. There he died on June 4, 1875, after a severe illness and a long agony.

EDUARD MÖRIKE has an oddly complex standing in the history of German literature. This corresponds exactly to the very many-sided nature of his personality. In certain respects he exemplifies, though late in time, the qualities which we nowadays generally associate with German classicism. He seems the most natural and legitimate poetic heir of Klopstock and Goethe. However, it would be possible to claim with equal justice that Mörike, though roughly a generation younger than the German romantic poets, is still very close to them in spirit. This is plain to the reader of his poetry, which often corresponds exactly to what was attempted but not attained by the romantics. Mörike shows very little affinity on the whole with the up-and-coming realist movement in literature, and he shows no connexion at all with the political poets of the Jung Deutschland movement. He is often contrasted with Heine, and indeed it would be difficult to find two more diametrically opposed personalities among German poets of the first half of the nineteenth century.

Mörike is a favourite poet among the Swabians and indeed is well loved everywhere in Germany. Like Schiller and Hölderlin he was a Württemberg man, and along with them he is the greatest among Swabian poets. His personality is completely different from that of Schiller, who tried desperately to realise his poetic mission in the public terms of stageworthy dramas and altogether desired to leave his mark in the world. He differs sharply from Hölderlin

209

too, who pursued truth and beauty with a conscious and deliberate, striving single-mindedness that soon destroyed him. These differences of personality were evident in the case of the latter two men from a tender age;[1] it must give the Swabians considerable satisfaction to reflect how diverse are the qualities of their great poets.

Mörike was born into a comfortable and happy doctor's family in Ludwigsburg near Stuttgart on September 8, 1804. When he was still a schoolboy in mid-career his father died and his family moved to Stuttgart where Eduard was taken under the wing of his uncle Georgii, a cultured and kindly person of whom the boy was very fond. Although he was never ambitious enough to be a "high flier" at school he managed to gain admission to the Urach Seminary, one of the Church boarding schools which formed an important part of the educational scene in Württemberg. These schools play a major role in the intellectual and artistic life of Württemberg and even Germany as a whole in the early years of the nineteenth century. Not only did some outstanding men serve in them as masters, but they also seem to have attracted as pupils an altogether disproportionate number of the most outstanding talents. When one reflects that Hölderlin was at school with Hegel and that Mörike was at school with the poets Waiblinger, Amandus Bauer and Hartlaub one gains some idea of the quality of the milieu in which Mörike was educated. As well as a very humane grounding in the Latin and Greek classics, music, German poetry, philosophy and history were well taught. The church in Württemberg must have had some pastors of very respectable intellectual calibre in 1800–50.

In 1822 Mörike moved on to the Tübingen Stift where he did not particularly distinguish himself, although as at school he was very well liked. In the following year during the Easter holidays at Ludwigsburg he came to know the lovely but unbalanced Maria Meyer, the daughter of a well-to-do family in Schaffhausen. His love for this woman was a deeply disturbing experience which upset the tranquil progress of his life and made Mörike aware for perhaps the first time of the daemonic depths of existence and of the powerful force of passion. After this Mörike studied to avoid a repetition of this kind of experience. He managed to bring his theological studies to a safe conclusion, but he could never be quite the same person after Maria Meyer.

The details of his seemingly endless series of curacies in Swabian villages are unimportant, but the fact stands out that Mörike did not manage to gain a living in the normal length of time. Of his slow professional progress, as well as of his broken engagement to his worthy but rather Philistine cousin, Luise Rau, it can be said that these things were the scarcely surprising result of a completely unworldly and unstriving life. Mörike was a sensitive and lovable man, who had a complete lack of concern for success, and people who considered ordered activity important must have found him trying at times. The church authorities treated him with considerable benevolence, even allowing him to retire on a small pension at the early age of thirty-nine. Endearing qualities were his great talent for friendship and his love and loyalty towards his own family, with whom he was always united by more than ordinary bonds of affection.

Mörike's comparatively late marriage to a Catholic lady, Margarete von Speeth, may seem a surprise. Yet he had always been attracted by the sensuous appeal of the Catholic ritual, and we may be certain that Margarete's neat, rather fastidious ways and aristocratic origins were attractive to this curiously unsimple Württemberg parson. It has often been suggested that Mörike was pagan rather than Christian in his essence. I am sure that doctrinally he would have felt bound to the Württemberg brand of Lutheran Protestantism, but I am also convinced that Mörike's most noticeable religious traits were a great personal kindliness and an openness to all the influences which might loosely be grouped together under the headings of religion, nature and art. If this might mean that he was as open to the direct appeal of nature as he was to specific Christian doctrines, then perhaps his confrères might occasionally have doubted his orthodoxy, in as much as any short-cut to the religious life is always anathema to the cleric, even if the short-cut should turn out to be the better way. Mörike was the kind of man whose charmed innocence saw no contradiction or inconsistency in believing at one and the same time in the values of ancient Greece and of Christianity. Unlike Hölderlin, who allowed his split personality to be reflected in the opposing values of Hellas and Christianity Mörike manages to believe simultaneously and on the whole comfortably in both sets of values at once. In the nature mysticism of his poetry there is room at one and the same time for these seemingly irreconcilable elements which coexist in the artist's mind as easily as they do in this diverse and contradictory world. The ups and downs of Mörike's rather tormented marriage—the presence in the household of his sister Klärchen cannot have made life easy for Margarete—must certainly have absorbed a good deal of the ageing poet's energies, and perhaps it partly explains the artistic sterility of his later years (after *Mozart auf der Reise nach Prag*). Yet a poet who had something more to say would have still contrived to say it, and Margarete should certainly not be blamed for not always being able to put up with a completely insupportable situation. It is good to be able to record that the couple, having in old age decided to split forces, were again reconciled as the poet lay dying. Mörike's later years were somewhat austere and poverty-stricken, and he was obliged to take a very undemanding post as Tutor in German Literature at a Stuttgart girls' school from 1851 to 1866.

Mörike's poetry reflects the many facets of his complicated personality. The aspect which he most willingly displayed to the world of the comfortable, slightly humorous poet of Swabian domesticity, the very incarnation of *Biedermeier* poetic art, the parson poet composing verses cosily in his study while outside the bees hummed and the local rustics carried on contentedly with their seasonal tasks undoubtedly forms part of the truth. Because he reflects the rural Swabia of a century or so ago in an often slightly idealising manner, his fellow-Swabians have taken him to their hearts. They feel him to be one of them, if not by family origin, by education, upbringing and inclination. His profession as a rural vicar, however unenthusiastically exercised, has thoroughly acquainted him with the lives of all sorts of Swabians and he views their occupations, interests and foibles with tolerant, understanding interest. The most famous poem he wrote in this vein is *Der alte Turmhahn* which tells in agreeable near-doggerel of his sentimental purchase of the old weathercock from his church tower. He placed it on top of the stove in his vicarage study. The poem purports to be spoken in the first person by the weather-cock, which tells of its own life and that of its new owner; it also seems to have observed the doings of the local people with a good deal of sly humour. Mörike evidently surveys his own life and doings with considerable detachment and even ironic superiority. The description of the vicar rather reluctantly writing his sermon on a Friday evening ("anderst mag's nicht sein") impresses itself on the memory.

Among other poems in the same vein one remembers *Häusliche Szene*, a humorous dialogue in hexameters between an eccentric middle-aged schoolmaster with an obsession for brewing vinegar and his good-natured and long-suffering young wife. Mörike very evidently knows his people and regards them with kindly understanding but he is far from blind to their shortcomings. His humour can also take a less kindly and tolerant form; in *Abschied* he allows himself the luxury of kicking his reviewer downstairs after the reviewer has paid a social call and commented on the size of his nose. This poem is attractively written in rhyming couplets with lines of varying length; the undignified descent of the reviewer is well communicated in the last few jerky and bumpy lines. A few poems take the peasants sharply to task for their less endearing ways, for instance *Pastoral-Erfahrung* and *Gute Lehre*. The former poem rather affectionately describes the naïve naughtiness of Mörike's parishioners, who steal his lettuces on a Saturday night, and in church on Sunday expect the sermon to provide them with the sharpness of vinegar and the smoothness of oil—a perfect dressing for the lettuce. *Gute Lehre* exposes the ungraciousness and philistinism of the people who are not capable of appreciating the beauty or the rights of other creatures in nature. All these poems and many others like them exemplify one facet of Mörike's chameleon-like personality; the detached, kindly, generally humorous observer of other men's foibles and peculiarities, who sets down his experiences in a fluent and entertaining form which, however, seldom raises these poems above the level of charming trifles.

Mörike can strike the *Volkslied* note most authentically, too. From the German Romantic poets he may well have inherited his interest in and love of folk poetry, but he also had a great love of his fellow human beings, a natural affinity with the sources of popular poetry and a sensitive appreciation of the joys and sorrows, the range of experience and the forms of expression of ordinary people. *Das verlassene Mägdlein*, a poem in four short stanzas, perfectly expresses the distress of the deserted servant-girl, sorrowing over her faithless lover as she makes the fire. Because the poet can fully appreciate the girl's emotional situation as well as the circumstances of her job, because he deals in absolutely simple language with things familiar to her like cockcrow, the stars and flying sparks, this poem has a truth and aptness which surpass other poets' more ambitious but less genuine attempts to imitate the manner of the *Volkslied*.

Mörike was also well versed in popular legend and traditions, and in one poem after another he either retells familiar legends or invents new ones akin to them. Some of these poems have a force and vitality which demand reading aloud or a musical setting if they are to have their full effect. *Der Feuerreiter*, the legend concerning a mad young man who is attracted by any fire in the neighbourhood, is a case in point. This poem, with its swift, staccato movement, and the emphatic refrain "Hinterm Berg", changing in the last strophe to "Ruhe wohl" after the excitement of the fire is past, has a daemonic force which again suggests that even the compulsion which draws the *Feuerreiter* to the scene of the blaze is not wholly incomprehensible to the poet. As so often in Mörike's poetry,

one senses that the poet is aware of the susceptibility of human conduct to domination by irrational and uncontrollable forces. Even
if one views *Der Feuerreiter* in isolation something of the urgent
compulsion of which the young rider is a victim comes across unmistakably.

Another famous poem dealing with a legend is *Die Geister am
Mummelsee*. It is not difficult to imagine how changing light and
weather conditions have caused eerie legends to arise about lakes in
such secluded places. This poem opens with a question on a care-
free, unsuspecting note; the speaker clearly has no idea of the
ghostly ritual that is about to take place. The mounting sadness of
the supernatural spectacle is skilfully evoked by the poet's cunning
use of rhyme and rhythmic resources—especially the very short
penultimate line of each stanza has an incantatory force which adds
greatly to the effect of the poem. The spirit king's burial is not
described in detail; we catch only a glimpse of his sad, radiant
queen, and the throngs of softly praying mourners appear only
momentarily; then the waters open and the mourning multitude
disappear. For a while their singing is still just audible. The events
down below cause the water to show strange, dancing lights as if
it were ablaze. The watchers, alarmed by the thought of the spirits'
return to the surface, rush from the scene. The reader, enthralled
by the poetic power of these verses, finds himself at the least strongly
aware of the hostile and dangerous forces threatening Man's existence; the poem conveys a sense of menace and insecurity akin to
that inducd by Goethe's *Erlkönig or Der Fischer*.

Other poems give expression to less frightening and disturbing
legends. *Schön-Rohtraut* forms an enchanting variation on the age-
old theme of the princess who loves her gamekeeper—and surely
most readers will agree that the fulfilment of this shy and modest
young man's dream of kissing the princess leaves more to the imagination and is therefore aesthetically more satisfying than D. H.
Lawrence's ruthlessly comprehensive narration of a gamekeeper's
amorous exploits with his employer's wife. Here, as often, Mörike
uses archaic and traditional forms of expression from the folk ballad
in the most natural way. In a different vein altogether are the two
songs of the robber chief, Jung Volker, the *Gesang der Räuber* and
Jung Volkers Lied. These are gay, wild, abandoned songs, full of
amoral energy and drive, not really quite what one would expect
from the pen of a young clergyman. Once again, as so often, in
the *Gesang der Räuber* Mörike uses an alliterative refrain ("Fiedel
und die Flint!") to striking effect.

All the poems so far mentioned show Mörike treating themes and employing verse forms which had often been used before; he is on the whole not breaking new ground, although his superior poetic talent makes his imitations of folk songs and ballads based on folk motifs far more natural and seemingly organic growths than those of, for example, his fellow-countryman and contemporary, Ludwig Uhland. The next group of poems for discussion shows Mörike in a very different light, and indeed illustrates an aspect of his poetic personality which was for many years not generally recognised. Mörike is more aware than most poets of both the heights and the depths of human experience. His poetic vision can be and quite often is of an intensity and power which sets him apart from lesser poets and justifies his claim to be regarded as Goethe's near poetic kinsman. The Germans like to call this area of human experience "dämonisch", but in a way this is begging the question, and we should try to isolate those elements in Mörike's poetry which place him in a special, very high category among German poets. Perhaps this can best be done by looking more closely at certain examples of his work.

An einem Wintermorgen vor Sonnenaufgang, written when he was scarcely twenty-one, represents one of Mörike's rare attempts to communicate a moment of preternatural illumination. The glad sense of release, the sudden brightness and the unexpected, dramatic merging of various elements of Christian and pagan religious experience, which are linked by the emotion of joy,—all this is sparked off by the sensation of awakening, on a dark winter morning. Mörike, a poet generally given to understatement, startles us into closer attention here by using such powerful expressions as "Wollust" and "glühe", words which might indeed be small coin in the hands of certain poets, but which when used by him must certainly convey a very powerful meaning. We are reminded in the following stanza of various other poets' attempts to convey the feeling of pure exposure to insights seldom given to mortal man; the "Krystall" of Stanza 2,1.1, may remind us of Shelley's famous lines in *Adonais* :

> Life like a dome of many-coloured glass
> Stains the white radiance of eternity,

or of Goethes writing in Faust II, *Dämmerung*, last line :

> Am farbigen Abglanz haben wir das Leben[2]

For Mörike, at this moment, all the distorting and discolouring elements have been removed and his soul is directly exposed to some most sublime influence. In the following lines he uses images akin to those employed by Goethe, Donne or Wordsworth to communicate the incommunicable. We may not be able fully to apprehend the exquisitely exciting experience which prompted this poem, but in the various striking images used by Mörike we gain at least some inkling of its power and immediacy. When Mörike says:

> "Die Seele fliegt, soweit der Himmel reicht,
> Der Genius jauchzt in mir,"

we know that this is not humbug; this is the plain truth, for Mörike was not the man for pretence.

From the higher reality of his morning vision the poet returns to the ordinary world in the final stanza. Yet even the ordinary world has acquired some reflected glory from the higher reality, as we realise from Mörike's description of dawn. The poet has been greatly moved, whether by the subconscious memory of a past blessed state or by the promise of such a state in the future he cannot say. He cannot retain the magic of that unexpected, marvellous moment; but the day's awakening has given him both strength and ability to go on living. Mörike is always acutely responsive to nature, but it is often solitude and darkness or semi-darkness which can most readily stir his being.

Another poem in which the reader becomes aware of Mörike's acute sensitivity to Nature is *Die schöne Buche* (1842). This is a much later poem, and differs from the *Wintermorgen* and many other poems inspired by Nature in that it actually describes fairly closely the beech tree which is its subject. To be more exact, the tree itself is sketched briefly, but Mörike does explain to us how it is set in the middle of a green carpet of grass, with a ring of small bushes at the perimeter of the circle; further from the beech the other vegetation becomes taller and more considerable, until at last one sees other large trees. One has the impression that the description of the scene is offered only as a preliminary to the festal moment of full appreciation, when the poet's breath is taken away by the beauty of the scene and he is overcome by the sheer beauty of this magic circle. On this occasion Mörike does not endeavour to communicate by any approximately suggestive image what the aesthetic experience is like, yet one realises that although the experience has been brief it has been of rare intensity. The poem is written in most harmonious hexameters, which fittingly contain the almost religious emotion of Mörike's aesthetic experience. Mörike was capable at fairly frequent intervals of moments of "exaltation and ecstasy",[3] and when these came upon him he

willingly surrendered himself to the thrill of enhanced awareness
and forgot this world.

Another poem from the same middle period of his life is *Auf eine
Christblume*. Here Mörike becomes ever more intensely preoccupied
with the nature of the flower and succeeds well in communicating
his reflections. The innermost essence of the flower is hard to
apprehend, but Mörike strives to get as near it as possible. His
whole endeavour is here directed to grasping the particular magic
of the Christmas rose, not to describing its physical aspect only but
its individuality and its spiritual meaning. The rose yields up its
innermost secrets to the close observer; through the eye the poet
can feel himself into the very heart of his subject. Once again we
realise how much the flower matters to the poet; for a time it has
constituted the exclusive focus of all his attention to the point
where the fusion between subject, poet and universe becomes complete. Mörike's dedicated contemplation has not only enabled him
to write a beautiful poem, but it has also helped him to transcend
the limitations of his own individuality through complete absorp-
tion in something else. On this occasion he uses rhyming iambic
pentameters to achieve a perfect formal setting for his musings on
the nature of the flower. Many years before Rilke Mörike was
already using with complete mastery the techniques with which
we are familiar in the *Neue Gedichte*.

Mörike's love for Maria Meyer not only exercised a generally
enlarging effect on his personality and made him tend to avoid exposure to spiritually disturbing experiences, but it produced its
direct poetic harvest in the form of several poems, the most famous
of which are the cycle of five poems printed for the first time in
Maler Nolten as Peregrina. These poems, originally first written
in 1824, were revised more than once and the version we generally
find in editions of Mörike's poems is a later one. Even the first short
poem in its unambitious metre soon begins to express the ambivalence of Mörike's feeling for Maria, his fear of becoming involved
with her set against the almost irresistible attraction of her personality. The poet's mixed feelings about this girl are drastically
conveyed in the final line of the poem :

Reichst lächelnd mir den Tod im Kelch der Sünden.[4]

The second poem of the cycle forms a sort of daemonic epithal-
amion. Perhaps expressing the poet's wild, uncontrollable emotion,
the metre becomes much freer, although still strongly rhythmical.
The account of the wedding feast shows some curious features, the
garden house with the twelve brazen serpents upholding its roof,

surely a suspicious circumstance, and then the bride herself, clad all in black except for the scarlet cloth round her head. The couple go in to the banquet in the decorated hall and presently slip away to enjoy one another's love in idyllic natural surroundings—this description of love's fulfilment is both restrained and wonderfully effective. Despite the bride's strange choice of colours for her dress —red is the harlot's colour, not the bride's—nothing at this stage diminishes the pure joy of their love, and the last line of this poem shows the poet setting the seal on the relationship by taking the girl to live in his house.

The third poem, still in free verse, tells of the horrors of discovery and disillusionment. Mörike's use of strong terms:

Schaudernd entdeckt' ich verjährten *Betrug*,[5]

indicates the strength of his feeling of outrage and injured innocence. And yet he senses, despite his harsh judgment and condemnation of the girl, that she loves him and that a special, indissoluble relationship will always exist between her and him. The memory of his first finding her, in romantic, fairy-tale-like circumstances, will never leave him, and however much he may try to forget her, he will never succeed. The see-sawing of the poet's emotions is well expressed in the fluctuations of length and rhythmical beat of the verse lines. He knows he could not resist her if she returned to him.

The fourth poem, written in rhyming, more regular lines, reveals the power that the poet's love still exercises over his heart. It tells of an imaginary return of the girl to her lover; they sit for a time grieving and wounding one another by their silence; then suddenly he weeps and the ice is broken.

The fifth poem, a sonnet, sums up and records the whole experience. Intellectually, the poet is fully aware of his beloved's weakness; he even admits that she was mad. Yet even this knowledge by no means impairs his love for her. He knows now that she can never love him wholly and solely, that she will leave him and never return again and the knowledge pains him ineffably. It is as though he needed to contain his intellectually accurate analysis of the situation in lines which at the same time are charged with anguish.

The *Peregrina* poems have been dealt with at slightly greater length because they do illustrate very fully and movingly Mörike's awareness and fear of passion on the one hand, and the irresistible fascination for him of the mysterious and daemonic. In spirit they are very close to the novel *Maler Nolten*, of which they form part, yet they form a completely characteristic expression of the poet's early torment, an aspect of his inner life and personality just as much as the rare moments of insight and inspiration underlying poems like *An einem Wintermorgen vor Sonnenaufgang.*

Mörike's reaction to the strain and excitement of experiences like that of *Peregrina* was to pray for freedom from these harrowing stresses. He preferred to avoid exposing his soul to these hazards, no doubt from a feeling that he was not certain of being able to emerge from them unscathed. Certainly his love for Maria Meyer enriched his whole life and broadened his sympathies in the end— *Maler Nolten* leaves us in no doubt about this, but it also hurt him, and he could not bear the thought of a repetition. This explains the tone of the famous and utterly characteristic little *Gebet* of 1832, in which Mörike, in all faith and piety prays God to give him no excess of joy or sorrow but to let his life be marked by gracious contentment; he is content to take whatever destiny God sends, but he would rather avoid the extremes of human experience.

On the whole Mörike wrote very little directly religious verse, although it is clear from the fervid tone of many nature poems that he does not distinguish between specifically religious verse and nature poetry. A poem such as *Auf eine Christblume* has a religious intensity which has more to do with an extreme reverence for Nature and a sensitive appreciation of her beauties than with any orthodox religiosity. However, Mörike did write, in addition to the *Gebet* already mentioned, a handful of other religious poems. Examples that readily spring to mind are *Zum neuen Jahr* (1833) and *Neue Liebe* (1846). It is fair to observe that despite the almost baroque charm of the New Year poem and the genuine devotion and piety which so clearly informs *Neue Liebe* there is not a trace of Protestant or even any Christian belief in either poem. They both show trust in God and a complete willingness to accept His purposes but unlike so much confessional poetry they at no point presume to interpret these purposes. *Neue Liebe* was directly inspired by Mörike's love for Margarete von Speeth.

Mörike sometimes wrote of elves and fairies, spirits and goblins and such trappings of the Romantic world of the imagination. He handles this delicate material with a light touch and enough humour to make us abandon our rational objections to this evidently unreal world. Examples of this kind of poem are *Elfenlied, Nixe Binsefuß, Der Zauberleuchtturm* and the *Mausfallen-Sprüchlein.*

Some of Mörike's poetry has a very strongly sensuous quality, which is scarcely found in any other German poet. Perhaps *Mein Fluß* (1828) exemplifies this aspect of Mörike's poetry more strikingly than any other poem. The highly developed tactile sense of the poet here becomes the principal agency through which he apprehends the whole of nature with almost mystical power. What begins as a hymn to the delightful coolness of the river in summer becomes a general song of joy in the universe and in love. Water, the single element, becomes the key to the poet's whole sense of belonging within a more general scheme of things. Another poem in which sensation plays a striking part is *Erstes Liebeslied eines Mädchens*, in which the daemonic, uncontrollable nature of love is communicated by means of the most arrestingly sensuous image.

Some aspects of Mörike's poetry have had perforce to be omitted from this survey. One might have mentioned the affectionate recollections such as *Besuch in Urach*, where the poet's yearning for union with Nature also plays a part, or another poem about a former cloister, *Bilder aus Bebenhausen*, written in graceful hexameters. Sometimes Mörike produces charmingly incongruous effects by the use of the hexameter for humorous purposes, as for instance in *Waldplage*, in its modest way perhaps recalling the techniques used in *The Rape of the Lock*. There are a number of short, unpretentious poems which are literally short exclamations of delight over an aspect of nature. There are the poems of the Orplid mythology, mysterious, beautiful, haunting, evocative. The *Märchen vom sichern Mann* is a charming piece of mythological nonsense with a particular appeal to anyone who knows the Swabian landscape. Mörike was a good classical scholar and translated many poems from the Latin and Greek with taste and discrimination. There is almost no end to the variety of theme, mood and treatment in this very rich and abundant poetic oeuvre. One of his most famous poems is *Denk es o Seele*, which stands at the end of *Mozart auf der Reise nach Prag*. This short reflective poem, which purports to be a Bohemian folk-song, sets out in eighteen short but pregnant lines the poet's awareness of the imminence of death and the uncertainty of life. The images he uses to indicate the inevitability and probable nearness of death are starkly simple, but from this very simplicity they derive their force. The rhymeless lines are almost conversational in tone, and the diminutives "Tännlein" and "Rösslein" do not fail to evoke a matter-of-fact, familiar atmosphere. Set against this is the finality of death, symbolised by the fir-tree which will become a coffin, the rose-bush which will decorate his grave, the merry, prancing horses which will solemnly and sedately lead his cortège.

As a young man still feeling his way in the profession of literature Mörike wrote his only novel, *Maler Nolten* (1832), which reflected his own life up to the age of about twenty-five or six. *Maler Nolten* is a tormented book and in writing it Mörike was plainly getting his own doubts and disharmonies under control. The work shows at great length how the daemonic early attachment of the successful young painter Nolten to the gypsy Elisabeth causes him to be lured to an early grave. The plot of *Nolten* is complicated but fragmentary, and the narrative technique falls short of what would normally be regarded as necessary in a novel nowadays. Mörike would on the whole not have found it easy to learn the craft of fiction from anyone writing in Germany in 1830. At least the reader's interest is maintained by the insight shown by the author into disordered and diseased states of mind. The action is constantly interrupted by elements which are not properly integrated into the work as a whole—poems, flash-backs, very detailed and rather indigestible descriptions of works of art, long reflective excursions, sections describing supernatural experiences and even a short drama. All this extraneous material makes the book too long and it suffers from a total lack of organisation. On the credit side, however, the work contains several very well-observed characters, Nolten himself with his pure artistic aspirations, his sense of his own limitations and the ever-present menace of his somewhat unstable personality, Larkens, the man who can live only by assuming the persona of other people, who suffers from melancholia and views the whole of life with a would-be superior irony, the beautiful Countess Constanze who seems to respond so readily to Nolten's love for her, the rather pathetic figure of little Agnes and the sinister gypsy, Elizabeth. The picture that emerges of life in a ducal court in early nineteenth century Germany rings true, and individual parts of the book show clearly that Mörike was a natural but undisciplined prose stylist of high quality. The poems in the book include some of Mörike's best—the *Peregrina-Lieder*, for instance, and the sonnets to Luise Rau, the *Feuerreiter* and more than a score of others. Mörike simply included within the text of the novel under one pretext or another the poems which he had written but not yet published elsewhere. It would be idle to pretend that *Nolten* is a very great work of literature; it owes something to *Wilhlem Meister* and to Hölderlin's *Hyperion* and to the German Romantic novel and can be compared to Keller's *Der grüne Heinrich* which appeared just over twenty years later. However, the novel is so much less organised and complete than Keller's that it suffers by comparison; also, the reader must admit that despite bright and interesting sections the total effect of *Nolten*, in which every major character dies in more or less depressing circumstances, is hardly calculated to provide entertainment or edification. Not surprisingly *Maler Nolten* had little success, although a few perceptive critics saw that a considerable talent lay concealed behind its romantic horrors and loose structure. For Mörike the writing of *Maler Nolten* was in the nature of a therapeutic exercise, which enabled him to get out of his system tendencies to mental illness. Nolten and Larkens die so that their author may live.

Mörike's next work of prose fiction, *Lucie Gelmeroth*, a much less ambitious undertaking, is at the same time far more successful. The *Novelle* orginally appeared in 1834 as *Miss Jenny Harrower*, but five years later Mörike re-issued it; he had renamed the story *Lucie Gelmeroth* and transferred it to a German setting. It tells how Lucie accuses herself of murder in order to protect the avenger of her sister's honour. The whole work shows a high degree of psychological perception, and Mörike very successfully delineates the heroine in her overwrought and near-hysterical state. The shorter form of the *Novelle* is much better suited to the author's talents, and it must be regretted that Mörlike did not write more works of this genre.

Among Mörike's other prose works *Das Stuttgarter Hutzelmännlein* deserves brief mention. This is a fairy story, told with great charm and skill in a language which is literally indistinguishable from that of the genuine *Volksmärchen*. Mörike makes the *Hutzelmännlein* introduce himself thus:

> Ein Kobold gut bin ich bekannt
> in dieser Stadt und weit im Land;
> meines Handwerks ein Schuster war
> gewiß vor siebenhundert Jahr.
> Das Hutzelbrot hab' ich erdacht,
> auch viel seltsame Streich' gemacht.[6]

The story then tells in prose of the delightfully whimsical activities of this good goblin. It is not surprising that Mörike has endeared himself to Swabian hearts with this tale.

Mörike's last great creative achievement was *Mozart auf der Reise nach Prag*, which he wrote in 1855 in readiness for the Mozart centenary of 1856. From an early age Mörike had loved and admired Mozart. His brother August's unexpected early death shortly after attending a performance of *Don Giovanni*, as well as the composer's own premature death, and above all, a feeling of deep affinity with Mozart's music made Mörike choose this material for his last and best prose work. The plot of the work is simple; it tells how Mozart goes to Prague with his wife Constanze for the

first performance of *Don Giovanni*. On the way by an amusing
accident he makes the acquaintance of a country gentleman and
his family, who invite him to join their circle and to play the piano
to them. Although it is clear that Mozart is at the height of his
creative powers and also at the summit of his career, a splendidly
vital, energetic and exceptionally gifted human being, Mörike indicates how death threatens him, too. The climax of the work
comes when Mozart plays the chorus from *Don Giovanni*, "Dein
Lachen endet vor der Morgenröte", to an audience hushed with
apprehension. The Bohemian folk-song which ends the *Novelle* so
appropriately has already been discussed. *Mozart auf der Reise
nach Prag* is Mörike's richest and most polished prose work, and is
certainly that which is most attractive to and accessible for for-
eigners.

Mörike occupies a special place among German poets of the
nineteenth century. He is a lyric poet of almost unparalleled range
and virtuosity, who has written a large number of the best poems
in the German language. His exceptional sensitivity to nature and
music and his responsiveness to every human situation are wedded
to an altogether unusual mastery of the forms of poetic expression.
More than any other nineteenth century German poet he succeeds
in assimilating and rendering personal to himself the world of folk-
song and folklore, but as we have seen, he is equally at home in the
very demanding arts of sonnet-writing and translation. His limitations are apparent when he attempts a longer prose work, but in
Mozart auf der Reise nach Prag he has offered a sensitive and
credible portrayal of Mozart and his world and contributed notably
to our understanding of the artistic personality. We must not allow
ourselves to be misled by his seemingly insignificant and unsuccessful life into underrating his genius; Mörike is a great and universal
poet who possesses the cardinal attribute of being a "vates" as well
as a master of form. This quality has nothing to do with wordly
success or even having a strong character or being in any obvious
sense one of the world's leaders, but it has a habit of being increasingly recognised with the passage of time, so that Mörike has now
come to be regarded as one of the handful of poets who have most
generously enriched German Literature.

NOTES

1.See J. M. Lindsay: "The Education of Hölderlin and Mörike" in *Modern Languages*, XLV, 2, June 1964.

2. In the coloured reflection we have life.

3. *Times Literary Supplement,* Leading Article, Friday, October 4, 1957.

4. You smilingly hand me death in the chalice of sin!

5. I *shudderingly* discovered long past *deception* (my italics).

6. A goblin good, I am known
   in this town and far afield in the country;
   I was a shoemaker by trade
   certainly seven hundred years ago.
   I invented *Hutzel*-bread.
   and have performed many queer tricks.

SELECT BIBLIOGRAPHY

Editions
Sämtliche Werke, 6 vols., ed: by R. Krauss, Leipzig, Hesse, 1905, and later editions.
Werke. Kritisch durchgesehene und erläuterte Ausgabe, 3 vols., ed. by Harry Mayne, Leipzig, Bibliographisches Institut, 1909: 2nd ed., 1914.
Sämtliche Werke, 1 vol., ed. by H. G. Göpfert, Munich, Hanser, 1954, 1958, 1964. The 1964 ed. is a great improvement on the earlier two.

A historical-critical edition of Mörike's works is in course of preparation by Hans-Henrik Krummacher. Herbert Meyer and Bernard Zeller in Marbach.

Letters
Briefe, 2 vols., ed. by K. Fischer and R. Krauss, Berlin, 1903.
Unveröffentlichte Briefe, ed. by Friedrich Seebass, 2nd ed., Stuttgart, 1945.

General Studies of Mörike
Hermann Fischer, *Eduard Mörike. Ein Lebensbild*. Stuttgart, 1881.
Karl Fischer, *Eduard Mörikes künstlerisches Schaffen*. Berlin, Otto Elsner, 1903.
Harry Mayne, *Eduard Mörike, sein Leben und Dichten,* 3rd and 4th ed., Berlin, Cotta, 1927. (Still the standard biography and absolutely reliable as far as factual information is concerned.)
Benno von Wiese, *Eduard Mörike,* Tübingen and Stuttgart, Rainer Wunderlich Verlag, 1950.

Margaret Mare, *Eduard Mörike*, London, Methuen, 1957.
S. S. Prawer, *Mörike und seine Leser. Versuch einer Wirkungsgeschichte*, Stuttgart, Klett, 1960. (Contains an excellent bibliography.)
Herbert Meyer, *Eduard Mörike*, 2nd ed., Stuttgart, Metzler, 1965.

On *Mozart auf der Reise nach Prag*
R. B. Farrell, *Mörike: Mozart auf der Reise nach Prag*, London, Edward Arnold, 1960.
Benno von Wiese, *Die deutsche Novelle*, Düsseldorf, August Bagel, 1965, pp. 213 ff.

On the poems
Attention is drawn to the useful bibliography on pp. 32–35 of Herbert Meyer's volume on Mörike in the *Sammlung Metzler*.

Jeremias Gotthelf

Jeremias Gotthelf

by J. R. FOSTER

In the first edition of J. G. Robertson's *History of German Literature,* published in 1902 and for many years the standard work on the subject in English, the Swiss novelist Jeremias Gotthelf was dismissed in half a dozen lines. Today it would hardly be an exaggeration to claim—echoing Goethe's famous prophecy about himself—that there is a new science called Gotthelf. The standard edition of his works already extends to forty volumes, with four more planned, new books on him are published almost annually (one of the most recent is in Japanese) and 1967 saw the timely appearance of a "summary of the state of Gotthelf studies".[1] All this is as it should be; Gotthelf is a writer of tremendous force and vitality whose partiality for larding his German with his native Berndeutsch must not be allowed to obscure his essential universality, even if it does erect a barrier—though by no means an insuperable one—to appreciation outside Switzerland and to translation into languages other than German.

The name Jeremias Gotthelf is a literary pseudonym, as is fairly obvious from its prophetic and biblical overtones. The real name of the man who chose to write under it was Albert Bitzius. Although Bitzius lived for most of his life in the country and wrote almost exclusively about country people, the Bitzius's (the name is a corruption of the Christian name Sulpicius) were in fact a patrician family from the city of Berne itself, where under the *ancien régime* they belonged to the circle of families entitled to hold all but the highest offices. Albert Bitzius was born in 1797 in the little country town of Murten, some twenty-five miles west of Berne, on the linguistic frontier between French and German-speaking Switzerland. His father was a pastor in the Bernese Church (a Calvinist Church that shows traces of Zwinglianism) and there never seems to have been any doubt that Albert would follow in his father's footsteps. After learning the elements of Greek and Latin from his own father, he went in 1812 to the "Green School" (the Gymnasium) in Berne, and on from there to the Academy, the forerunner of the University of Berne. He completed his theological studies successfully in 1820 and was appointed curate to his father in the parish of Utzenstorf, whither the latter had moved in 1805 when Murten was allotted by Napoleon's Act of Mediation to the Canton of Freiburg. However, Bitzius's formal education was not yet over, for in 1821 he took leave of absence from his pastoral duties and went off for a year to the University of Göttingen—much favoured at that time by students from Berne—to enlarge his theological and general knowledge. There he attended G. J. Planck's lectures on theology, read a good deal of Scott and developed an enthusiasm for Schiller, about the only classical German writer whose influence can be clearly traced in his work (in the historical tales). He rounded off his year at Göttingen with a trip to North Germany, penetrating as far north as the island of Rügen and returning home via Berlin, Leipzig, Dresden and Munich. It is worth laying some emphasis on the extent of Bitzius's formal education, for it reminds us that although he was thoroughly familiar with the Bernese farmer's life—the rectory at Utzenstorf had a farm attached to it —and tends to be described as a "novelist of peasant life" (which indeed, among other things, he was), his mental world is basically that of an educated upper-class urban Bernese, not that of a peasant. Similarly, although Bitzius emerged as a writer fairly late in life—he was nearly forty when he wrote his first novel—research has shown that it cannot be asserted, as it once was, that there are no signs of literary interests and activity in earlier years. If little is proved by the fact that in 1816 he won third prize at the Berne Academy for an essay on the subject "Ist sich das Wesen der Poesie der Alten und Neuern gleich? Zeichnet sich die neuere durch besondere Eigenschaften aus, and welches sind die Ursachen dieser Verschiedenheit?"[2], it is rather more significant that the papers he left behind after his death contained a number of unpublished early essays and reports of considerable interest (especially the *Gespräch der Reformatoren im Himmel* and the *Chronik von Lutzelflüh*), that his youthful sermons display an increasing clarity and rhetorical force, and that before he sat down to write his first novel he had contributed some twenty-five articles to the *Berner Volksfreund,* the organ of the moderate Liberals in the canton of Berne. Some of these Frühschriften would repay a good deal more study than they have yet received.

Back in Utzenstorf with his father, Bitzius threw himself with enthusiasm not only into the normal pastoral duties of a curate but also into the educational work that developed on a country clergyman in those days (the pastor was directly responsible for primary education in his parish). His father was a keen educationist who had had dealings with Pestalozzi, and his son inherited the interest to a marked degree. In fact, Karl Fehr[3] rightly speaks of Bitzius as possessed by the *furor paedagogicus,* and it is this enthusiasm for education that is the key to the eventual transformation of Albert Bitzius into Jeremias Gotthelf, or at any rate the trigger that started the process. A word is here necessary, if we are to see Bitzius's passionate interest in education in the proper perspective, on the social background to it. Up to 1798 Switzerland had been a loose confederation of independent cantons and subject territories, with full citizenship confined to the patrician oligarchies who ruled the capitals of the cantons; by 1831 not only had the subject territories been raised to the status of independent cantons but all the inhabitants of the individual cantons had full political and legal rights. The trouble was that a large proportion of the population, especially in the country, was not equipped to exercise its new responsibilities. People in Bitzius's position were acutely aware of this gap between duty and capacity, and the desire to fill it was the conscious aim that made Bitzius a writer.

When Bitzius's father died in 1824 his son did not succeed him as pastor of Utzenstorf because he had not yet served the required five years as a curate. Instead he was moved, still a curate, to the big parish of Herzogenbuchsee in the valley of the Aare, between Solothurn and Langenthal. It is interesting to note that during his early years here Bitzius had his only personal encounter with Pestalozzi. In 1826 Pestalozzi addressed the *Helvetische Gesellschaft* in Langenthal (it was in fact the last public speech he made), and the list of those present includes V(erbi) D(ivini) M(inister)Albert Bitzius.[4]

Bitzius's time at Herzogenbuchsee was on the whole not a success; he clashed with the local *Oberamtmann* or governor, Rudolf Emanuel von Effinger, over a proposal to build a new school (Bitzius was a man who liked his own way), and was dismissed from his post. But for the good offices of a friend in Berne he would have been sent to the lonely parish of Amsoldingen, near Thun; in fact the posting was cancelled and he was appointed instead to the Church of the Holy Spirit in Berne itself, the most important church in the city after the Minster. Bitzius had misgivings about this appointment because he did not possess a very good speaking voice for sermons. His misgivings were justified; the Church authorities were not satisfied with his efforts in Berne and a year and half later, on New Year's Day 1831, he found himself on his way to the remote country parish of Lützelflüh in the Emme valley, north-east of Berne, still a curate and in fact by now the oldest one in the canton. Bitzius was now thirty-three; he was a man of considerable ambition, as is clear from several passages in letters he wrote as a young man, and at this point in his life he could not have felt that he had achieved a great deal or that his prospects looked particularly encouraging. Nevertheless, it was in Lützelflüh that Bitzius was to find himself and to end his days. The rest of the story of the birth of Jeremias Gotthelf cannot be better told than in the words of a brief autobiography which Bitzius wrote in 1848: "After the death of Herr Fasnacht (the pastor of Lützelflüh) I was elected pastor of the parish.... A year later I married the grand-daughter of my last principal [i.e. Fasnacht], the daughter of Professor Zeender of Berne, who was famous in his time.

"At that period the Canton of Berne was the scene of various struggles, none of which was fought out with more bitterness than the educational one. As a member of the Cantonal School Board, as a lecturer at a refresher course [for teachers] which the Education Department arranged in Burgdorf, while Herr Fellenberg held an opposition course at Hofwyl, and later as a school inspector, I was to some extent involved in these struggles and broke more than one lance with Fellenberg.[5] This, and the character of my parish [the Emmental farmers were proud and reserved, and viewed their pastor, an 'outsider', with suspicion], which condemned me to a slow wait, to a kind of passivity, awoke in me more and more the urge to express myself in writing on matters concerning the people, although nothing was more contrary to my nature than sitting down to write. My nature had to submit; in July 1836 the continually increasing need broke out in the 'Bauernspiegel'. Since then there is no end to it, so that I am constantly amazed how a boy who could not keep his feet still could develop into a man who spends so much time sitting and writing".[6] The end in fact came some eighteen years after *Der Bauern-spiegel*, in 1854, by which time Bitzius had produced twelve novels (and half a thirteenth), about forty shorter tales and a considerable number of Kalendergeschichten or anecdotes, not to mention his political journalism, a fairly voluminous correspondence and the sermons he preached to his flock every Sunday.

D ER BAUERN-SPIEGEL (to give the title its original ortho-graphy) is an Ich-Roman, the autobiography of an orphan to whom Bitzius gave the name that he was to adopt as his permanent pseudonym. It begins with a memorable sentence of remarkable power :

Ich bin geboren in der Gemeinde Unverstand, in einem Jahre, welches man nicht zählte nach Christus.[7]

The habit of giving characters and places imaginary names indica-tive of their nature is one which Gotthelf shares with his contemp-oraries Trollope and Dickens; no doubt the farmers of Unverstand would have gladly supplied a school like Dotheboys Hall with skimmed milk and stale eggs. This first sentence sets the tone of the whole book, which deals almost exclusively with the darker side of rural life, the "Schattenseite", as Gotthelf calls it in his preface. He was writing primarily, as we have seen, to educate his fellow-countrymen, and he had to show them their faults before he dared to dwell on their virtues. Jeremias loses his father, a poverty-stricken tenant-farmer, early in life. The home is sold up and Jeremias is thrown on the parish, who board him out, as was the custom with orphans, with various farmers. Despised and ill-treated by most of them, Jeremias grows up with little faith in God or man. He falls in love with Anneli, a maid on a neighbouring farm, visits her in her room one night (in accordance with the custom of the "Kilt-gang", frowned upon by Gotthelf) and gets her with child. He determines to marry her, but Anneli dies in child-birth, thanks to the clumsy and brutal ignorance of a country doctor. Sick of life, Jeremias runs away to Paris, where he joins the Swiss guards of Charles X. There he makes friends with Bonjour, a veteran of Napoleon's Russian campaign, who restores his faith in life and makes a true Christian of him. With the fall of the Bourbons in 1830 Jeremias and Bonjour return to Switzerland. Jeremias falls ill, and on his recovery finds that Bonjour is dead and has left him some money. He looks round for some useful job under the new-born democracy, but is advised by a wise friend, a weights-and-measures inspector who is a mouthpiece for Bitzius's own views, that the democracy has not yet found itself and is not ready for the services of honest men. His friend suggests that he should settle down at some decent country inn, do a little unofficial educational work on the regular guests and write his autobiography. Jeremias follows this advice. He is about to be appointed parish clerk when he falls ill, his book just completed, with visions of Anneli before his eyes. This bare, compressed summary of *Der Bauernspiegel* naturally gives no idea of its power, which proceeds from its manner as much as from its matter. In this first novel Gotthelf's highly individual style is already almost fully developed. Sometimes terse, sometimes leisurely and rhetorical, it is always vivid and trenchant, like the Emmental dialect that it echoes and occasionally introduces word for word, as for example in a class-room scene, where any request for an explanation of the catechism is met with the sharp injunction : "Büb, lern du, das gaht di nüt a !"[8] As Gotthelf remarks, with a touch of the ironical humour that abounds in his novels,

> Das waren noch die guten, alten Zeiten, wo man in der Schule Religion lernte, und nur Religion. . . .[9]

Der Bauernspiegel brings in many themes treated in greater detail in later books : the meanness and avarice of many farmers, the unchristian treatment of the orphaned and the poor, the inadequacy of the primary schools and the superstitious conception of religion too often prevalent in the farm-houses. Indeed, as Carl Manuel first pointed out in his early but still pertinent biography of Bitzius (1861),

> Es [*der Bauernspiegel*] ist das Urbild und Vorbild, wir möchten fast sagen : das Programm aller seiner späteren Schriften. Seine wichtigsten späteren Bücher sind gleichsam schon *in nuce* in diesem ersten enthalten.[10]

Gotthelf's second novel, *Die Leiden und Freuden eines Schulmeisters*, (two volumes, 1838–39), takes up the school question. It describes the struggles of Peter Käser to teach reading, writing and the elements of religion to classes of a hundred or more, and to support a growing family on his miserably inadequate pay. Like *Der Bauernspiegel*, it emphasizes the darker side of Swiss country life. The third novel, *Uli der Knecht* (1841), and its later sequel,

Uli der Pächter (1848), are more mellow in tone. The indignation that had first driven Gotthelf to write had temporarily exhausted itself, and it is not until the course of political events roused his angry opposition that a note of bitterness again returns to his writing. The two Uli books portray the successful struggle of a farm labourer to improve his position in life. The next novel, *Anna Bäbi Jowäger* (two volumes, 1843–44), deals with the preference of the peasants for consulting quacks rather than qualified doctors, and was written at the request of the Bernese public health committee. A rich and many-stranded book, it contains amongst much else an interesting discussion between a country clergyman and his progressive doctor-nephew on the proper relationship between priest and doctor, and is in many ways the most profound of Gotthelf's novels. The most delicate in psychological analysis is *Geld und Geist* (1843–44), the story of the misery brought on a happy and prosperous family by a quarrel between the farmer and his wife about a sum of money the former loses through negligence. The knot is loosed by the wife's humility and her readiness to cast out the beam in her own eye first. *Geld und Geist* has been described by H. M. Waidson in an interesting comparison as a work of "classical simplicity", possessing "the inwardness and purity of Goethe's *Iphigenie auf Tauris* or *Torquato Tasso*—an action limited to a small number of characters who represent the highest ethical and cultural level attainable by the social group to which they belong".[11] *Jakobs des Handwerksgesellen Wanderungen durch die Schweiz* (1846–47) is the one novel with a theme totally outside Gotthelf's own experience and is less convincing than the rest, though often very entertaining. Like the last two novels, *Zeitgeist und Bernergeist* (1851) and *Die Erlebnisse eines Schuldenbauers* (1854), it reflects Gotthelf's alarm at contemporary political and social trends.

Of the three novels not so far mentioned, *Der Geldstag* (1845), *Käthi die Grossmutter* (1847) and *Die Käserei in der Vehfreude* (1849), the first two date from Gotthelf's mature middle period, while the last may be roughly described as a "political" novel, though it is a good deal more relaxed in tone than *Zeitgeist und Bernergeist* or *Die Erlebnisse eines Schuldenbauers*. The dates given in brackets after the names of the novels are in all cases those of publication, which usually followed fairly swiftly on composition, except in the case of the unfinished *Der Herr Esau*, written in 1844 but not published until 1922.

The main criticism that can be advanced against Gotthelf's novels is that they are formless. It is true that he is always ready—like

many eighteenth- and nineteenth-century novelists—to digress from
his narrative in order to discuss, usually in a didactic tone, any
subject that arouses his interest or indignation. It has in fact been
discovered that, on average, about one-tenth of each novel is taken
up by the author's reflections. But Gotthelf's work defies the application of ordinary canons (if such exist in the case of the novel)—
he has been described as an "erratic block" in the landscape of
German literature—and in most of these digressions the vigour of
his language and personality carries off what in a lesser writer
might well seem tedious and out-of-place. This formlessness reaches
its climax in the huge fragment *Der Herr Esau*, where after 500
pages of rumbustious description of the doings of three separate
families—those of a Radical politician, an old-fashioned aristocrat
and a prosperous farmer, all three presented almost as caricatures—
it is difficult to see where and how (if ever) the novel was going
to end. But it is only fair to Gotthelf to remember that he never
published *Der Herr Esau*. It would be equally possible, certainly
nowadays, to criticize others of the novels as too well made, in
so far as they are neatly tied up with happy endings. The fact
is that with Gotthelf, as with any important writer, a plot is only a
peg for the presentation of a view of life. Rudolf Hunziker gets near
the heart of the matter when he says in his notes to *Jakobs Wunde-
rungen* :

> "Gotthelf's Künstlernatur (war) nach ethischen, nicht nach
> ästhetischen Prinzipien orientiert. Ihm bedeutete stets die Sache,
> die zu sagen das Feuer seines lodernden Temperamentes ihn
> zwang, das Wesentliche. Hatte er jeweilen den stofflich—ethi-
> schen Plan gefasst, so war damit zugleich die Frage nach der Form
> zu einem guten Teil gelöst. Zu der Lehre, dass die gleichzeitige
> Konzeption, die aprioristische Vermählung von Inhalt und Form
> die natürliche Vorbedingung für die Entstehung eines Kunst-
> werks sei, bildet der Fall Gotthelf ein vortreffliches Para-
> digma."[12]

Gotthelf himself was little concerned with literary artistry as such;
he declares in the *Armennot*, a treatise on the problem of poverty
published in 1840, that he has found more intellect displayed in a
well-laid hedge than in many a book. Nevertheless, some of his
short stories do show a good deal of conventional artistry, especially
Die Schwarze Spinne (1842), a horrifying tale of a pact with the
devil, and *Das Erdbeeri Mareili* (1851) the charming little idyll of
a poor country girl who finds her niche in life as the lady's maid

of a woman whom she worships. It is significant that attempts to
trace links between Gotthelf and the literary movements of his time
find most of their supporting evidence in these shorter tales (many
of them can properly be described as *Novellen*, which meant less to
Gotthelf than his novels; he felt that his genius needed a big canvas.
There can be no question that the historical tales, the *Bilder und
Sagen aus der Schweiz*, are Romantic in inspiration; themes from
Scott's novels have been traced in some of them.[13] Attempts, on
the other hand, to classify stories like *Das Erdbeeri Mareili* as
"typically Biedermeier"[14] are less well-conceived; the theme of *Das
Erdbeeri Mareili* may be—coincidentally—Biedermeier, but the
language and style as a whole remain pure Gotthelf and highly
individual. The same is true of the almanac stories which Gotthelf
produced for the *Neuer Berner Kalender* from 1839 to 1844. In
editing an almanac Gotthelf was following in the footsteps of
Matthias Claudius, Johann Peter Hebel and many other lesser
writers too, but again he put his very personal stamp on the whole
project. As H. M. Waidson says,[15] the *Neuer Berner Kalender*
gives us a picture of Gotthelf's imaginative world in miniature.

The ground-note of all Gotthelf's work is a deeply-felt, undog-
matic Christianity expressed in straightforward and traditional
terms :

> Es ist und bleibt also das Christentun in vollem Sinne des
> Wortes der einzige wirksame Balsam für die eiternde Wunde
> [poverty and social discontent].
> "Christus ist und bleibt der einzige Heiland für die sieche
> Welt."[16]

As a young theological student, Gotthelf had given signs of a
fairly casual attitude to his chosen profession and shown less interest
in the subtleties of theology than in going out into society and
meeting people. He says in the short autobiography already mentioned :

> "Die Gesellschaft und namentlich die weibliche nahm mich
> mehr in Anspruch als die Wissenschaft."[17]

Here, by the way, we surely have a glimpse of that side of his
nature which made him into a novelist, and one with such sure
psychological insight. However, be that as it may, by the time
Albert Bitzius decided to turn himself into Jeremias Gotthelf,
Christianity had become a tried, tested and all-embracing view of
life which was to colour everything he wrote. As K. Guggisberg puts
it pregnantly in his introduction to the Frühschriften,

"Die reformierte Tradition Zwinglischer Observanz hat sich in ihm mit dem Herderschen Offenbarungsuniversalismus zu einem einheitlichen, Natur, Geschichte und Gegenwart umfassenden Wirklichkeitsverständnis verbunden."[18]

If a certain unresolved tension between an Old Testament and a New Testament conception of God is sometimes apparent, that is perhaps due to the Volksschriftsteller's need to frighten his readers from time to time—for their own good—with a little thunder from Sinai.

For Gotthelf, man is a creature of God, who had defined good and evil in his commandments and revealed himself more fully in the person and teaching of Christ. His presence can also be felt behind the whole visible world :

"Doch noch viele Engel gehen durch die Welt. Die Feuerflammen sind Engel des Herrn und auch die Wasserströme; Bettler sendet der Herr aus und ruft uns durch sie bald zur Weisheit, bald zur Barmherzigkeit. Steine legt uns der Herr in die Wege und lässt den Tau fallen zu unseren Füssen, alle sind Engel Gottes."[19]

Reminiscences of the Bible are common in Gotthelf's language and imagery. The world is "God's immense temple" and what we do in it decides not only our life here and now, but also what will happen to us for all eternity :

"Der Mensch ist nach dem Ebendbild Gottes geschaffen; nach der Herstellung dieses Ebenbildes soll der Christ streben, er soll versuchen, göttlich zu leben im sterblichen Körper, die Erde zu einem Vorhofe des Himmels zu machen."[20]

When Uli realised that he had been living a worthless life,

"Es kam ihm vor, als ob da zwei Mächte sich um seine Seele stritten, fast gleichsam ein guter und ein böser Engel, und jeder ihn haben wollte."[21]

In spite of the "als ob" and the "gleichsam"—the fundamentalist bowing to rationalist—there is no confusion in Gotthelf's world between good and evil, although they may sometimes be closely intertwined and difficult to differentiate. Behind his characters stand heaven, hell and eternity. Good is compliance with God's will, and evil opposition to it. Evil may spring from inside, from man's naturally weak and sinful nature, which Gotthelf strongly emphasises :

"Was ists nun aber, das eine, welches die äusserlich so ver-
schieden gestellten Menschen auf die gleiche Stufe bringt, in
ihren Verhältnissen zu ihren Mitmenschen innerlich so gleich-
macht? Es ist die Leidenschaft, das Laster, die übermächtig
gewordene Sinnlichkeit, der alte Mensch, der jede Hülle abge-
worfen, alle Rücksichten überwunden hat. Es ist dieser alte
Mensch, der Gott und Nächsten hasset, untüchtig ist zu allem
Guten und geneigt zu allem Bösen."[22]

The novels contain many characters enslaved to these evil instincts : the Dorngrutbauer in *Geld und Geist* more or less selling
his daughter to Kellerjoggi, Johannes in *Uli der Pächter* reviling his
dead father after bleeding him white while he lived, the lazy innkeeper Steffen and his wife Eisi in *Der Geldstag* living for nothing
but their own comfort. Even those in whom the new man has
already stirred may fall back into serious sin; Uli becomes a cheat
and perjurer. Not that the tone of the novels is pessimistic; Christ
has broken the power of evil. In the last resort, of course, evil always
springs from inside the individual, but it can come from outside in
the sense of spreading from one set of persons to others. This,
Gotthelf felt, was happening in the political life of the Canton of
Berne, and of Switzerland as a whole, in his own day. He was no
mere reactionary and as an enlightened Liberal had welcomed the
"new order" of 1831, but in the rise of Communism, and more
urgently Radicalism, he saw the traditional Christian way of life
of his countrymen threatened. His attack on Communism is the
novel *Jakobs Wanderungen*; his long struggle against the Radical
politicians who governed Berne from 1838 to 1850 reaches its
climax in *Zeitgeist und Bernergeist*. This unyielding, obsessional
opposition to the materialistic tendencies of the time as they
appeared in microcosm in Switzerland is one of the things that make
Gotthelf a particularly interesting figure. In many respects his attitude was an exaggerated one; but he did point to the dangers to
society implicit in Radicalism (Communism, of course, was still in
its infancy and at that time a less pressing danger) with prophetic
rightness, and studied moderation is not to be expected of prophets.
Even Gottfried Keller, who was on the other side of the fence politically (though he was not blind to Gotthelf's purely literary gifts),
was prepared to admit by the time he wrote *Martin Salander* that
"progress"—a Radical watchword mercilessly guyed by Gotthelf—
had its limitations as an ideal.

It has to be remembered that in those days Radicalism signified
for contemporaries more or less what Communism signifies for us

today. It implied a philosophical as well as a political standpoint, and one that was quite contrary to the traditional Christian view of life. The Liberals of the thirties had put the individual before the State, which, with Montesquieu, they regarded as a necessary evil, whose main function was to protect the liberty and rights of the individual. The Radicals of the forties gave the State a more positive function. Their thinking was largely based on that of Hegel, who regarded history as the progressive self-revelation of the universal spirit and the Prussian State as its most perfect embodiment so far. But the real prop of Radicalism was Hegel's critic Feuerbach, who changed the whole character of his predecessor's system by doing away with God and asserting that the decisive factor in human existence was physical environment. His theory that religions are merely attempts to provide imaginary compensation for real misery was to have a profound effect on Marx, Engels and Lenin. It would be futile to pretend that the reforming spirit of Radicalism produced no beneficent results, but nothing has occurred in the century since Gotthelf's death to prove that he was wrong in opposing its materialism, which he saw, rightly or wrongly, as liable to affect every aspect of life. He says in the preface to the novel *Zeitgeist und Bernergeist*:

> "Wer mit Liebe am Volke hängt, klar in dessen Leben sicht, der muss überall mit der radikalen Politik feindlich zusammentreffen, denn dieselbe ist eigentlich keine Politik, sondern eine eigene Lebens—und Weltanschauung, die alle Verhältnisse einfasst, der ganzen Menschheit sich bemächtigen will.[23]

Zeitgeist und Bernergeist, perceptively described by H. M. Waidson as "an eschatological novel", may be regarded as Gotthelf's final reckoning with Radicalism. It was written to support the Liberals (who were now in effect the conservative party) in the electoral campaign of 1850, but did not appear until after their victory. Like *Jakobs Wanderungen* (where we never learn what craft it is precisely that James the Journeyman is supposed to ply), it suffers from the schematic construction always liable to spoil tendentious books (usually, once Gotthelf began to write, his joy in creation swamped his conscious aims, so that what was planned as a short story would end as a full-length novel), but remains an impressive summary in plastic form of his beliefs about the nature and purpose of human life. It is the story of two families, those of Ankenbenz and Hunghans. Friends from boyhood, these two are the richest and most respected farmers in the village of Küchliwyl. When the book opens, a shadow is about to cloud the two men's friendship. Hunghan's

wife confides to Benz's wife that her husband is neglecting his family
and his farm in favour of politics, in which he supports the Radicals. The rest of the book describes how Hans gradually ruins himself by his devotion to Radicalism. Not until his wife has died from
worry and his favourite son from a stroke at a drinking-party does
he realise the error of his ways and decide to mend them. His old
friend Benz, who has quietly remained a staunch Conservative, is
only too glad to help him make a fresh start. Only the worst side
of Radicalism is shown in the book, and Gotthelf admits as much
in the preface, where he declares that he has no quarrel with the
honest men in the Radical Party. The politicians who lure Hunghans away from his wife and family are depicted as godless, plea-
sure-seeking careerists, whose motto is "Look after yourself first".
One day Ankenbenz meets Hunghans and his Radical friends at an
inn, and one of the politicians describes his conception of religious
freedom thus :

> "Politische Freiheit ist ein Unding ohne religiöse Freiheit, und
> die religiöse Freiheit besteht nicht darin, dass jeder glauben kann
> was er will, sondern darin, dass keiner mehr einen Glauben hat,
> anders zu handeln als Naturgemäss, keiner mehr an ein zukünftig
> Leben denkt . . ."[24]

Benz walks home reflecting with horror on the idea of a life
without God. The most convincing parts of the book, considered
purely as a novel, are the pictures of Benz and his wife and children
at home. They form one of those old-established farming families
that Gotthelf excelled in portraying.

But before we write off *Zeitgeist und Bernergeist* as, artistically,
not a complete success, it is worth pausing to consider just what
artistic category Gotthelf fits into, if any. With his scathing denun-
ciations of the times in which he lived and his large output of political journalism, he seems to me to be a figure who can be as well
compared with a Juvenal, a Savonarola or a Karl Kraus as with
other novelists. In his lighthearted moments (and there are plenty
of these) there is almost a touch—ludicrous though it may sound in
this context—of Gilbert and Sullivan. In the last analysis he is
simply *sui generis*.

Nevertheless, for much of the time he is also a superb novelist
who possesses the one gift essential to a novelist—*pace* modern
literary theory and champions of the New Novel—that of being
able to create convincing characters and to place them in a realistic
setting; in other words, the gift of creating a coherent world of his
own. Gotthelf possessed this gift in such abundant measure that he

was able to sit down some time after completing a story and continue it quite effortlessly, almost, it would seem, *ad infinitum*; he
added in this way two further long sections to the original *Geld und
Geist* and talked at one time of adding a fourth; and *Uli der
Pächter*, the sequel to *Uli der Krecht*, was writen some seven years
after the original novel.

Gotthelf unfolds before us a living panorama of a people whose
life he thoroughly understood (he was as good a judge of a horse
or a cow as any of his parishioners) and with whose attitude to it he
sympathised. It is a picture of a world of farmers and country
tradesmen—some poor, some rich—engaged in the essential business of life: working, eating, sleeping, marrying, dying. No
romantic halo hovers over the countryman's life; a farmer's prosperity is measured by the size of his manure heap, and on at least
two occasions people fall into the ponds of liquid manure that
surround the heaps. On the other hand, farming is not regarded
as a sordid round of unsatisfying toil; it is a hard but interesting
life accepted as a matter of course, the fundamental form of civilised life. The unit is the family, with, in the richer ones, the
labourers and maids who live in the farmhouse. This society is not
a matriarchy, but the farmer's wife has an important part to play,
knows it, and is swift to dominate a shiftless husband. Marriages are
arranged preferably for love, but with an eye to convenience. The
Emmental farmer's attitude to marriage is amusingly illustrated in
the short story *Wie Joggeli eine Frau sucht*; a rich young farmer
does his wooing disguised as a tinker, so that he can see the local
young ladies at work in their homes. The outward sign that all is
well with a family's spiritual condition is attendance at church on
Sunday; Änneli, in *Geld und Geist*, is reconciled to her husband
after a Sunday sermon. Round this central core of the family
farm in the Emmental or Oberaargau stand pictures of the other
aspects of country life: the village schoolmaster's home in *Die
Leiden und Freuden eines Schulmeisters*, the inn in *Der Geldstag*,
the vicarage in *Anne Babi Jowäger*, village life as a whole in *Die
Käserei in der Vehfreude*, which describes, with a wealth of expert
knowledge, the establishment of a cheese co-operative. The details
are filled in by the short stories, which provide vignettes of almost
every country trade and delve back as well into the history and
legends of this long-established and stable society, a society with
which Gotthelf has a sort of love-hate relationship, feeling that it
needs reform as well as defence.

For Gotthelf is no mere Heimatkünstler or sentimental chronicler
of rural life; these country scenes and country people are simply the

particular form of life which he knows best and in which as an artist he therefore necessarily clothes this own enormously powerful vision of life, a vision based on a deep and subtle understanding of human nature.

It is the same with his use of dialect. Gotthelf's Berndeutsch is not something that he introduces into his Hochdeutsch at nicely calculated intervals to add charming touches of verisimilitude; his characters rise up before his eyes speaking as they would in everyday life, and he cannot at these moments do anything but write Berndeutsch. Here again, form and content are one. In so far as dialect invades the narrative as opposed to the dialogue (which occupies, on an average, roughly two-fifths of each novel,[25] it is again because Berndeutsch terms and forms are the most concrete and vigorous means at Gotthelf's disposal for expressing the ideas he has in mind. Gotthelf made the point himself in a letter to I. Gersdorf :

"Ebenso will ich nie im Dialekt schreiben, und auf den ersten zwanzig Seiten wird man wenig davon merken, nachher werde ich dazu gezwungen, ich mag wollen oder nicht, und vieles lässt sich freilich nur im Dialekt treu geben. Zudem ist unser Dialekt wirklich gar bündig und kräftig, und manches verdiente in den allgemeinen deutschen Sprachschatz aufgenommen zu werden."[26]

He tried at times to produce versions of his work—*Uli der Knecht,* for example—with the Berndeutsch eliminated, for the benefit of the North German public, with whom he scored quite a hit in his lifetime. The result was not a success; most of the speed and vigour has gone. For instance, "Dein Hudeln kömmt mir zu oft wieder" expands into the dull paraphrase, "Deine Nachtschwärmereien und dein Betrinken kommen mir zu oft wieder".[27] Not that Gotthelf is a dialect writer in the normal sense of the term; his language is a Mischsprache that swings constantly between the two poles of Hochdeutsch and Berndeutsch—this is part of its fascination—and is really his own creation. The early twentieth-century French critic Muret saw this :

"En matière de langage, Gotthelf doit être considéré comme un génie créateur."

Walter Muschg is even more enthusiastic, and more specific :

"Sein Berndeutsch ist monumental, von einem Riesen geprägt, es setzt sich nur zur Hälfte aus dem mundartlich Geläufigen zusammen. Die andere, grössere Hälfte war vor ihm und nach ihm niemals da. Sein Sprachgefühl hat den Dialekt in eine Sphäre weggehoben, die nur vom Schöpfer her überschaut und begriffen werden kann.[28]

In this domain it is hardly too much to compare Gotthelf with Luther, to whom, as Guggisberg has pointed out,[29] he is remarkably similar in character and temperament. In the *Gespräch der Reformatoren im Himmel* it is Luther who gets all the best lines, like the splendidly Gotthelfian challenge :

"Wisst ihr auch, was Reformation ist? Die endet sich nie."[30]

Of course, Gotthelf's use of dialect does put difficulties in the way of the non-Swiss reader—what is needed is an edition of the novels with notes at the foot of each page, so that the reader is not held up—but it has not prevented him from being translated into French, Italian, Dutch, Danish, Swedish, Finnish, Norwegian, Hungarian and English.[31] Most of the English translations date from the nineteenth century and are a bit heavy-handed, but a very effective version of *Die schwarze Spinne* appeared only a few years ago.[32] Dialect presents less of a problem in the shorter stories because it appears much less frequently than in the novels; sometimes hardly at all.

Gotthelf has had no real literary progeny because he is quite literally inimitable, but Strindberg's second novel, *Hemsöborna,* seems to have been modelled on *Uli der Knecht* (Strindberg came across Gotthelf's work while living in Switzerland),[33] and Thomas Mann has described how he read *Uli* and its sequel while writing *Doktor Faustus*, "in order to keep in touch with great narrative literature".[34] In Switzerland Gotthelf has been for many years now a popular classic, with all kinds of paper-back editions of individual stories on sale in every bookshop. The centenary of his death in 1954 provoked a number of radio and film adaptations, some of them, naturally enough, conveying little more than the plot of the particular stories on which they were based. As Karl Fehr says,[35] Gotthelf is a mine of poetic beauty—and of religious, psychological and ethical wisdom—that is far from being exhausted; it is the scholar's job, especially as we move further and further away from Gotthelf's own age, to ensure that the true nature of his greatness is not lost from sight.

NOTES AND TRANSLATIONS

N.B. SW = Gotthelf's *Sämtliche Werke,* ed. by R. Hunziker and H. Bloesch, 24 volumes and 16 supplementary vols., Zürich, 1911 ff.

1. Karl Fehr, *Jeremias Gotthelf (Albert Bitzius),* Sammlung Metzler, J. B. Metzlersche Verlag, Stuttgart, 1967.

2. "Is ancient and modern poetry similar in nature? Is modern poetry distinguished by special characteristics, and what are the reasons for this difference?"

3. K. Fehr, op. cit., p. 38.

4. *Verhandlungen der Helvetischen Gesellschaft zu Langenthal im Jahre 1826,* quoted by Bloesch, *Jeremias Gotthelf. Unbekanntes und Ungedrucktes über Pestalozzi, Fellenberg und die bernische Schule,* Berne, 1938.

5. Philipp Emanuel von Fellenberg (1791-1844): a Swiss educationist with an international reputation at the time. Bitzius disliked the amount of influence he wielded in Berne and considered his rationalist approach harmful to religious life.

6. *Selbstbiographie, in Jeremias Gotthelfs Persönlichkeit,* ed. by W. Muschg, Verlag Benno Schwabe & Co., Klosterberg, Bâle, 1944, p. 26. Gotthelf wrote this compressed autobiography at the request of G. L. Meyer von Knonau, archivist of Zürich, for a handbook on Switzerland which was never in fact published.

7. SW, vol. 1, p. 7. Almost untranslatable. "I was born in the parish of No-sense, in a year which was not reckoned as one of our Lord's."

8. SW, vol. 1, p. 79. "You just learn, boy; that doesn't concern you."

9. "It was still the good old days, when one learned religion at school, and only religion..."

10. C. Manuel, *Jeremias Gotthelf, sein Leben und seine Schriften,* reprinted by the Eugen Rentsch Verlag, Erlenbach–Zurich, 1922, p. 52. "It is the archetype and prototype, one might almost say the programme of all his later writings. The most important of his later books are already contained *in nuce,* so to speak, in this first one".

11. H. M. Waidson, *Jeremias Gotthelf, An Introduction to the Swiss Novelist,* Oxford, Blackwell, 1953, p. 84.

12. R. Hunziker in SW 9, p. 510: "Gotthelf's artistic nature was guided not by aesthetic but by ethical principles. To him, what his fiery temperament compelled him to say was always the essential thing. Once he had decided on the content and ethical theme [of a story] the question of form was already largely resolved. The case of Gotthelf is an excellent example of the doctrine that simultaneous conception, the *a priori* marriage of content and form, is the natural precondition for the birth of a work of art."

13. T. Salfinger, *Gotthelf und die Romantik,* Bâle, 1945, pp. 123 f.

14. F. Sengle, *Zum Wandel des Gotthelfbildes,* GRM, 1957, p. 248.

15. H. M. Waidson, op. cit., p. 158.

16. SW 15, p. 255 (Addendum to *Die Armennot*): "Christianity in the full sense of the word is and remains the only effective balm for the festering wound. Christ is and remains the only saviour for this sick world."

17. "Society, especially feminine society, made more demands on my time than scholarship."

18. SW, supp. vol. 12, p. 8. A Tacitean summary that almost defies translation. "The tradition of the Reformation in its Zwinglian form united in him with Herder's notion of universal revelation to form a unified view of reality embracing nature, history and the contemporary world."

19. SW, 3, p. 156. "Many angels still walk through the world. Flames are angels of the Lord, and streams, too; the Lord sends out beggars and through them He calls us now to wisdom, now to mercy. The Lord lays stones in our path and drops the dew at our feet; all are angels of the Lord."

20. SW 15, p. 97. "Man is created in God's likeness; the Christian should strive after the restoration of this likeness, he should try to live a godlike life in this mortal body and to make this earth a forecourt to heaven."

21. SW 4, p. 46. "It seemed to him as if two powers were striving for his soul, almost as it were a good and a bad angel, and each wanted to possess him."

22. SW 13, p. 361. "What is it, the one thing that reduces men who are superficially quite different to the same level, and makes them so alike in their relations with their fellow-men? It is passion, vice, sensuality triumphant, the old Adam, who has cast off every veil and conquered every scruple. It is this old Adam that hates God and neighbour, is incapable of any good and inclined to every sort of evil."

23. SW 13, p. 9. "Whoever is fond of the people and sees clearly into its life must clash with Radicalism, for it is not merely a political standpoint, but a whole philosophy of life that affects every human relationship, that wishes to gain control of the whole human race."

24. SW, vol. 13, p. 200. "Political freedom is useless without religious freedom, and religious freedom does not consist in everyone's believing what he likes, but in no one's any longer believing in anything but a natural mode of life without any thought of a life to come..."

25. A. Reber, *Stil und Bedeutung des Gesprächs im Werke Jeremias Gotthelfs*, Walter de Gruyter & Co., Berlin, 1967, p. 23.

26. SW, supp. vol. 5, p. 335. "Similarly, I never set out to write in dialect, and in the first twenty pages little of it will be noticed; after that I am compelled to do so whether I want to or not; and certainly many things can only be rendered truly in dialect. Moreover, our dialect is very succinct and forceful, and many expressions would merit being incorporated in the general German vocabulary."

27. *Uli der Knecht*, North German, "bowdlerised" version published by Springer, p. 3. Quoted by A. Reber, op. cit., p. 80.

28. Gabriel Muret, *Jérémie Gotthelf*, Librairie Félix Alcan, Paris, 1913, p. 443; W. Muschg, *Gotthelf. Die Geheimnisse des Erzählers*, C. H. Beck'sche Verlangsbuchhandlung, Munich, 1931, p. 447. "His Berndeutsch is monumental, coined by a giant; it is only half composed of current dialect. The other, greater half never existed before or after him. His feeling for language lifted the dialect into a sphere which can only be surveyed and understood by the creator."

29. K. Guggisberg, *Jeremias Gotthelf. Christentum und Leben*, Max Niehans Verlag, Zürich and Leipzig, 1939, p. 53.

30. SW, supp. vol. 12, p. 186. "Do you really know what reformation is? That is something that never ends."

31. H. M. Waidson, *Jeremias Gotthelf's Reception in Britain and America*, Modern Language Review, vol. 43, Cambridge, 1948; J. R. Foster, *Jeremias Gotthelf's Reputation Outside Switzerland*, German Life and Letters, 1955.

32. The Black Spider, trans. by H. M. Waidson, Calder, London.

33. M. Lamm, *August Strindberg*, Stockholm, 1940, vol. 1, pp. 378 ff.

34. Th. Mann, *Die Entstehung des Doktor Faustus*, Bermann-Fischer Verlag, 1949, p. 60.

35. K. Fehr, op. cit., p. 96.

SELECT BIBLIOGRAPHY

Editions
Sämtliche Werke in 24 Bänden. In Verbindung mit der Familie Bitzius und mit Unterstützung des Kantons Bern, edited by R. Hunziker and H. Bloesch and, since their deaths, by K. Guggisberg and W. Juker. 24 vols. and 16 supplementary vols., with 4 more planned. Eugen Rentsch Verlag, Erlenbach bei Zürich, 1911 ff. The same publishers also produce a cheaper version of the main volumes of this standard edition, with the same text but without the critical apparatus and notes.
Jeremias Gotthelfs Werke in 20 Bänden, ed. by W. Muschg, Verlag Birkhäuser, Bâle, 1948 ff.

Biographies
K. Fehr, *Jeremias Gotthelf*, 1954. Very comprehensive; makes use of newly discovered material.
R. Hunziker, *Jeremias Gotthelf* (Die Schweiz im deutschen Geistesleben, Bd. 50/51), 1927.
W. Muschg (ed.), *Jeremias Gotthelfs Persönlichkeit. Erinnerungen von Zeitgenossen*, Verlag Benno Schwabe & Co., Klosterberg, Bâle, 1944.

General Critical Studies
W. Günther, *Der ewige Gotthelf*, Eugen Rentsch Verlag, Erlenbach-Zürich, 1934; 2nd, revised and enlarged endition, 1954. Very good

literary appreciation; corrects the balance disturbed by W. Muschg's largely psycho-analytical study (see below).

G. Muret, *Jérémie Gotthelf. Sa vie et ses œuvres*, Librairie Félix Alcan, Paris, 1913. An early product of the resurgence of interest in Gotthelf; very thorough and still useful.

W. Muschg, *Gotthelf. Die Geheimnisse des Erzählers*, C. H. Beck'sche Verlagsbuchhandlung, Munich, 1931; 2nd edition, 1967. Profound and illuminating; lays a little too much emphasis on the psycho-analytical approach.

W. Muschg, *Jeremias Gotthelf. Eine Einführung in seine Werke*, A. Francke, (Dalp-Taschenbücher, vol. 303), Berne, 1954; 2nd ed. (Sammlung Dalp. vol. 63), 1960. Mellower and more balanced than Muschg's original study; consists mainly of the prefaces to the 20-volume Birkhäuser Klassiker edition of Gotthelf (see above).

H. M. Waidson, *Jeremias Gotthelf. An Introduction to the Swiss Novelist*, Blackwell, Oxford, 1953. Comprehensive, thorough and balanced; highly esteemed by Swiss Gotthelf scholars.

Gotthelf's Religion and Philosophy

E. Buess, *Jeremias Gotthelf. Sein Gottes- und Menschenverständnis*, Evangelischer Verlag, Zollikon-Zürich, 1948.

K. Guggisberg, *Jeremias Gotthelf. Christentum und Leben*, Max Niehans Verlag, Zürich and Leipzig, 1939.

D. Schmidt, *Der natürliche Mensch. Ein Versuch über Gotthelf*, Giessener Beitr. z. dt. Philologie 76, 1940.

Language and Style

E. Fankhäuser, *Die Flexion des Berner Dialekts nach Jeremias Gotthelf*, Lausanne, 1898.

L. W. Forster, *The Language in German Switzerland*, German Life and Letters, Vol. IV, Oxford, 1939.

F. Hubert-Renfer, *Berndeutsch und Hochdeutsch im Werk Jeremias Gotthelfs*, Berner Zeitschrift für Geschichte und Heimatkunde 17, 1955, No 1.

R. Hunziker, Supplementary essay (on Gotthelf's use of language) in *Jakobs des Handwerksgesellen Wanderungen durch die Schweiz*, SW, vol. 9, pp. 504-533.

A. Reber, *Stil und Bedeutung des Gesprächs im Werke Jeremias Gotthelfs*, Walter de Gruyter & Co., Berlin, 1967.

Miscellaneous

K. Fehr, *Jeremias Gotthelf (Albert Bitzius)*, J. B. Metzlersche Verlagsbuchhandlung, Stuttgart, 1967. A concise summary of the present state of Gotthelf studies; good bibliography.

W. Günther, *Neue Gotthelf-Studien*, Francke Verlag, Berne, 1958. Essays on various aspects of Gotthelf's work.

W. Laedrach (ed.) *Führer zu Gotthelf und Gotthelfstätten,* Francke Verlag, Berne, 1954. Essays by various hands.

W. Laedrach, *Jeremias Gotthelf in Lützelflüh,* Verlag Paul Haupt, Berne, Berner Heimatbücher No 9, no date. Brief introduction (including Gotthelf's autobiography) followed by an interesting collection of photographs of places associated with Gotthelf.

Wilhelm Raabe

Wilhelm Raabe

by JAMES H. REID

Wilhelm Raabe was born in Eschershausen, a village in the hilly country of the upper reaches of the Weser, on September 8, 1831. His ancestors had been miners in the Harz; a great-grandfather was a civil servant of some literary talents. His father, a minor legal official, died in 1840; Raabe was very closely attached to his mother, Auguste Raabe, née Jeep, to her death in 1874. After adequate primary schooling in Holzminden and Stadtoldendorf, he went to the Gymnasium at Wolfen-büttel, but he made little progress there and left in 1849 without attempting his Abitur. For the next four years he was an apprentice bookseller in Magdeburg, unhappy and isolated for most of the time, and he returned home to Wolfenbüttel in 1853, ill and with very little prospects. Two lonely years at the University of Berlin ended in his discovery of his literary talents, when *Die Chronik der Sperlingsgasse* proved a success. The rest of his uneventful life he devoted to literature. In 1862 he married Bertha Leiste and lived with her in Stuttgart until 1870, when, disappointed with his failure to win recognition in the literary atmosphere there, he moved north again, taking up residence in Brunswick, where he died on November 15, 1910. He had four daughters, the youngest of whom died very suddenly in 1892 at the age of sixteen, a shock which was the more poignant in that it came when Raabe seemed at last on the point of achieving a break-through in his relations with the public.

"ZU spät im Jahre" :[1] the narrator of *Prinzessin Fisch* at first contemplated giving his novel this title. It is about a boy, Theodor Rodburg, who was born many years later than his youngest sister, when his father was well over sixty and neither expecting nor desiring any addition to an already large family. All the brothers and sisters settle into bourgeois society without difficulty, but Theodor has problems; he has been born out of time and remains "out of time".

Wilhelm Raabe, the author of *Prinzessin Fisch*, was "out of time" throughout his life. He was born in 1831, at, as subsequently appeared, a peculiarly unfruitful moment for future German writers. The only other major figure born within ten years of this date was Conrad Ferdinand Meyer; Gottfried Keller and Theodor Fontane were twelve years older, Nietzsche thirteen years younger, and Gerhard Hauptmann, the next important man of letters, was

not born until 1862. Literary historians have difficulty in fitting
Raabe into the appropriate pigeon-hole. A recent English publication on the period 1871–1945[2] makes no mention of Raabe at all,
although all his major works were written in this time. *Das Odfeld,*
for example, appeared in the year of *Vor Sonnenaufgang* (1889),
Hastenbeck was published barely two years before *Buddenbrooks*
(1899), while *Stopfkuchen,* possibly Raabe's greatest novel, came
out in the same year as Wedekind's *Frühlings Erwachen,* Hofmannsthal's *Gestern* and Hauptmann's *De Waber* (1891). Nor is it
simply that Raabe represents an older tradition which happened
to run on into these later years. On the contrary, in the last twenty
years it has been becoming increasingly clear that Raabe's later
novels point forward to the "innovations" of the twentieth century,
to Faulkner, Virginia Woolf and Thomas Mann. Not the members
of the Naturalist movement, although "Bleibtreu und Genossen"
received all the publicity,[3] but Wilhelm Raabe was the true por-
trayer of the German industrial revolution—his *Pfisters Mühle*
(1883–84), interestingly enough, was rejected by the first publisher
because of its "bad odours"—and, what is more important, the only
one to devise the appropriate means of presenting this revolution
in terms of literature.

During his life-time Raabe was out of step with developments,
both in his own failure to recognise important literary trends outside
his own and in the failure of the general public and the established
critics to recognise his worth. In the first respect he differed strikingly from Theodor Fontane, with whom he had otherwise many
similarities; while Fontane was a highly perceptive literary critic,
very much in touch with the new generation of writers, Raabe rejected his younger contemporaries and their tastes out of hand. His
correspondence practically ignores all the important figures of the
1890s. Unlike Fontane, Raabe was a novelist pure and simple. He
was not a "man of letters" in the wider sense. His few poems belong to his earliest years and he later wished them to be ignored;
plans to write drama were made only in 1863–64 and never carried
out. More striking, however, is the lack of any by-products to his
novels : he wrote no theoretical essays or pieces of literary criticism,
nor even articles of a general nature. There is no parallel in Raabe
to the essays which form such an important part of the works of
Schiller or Thomas Mann. All that we have apart from the novels
and short stories are a few notebooks, cursory diary entries, which
mainly register the day of commencement and completion of his
works, and a correspondence which suggests little genius. Raabe
spent most of his life in non-literary surroundings. He went to Stutt-

gart in 1862 looking for more congenial company and more sympathetic publishers, found neither and returned North in 1870 to the unliterary town of Brunswick. Added to this isolation from his contemporaries was the failure of the public to appreciate his peculiar kind of literature; the critics, once he had stopped writing stories like his first one, ignored him completely. For Raabe, possibly more than any other writer, suffered throughout his life from the success of his first publication. *Die Chronik der Sperlingsgasse*, which appeared in 1856, is a sentimental-cum-humorous piece of Biedermeier literature, which rapidly became one of the favourite books of the German bourgeoisie; Hermann Hesse reported finding it among his mother's books when he was learning to read, and it is still a favourite present for aunts to give children at Confirmation. On the strength of the book's success Raabe decided to become a professional writer. But the public failed to follow his development. Only *Der Hungerpastor* (1862–63) approached the popular success of the first work, and both Raabe reckoned later to his juvenilia. He went on to write novel after novel for forty years, almost without respite, as his diary shows, in order to survive and support his family. Not until his sixtieth birthday was much official notice taken of him; thereafter he gradually received more and more recognition, but not, as he complained, in the form of an increased sale of his books!

The red herring of "Heimatdichtung" was one of the first interpretations to lead critics astray when they did eventually occupy themselves with Raabe's works. Most of the stories are set in the identifiable district where Raabe spent his youth, the Harz and the mountainous country along the Weser. In his last years he found Gustav Frenssen, one of the typical "Heimatdichter", being described as a second Raabe, and Josef Nadler was quick to take up the trail. Only in recent years has a more universal picture of the writer emerged, with admiration coming from critics of as diverse ideologies as Georg Lukács and Hermann Pongs. The division of Germany has divided the Raabe critics—like everything else —into two camps. In the East stress is laid on the social aspect of his work, its reflection of the age in which he lived and his criticism of that age; in the West this tends to be dismissed as less important and attention is drawn to the more formal and metaphysical aspects of his presentation of man in the world. The division was already present before the war, however, as the following quotations show :

Weder die großen politischen Vorgänge seit 1848 noch die geistigen Ereignisse der Zeit haben einen tieferen Nachhall hinterlassen. (Fritz Martini, 1933)[4]

Wie steht nun Raabe zu den Zentralfragen dieser historischen Entwicklung [1789–1871]? Sie spielen in seinen Werken ... eine sehr große, ja, ausschlaggebende Rolle. (Georg Lukács, 1939).[5]

It is true that there are metaphysical implications in Raabe's novels—as in most German novels. From this point of view Raabe's novels are centred on the questions: How meaningful is the universe in which man finds himself? Is there any relation between our conception of value and the way in which the universe actually works? Again and again reading Raabe's mature novels one is confronted with an expression implying the absurdity of human aspirations. *Der Schüdderump* (1867–69) has long been recognised as Raabe's most pessimistic novel in its conviction that the world is ruled by "die Kanaille". But later works merely change the emphasis. Quoting a passage from Lessing, the narrator of *Horacker* (1875) comments:

Ach, die Welt ist eben ohne jegliche Rücksicht auf das Sittengesetz und die Ästhetik ganz antiquarisch, das heißt vom Anfang an darauf gegründet, daß eine Spinne die andere frißt![6]

Frau Wackerhahn, the central figure of *Hastenbeck*, knows all about "der Welt Viehheit";[7] in the end she has helped two young lovers to come together "und das Elend weiterzugeben auf Erden".[8] This conception of life as "Elend" is a leitmotiv of Raabe's works, to be found, for example, in *Meister Autor* (1872–73) and *Deutscher Adel* (1876–77); *Else von der Tanne* (1863–64), one of Raabe's grimmest stories, purports to have been written by the pastor "im Elend", Elend being a place in the Harz mountains familiar to readers of Goethe's *Faust*! The absurdity of life is perhaps clearest in Raabe's historical novels, especially *Das Odfeld* (1886–87) and *Hastenbeck*, which portray life as a "war of each against everyone". These are novels on the Seven Years' War, but Raabe described his contemporaries as "das kriegsgewohnte, eiserne Geschlecht der zweiten Hälfte des neunzehnten Jahrhunderts" (*Deutscher Adel*).[9] *Das Odfeld* opens with a portent: two flocks of crows do battle in the air above the place where on the following day the rival armies will clash. Buchius, a redundant schoolmaster, witnesses the portent and takes a wounded crow home with him to care for it. He becomes involved in the battle, and after various turns of fortune returns home in the evening to find the place devastated by looters; only his room has escaped their notice. But when he enters he finds it in indescribable confusion; the crow he befriended has completed man's destruction. The hostility or at least indifference of nature as incorporated here in the crow is a frequent motif of Raabe's writings and one which both distinguishes him from the Romantics and points at the essential homelessness of man "auf der närrischen Erde"[10] (*Prinzessin Fisch*, 1881–82). Theodor Rodburg learns in the end that there is no such thing as "home"—what is usually felt to be the peculiarly twentieth-century phenomenon of "der unbehauste Mensch"[11] is thus expressed already by Raabe. Both *Zum wilden Mann* (1873) and *Deutscher Adel* scoff at the Romantic notion that man can find consolation in nature and "die große, schöne Gleichgültigkeit der Natur"[12] is a theme of *Unruhige Gäste* (1884).

The element of absurdity in human life presented in Raabe's works can be overstressed. *Prinzessin Fisch* takes as its leitmotiv the "Zusammenhang der Dinge",[13] implying an overall pattern in life which is present even if man can but dimly perceive it. The term "Fate", which occurs very frequently in Raabe's novels, similarly suggests that life has meaning, although man himself has little control over his destiny; this motif is given an interesting twist when, in *Prinzessin Fisch*, Raabe compares the narrator of a novel to the three Fates—the consistent use of an omniscient narrator itself implies an overall pattern in life. A related motif is that of life as a play on the stage, found in *Unruhige Gäste*, in *Die Akten des Vogelsangs* (1893–95) and especially in *Im alten Eisen* (1884–86), where two of the protagonists have previously been connected with the theatre. In *Die Akten des Vogelsangs*, however, the "Tragikomödie des Daseins"[14] tends at times more to resemble the Theatre of the Absurd: for Velten Andres, as for Talbot in Schiller's *Die Jungfrau von Orleans*, the world is ruled by "der Narrenkönig".[15]

What is important and original in Raabe's writings is that he binds these metaphysical problems into a precisely described social and historical milieu. Raabe's heroes are not wrestling with the world in a social vacuum as the heroes of the German novels of the earlier part of the nineteenth century often seem to be; they are on the contrary preoccupied with a vital social problem, which has not lost its actuality since Raabe's day. Viewed from this angle, Raabe's basic theme is the question : How is it possible for the individual to retain his individuality—and therefore his humanity—in the face of ever-increasing industrialisation, standardisation, rationalisation?

Raabe himself denied wishing to write a "Zeitroman". Nevertheless his novels are highly significant depictions of their age. Raabe was remarkably well informed on all that was going on around him and for a time he was committed to a specific political cause. The "Nationalverein" was founded in Frankfurt-am-Main in September 1859 specifically to further the cause of German unity and had at the height of its popularity about 40,000 members. It was frowned on by the authorities, especially in Hanover, and membership in the days of the paternalistic "Kleinstaat" was felt to be incompatible with service of the State. Raabe became a member of the local group in Wolfenbüttel in April 1860 and was present at the first general meeting of the society in Coburg in September of the same year. Thirty years later in the novel *Gutmanns Reisen* (1890–91) Raabe described the assembly from the perspective of a number of individuals from various parts of Germany and Austria. The "Nationalverein" and all it stood for is undoubtedly the most important political factor in Raabe's writings. For only a unified Germany which had overcome the provincialism described in *Abu Telfan* (1865–67) could provide the background of a social community in which the human values for which literature stands have their rightful place. From this standpoint alone is it possible for us today to understand Raabe's enthusiasm for the Prussian wars of 1866 and 1870–71. He as a North German experienced the former in Stuttgart, where South German particularism favoured France rather than German-speaking Prussia, and he got into trouble over his Prussian sympathies. Raabe's admiration for Bismarck is to be seen in this light also. It is unfortunate that his enthusiasm for the cause of German unity took him so far as what appears in some of his letters as downright jingoism or at best narrow-mindedness. When Sacher-Masoch invited him in 1881 to contribute to his specifically "international" periodical *Auf der Höhe*, Raabe refused :

> Je weniger *heute* das Deutsche Volk sich seinen frühern internationalen Zuvorkommenheiten hingiebt, desto besser![16]

In Raabe's defence it can be pointed out that there was some justification in shunning attempts at superficial international harmony and unity before Germans themselves had been genuinely united, and attention is worth drawing to the passage in *Abu Telfan* which looks forward to a time when "die Vereinigten Staaten von Europa" will be "dieser glückselige und wahrhaft normale Zustand";[17] a letter of 1885 suggests that Germany was not yet worthy of a place in the "United States of the Universe".

In the event Raabe was disappointed in the quality of German unity after 1871. No great spiritual rebirth of the nation took place and Raabe, who had hoped that the Germans would at last have time for his books, was quickly disillusioned. The two novels which deal most directly with the cause of German unity both clearly show this disillusionment. *Der Dräumling* (1870–71) describes a small North German town preparing to celebrate the hundredth anniversary of the birth of Friedrich Schiller, the greatest poet of German national unity. While the schoolmaster is determined to make it a great occasion with a pageant, speeches and the public recital of poems by Schiller and himself, the local ratepayers are much more concerned about how much this will cost them than about the poet himself or anything he stands for. *Der Dräumling* was written during the war which Raabe hoped would fulfil his dreams; that it presents such an ironic view of the people who had to carry the dream into effect suggests that as a novelist he was more clear-sighted than as a private individual. *Gutmanns Reisen* adds an epilogue to the cause of German unity. The convocation of the "Nationalverein" is relativised by reference to the shy love-affair it sparks off between two of the participants; this, Raabe implies, is much more productive of unity than all the enthusiastic speeches.

The reason for Raabe's disillusionment, implied in *Der Dräumling*, is stated specifically in the 1890 preface to the second edition of *Christoph Pechlin* (1871–72):

> Die Wunden der Helden waren noch nicht verharscht, die Tränen der Kinder, der Mütter, der Gattinnen, der Bräute und Schwestern noch nicht getrocknet, die Gräber der Gefallenen noch nicht übergrünt; aber in Deutschland ging's schon—so früh nach dem furchtbaren Kriege und schweren Siege—recht wunderlich her. Wie während oder nach einer großen Feuersbrunst in der Gasse ein Sirupsfaß platzt, und der Pöbel und die Buben anfangen, zu lecken; so war im deutschen Volke der Geldsack aufgegangen, und die Taler rollten auch in den Gossen, und nur zu viele Hände griffen auch dort danach. Es hatte fast den Anschein, als sollte dieses der größte Gewinn sein, den das geeinigte Vaterland aus seinem großem Erfolge in der Weltgeschichte hervorholen könnte![18]

Preoccupation with the material benefits of political unification had made the Germans lose sight of spiritual values. Already in *Der Schüdderump*, written between the wars and published in 1870, materialism is seen as the supreme evil and is linked with death itself. The striking image which Raabe uses in this novel is that of the plague-cart, "der Schüdderump", to which the narrator refers again and again. The symbol relates to death, but specifically to material, physical death and can therefore be associated with Dietrich Häußler, the sometime barber of Krodebeck, who makes his fortune in the South and returns to claim his lovely grand-daughter, an asset which he wishes to realise by selling her off to an important business connection. *Meister Autor* too deals with the corrupting power of money. Unlike Tonie Häußler, Gertrud Tofote is seduced by her fortune, estranged from her former friends and protectors and lost to materialist, mindless society. Where this novel presents an advance on the previous one is in the figure of the narrator, a Herr von Schmidt, who, far from rescuing Gertrud, himself succumbs to the enticements of society.

The years 1870–1914 laid the foundations of modern Germany. During this time the industrial revolution took place, turning Germany from a predominantly rural into a predominantly urban country— in 1871 only 36 per cent of the population lived in towns of more than 2000 inhabitants; by 1910 it was 60 per cent—and making Germany the largest producer of steel and chemicals in Europe. Raabe was thus writing his best novels in a rapidly changing society. Here we must differ from Barker Fairley, who claims that few of Raabe's novels, despite their exact dating in the course of the narrative, are necessarily connected to a specific time in history, and furthermore that Raabe never gives us the sense of impending change, of something nearing its end.[19] *Pfisters Mühle*, which Fairley admits as an exception, describes very poignantly the effects of the industrial revolution on the old Germany with the idyllic mill and its chestnut trees, the students and the open-air restaurant. But this is a theme to be found also in *Meister Autor* with its lament over the demolition of picturesque medieval build-ings to facilitate access to the railway station and the destruction of a rococo house and garden to make way for a main road. Great stress is laid at the beginning of *Horacker* on the fact that Ecker-busch is the last holder of his office, the post of "Konrektor" having since been abolished; at the close of the novel this theme is taken up again in the remark by Nagelmann to Neubauer, both repre-sentatives of the new order (the latter's name is obviously import-ant) :

> Alle diese grauköpfigen, muntern Kerle hier herum hängen merk-würdig freundschaftlich miteinander zusammen. Daß wir jetzigen Leute diese heitern, naiven Zustände aufrechterhalten werden, scheint mir lieder unwahrscheinlich.[20]

In *Alte Nester* (1877–79) a road now runs through the place where the nut-trees of the protagonists' idyllic childhood stood. *Das Horn von Wanza* (1879–80) takes its title from the horn which the night-watchman is no longer allowed to blow to mark the hours of the night; it has been replaced by a whistle in the cause of "progress". *Prinzessin Fisch* describes the coming of the tourist traffic to the sleepy town of Ilmenthal—satire of modern mass tourism is also to be found in *Unruhige Gäste*; at the same time industrial progress causes the romantic Ilme to be tamed to provide power for a paper works. *Die Akten des Vogelsangs* shows the process of industrialisation and urbanisation which turn the idyllic Vogelsang suburb into a noisy and noisome place dominated by factories and a fairground. Even in *Stopfkuchen*, where time seems mostly to stand still, we can detect impending change. Schaumann complains that the hedges under which he used to lie as a boy are gradually being replaced by walks and fences. Moreover, although he has overcome the world, his triumph is but precarious; he is childless, whereas Eduard, the worldly-wise, returns to his wife and children, and the novel ends with the clamouring of Eduard's children. His is the tradition which will continue.

Raabe is thus keenly aware of the transitional nature of the age he is describing. But he is not simply the "laudator temporis acti", as Lukács describes him.[21] On the contrary, he postulates the necessity of development. *Alte Nester* is at least partly about this necessity and the impropriety of trying to cling to the past. This is made clear in the fate of Ewald Sixtus. During his exile Ewald has been planning to restore the past, to marry Irene Everstein and reinstate her in her father's mansion. But the mansion proves to be quite uninhabitable and its only proper use can be in the cause of progress: it is pulled down and used as material for a bridge across the Weser. Sophie Grünhage puts Raabe's standpoint as clearly as anybody in *Das Horn von Wanza*, when, complaining about the abolition of the night-watchman's horn and the German orthographic reform, she says to her nephew:

> Kind, Kind, ich will euch gewiß nicht das Recht nehmen, in den Tagen zu leben, wie sie jetzt sind, und auf sie zu schwören; aber manchmal meine ich doch, ein wenig mehr Rücksicht auf das Alte könntet ihr auch nehmen.[22]

For one of Raabe's main aims is to rescue what is valuable from the past into a present which is ever more inclined to forget it.

In this aim we have the real reason for the complicated time structures of Raabe's later novels which have so struck readers from Erwin Rohde in 1877 to the present day. Raabe tends to concentrate the external "action" of his stories into a short space, a few

days in *Im alten Eisen* and *Das Horn von Wanza*, a short holiday
in *Pfisters Mühle*, a single day in *Horacker, Das Odfeld* and *Stopfkuchen*. At the same time, by various devices he extends this period
deep into the past, so that past and present merge into one. In
these works, especially the last-named, he is anticipating the "spatial
form" of such twentieth-century novels as *Mrs Dalloway* and
Ulysses, which, in the words of Joseph Frank, "the reader is intended to apprehend ... in a moment of a time, rather than as a
sequence."[23] The internal system of references and cross-references,
of symbols and counter-symbols, is in other words more important
than the external system of time by the clock. The "nüchterne
Muse des Nacheinander" is replaced by the "Göttin des Durchein-
ander"[24] (*Der Dräumling*). Thus *Stopfkuchen* is, superficially, the
account of the last day of Eduard's visit to his native Germany.
But at least five different levels of time can be distinguished in the
story: the time of Eduard's writing about his experiences as he
voyages back from Hamburg to Cape Town; the time of the day
he is describing; the time of the story which his friend Schaumann
related to him on that day; the time when the Rote Schanze was
built during the Seven Years' War; and finally prehistoric time,
the time of the giant sloth whose fossilised remains are in Schaumann's collection. As Schaumann himself is both the giant sloth and
Prince Xaver of the Seven Years' War, we can see how complex the
system of references can become. Related to this technique of the
mingling of time levels is the important use of leitmotivs. In *Stopfkuchen* the motto "Gehe aus dem Kasten"[25] is one such: a quota-
tion from Noah, it might seem to refer to what Eduard has done,
namely to emigrate and colonise the earth and at one point Eduard
calls his ship an "ark"; but Eduard as little as any of the other
philistines has left the herd and it is stay-at-home Schaumann who
has been most true to his maxim. In *Unruhige Gäste* the leitmotivs
of light and shadow play an important role, while *Die Akten des
Vogelsangs* makes great use of the tree-motiv: the trees of the
Vogelsang, which yield to industrial development, the tree from
which Helene Trotzendorff is rescued by Velten Andres, the Tree
Yggdrasill, the Tree of Life, in which Andres in turn has become
inextricably lost. And finally in this connection the quotations
which Raabe introduces so generously in all his novels, requiring
his readers at times to be encyclopedically well-read, extend the
leitmotiv technique on to a universal level. They further relativise
the temporal aspects of the story and provide yet another super-
structure of references. *Prinzessin Fisch* makes this function clear
when Bruseberger tells Theodor:

Es wiederholt sich alles in der Welt, auch die Geschichte von der Zauberprinzessin in eurem alten Homer, und selbst die gelehrtesten Gymnasiumsprofessoren können noch für einen Moment in die Falle gehen und alle ihre neun Musen aus einem Sumpfe auffischen wollen.[26]

Das Odfeld provides the most obvious examples of history repeating itself : the Seven Years' War is merely another version of the Thirty Years' War, of the wars of the Franks against the Saxons and of the Romans against the Cheruskans. In other words, Raabe's stories do not relate an action during which something new takes place, but are about the general human situation as it has always been. He emphatically contradicts the typical nineteenth-century facile belief in progress.

These structures successfully reflect the situation of Raabe's own day. For if industrialisation and urbanisation meant the end of the old Germany with its organic traditions which had grown and developed gradually over a long stretch of time, then they had also in a sense put an end to the whole conception of time as a maturing process. The "Entwicklungsroman"[27] which is so peculiar to German literature of the first two-thirds of the nineteenth-century depends on this conception of time and becomes therefore less and less appropriate as a vehicle of expression. This can be seen in Raabe's own "Entwicklungsroman", *Der Hungerpastor,* which belongs to his early period and is among the works he repudiated later. It is a poor example of the type, much of it derivative, and its ideology was later to be reversed in the maturer novels. Henriette Trublet, the French good-time girl, is damned as a "sinner" and eventually reformed; her counterpart in *Im alten Eisen* is truly humane and Raabe expressly refuses to have her reformed in the end to suit his readers. "Stopfkuchen" was actually intended by his parents to become a "Hungerpastor", but did not and the Faustian ideology of Hans Unwirrsch's "Streben nach oben"[28] is turned upside-down by Schaumann, the "giant sloth". Industrialisation is presented in *Der Hungerpastor* in one short episode and Berlin plays an important—negative—part, but Raabe fails to see the consequences of these developments for his literature. A trite ideology and a trite form go hand in hand. Raabe later abandoned the "Entwicklungsroman" form, which was by this time as doomed as the Vogelsang suburb. *Alte Nester* provides the nearest equivalent in the later works. Just Everstein, the counterpart of Ewald Sixtus, also returns from emigration, but succeeds in restoring the old peasant traditions of his "Steinhof". This search for salvation on the land, however, is fortunately an isolated instance in Raabe; it would otherwise have brought him dangerously close to the "Heimatkünstler" and their followers in the Third Reich.

As we have seen, Raabe is not simply content to keep up with his times. He is also concerned with saving what can be saved from the past. For this purpose his narrative structures serve equally admirably. Concentration of the external "action" goes hand in hand with extension of it into the past; this is as true of *Das Horn von Wanza, Im alten Eisen* and *Stopfkuchen* as it is of *Mrs Dalloway* and the contemporary novels of Heinrich Böll. Memory plays a very important part in Raabe's works and is linked to his attack on contemporary philistine Germans, who, as the already quoted passage from the preface to *Christoph Pechlin* declares, were quick to forget the wounds still bleeding from the 1870–71 war in order to reap the material benefits of victory. Ludolf Amelung in *Villa Schönow* (1882–83) dies ten years after of wounds received in France, and his unhappy fate leaves the community in some embarrassment: on the one hand they are delighted at the opportunity of holding a patriotic demonstration at the funeral, on the other they are unwilling to do anything practical to help Amelung's younger brother, who has now been left completely alone. Apart from the more immediate past, it is the Wars of Liberation at the beginning of the century which stand out most clearly for Raabe's heroes from Wassertreter in *Abu Telfan*, who afterwards participated in the German students' Wartburg convention and was imprisoned in the reaction which followed under Metternich—the "Wartburgfest" is an important point of reference in *Horacker*—via von Glaubigern in *Der Schüdderump* to Marten Marten of *Das Horn von Wanza*, who still limps fifty years after from a wound received in the wars: this limp itself is Raabe's symbol for the way in which the past lives in the present. The Wars of Liberation are important for Raabe as representing a time when the Germans were, however briefly, united. The revolution of 1848 is, as Lukács points out, much less important. Only in *Gutmanns Reisen* do we find a relic of this revolution in the person of Alois von Pärnreuther, an Austrian who had been Willi Gutmann's boyhood hero, but has now turned into a bald, fat and very placid Viennese wine-merchant. In this way Raabe, rightly or wrongly, presents 1848 as something which does *not* live on in the present.

Raabe's diagnosis of his age as one of transition from a rural society of organic traditions into an unhistorical, industrial one is reflected in other ways too. The most important of these relates to his presentation of character. Industrialisation and urbanisation have had two at first sight contradictory effects on humanity. On the one hand the flight from the country into the anonymity of the towns meant that community life was broken up and the individual thrown back on himself. On the other, the loss of any personal relationship between the craftsman and his work brought standardisation and the individual's personal loss of identity. Both of these effects are reflected in Raabe's eccentric heroes. In Raabe's early works community and communication are guaranteed by the restricted locality in which the characters live, the Sperlingsgasse in the first story, the Kröppelstraße in *Der Hungerpastor*, which represents for Hans throughout a haven of wholeness. Raabe's espousal of the cause of German unity may be regarded as his desire to strengthen this sense of community on a national level,[29] a desire which, however, was not fulfilled. The later novels lack the ideal community of the early works and *Die Akten des Vogelsangs* provides a striking counterpart to *Der Hungerpastor* in this respect. The Vogelsang suburb, where all were as one family, is destroyed and the concept of "neighbourhood" lost. Krumhardt reflects :

> Die Nachbarschaft! Ein Wort, das leider Gottes immer mehr Menschen zu einem Begriff wird, in den sie sich nur mühsam und mit Aufbietung von Nachdenken und Überdenken von allerlei behaglicher Lektüre hineinzufinden wissen. Unsereinem, der noch eine Nachbarschaft hatte, geht immer ein Schauder über, wenn er hört oder liest, daß wieder eine Stadt im deutschen Volk das erste Hunderttausend ihrer Einwohnerzahl überschritten habe, somit eine Großstadt und aller Ehren und Vorzüge einer solchen teilhaftig geworden sei, um das Nachbarschaftsgefühl dafür hinzugeben.[30]

The most striking and intense description of urban non-community is to be found in *Im alten Eisen*, in which two young children are left for three days and nights in an enormous Berlin tenement full of people—the description is at times reminiscent of parts of Kafka's *Der Prozeß*—but with only their dead mother for company. The second effect, standardisation, is seen mainly as bureaucracy. Krumhardt's tidy, bureaucratic mind has difficulty in following the eccentricities of his non-conformist friend Velten. The first part of *Unruhige Gäste* hinges on the refusal of Volkmar Fuchs to conform to the demands of bureaucracy and allow his dead wife to be buried in the churchyard by those who had refused to give her a decent life but now insist on giving her a "decent" burial—that Volkmar in the end becomes as much a philistine as the rest is a particularly effective comment on the difficulty of individualism in a society whose motto, according to *Horacker*, is the jingle :

> Stramm, stramm, stramm;
> Alles über einen Kamm.[31]

Against these conditions Raabe sets his eccentric heroes. Autor Kunemund of *Meister Autor* introduces himself with the words :

> Ich verstehe die Welt wohl noch, aber sie versteht mich nicht mehr, und so werden wir wohl nie mehr so zusammenkommen, wie damals, als wir beide noch jünger waren.[32]

Eckerbusch and Windwebel of *Horacker* are two schoolmasters whom nobody takes seriously. Sophie Grünhage of *Das Horn von Wanza* is an elderly, solitary widow, her friend Marten Marten likewise does not "belong". Heinrich Schaumann of *Stopfkuchen* is the most obvious "outsider" : he has followed his motto "Gehe aus dem Kasten", has abandoned the philistine herd and taken up residence in an old redoubt outside the town, from which he metaphorically bombards the bourgeois as his predecessor had done in the Seven Years' War. In the historical novels too humanity is found only among the social outcasts : Buchius of *Das Odfeld*, who was left behind when his school moved to a safer place, and Frau Wackerhahn of *Hastenbeck*, who, like Stopfkuchen, lives well apart from the villagers in an old tower and enjoys the reputation of a witch. The chief function of these eccentrics is to hold up a mirror to society : true humanity is to be found only outside society. And in this way too Raabe is indirectly reflecting the standardisation and loss of individuality in modern society; those who belong are faceless ghosts.

Here is Raabe's answer to the problem posed earlier. Individuality and humanity can be preserved in an industrial age only in spite of society, by remaining, spiritually at least, outside it. This is, of course, a form of resignation. Raabe has no political solution to offer after the collapse of his hopes in 1871. He ignores the rise of socialism, speaks with scorn of the future "Bebel State", and in a letter to Clara Zetkin writes of having no intention of helping the Social-Democratic vision on its way.[32a] In spite of his theme, the industrialisation of Germany, his characters are taken from a very narrow social range, mainly the lower middle-class professions : parsons, teachers, the occasional civil servant, doctor, professor. There are a few craftsmen among his positive characters : a bookbinder in *Prinzessin Fisch*, a carpenter in *Unruhige Gäste*. One or two villainous industrialists and business-people (*Der Hungerpastor*,

Der Dräumling) are to be found, but no artisans, no factory-workers, not even in those novels, like *Im alten Eisen*, which are set in proletarian Berlin. This lack in itself is significant as a negative indication of Raabe's view of the standardisation and depersonalisation caused by industry : "individuals" in Raabe's sense can be found only among the intellectuals and archaic craftsmen outside the factories, which are thereby indirectly indicted. Nevertheless, Raabe's reaction to his society can be described as a kind of "innere Emigration"[33] not very different from that of the more respectable writers in Hitler's Reich. The "Katzenmühle" to which everybody retreats at the end of *Abu Telfan* is an obviously facile Utopia. More important are the later figures who remain in society while detaching themselves from it mentally. Even Schaumann is a respected, if odd, figure of the "Stammlokal" life of the town; the philistines merely fail to notice that he is laughing at them all the time when he invites them to his wedding or when he tells his story to Eduard with the express intention of letting the barmaid overhear it, so that the news can be spread in the way the philistines appreciate—by rumour. That Raabe was aware of the basic sterility of this attitude is implied, as we have seen, in his insistence on the archaic nature of his heroes. To that extent he is completely honest in his presentation of the conflict between individual and society.

In conclusion we may ask to what extent Raabe is a "modern" writer. His basic theme is as appropriate today as it was then : individuality and mass society are the antinomies with which all modern literature has to wrestle. His forms equally anticipate those of the twentieth-century novel : spatial form, confusion of time sequences reflect then as now the loss of traditions. Inner monologues have been found in his last, incomplete novel *Altershausen* (begun 1899). The frequent adoption of the dramatised narrator, whereby the narrator himself is a member of the bourgeois, philistine society, an "insider", and is describing the life of one who is his complete opposite (*Meister Autor, Alte Nester, Stopfkuchen, Die Akten des Vogelsangs*) anticipates Thomas Mann's narrative technique in *Doktor Faustus*, not in any "naive" way as Roy Pascal believes, but in full awareness of the implications of this dualism.[34]

On the other hand, it must be recognised that most of the material on which Raabe bases his plots is definitely of the nineteenth century. In *Das Horn von Wanza* the voices at the town council meeting when the request to reintroduce the nightwatchman's horn is rejected could very well have been raised at a contemporary debate on subsidies for the local playhouse; but in fact

we are dealing with a long-defunct custom. David Daiches suggests
that the twentieth-century novelist, unlike his nineteenth-century
predecessor, cannot draw on the "public sense of significance",
which he defines in terms of "marriage, property or a deliberate
change of environment".[35] Daiches is writing about the English
novel, and German novelists have in general lacked the "public
sense of significance" for historical and social reasons—chiefly the
lack of a nation-wide society. Nevertheless it is interesting to examine
the three motifs mentioned by Daiches in Raabe's work. Marriage
as the culmination of an action consisting in the surmounting of
barriers to love—Aldous Huxley's "Obstacle Race"—is surprisingly
seldom in his stories; his plots generally contain the love-interest but
few depend on it. The other two motifs are much more prominent.
The importance of property, of building and destroying has already
been analysed in connection with Raabe's portrait of the industrial
revolution. Emigration, a physical change of environment, is perhaps even more decisive. Again and again the action of Raabe's
novels is set in motion by the return of an emigrant : *Abu Telfan,
Der Schüdderump, Zum wilden Mann, Deutscher Adel, Alte Nester,
Prinzessin Fisch, Stopfkuchen. Der Dräumling* and *Unruhige Gäste*
reunite two old friends, *Das Horn von Wanza* is about a journey to
an old aunt and various homecomings are recounted in the course
of it. Emigration was of course part of the German way of life in
the nineteenth century, but the frequency of the motif in Raabe
seems significant.

What is striking about the two motifs is the way in which Raabe
dissociates himself from them. What he is really saying is : These
are things which people set great store by, but in reality they are
not essential at all. *Stopfkuchen* culminates in Eduard's recognition:

> Ja, im Grunde läuft es doch auf ein und dasselbe hinaus, ob man
> unter der Hecke liegenbleibt und das Abenteuer der Welt an sich
> herankommen läßt oder ob man sich von seinem guten Freunde
> Fritze Störzer und dessen altem Le Vaillant und Johann Reinhold
> Forster hinausschicken läßt, um es draußen auf den Wassern
> und in den Wüsten aufzusuchen![36]

On property the most important gestures are made by Velten
Andres, "der eigenstumsmüde Mann",[37] who on his mother's death
destroys her personal belongings and gives away the rest to anyone
who desires it. This action shocks Krumhardt and especially Krumhardt's wife, who finds it lacking in piety—in fact Velten is partly
influenced by exaggerated piety, dreading the thought that strangers

might make free with his mother's most personal possessions—and she exclaims to her husband that she hopes he will never treat her and their child in the way Andres has treated his mother's property. Frau Krumhardt is usually taken to be Raabe's mouthpiece at this point, the voice of common sense. But this cannot surely be the case. For Frau Krumhardt is thereby equating people with property, with things—her husband too praises God for what he has received "an sicherem Eigentum",[38] namely his wife! Raabe would be the last to equate people with things. A better clue to Raabe's attitude to property is to be found in *Prinzessin Fisch*, when Baumann, a much more credible person than Frau Krumhardt, tells Theodor, "daß es im Zusammenhange der Dinge und Wissenschaften gar kein Eigentum gibt".[39] Frau Krumhardt's bourgeois values are what Raabe is calling in question, not only here but as early as *Abu Telfan* in the indictment of society by Kind and Fehleysen.

Even in these respects Raabe thus remains remarkably forward-looking. Like his own protagonists the man who in his life-time appeared to be quite out of step with his age was in reality more closely in touch with it, a more clear-sighted and incorruptible on-looker than perhaps any one of his contemporaries among German writers. He was and is certainly the most inexhaustible of novelists.

TRANSLATIONS AND NOTES

1. Too late in the year, i.e. out of time.

2. Ronald Gray, *The German Tradition in Literature 1871–1945*, Cambridge University Press, 1965.

3. Bleibtreu and Company. Letter to Siegmund Schott, 21.2.1891.

4. Neither the great political developments since 1848 nor the intellectual events of the age left any echo. "Wilhelm Raabe und das XIX. Jahrhundert", *Zeitschrift für deutsche Philologie*, 58 (1933), p. 327.

5. How does Raabe stand with regard to the central questions of this historic development? They play a very great, even decisive role in his works. *Deutsche Realisten des 19. Jahrhunderts*, Berne, Francke 1951, p. 233.

6. Alas, the world, ignoring the moral law and aesthetics entirely, is quite old-fashioned, that is to say, founded from the beginning on the principle that one spider eats another.

7. The world's bestiality.

8. And to pass on the misery on earth.

9. The war-wonted, iron race of the second half of the nineteenth century.

10. On the foolish earth.

11. Homeless Man, the title of a book on modern literature by Hans Egon Holthusen, Munich, 1951.

12. The great, beautiful indifference of nature.

13. The context of things.

14. The tragi-comedy of life.

15. The King of Fools—cf *Die Jungfrau von Orleans,* III, 6.

16. The less *today* the German people pander to their former international obsequiousness the better!

17. The United States of Europe... this blissful and truly normal condition.

18. The wounds of the heroes had not yet healed, the tears of the children, the mothers, the wives, the brides and sisters had not yet dried, the graves of the fallen were not yet green; but already in Germany—so soon after the fearful war and arduous victory—things were happening in an odd manner. Just as during or after a great fire a barrel of treacle bursts in the street and the mob and the little boys began to lick; so in the German people the money-bag had opened and the dollars too were rolling about in the gutters and all too many hands clutched out at them too. It almost looked as if this was to be the extent of the profit that the united Fatherland was to gather from its great success in world history!

19. *Wilhelm Raabe. An Introduction to his Novels,* Clarendon Press, 1961, pp. 256, 259.

20. All these grey-headed jolly chaps about here hang together in a remarkably friendly way. I'm afraid it's improbable that we people of today will keep up these happy, naive conditions.

21. *Essays on Thomas Mann,* tr. Stanley Mitchell, Merlin Press, 1964, p. 21.

22. Child, child, I certainly don't want to deny your right to live in the present and according to the present; but sometimes I must say you might have a little more consideration for older things.

23. "Spatial form in modern literature", in: *Criticism. The Foundations of Modern Literary Judgment,* ed. Schorer, Miles, McKenzie, revised edn, New York, 1958, p. 381.

24. The sober-minded muse of things in succession... the goddess of things all at once (Barker Fairley's translation, op. cit., p. 200).

25. Go forth of the ark (*Genesis,* viii. 16).

26. Everything repeats itself in the world, even the story of the magic princess in your old Homer, and even the most learned grammar school teachers can still momentarily fall into the trap and try to fish all their nine muses at once out of a marsh.

27. The novel which describes an individual's development.

28. Striving upwards.

29. Cf. Herman Meyer, *Der Sonderling in der deutschen Dichtung,* 2nd edn, Munich, Hanser 1963, p. 289.

30. Neighbourhood! A word that alas is for more and more people turning into a concept to which they can give meaning only with diffi-

culty and after much thought and reflection on all kinds of old-fashioned books. We who have known a neighbourhood always shudder when we hear or read that the population of yet another German town has passed the first hundred thousand, thereby becoming a city and enjoying all the honours and advantages of such for the loss of the feeling of neighbourhood.

31. Perhaps: Stand at attention! All will be uniform.

32. I probably still understand the world, but it no longer understands me, and so we shall probably never again come together as we did in earlier days when we were both younger.

32a. August Bebel (1840–1913), one of the leaders of the German Socialist Movement; Clara Zetkin (1857–1933), then editor of the Social-Democrat periodical for women *Die Gleichheit* later a Communist member of the Reichstag.

33. Emigration into the interior, i.e. of the mind.

34. *The German Novel. Studies,* Manchester University Press, 1956, p. 174. Cf Raabe's letter to Edmund Sträter, 5.2.1890, on the function of the narrator in *Meister Autor.*

35. *The Present Age. After 1920,* Cresset Press, 1958, p. 92.

36. Yes, ultimately it's all the same whether you lie under a hedge and let the world's adventures come to you or whether you let yourself be sent by your good friend Fritz Störzer and his old Le Vaillant and Johann Reinhold Forster out into the world to seek them outside on the waters and in the deserts.

37. The man tired of property.

38. As far as secure property is concerned.

39. That in the context of things and sciences there is no property.

SELECT BIBLIOGRAPHY

The definitive edition of Raabe's works is now almost complete:

Wilhelm Raabe: *Sämtliche Werke.* Historisch-kritische Ausgabe, im Auftrag der Braunschweigischen Wissenschaftlichen Gesellschaft herausgegeben von Karl Hoppe, Freiburg i. Br./Braunschweig, Klemm, later Göttingen, Vandenhoeck & Ruprecht, 1951 ff. Twenty volumes.

This has largely superseded the earlier:

Wilhelm Raabe: *Sämtliche Werke,* Berlin-Grunewald, Klemm, 1913–16. Eighteen volumes in three series.

A selection of Raabe's correspondence:

"In alls gedultig". Briefe Wilhelm Raabes (1842–1910), ed. Wilhelm Fehse, Berlin, Grote'sche Verlagsbuchhandlung, 1940.

The most complete bibliography is:

Fritz Meyen: *Wilhelm Raabe Bibbliographie*, Freiburg i. Br./Braunschweig, Klemm, 1955.

Further bibliographical data can be found in:

Jahrbuch der Raabe-Gesellschaft, Braunschweig 1961 ff.

The following books and articles are important:

Barker Fairley, "The Modernity of Wilhelm Raabe", in: *German Studies presented to L. A. Willoughby*, Oxford, 1952.
Barker Fairley, *Wilhelm Raabe. An Introduction to his Novels*, Clarendon Press, 1961.
Wilhelm Fehse, *Wilhelm Raabe. Sein Leben und seine Werke*, Braunschweig, Viebig, 1937.
Herman Helmers, *Die bildenden Mächte in den Romanen Wilhelm Raabes*, Weinheim (Bergstr.) 1960.
Herman Helmers, "Die Figur des Erzählers bei Raabe", in: *Jahrbuch der Raabe-Gesellschaft*, 1965.
Walther Killy, "Geschichte gegen die Geschichte. Raabe: 'Das Odfeld' ", in: *Wirklichkeit und Kunstcharakter. Neun Romane des 19. Jahrhunderts*, München, Beck, 1963.
Georg Lukács, *Deutsche Realisten des 19. Jahrhunderts*, Berne, Francke 1951.
Frank C. Maatje, "Ein früher Ansatz zur 'Stream of consciousness'— Dichtung: Wilhelm Raabes 'Altershausen' ", in: *Neophilologus* 45 (1961).
Fritz Martini, "Wilhelm Raabe und das XIX. Jahrhundert", in: *Zeitschrift für deutsche Philologie* 58 (1933).
Fritz Martini, "Das Problem des Realismus im 19. Jahrhundert und die Dichtung Wilhelm Raabes", in: *Euphorion* 36 (1935).
Fritz Martini, "Deutsche Literatur in der Zeit des 'bürgerlichen Realismus'. Ein Literaturbericht, in: *Deutsche Vierteljahrsschrift für Literaturwissenschaft und Geistesgeschichte*, 34 (1960).
Gerhart Mayer, *Die geistige Entwicklung Wilhelm Raabes. Dargestellt unter besonderer Berüucksichtigung seines Verhältnisses zur Philosophie*, Göttingen, Vandenhoeck & Ruprecht, 1960.
Herman Meyer, *Der Sonderling in der deutschen Dichtung* (1943), 2nd edn., München, Hanser, 1963.
Herman Meyer, "Raum und Zeit in Wilhelm Raabes Erzählkunst", in: *Deutsche Vierteljahrsschrift für Literaturwissenschaft und Geistesgeschichte* 27 (1953).
Herman Meyer, *Das Zitat in der Erzählkunst. Zur Geschichte und Poetik des europäischen Romans*, Stuttgart, Metzler, 1961.
Hubert Ohl, "Eduards Heimkehr oder Le Vaillant und das Riesenfaultier. Zu Wilhelm Raabes 'Stopfkuchen' ", in: *Jahrbuch der deutschen Schiller-Gesellschaft* 8 (1964).

Hans Oppermann, "Zum Problem der Zeit bei Wilhelm Raabe", in: *Jahrbuch der Raabe-Gesellschaft*, 1964.

Roy Pascal, "The Reminiscence Technique in Raabe", in: *Modern Language Review* 49 (1954).

Roy Pascal, *The German Novel. Studies,* Manchester University Press, 1956.

Hermann Pongs, *Wilhelm Raabe. Leben und Werk,* Heidelberg, Quelle & Meyer, 1958.

Johann Nestroy

Johann Nestroy

by GERTRUD SEIDMANN

"Samstag den 24. August 1822. Im k.k. Hoftheater nächst dem Kärnthnerthore. Die Zauberflöte. Große Oper in zwey Aufzügen, von Emanuel Schikaneder, Musik von W. A. Mozart ... Herr Nestroy wird in der Rolle des Sarastro seinen ersten theatralischen Versuch wagen, und empfiehlt sich der Nachsicht des Publikums."[1]

This advertisement marked the beginning of a life in the theatre which was to span forty years, during which Johann Nestroy was to play 879 parts and to write over eighty works for the stage. Born in Vienna in 1801, the son of a lawyer not long settled in the capital (the family originated from Bohemia), he gave up his own law studies after a successful trial début in Mozart's opera, when he was offered a two-year contract as a singer at the Court Opera House. But the following year, wanting to get married, he asked to be released from his engagement, and left Vienna for better pay and more varied experience elsewhere: his début on a famous stage had given him an advantageous start. He joined first the German Theatre in Amsterdam, then the National Theatre in Brünn, where both opera and drama were performed, and was soon found to be a versatile actor with a facility for learning new parts and a good-natured willingness to take over at short notice. Thus he soon acquired a large repertory, in which spoken parts, and more and more comic ones, began to predominate (for a register of the parts he played, see *Sämtliche Werke*, vol. 15, p. 431 ff.). His Brünn contract, however, was forcibly annulled by the Austrian police for offences against the censorship laws and "disrespect towards the audience"—a forctaste of a lifetime's skirmishes with the authorities.

His next engagement was at the Graz and Pressburg theatres, then under joint management; and now he reached a significant turning-point in his life: on December 15, 1827, he made his first appearance as Sansquartier in Angély's farce *Mädchen in Uniform*, a role which he made famous; and on the same evening he made his bow as a playwright with the one-act farce *Der Zettelträger Papp*, in which he played the title-role. The same year his wife had left him for another man, and not long after he settled down to a sometimes stormy, but, despite his numerous escapades, enduring association with the actress Marie Weiler, who continued acting with him for many years, while seeing to the upbringing of his son Gustav, and later of their own two children, subsequently legitimised (Austria did not permit the re-marriage of divorced

275

persons). She also looked capably after their finances, the acquisition of a nice competence and some property, and eventually even the management of the theatre, with which Nestroy was entrusted towards the end of his career.

In 1831, Nestroy sought an engagement in Vienna again. By now he commanded as many as 450 parts and had shown a decided comic gift; and after some fairly hard bargaining he finally contracted himself to one of Vienna's most successful theatrical entrepreneurs, the actor-manager Carl Carl, who then controlled the Theater an der Wien. Thus at last, at the age of thirty, began his association with the *Wiener Volkstheater* with which his name is associated.

Carl engaged him both as an actor and as one of the house playwrights of whom the Vienna stage, given its relatively small but theatre-hungry public, had constant need: it is a measure of its appetite that of Nestroy's immediate predecessors in the Popular genre, Carl Meisl wrote 177, Alois Gleich 220 plays, and his contemporary Eduard Bauernfeld, the favoured comedy author of the "legitimate" stage of the Hof-Burgtheater, forty-three. Nestroy spent the rest of his professional life with the same management, moving with it in the forties to the Theater in der Leopoldstadt, subsequently rebuilt and re-named Carltheater, and after Carl's death briefly managed by him; his life almost entirely filled by the theatre where, too, he sought not only his passing affaires but those enduring friendships to which the sparse remains of his correspondence testify.

He continued to travel a certain amount; as his star rose, he was in demand for guest performances in other cities, both within the Austrian Empire and beyond its frontiers, in Hamburg, Frankfurt, Berlin, Munich; on holidays he travelled to Paris, North Germany, and the Netherlands; in later years he liked to spend them in Ischl, where the Emperor had a summer villa, and on Heligoland, where he enjoyed the peace and the fishing (letter of 11.vii.1848). For his retirement he chose Graz: he survived it only a matter of months, dying, at the age of sixty-one, from the effects of a stroke.

I F for many of his contemporaries Nestroy was simply a brilliant entertainer, whose plays would disappear with the performers for whom they served as vehicles, he nevertheless excited violent partisanships for and against, in a city which took its theatre-going seriously.

Success or failure of a new work were never left in doubt by vocal first-night audiences, and figures for subsequent performances tell their own story (collected in *S. Werke,* vol. 15, p. 399 ff.). The critics voiced their opinions primarily in Adolf Bäuerle's *Theater-Zeitung* and M. G. Saphir's *Humorist,* and many a contemporary memoirist recorded the scene. Those who appreciated Nestroy's genius, such as Prince Friedrich von Schwarzenberg and Friedrich

Hebbel (quoted in Basil, p. 169 f.) or Eduard von Bauernfeld (*Aus Alt- und Neu-Wien, Ges. Schriften*, 1872/3, vol. 12, p. 53 ff.), praised his brilliant intellect and wit; though Bauernfeld, who lauds the probity of his private character, deplores the debasing vulgarity he sees in the actor and playwright, "der crasse Egoismus im Bunde mit der gröbsten Sinnlichkeit"[2] and Adam Müller-Guttenbrunn (*Im Jahrhundert Grillparzers*, Wien, 1895, p. 115) refers to the "Cyniker" who debased the Popular stage. Nestroy's adversaries tended to suggest that the playwright's bitter satire was destroying the good-natured *Gemütlichkeit* of the Viennese,—a process more properly attributable to economic and political events. Even on the stage of the *Volkstheater*, Nestroy's figures were hardly the first to satirize the less admirable citizens of this "Capua der Geister",[3] for Adolf Bäuerle's Staberl in *Die Bürger von Wien* (1813) was a true forerunner of Nestroy's "liederliche Gesellen".[4] A convenient stalking-horse for these criticisms was found in the personality and work of Ferdinand Raimund, a decade older than Nestroy, and already the leading comic actor of the famous Theater in der Leopoldstadt, when Nestroy made his debut at the rival Theater im Freihaus an der Wien.

Raimund, too, had taken the step, to him far more difficult, from acting to writing; and his genius was indeed very different from that of Nestroy, rooted, as it was, in an earlier, more naive period of the Viennese stage. All his works, including his high-flown but unsuccessful attempts at tragedy, belong to the traditional genre of the *Zauberstück*, the machine-play, in which earthly and super-natural forces intermingle to hold an audience rapt before surprising stage-effects. (Collection of texts in the series *Barocktradition im österreichisch-bayrischen Volkstheater*, ed. O. Rommel, in *Deutsche Literatur, Reihe Barock*, vols. 1–5, 1935–39). The charm of Rai-mund's plays lies in the handful of fully rounded character-studies he wrote for himself, such as the misanthropist of *Alpenkönig und Menschenfeind* (1828) and especially the faithful Valentin of *Der Verschwender* (1834), with his appealing simple philosophy, his warmheartedness and his down-to-earth humour; and in the uniquely touching, perfectly and poetically realized allegory of a figure like his "Jugend". Their appeal resembles that of the *Volks-lied* which, in their pleasing musical settings, Youth's "Brüderlein fein" and Valentin's "Hobellied" have in the course of time become famous.

Nestroy's works do indeed breathe an entirely different spirit, and Raimund is reported (e.g. by Bauernfeld, loc. cit.) to have shuddered at his rival's vulgarity. When Raimund, a chronic depressive, took his own life in 1836, at the height of his fame, gossip was not slow to make Nestroy's rising star responsible for this suicide (see e.g. Holtei—hardly an impartial critic, as he had smarted under Nestroy's successful parodies of his sentimental dramas—, quoted in Basil, p. 171). These contemporary partisanships re-echoed for a long time (Karl Holl's *Geschichte des deutschen Lustspiels,* 1923, and Josef Nadler's *Literaturgeschichte Österreichs,* 1951, both refer to Nestroy's *Lumpazivagabundus,* performed in 1833 and based on an earlier sketch, in its turn derived from a model by Gleich, as a vulgar parody of *Der Verschwender* of 1834); and posterity was a little slower to recognize Nestroy than Raimund, who received the accolade of performance at the Burgtheater ten years earlier—in both cases long after the authors' deaths. A first collected edition of Nestroy's works (ed. by V. Chiavacci and Ludwig Ganghofer), with a biographical and critical essay by Moritz Necker, appeared in 1890–91.

Any study of his whole *oeuvre* will reveal weaknesses and evidence of haste, and both juvenilia and such a late work as *Häuptling Abendwind* (1862) have little of the appeal of the plays Nestroy wrote in his most creative period, from the late 'thirties to the early 'fifties, during which he shows a constantly renewed inventiveness and a sparkling wit in even the slighter occasional pieces. Occasional, in a sense, they all were, written for the actors of Director Carl's company; but they presupposed, or perhaps elicited, a variety of acting styles, from the travestied magicians and immortals, conversing in Viennese dialect, of the *Zauberposse,* to the *Volksstück* which announces the serious moral purpose of an Anzengruber, from the traditional comic style of the extempore *Stegreifkomödie* to political satire, from the gay comedy of intrigue and imbroglio to the parody of high drama. The handful of plays to be discussed in greater detail below is to give some idea of this variety.

Nestroy takes his material where he finds it, from older comedies, current successes on foreign stages, collections of folk tales, or the latest sensational novel. As he is a practical man of the theatre, the form, in which he casts it, is largely determined by the tradition of the Volkstheater within which he works; as an Austrian writer, he is limited by the pressure of the political circumstances of the day; as a salaried *Bühnendichter,* he plans and drafts his plays first in terms of the actors for whom they are written. Although the comedies have long survived their first interpreters, an idea of the appearance and the acting style of the principal pair of comedians for whom they were written helps to visualize the intended stage effect.

The star of the Theater an der Wien, when Nestroy joined it, was Wenzel Scholz, until his death in 1857 Nestroy's constant partner on the stage. He has been described (O. Rommel in *Einbegleitung* to *Einen Jux will er sich machen*, 1923, p. 120 f.) as one of those comedians who barely need to "act", the very appearance conveying the essence of a certain type of comic. Engravings of stage scenes (reproductions in O. Basil) show him, short and corpulent, sometimes in exaggerated movement, on his face an expression of stolid stupidity or of exaggerated surprise : a Pulcinella or a Sancho Panza. Nestroy sometimes uses him for fairly obvious effects : in *Lumpazivagabundus*, playing on the contrast between appearance and character, he writes for Scholz the part of the tailor Zwirn ("Thread"); stage directions describe him as perpetually in motion, he is forever ready to dance, "schlägt ungeheuere Fußtriller",[5] and is particularly boastful of his successes with the ladies, "Ich könnt' euch meine Amouren bataillonsweis aufmarschieren lassen"[6]—quite in the succession of the eighteenth century's Hanswurst "der übel belohnte Liebhaber vieler Weibsbilder",[7] a predecessor he also resembles by his infantile traits, his nonsense talk, and his inability to think further than the moment; and Nestroy provides him with many opportunities for the traditional *Tazzi* of the old extempore comedy. In *Zu ebener Erde und im ersten Stock* Scholz played the poor *Tandler* (old clothes-man) and sighing lover Damian Stutzl, "eine ungesättigte Leidenschaft"[8] and raging jealousy in his heart; one may imagine the effect made by the contrast between his appearance and his words, "Das hat schon frische, feste Leut' zusammg'rissen, was hab ich erst zu erwarten, der ich schon so viele Jahre auf'm Tandelmarkt bin."[9]

Other Scholz parts, such as the bootblack Hutzibutz of *Das Haus der Temperamente*, or Klaus, the malicious but easily deceived servant of the forces of reaction in *Freiheit in Krähwinkel*, make the most of the combination of stupidity and conceit which the comedian knew so well to portray; but to savour fully the figure of Melchior in *Einen Jux will er sich machen*, with his repetitive tags, "Das is klassisch!"[10] or "Es is ein wahres Glück, daß Euer Gnaden mich haben"[10]—it is instructive to read of the inimitable effects the actor managed to produce from the repetition of one single phrase (O. Rommel, loc. cit.). One of Scholz' most remarkable roles, though, must have been the more-than-lifesize Holofernes in Nestroy's parody of Hebbel's *Judith*.

In many of his plays, Nestroy's own part is the perfect foil and counterpart to Scholz', for which his appearance and his natural acting style, underlined by costume and make-up, almost seem to have predestined him. Theatrical engravings and contemporary descriptions (reproductions, and descriptions quoted, in Basil) combine to give a striking picture of a man extremely tall and thin, with expressive gestures of arms and hands; several excellent photographs show a strong face with a long nose, jutting chin, beetling black eyebrows and lively, dark, piercingly intelligent eyes. The piled-on adjectives and neologisms, the complicated similes, the immensely long bravura sentences he writes for his own parts, give ample testimony of the acrobatic facility of his tongue. These traits he exploits in such parts as the intriguing valet Johann in *Zu ebener Erde* and the similar part of Schlankel in *Das Haus der Temperamente,* both times a foil to Scholz' part. If here he trades on his natural gifts to play the traditional *Intrigant* who sets the farce in motion, one of his most famous, yet among the earliest character parts he wrote for himself, went far to reinforce a stage personality sometimes described as "daemonic" : this was the part of the cobbler Knieriem in *Lumpazivagabundus,* a grotesque figure living only for drink and astronomy. Many of those who have spoken of his "vulgar cynicism" must have had this drink-sodden figure in mind. But he wrote many parts for himself which are of an entirely different character. The hero-heroine of *Judith und Holofernes*—in the parody a disguised male Joab—gave opportunities for clowning; the Mussi Weinberl of *Jux* is a gay and debonair young man, the journalist Eberhard Ultra of *Freiheit in Krähwinkel,* one of his happiest roles, the embodiment of freedom-loving optimism and enlightenment; but into the title-roles of *Der Unbedeutende* or *Der alte Mann mit der jungen Frau* there enters a new element of psychological realism, very different from the stock comic character or intriguer of farce, who belongs so much more obviously to the ancient tradition in which the Viennese Popular Theatre was rooted.

At the time of Nestroy's stage debut this flourished at several suburban *Vorstadttheater,* having been driven from the stage of the Court Theatre in 1770 by a *Wiener Hanswurststreit,* long after Gottsched's reforms. But the theatre of entertainment, centred on the *Komische Person,* the successors of J. A. Stranitzky's Hanswurst (first established at the Kärntnertortheater in 1712) and his later companion, the actor Kurz' Bernardon, had soon found a refuge in the theatres outside the walls, of which the most important were those in der Josefstadt, an der Wien, and, for long the most successful, in der Leopoldstadt. (Texts, *Wiener Haupt- und Staatsaktionen,* intro. and ed. by Rudolf Payer von Thurn, Wien 1908–10, *Wiener Neudrucke,* vol. 2, 4, 1883, *Der weiland Kasperl,* by Gustav Gugitz,

Wien, 1920, *Raimunds Vorgänger*, by Rudolf Fürst, Berlin 1907, *Barocktradition im ö.-b. Volkstheater*, s. above: *description, Deutsch-Österreichische Literaturgeschichte*, by J. W. Nagl, Jakob Zeidler and Eduard Castle, Wien 1899–1937.) In der Leopoldstadt ruled the actor La Roche as Kasperle, of whom the Eipeldauer's letters relate, "(Er) kommt mir vor wie's liebe Brot, das man nicht satt wird"[11] quoted Nagl-Zeidler-Castle II., p. 480), to whose "Ritter- und Geisterstücke"[12] Grillparzer remembers being taken as a child (*Sämmtliche Werke*, Stuttgart 1872, p. 14).

One of Kasperle's favourite vehicles was the *Zauberstück*, where the attractions of the comic figure was enhanced by baroque elements of stage machinery and stage surprise, by an element of parody, or rather travesty, which at the same time mocked this world, and last, but not least, by the appeal of their music—a mixture still effective in the Savoy operas. If Haydn had provided the music for "Der neue krumme Teufel", (1751) the gifted and prolific Wenzel Müller wrote, amongst many others, the settings for *Kaspar der Fagottist oder die Zauberzither* which, like *Kaspar der Vogelkrämer* (Papageno's trade) appeared in 1791, the same year in which *Die Zauberflöte*, with a libretto by Emanuel Schikaneder, was first performed at the Theater an der Wien.

After the death of La Roche, after Anton Hasenhut's Thaddädl, the vogue of the *Zauberstück* seemed to wane, especially following the success of a new *Komische Person*, Bäuerle's parapluie-maker Staberl, created by the actor Ignaz Schuster in *Die Bürger von Wien* (1813), which was succeeded by a host of imitations and a new predilection for a *Lokalposse* in which the audience could enjoy the mocking of its own manners and modes, as it did in the contemporary letters of the "Eipeldauer" : but the rising star of Raimund gave the genre, and with it the Theater in der Leopoldstadt, a new lease of life in the 'twenties and 'thirties, despite the grumblings of the critics.

Nestroy's own beginnings as a playwright, too, lay in the genre of the *Zauberstück*, in which he gained his first great success in Vienna with *Lumpazivagabundus oder Das liederliche Kleeblatt*[19] (1833). The farce begins with a bet between the spirit Lumpazivagabundus, a travestied Mephisto figure, who describes himself as "Beherrscher des lustigen Elends, Beschützer der Spieler, Protektor der Trinker",[14] and the fairy Fortuna : he vows that three of his votaries, however favoured by fortune, will forever remain dissolute rakes. At once the scene changes to Earth, and there enter, in turn, the three "liederliche Gesellen" : Leim, the carpenter (written for

Director Carl), Knieriem, the cobbler—Nestroy's role—and lastly, Zwirn, the tailor—Scholz' star part; three poor wandering journeymen, each introducing himself in his trade character, with a song or a monologue in the fashion by now traditional. The carpenter, the most respectable of the three, is overcome by sudden melancholy whenever he remembers faithless Peppi, his master's daughter who, he believes, has married another; the tailor, devoted to dancing and the ladies, is animated by a colossal vanity—waking up in the straw of the village inn he calls for a mirror and some Eau de Cologne"; while the cobbler has only two ruling passions : drink and astronomy, which complement each other, for late at night, when he has been thrown out of the tavern, he has opportunities for studying the starry firmament and thus he knows that "der Komet" will soon destroy the world—enough to drive a man to drink.

In the inn, to which the three repair, they hear of a lottery which is to be drawn on the morrow, and in which one hundred thousand thalers are to be won. Knieriem immediately translates into his own currency, "Hunderttausand Taler! Das gibt über a Million Maß G'mischt's",[15] before they settle down to sleep and, guided by Fortuna, to dream of the lucky number. The comic vicissitudes they still have to undergo before their fortunes are really assured, the comedians' crosstalk, and Zwirn's naughty *lazzi*, ensure that the audience is still kept at a pitch of comic tension. The second act is mostly Zwirn's who, now that he is rich, is indulging his tastes for Society and a gay life, not without continually giving himself away as the *ci-devant* tailor : "Marschieren Sie, sonst wirf ich Ihnen ein Bögeleisen nach!"[16] he threatens when he feels himself insulted— the very substitution of an "ö" for an "ü" an indication of his efforts at gentility.

The third act brings the three together again, as they had sworn, a year after their lucky win : honest Leim is now prospering and happy with his Peppi—it had all been a misunderstanding—but the other two have wasted their fortunes and sunk lower and lower : Zwirn now cannot keep his hands even off his friend's wife, and Knieriem has passed from beer to an immense thirst for spirits, but still believes in the imminent destruction of the world by the Comet : "Die Welt steht auf kein' Fall mehr lang"[17] is the burden of the *Kometenlied,* the first of the famous and much quoted *Couplets* in which the comedian was to comment on the modes and mores of his times. Nestroy's jolly rake of Act I has become a disgusting sot. Yet this "modern morality" is suddenly and perfunctorily brought to a happy close by the intervention of the Spirit of Love : a rapid stage transformation shows the two dissolute cronies, too, most improbably in a state of happy domesticity. This improbability the author speedily ignored, with a continuation written the following year, in which all three—including Leim—with their families, are sunk even lower from their spurious respectability. These perfunctory endings we shall meet again. Nestroy rarely takes the trouble to prepare the inevitable happy conclusion of a farce; he mocks at himself when he makes his Mussi Weinberl remark at just such another denouement in *Einen Jux will er sich machen*: "Also hat sich der Fall schon wieder ereignet? Nein, was's Jahr Onkel und Tanten sterben müssen, bloß damit alles gut ausgeht—!"[(18)]

It is fairly apparent that Nestroy's interest in this *Zauberposse* was centred on the contrasted character-parts, on the comic dialogue and situations, on his own role as "Raisonneur", the commentator on the follies of the world around him, in the *Couplet*: least of all on the magic world which gives the genre its name. His earliest attempts in this type of comedy still show him interested in the opportunities it offers for stage display: *Der Tod am Hochzeitstage* (1829) contains, Raimund-fashion, a whole page of stage directions for the dwelling of the Queen of Dreams, with a host of allegorical props, such as a black watering-can with silver magic symbols for the watering of black and white poppies and there are "transformations" and "tableaux". In *Lumpazivagabundus* such stage effects are almost non-existent, some were cut even between manuscript and stage version. The comic effects to be obtained from a travestied Viennese world of immortals he neglected here entirely, except for the brief appearance of the eponymous "hero" himself, whose name is said to have struck Raimund as inexpressibly vulgar. The only purpose of the magic world in this comedy is to serve as a dramatic lever, and as a convenient framework for a *Schubladenstück* linking together three successive episodes in the careers of his comic trio, similar to the occasional use to which it had already been put by some of his predecessors, as by Bäuerle in *Wien, Paris, London und Konstantinopel* (1823), or in Meisl's *1723, 1823, 1923*. It is hardly surprising, then, that after the failure of a very few subsequent *Zauberstücke*—despite the continued success of *Lumpazivagabundus*—Nestroy soon dropped almost entirely what by then had become a dreary device.

One other traditional genre, which sometimes filled the *Wiener Volkstheater* for weeks on end, was Parody. Various writers have tried to attribute this predilection to a specifically Austrian gift for irony (Nagl-Zeidler-Castle, vol. 1, p. 382) to the influence of Austrian history (H. Cysarz, in *Die Barockdichtung*, 1924, p. 227), or the way of life of its people (O. Rommel in *S. Werke*, vol. 15,

p. 74); the tradition certainly extends from a comic "Amphitruo" and other burlesques on mythological themes, performed by Stranitzky's company, well into the nineteenth century. Among Nestroy's older contemporaries the author Carl Meisl was particularly prolific in this field. His *Orpheus und Eurydike* and *Die Entführung der Prinzessin Europa* transport us to a Viennese Olympus, with Bacchus a vintner, Adonis a dandy, and Pan a timber-merchant; Joachim Perinet produced "caricature operas" in his *Ariadne* and *Telemach* for the Theater in der Leopoldstadt. The genre is not dissimilar from Offenbach's operetta, and Nestroy in his own repertory spanned the generations between Meisl's and Offenbach's Jupiter, which he created for Vienna in 1860 as one of his last parts.

But the mythological world of the *opera seria* was not the only one to be burlesqued : well-known literary works were equally mercilessly—and speedily—travestied. Perinet's *Hamlet, Prinz vom Tandelmarkt*, Gleich's *Fiesko der Salamikrämer* and Bäuerle's *Maria Stuttgardt* employ exactly the same means to bring the heroes and heroines of high tragedy down to a local world of Viennese drolls, in which Fiesko's sole desire is to become a master sausage-maker, Characteristic Viennese types such as the proverbially quarrelsome "Sesseltrager" (chair-men) appear, and local events and customs are once again introduced for the delectation of the audience, with a star part for the principal comedian of the day. Such immediate translations to the local scene represent a recognition of merit rather than the criticism of true parody; they also, as has been remarked, presuppose an audience familiar, if not with every one of the models, then at least with the type.

There were, however, other parodies which merit the name better Kurz' *Bernardon die getreue Prinzessin Pumphia* (1765) was announced as a "Critique oder Parodie über die sonst von vielen teutschen Truppen sehr übel vorgestellten Tragödien".[19] This mocks at the weaknesses of the "regular" post-Gottschedian tragedy : the artificial exposition, the contrived entrances and exits, the role of the confidant, and the violence done to commonsense by an artificially imposed unity of place (a fortress is brought on stage and placed over the captured general's head).

The actor Nestroy was naturally familiar with the genre : while still singing in opera, he was already taking part in *Staberl als Freischütz* and other parodies. His early experience was no doubt instrumental in making his opera parodies—of *Robert le Diable*, of *Zampa*, of *Martha*, even of the early Wagner, doubly effective. In *Adelheid, die verfolgte Wittib* (1832, his first work for the Theatre an der Wien) he parodied a ballet; with *Weder Lorbeerbaum noch Bettelstab* (1835) and *Die verhängnisvolle Faschingsnacht* (1839) two of Holtei's sentimental dramas. In some of these works Nestroy already departs from the easy laughs of travesty and achieves a more pointed "Critique". His *Robert der Teuxels* motto "Nur Böses!"[20] became proverbial. His outstanding essay in this genre however was his parody of Hebbel's early tragedy *Judith* which had its first performance at the Burgtheater in 1849. Nestroy's parody for the *Volkstheater* followed apace, and found its mark.

The tragic problem of Hebbel's heroine he ignores; by turning her into a disguised "hero" Joab—Nestroy's own part—he strikes a note of simple fun reminiscent of Kurz' *Princess*. The parodist's target is, first of all, Hebbel's desire to make his Bethulians represent the "Grundgedanken des Judentums".[21] His Bethulians are visionaries, God's People in dire need and oppressed. Nestroy's are representatives of the citizens of the Leopoldstadt suburb whom he knew so well, speaking the typical *Jargon* of the Viennese Jews, recognisable in print by its sentence structure: "Aber werden sie stehn bleiben draußen? Nein, sie werden dringen herein."[22] Business and finance are never far from their thoughts. This is how the High Priest laments over the dreadful times: "Joab, in was bist du gekommen für einer abscheulichen Period! Greuel der Verwüstung in Israel, Erdbeben in der Handelswelt, die festesten Häuser stürzen übereinander!"[23] Speaking of Holofernes, Jojakim says: "Sie sind ihm alle zinsbar, die Könige der Erde." Joab: "Was zinsbar? Is er der Hausherr?".[24]

Crowd scenes introduce the citizens of Bethulia at their military drill: an exercise of a very democratic cast. Corporal Assad: "Marsch!" Recruit Hosea: "Wohin?"—Assad: "Habt Acht!" Ammon: "Ich bin neugierig auf was?"—Assad: "Links g'schaut!" Hosea: "Warum?"[25]—The Hebrew warriors are also depicted in Joab's song and monologue (Scene 14).

The cunning Jew had been a stock figure of the Wiener Volkstheater, like the honest Tyrolean and other national stereotypes: but Nestroy's jokes are far more reminiscent of those invented and enjoyed by Jews themselves—who incidentally made up a conspicuous part of his public.

If Nestroy's Bethulians from the Leopoldstadt are a novel variation on the local Viennese figures of burlesque and travesty, Hebbel's more than life-size Holofernes in the young man's first drama is a character who might be said to bear the seeds of risibility within himself. "Immer neigte er in seinen Stoffen zum Ungeheuerlichen, das alles auf die äußerste Spitze treibt",[26] says Fritz Martini on the subject of *Judith* (*Deutsche Literaturgeschichte*, 9th ed., Stuttgart, 1958, p. 373); and this Hercules of a man, tyrannical, wilful, the master of all he surveys, but demonstrating his powers chiefly in ordering the occasional beheading of an underling, unless superlatively well acted, can easily make an involuntarily comic effect, and thus offers the parodist a broad target.

Nestroy's chorus announces, "Er ist der Feinde Schrecken, Schrecken, Schrecken",[27] and his intimates relate with bated breath : "Mir sagte sein Kämmerling, daß er mit dem linken Fuß aufgestanden."—"An solchen Tagen ist immer seine rechte Hand zu fürchten."[28] But the parodist makes his happiest play with the introspective cast of mind of Hebbel's hero, who is forever observing and analysing himself, a feature he happens to share with the traditional *Komische Person*, but particularly with Nestroy's own creations. "Zittere !" exclaims his Bertram in *Robert der Teuxel*, "Ich bin gar ein kurioses Wesen !"[29] Hebbel's Holofernes bears some resemblance to such a figure when he says : "Das ist die Kunst, sich nicht auslernen zu lassen"[30] (Act I), or : "Das freut mich am meisten, daß ich nicht weiß, woher ich kam"[31] (Act IV). On a sacrifice to Jehovah : "Ein Mann bringt's dir, und ein solcher, der's nicht nötig hätte"[32] (Act V). Mocking Hebbel's Holofernes who says : "Den Holofernes töten, . . . Dazu könnt' ich mich selber verführen lassen, wenn ich nicht wäre, der ich bin"[33] (Act V), Nestroy coins the superb phrase for Scholz-Holofernes : "Ich glaube von jedem Menschen das Schlechteste, auch von mir, und ich hab mich noch selten getäuscht."[34] A distinct affinity between the language of Hebbel and that of Nestroy, in the tendency of both towards the extended metaphorical phrase on the one hand, towards a pointed aphorism on the other, is deserving of notice. Perhaps this explains why Hebbel was one of those who appreciated Nestroy's genius. Preferring, he writes (quoted Basil, p. 171), good farce to mediocre tragedy, he comments that "sicher wird ein Kunstverständiger für einen einzigen Nestroyschen Witz de première qualité eine Million gewöhnlicher Jamben hingeben".[35] The parody appeared at first anonymously.

If his essays in the *Zauberposse* and in Parody exhibit most clearly Nestroy's roots in the traditional forms of the *Wiener Volkstheater*, he pleased not only the public, but the critics, too, with *Zu ebener Erde und im ersten Stock*[36] (1835), in which they thought they saw the serious *Volksstück* with a didactic tendency which they were increasingly demanding, attacking the playwrights of the Popular stage—including Raimund—for their levity. In this new play, where on a horizontally divided stage Nestroy plays on the contrast between the poor on the groundfloor and the rich on the *piano nobile*, he was held to have painted a realistically observed picture from true life, and pointed a moral.

As a matter of fact, realistic local colour was not unknown in either the *Zauberstück* or Parody : as we have seen, one of the attractions of these genres was this very intermingling of types and manners of the real world with the supernatural world of magic. Already Hafner's *Bürgerliche Dame* had satirized mid-eighteenth century life in Vienna, and we see the rise of a periodical literature and its didactic tendencies mirrored in such plays as Eberl's *Die Negozianten oder Warnung für junge Leute* (1791), or Gewey's *Modesitten* (1800), while "noble savages" such as "der Viehhändler aus Ober-Österreich"[37] or "der Tiroler Wastl"[37] show up big city life, like the Eipeldauer in his letters; the existence of national stereotypes has already been commented on.

It is generally assumed that such tentative feelers towards a greater realism led no further because of the overwhelming success of Kasperle, who belonged to the timeless, totally unrealistic world of farce and extempore comedy. Nevertheless, at the Leopoldstädter Theater itself a new generation of comics had already begun to create more localised, more realistic types. A decisive step in this direction seemed to be taken by Bäuerle's *Die Bürger von Wien* (1813), which mirrors the patriotic feelings of those stirring days after Napoleon's defeat, and presents the citizens of Vienna as a worthy, self-confident community, to which the parasitic "para-pluie-maker" Staberl, as portrayed by Ignaz Schuster, formed a comic contrast. Yet the overwhelming success of the play was made, not by the background of worthies, but by this comic figure, who was after all a brother under the skin of Hanswurst the "Sauabschneider" (sow-butcher) or Kaspar the bassoon-player, and was speedily imitated by a whole host of similar comic figures; spot-removers, dessert-bakers, stocking-knitters, a fiddler Kratzerl, or Raimund's Barometermacher Quecksilber, who pursue their eccentric trades (provided they have not already failed in them) solely for the purpose of their introductory song and some comic dialogue.

Nestroy's poor family *zu ebener Erde*, if their trade suspiciously resembles those others—they are *Tandler*, old clothes' and rag dealers—are at any rate seen in their home, they evidently live on their meagre earnings, and their financial worries seem very real. Their trade even plays a part in the plot, for the honest *Tandler* is rewarded when some money, forgotten in an old coat, is discovered, and gives him his first taste of prosperity, while the rich financier Goldfuchs *im ersten Stock* is ruined by certain unfortunate financial transactions. In contrast to the timeless farce, where lovers only live for their love, and fathers can devote themselves entirely to the guarding of daughters and wards, the scene here graphically depicts the city's cruel contiguity of rich and poor, of hunger and wasteful abundance.

A closer look, though, reveals the ancient plot: poor Adolf Schlucker loves rich Emilie Goldfuchs; the parents' disapproval and the social gulf provide the necessary obstacles; and a sly intriguing servant and poor lovesick Damian Stutzl are the contrasting pair of comedians. But the wheel of fortune turns: the rich are impoverished, the poor find themselves suddenly rich—once again by means of a lottery, though chance, not magic, brings this about—and poor Adolf turns out to be the son of a nabob— indeed, "der Fall hat sich schon wieder ereignet",[38] and we see at last not only the lovers united, but the Schlucker family moving into the first floor vacated by Goldfuchs, who is forced to descend to the poor man's groundfloor dwelling.

Nestroy's own part of the intriguing servant follows on the whole conventional lines, although there are nice touches of "realism" here, too, in his change of tone when his master has become impoverished. Damian Stutzl, the lovelorn *Tandler*, though, is a delightfully drawn figure, his corpulent body inhabited by a speculative spirit: "Es ist ein Unterschied zwischen Bäck und Bäck, es ist eine Differenz zwischen Fleischhacker und Fleischhacker, aber der Abstand, der zwischen Tandler und Tandler ist, der geht schon ins Unberechenbare hinein."[39] He is evidently a reader,—he discloses that "Auf'm Ofenmäuerl drin liegt der Abälard und die Heloise"[40] —and potentially an author: he plans to issue, by subscription, a "Systematische Anleitung zur Lumpen—und Fetzenkunde".[41] If that, too, fails, it will be the end for him, for he is certain to be "vom Schicksal bestimmt, das verworfenste Individuum der untersten Gattung zu sein".[42]

The other members of the *Tandler*'s family, too, are drawn with loving care: the domineering head of the household, the two women, especially Damian's adored Salerl, a real "resche Wienerin";[43] and even the three small children are lovingly differentiated and have their telling lines: as the family prepares to move upstairs, the mother asks: "Hat kein's was vergessen?" Seppel, carrying a broken toy horse, replies, "Nein, das Notwendigste haben wir schon."[44]

The outstanding feature of this comedy, though, is the use Nestroy makes of the horizontally divided stage, from which he squeezes the utmost in irony, in comic situations, and in stage effects. He employs it for a sentimentally touching scene, where in the finale of Act I the rich man's boards groan under choice meats, and even the servants regale themselves with champagne, while at the same time the poor family below says grace over dry bread and water (see the theatrical print reproduced in Basil, p. 93). But more often the contrast will be a comic one. Thus in the very first scene the demands of the creditors below, "Wird's endlich werden oder nicht? Wann kriegn wir unser Geld?"[45] interlock and rhyme neatly with the words of the servants upstairs preparing the banquet: "Nur hurtig, fleißig, zaudert nicht, Die Tafel trägt uns Geld" ... "Ich hab' fünf Gulden dreißig Kreuzer z'krieg'n!— "Heut' muß der Tisch sich völlig bie'gn",[45] etc. The exclamations of the card-players in the rich man's home, "Meine Coeur-Dame werd' ich verlieren", "Coeur ist Atout"[46]—make a pointed commentary to the feelings of the youthful lover below; and the two comics make their entrances simultaneously, Damian below to a melancholy tune, Johann upstairs to a vivacious one, and proclaim their introductory and *Antrittslieder* monologues alternately.

Nestroy draws a different effect from his divided stage in the sequence of scenes (Act I, 12–17) where the familiar device of a love-letter falling into the wrong hands is demonstrated before the very eyes of the audience: as Emilie's letter to Adolf is let down on a string from a first floor window, Father Schlucker intercepts it; as she sighs, "Jetzt wird mein Adolf ihn lesen",[47] the old man angrily reads it aloud; but a second letter, destined by jealous Damian for the would-be seducer of his Salerl, ensures that Emilie imagines she receives, after all, the reply she had hoped for.

But these devices are not overworked: sequences of scenes will be concentrated on one part of the stage, as at the beginning of the third act; then there are new possibilities to be drawn from the setting, as the two comedians change places, for Johann has an eye to brisk Salerl, while Damian, in a temporary access of faithlessness, thinks of deserting her for Emilie's pretty maid and confidante. Finally, however, as the newly enriched triumphantly move into the grand apartment on the first floor, while the ruined financier finds a refuge on the ground floor they have vacated, the reversal of fortune is as visibly demonstrated on this divided stage as in a medieval allegory.

Nevertheless, to stress only this latter aspect, and to see in this farce primarily a "volkserzieherische Tendenz"[48] is surely to underrate both the comic features that link it closely to Nestroy's other works, and the outstanding attraction the device of the divided stage seems to have held for him. A subsequent "dramatisches

Gemälde"[49] *Der Treulose oder Saat und Ernte* in which he attempted more truly a *Sittenstück* was a resounding failure, and we find the playwright abandoning the serious *Volksstück* for many years, and turning back once more to the opposite pole, to pure farce; and with *Das Haus der Temperamente*[50] (1837) to almost the quintessence of the form.

Here we are in purest theatreland, where all maidens are beautiful, all fathers cruel, all maids coquettish, and all lovers finally united, and the action set in motion by a clever arch-intriguer, followed by a stupid, but ever hopeful imitator : the Zannipair of the Commedia dell'Arte, which had long been at home in Vienna. Stranitzky himself had at one time shared the Kärntnertor-theater with one of the "wälsche Truppen" whose comic art was carried on well into the nineteenth century by the pantomime company of the Leopoldstädtertheater, and echoed by the traces it left in *opera buffa* as well as in the indigenous forms of the *Wiener Volkstheater*. In their essentials, the plots of almost all of Nestroy's farces can be related to the traditional ones of extempore comedy, but in *Das Haus der Temperamente*, instead of clothing it in the verisimilitude of recognisable local figures, Nestroy wilfully exposes the bare mechanism of his plot by type-figures (representing the four temperaments), and not once, but four times, on a stage divided, this time, into four quarters : the upper left belongs to choleric Braus, the upper right to phlegmatic Fad, the lower left to melancholic Trüb, and the lower right quarter to sanguine Froh, each quarter-stage painted a suitably symbolic colour, and each containing some simple, but significant prop : here a mirror, for Demoiselle Froh to admire herself in; there an armchair for Father Fad's nap.

If the four families re-enact identical plots, Nestroy's wit makes the most of their temperamentally contrasting reactions. Froh's daughter enters with the words, "Na, wie g'fall ich Ihnen in dem Anzug, Papa?",[51] while the parallel scene in the Trüb family begins with the following exchange : Father Trüb : "Hat dein Schmerz heute einen besonderen Grund?"—Daughter : "Ist nicht der Schmerz der tiefste, welcher grundlos ist?"[52] Have the fathers destined their daughters for matrimony? This is how they announce the news : Trüb : "Laß heute der Freude Sonnenblick durch der Tränen Nebelschleier dringen, dir winkt ein Myrtenkranz." Fad : "Was hab ich denn sagen wollen? Ja richtig, du wirst die Tag heiraten."[53]

But Nestroy-Schlankel sets his intrigues in motion, Scholz-Hutzibutz panting behind, and Braus' friend Sturm arrives mis-

takenly in the Fads' apartment, while Froh is forced to listen to a
reading from a "Traueralbum für Schwermütige oder Sammlung
trüber Gedanken",[54] which would have been meat and drink to
Trüb. Once again it is Nestroy's stagecraft which delights : with the
ease of a juggler he manipulates his players on this fourfold stage,
sends the two comics on their peregrinations from one family to the
other, re-sorts the groupings so that suddenly all the fathers meet
in one apartment, all the sighing lovers in a second, all the
daughters in the third, and the two comics with the soubrette in
the fourth (this scene is reproduced in Basil, p. 97); and, as in *Zu
ebener Erde* ... allows the audience to relate ostensibly unconnected speeches. He was to use similar devices twice more : the two
Dramatische Zimmerherrn of his Prologue to a "Quodlibet" (the
popular device by which an actor's favourite roles were linked
together into an evening's entertainment), a tragic actor and a
comedian, rehearse their parts in the same room, and once again
their speeches form a significant commentary on each other; and
in the late play *Umsonst* (1857) Nestroy employs a vertically
divided stage. He quite evidently took pleasure in such parallelism,
which allowed him to indulge an inclination towards antithesis and
irony, and at the same time to demonstrate all the skills of his stage
technique—and never more so than in *Das Haus der Temperamente*, where an abstract idea is turned convincingly into an embodied witticism.

The following decade is perhaps the richest, most happily productive of Nestroy's writing, in spite of the added burden Carl's
acquisition of the Theater in der Leopoldstadt laid on his actors :
from the beginning of 1839 until April 1845 they were employed
at both his theatres, and there were times when Nestroy was on the
stage night after night, as well as rehearsing new parts. To this
period belong two of the comedies which show him at the height of
his powers, *Der Zerrissene* (1844), and the evergreen *Einen Jux
will er sich machen*[54] (1842).

In this comedy the "mordant cynic" of the Nestroy-legend played
"Mussi" (Monsieur) Weinberl, a gentle philosopher from behind
the counter, thoughtful yet debonair, with a ready wit, the soul of
honesty, but dreaming, for once in his life, to have one real "adventure", a *Jux*, before settling down to a hardworking partnership
with Herr Zangler, the owner of the "Gomischtwarenhandlung",
the all-purpose village-store where he works—and adventures
rain down on him and his apprentice-companion thick and fast;
impersonations, concealments, disguises, sudden flight, handsome
ladies, wicked burglars, discoveries and last-minute escapes,—until

all find themselves, breathless, united in yet another surprisingly sudden happy ending, to be mocked at by the playwright himself. The comic of situation is richly exploited; and beside the richly rounded character of Mussi Weinberl there is the Cherubino-like figure of the apprentice Christopherl (traditionally played as a *Hosenrolle* by a comedienne), the stern father, the sighing lovers, the modiste Madame Knorr, object of Herr Zangler's affections, and Frau von Fischer, "a widow", whom the imbroglio created by Mussi Weinberl leads into his own arms; and, among the sharply delineated figures on the fringes of the plot, first and foremost Scholz' odd-job-man Melchior, simple-minded but conceited, with his standing tags and his good-humoured impertinence; but there are some gems also among the tiny roles, Frau Gertrud, the house-keeper, Fräulein Blumenblatt, who so surprisingly takes pity on the eloping lovers for "der Mann, der mich liebte ... War auch für's Entfliehen eingenommen Wie Sie, nur mit dem Unterschied, daß er allein geflohen ist",[55] and even the tailor who arrives—late— with Zangler's new gala uniform.

One and all their author endows them with his own readiness of tongue and wit, in a dialogue which positively scintillates with comic invention. Brisk repartee is the order of the day : here the poor suitor pleads his cause with the father of his adored : "Meine Tante in Brüssel ist reich".—"Gratulier."—"Ich werde sie beerben." —"Aber wann?"[56] The old *Hausknecht*, Melchior's predecessor, departs, demanding his wages (and a tip): "Ich hab' heut vor vierzehn Tagen aufg'sagt..."[57] Zangler reminds him; "Übrigens irr' Er sich nicht, ich hab' Ihm aufg'sagt, nicht Er mir."—"Kann sein. Ich hab' aber z'erst durch Nachlässigkeit und Unwillen zu erkennen geb'n, daß mir der Dienst nit mehr g'fallt; daß Sie dann g'sagt hab'n, ich kann mich in vierzehn Tagen zum Teufel schern, das war nur eine natürliche Folge davon."[57] A simple pun on "schwärmen"[58] is developed to fall naturally into line with the drawing of a character : Zangler's lovelorn daughter is reported to be in the garden near the bee-hives, "Ich glaub bloß deswegen, weil die Bienen schwärmen. Soll sich ein Beispiel nehmen, das sind nur Tiere und schwärmen auf eine so nützliche Weise..."[58] The cunningly developed play on words forms the basis of a whole scene, when Weinberl and Christopherl, in constant danger of being shown up as impostors, desperately try to keep up a bold front (Act II, 7); above all it forms the slender basis on which Nestroy constructs the whole airy phantasy of Mussi Weinberl's entrance song and monologue, a brilliant play on the manifold senses of "handeln" and "Handlung".[59] " 'Ich hab' dich g'wiß',—

sagt eine Braut, Indem sie so auf'n Bräut'gam schaut, 'In zwanzig
Jahrn wie heut so gern.'—Da wird wohl auch was g'handelt
wern."[59] Thus runs the burden of the *Couplet*, and the monologue
is an extended philosophic reflection on the contrast between "der
Handelsstand" (the world of commerce) and the generality of men.
"Schaun wir auf'n Handelsstand, wie viel gibt's da Großhandlungen, und schaun wir auf die Menschheit, wie wenig große Handlungen kommen da vor . . .—Jetzt, wenn man erst die Handlungen
der Menschheit mit Gas beleuchten wollt'—ich frag', wie viele
menschliche Handlungen halten denn eine Beleuchtung aus wie
eine Handlung auf'n Stock-im-Eisen-Platz?"[60]

The part is rich in passages where the actor Nestroy could
demonstrate the remarkable agility of his tongue, as in the delightful picture he draws of a busy day with " 's ganze G'wölb voll
Leut' "[61] which he draws for Christopherl's benefit (Act I, II), ending, after the verbal description of mounting chaos has come to a
climax, with the words,—"in solchen Momenten muß der Kommis
zeigen, was ein Kommis ist . . . und mit einer ruhigen, ans Uner-
trägliche grenzenden Gelassenheit eins nach'm andern bedienen."[62]
But it is in the extended metaphorical reflections, where a character
tries to express his deepest feelings in the language of his everyday
life and trade, which comes most naturally to him, that Nestroy's
abundant comic inventiveness and wit flow most richly, as in the
moment when Weinberl opens his heart to Christopherl :

"Glauben Sie mir, junger Mann! Der Kommis hat auch
Stunden, wo er sich auf ein Zuckerfaß lehnt und in süße Träumer-
eien versinkt; da fallt es ihm dann wie ein Fünfundzwanzig-Pfund-
Gewicht aufs Herz, daß er von Jugend auf ans G'wölb gefesselt
war wie ein Blassel an die Hütten. Wenn man nur aus unkompletten
Makulaturbüchern etwas vom Weltleben weiß, wenn man den
Sonnenaufgang nur vom Bodenfenster, die Abendröte nur aus
Erzählungen der Kunderschaft kennt, da bleibt eine Leere im
Innern, die alle Ölfässer des Südens, alle Heringsfässer des Nordens
nicht ausfüllen, eine Abgeschmacktheit, die alle Muskatblüt'
Indiens nicht würzen kann."[63]

Otto Rommel says of this comedy, "Man kann sich kein köst-
licheres Fastnachtstück denken" (in the edition of 1923, p. 122).[64]
It lives on, not only in the repertories of Vienna's theatres and in
the film made of the Burgtheater's production (with Josef Meinrad
as Weinberl and Inge Konradi as Christopherl), but in Thornton
Wilder's "The Matchmaker" and in the Musical "Hello Dolly!",
in its turn based on Wilder's play.

Nestroy himself, though, turned to a new field in the brief period after the revolution of March 1848, when for a time freedom of speech was permissible on the stage : to political satire. Otto Basil tends to agree with Rommel, that, in spite of political undertones perceptible even in earlier plays, the satirist was not the man to wish to reform the world and devote himself primarily to a political aim; nevertheless, neither his avidity to avail himself of the new freedom, not the constant pressure exerted on the playwright during his most creative years in this "classic example of a police state" (A. J. P. Taylor in *The Habsburg Monarchy 1815–1918*, 1941, p. 31), should be underrated. Throughout Austria the liberalism which had dawned in the days of Joseph II was rigorously suppressed during the first half of the nineteenth century, especially during the *régime* associated with the name of Prince Metternich. An extensive system of police and informers guarded the preservation of the *status quo*, and the strictest censorship watched over those who lived by the spoken or written word. The expression of political opinion, even of the most loyal patriotic sentiments, as Grillparzer's unhappy experiences show, was strictly forbidden; but the censorship went far beyond this,—nothing could be allowed that might be interpreted as "offensive" to any existing institution, a respected trade, or least of all one of the nations so precariously held together in this vast empire; the Censor moreover watched over the preservation of morals and decency, and with his stamp of "typum non meretur" even acted as an arbiter of artistic merit. There was no appeal against his capriciousness to the letter of a law which had never been made public.

This censorship struck particularly hard at the Popular stage where not only the playwright's sallies, but an actor's improvised "extempores", or simply a comedian's gesture, a wink, or a significant stress on a word, could in a moment undo the work of the blue pencil. Nestroy had begun to suffer from the attentions of the police as soon as he established himself as a comic actor; his engagement at Brünn, as we have seen, was forcibly brought to a close for such persistent "extemporising", a habit of which his quick wit and ready tongue could not easily rid themselves. After he had reached Vienna, his career was punctuated by admonitions and fines, and during the run of *Zu ebener Erde* ..., while the critics were acclaiming the serious *Volksdichter*, he had to undergo five days' imprisonment for various "offences",—an imprisonment which he seems to have borne with his customary god humour, as witness a letter dated from "Zwing-Uri" in which he describes how "Nur selten bringt das sanfte Himmelblau eines bedienenden Polizeimannes eine Abwechslung in das einförmige Weiß meines Turmgemaches".[65] He continues, an offending critic in mind, "Wie mir in müßigen Stunden mancherlei treffende Gedanken kommen, so ist mir eine ganz originelle Art von Ohrfeigen eingefallen . . ."[65]

Yet the mere existence of this official pressure was a constant factor at the back of his work; his manuscripts show the meticulous pre-censorship he applied to the ideas which flowed so freely from his imagination. If nothing reported from Nestroy's lips quite matches the horror of Grillparzer's "Die Zensur hat mich umgebracht" (in Beethoven's conversation notebook of 10. iv. 1826),[66] his biting description of the Censor as this "Mensch gewordenen Bleistift, diesem Krokodil, das an den Ufern des Ideenstromes lagert und den darin schwimmenden Literaten die Köpf abbeißt"[67] seems to come from the heart. It appears in *Freiheit in Krähwinkel*[68] (1848), one of the three political satires he wrote during the months following the revolution which drove Metternich into exile and brought a young Emperor to the throne.

In this play, which re-enacts, in miniature form, all the stirring events of the Vienna March days in the Krähwinkel, which had, since Kotzebue, served as the background to many a burlesque farce, he wrote for himself one of his gayest parts, the revolutionary journalist Eberhard Ultra, successful leader of a bloodless revolution, successful wooer of spirited Frau von Frankenfrey, a bold fighter for freedom and progress—however neatly the satirist pins down the Viennese *Bürger* complaining, when the forces of reaction catch up with him, "und wenn ich noch was getan hätt', aber gar nix als zug'schaut bei der Revolution . . ."[69] In *Lady und Schneider* of the following year the satirist, impartially distributing his blows to right and left, wherever folly seems to rear its head, appears firmly on the side of property : "Ah, wenn d'Freiheit Kommunismus wird, nein, Da hört es auf, ein Vergnügen zu sein."[70] Yet *Der alte Mann mit der jungen Frau,* written the same year but unperformable in the playwright's lifetime, combines with a serious treatment of the problem indicated in the title, the story of a man rescued from political persecution. With *Der Unbedeutende* (1846), *Der Schützling* (1847) and *Kampl* (1852) it forms a small group of plays which indicate that, more than ten years after *Zu ebener Erde . . .*, an older Nestroy does indeed approach a *Volksstück* which throws a more serious light on social and political evils than the familiar satire or manners and modes.

Grillparzer once called the productions of the Viennese Popular Stage "dramatische Konzertstücke, die, bei schwacher Versinnlichung von Seite des Verfassers, dem Schauspieler Gelegenheit bieten, in der Entwicklung seines eigenen Talentes Halt und Verbindung zu suchen und zu finden."[71] Nestroy's comedies, as we have seen, are fully scored, evidence, not of "schwacher Versinnlichung", but on the contrary, of the most vivid comic and dramatic imagination. To this, his honoured place in the repertory of the Vienna theatres, as well as the serious critical attention paid to his writings, beginning with the appearance of the first collected edition in 1890–91, bear ample testimony. The common reader may wish to agree with the conclusion of Alfred Polgar's essay on Nestroy that "Nestroy's Dichtung ist das schönste Monument, das je dem Mutterwitz eines Volkes errichtet wurde."[72]

TRANSLATIONS

1. Saturday, August 24, 1822. At the Imperial and Royal Court Theatre at the Kärntner Gate. The Magic Flute. Grand Opera in two Acts, by Emanuel Schikaneder. Music by W. A. Mozart . . . Herr Nestroy will make his theatrical debut in the role of Sarastro and recommends himself to the favour of a generous public.

2. Crass egoism in leave with the coarsest sensuality.

3. Capua of the spirit.

4. Rakes.

5. Makes immense fouettés.

6. I could parade my amours for you by the battalion.

7. The poorly rewarded lover of many women.

8. An unrequited passion.

9. Strong, healthy men have been struck down by this, what can I expect, after so many years in the rag-market.

10. That is classic. How very fortunate for Your Honour to have my assistance.

11. He is like the daily bread, one never gets tired of him.

12. Plays of chivalry and ghosts.

13. Lumpazivagabundus or The Three Rakes.

14. Ruler of gay poverty, guiding spirit of gamblers, protector of drinkers.

15. A hundred thousand thalers! That would buy over a million quarts of ale.

16. Get out, or I'll let you have it with a smoothing-iron.

17. The world (or, depending on the stress, *this* world) is not going to last much longer.

18. Well, well, so it has happened again? What a number of uncles and aunts have to die each year, only to make everything end happily—

19. Critique or parody of the tragedies usually very ill performed by many German companies.

20. Only evil!

21. The soul of Judaism.

22. But will they remain outside? No, they will force their way in.

23. Joab, in what terrible times you have come! Horrors of destruction in Israel, tremors in the commercial world, the strongest houses are collapsing!

24. (Pun on *Zins*: tribute/rent.) They all have to pay him *Zins*, the Kings of the World.—Why *Zins*? Is he the landlord?

25. Quick march!—Where to?... Atten'shun!—I wonder what for? ... Eyes left!—Why?

26. His subjects always inclined towards the monstrous, which carries everything to an extreme.

27. He is the terror, terror, terror of his enemies.

28. I was told by his chamberlain that he got out of bed on his left foot (i.e. "on the wrong side"). On such days his right hand is much to be feared.

29. Tremble! I am a most curious being.

30. Therein lies the art; to be inscrutable.

31. My greatest joy is that I do not know whence I came.

32. A man brings it to you, who needn't have troubled.

33. Kill Holofernes ... I could almost let myself be persuaded to do it, if I were not who I am.

34. I believe the worst of every man, including myself, and I have seldom been mistaken.

35. A connoisseur will surely give a million ordinary iambics for one sole witticism by Nestroy.

36. Ground floor and first floor.

37. The cattle-dealer from Upper Austria; Wastl from the Tyrol.

38. It has happened again.

39. There are bakers,—and bakers, there are butchers,—and butchers, but the gulf that exists between one old clothes-man and another is unfathomable.

40. "Abelard and Heloise" is lying on the shelf behind the stove.

41. Systematic Introduction to the Science of Rags and Tatters.

42. Destined by Fate to be the most despicable specimen of the lowliest species.

43. Brisk Viennese girl.

44. Has no one forgotten anything?—No, we have got the most essential things.

45. Howabout it, then? When shall we get our money back?—Quick, hurry, get busy. We shall make money out of this dinner. ... You owe me five Gulden thirty Kreuzer!—Today the stable must groan under all the food.

46. I shall lose my Dame of Hearts.—Hearts are trumps.

47. Now my Adolf will read it.

48. Didactic tendency.

49. Dramatic painting.

50. The House of the Temperaments.

51. Well, how do you like me in this dress, Papa?

52. Is there a particular reason for your grief today? Does not that grief go deepest, which *has* no reason?

53. Let the sunray of joy pierce the mist of tears today, a crown of myrtle shall be thine.—What was I going to say? Oh yes, you'll be getting married one of these days.

54. Mourning Album for the Melancholy, or A Collection of Sad Thoughts.

55. The man who loved me ... was all for stealing away and eloping, too, the only difference was, he stole away alone.

56. My aunt in Brussels is rich.—Congratulations.—I shall inherit her fortune.—When?

57. I gave notice a fortnight ago.—By the way, don't make a mistake, it was I who gave notice, not you.—Maybe. But I first showed by negligence and laziness that I did not like my service here any more; that you then said, I can go to the devil in a fortnight's time, was only the natural consequence of my action.

58. (*schwärmen*: to be love-sick/to swarm.) I think it is only because the bees *schwärmen*. She ought to follow their example, they are only insects and *schwärmen* in such a useful manner.

59. (*handeln:* to trade/bargain/act; *Handlung:* shop/action.) I am sure, says the bride, looking at her bridegroom like this, I shall love you just as much twenty years hence.—Well, she won't necessarily stick to that figure.

60. If we look at the commercial world, how many *Großhandlungen* (wholesalers) there are, and if we look at Humanity, how few *große Handlungen* (great actions) do we see ... And if one were to light up the *Handlungen* of men with gas,—I ask you, how many human *Handlungen* (actions) would stand the brilliant light of a *Handlung* (shop) on the Stock-im-Eisen square?

61. The whole (basement) shop full of people.

62. At such moments the salesman must show the very essence of salesmanship ... and with a calm bordering on the unbearable serve each customer in turn.

63. Believe me, young man! The salesman, too, has his moments, when he leans against a sugar barrel and loses himself in sweet dreams; then he feels crushed as by a twenty-five pound weight, at the thought that from his youth he has been chained to the shop like a watchdog to his hut. If one only knows the world from half-torn papers used for wrapping, if one knows the sunrise only through an attic window, the glow of the evening sky only through what the customers tell one, there remains an emptiness in one's heart, which all the oil-barrels of the South, all the herring-barrels of the North cannot fill, a dullness of taste, which no muscatel from India can spice.

64. It is impossible to think of a gayer carnival play.

65. Only rarely does the gentle azure of a policeman on duty bring some colour into the monotonous white of my dungeon.—As in hours of leisure I often have good ideas, I have just thought of a most original type of box on the ear.

66. The Censorship has killed me.
67. This pencil turned into a man, this crocodile which lies in wait on the banks of the River of Ideas and bites off the heads of the authors who swim in it.
68. Freedom in Krähwinkel.
69. As though I had *done* something, but I only stood and watched this revolution.
70. No, when Freedom turns to Communism, That's the end of all pleasure in it.
71. Dramatic concertos, which, only sketched in outline by the author, give the actor an opportunity to seek, and find, a handhold and a connecting link for the development of his own talent.
72. Nestroy's writings are the finest monument ever put up to a people's natural mother-wit. (Alfred Polgar; Auswahlband, Berlin 1930, p. 176 ff.)

BIBLIOGRAPHY
Works
Sämtliche Werke. Historisch-kritische Gesamtausgabe, hg. von Fritz Brukner und Otto Rommel, Wien, 1923–1930, 15 vols. Vol. 15 contains O. Rommel's monograph *"Johann Nestroy. Ein Beitrag zur Geschichte der Wiener Volkskomik"*.
Gesammelte Werke. Hg. von Otto Rommel, Wien, 1948/9, 6 vols. Photostatic reproduction, Wien, 1962. (Revised selection, based on *Sämtliche Werke*.)

Letters
Johann Nestroys gesammelte Briefe (*1831–1862*). *Nestroy und seine Bühne im Jahre 1848*. Hg. von Fritz Brukner, Wien, 1938.

Biographical and critical literature
Basil, Otto, *Johann Nestroy in Selbstzeugnissen und Bilddokumenten*. Reinbek bei Hamburg, 1967. (Rowohlts Monographien Nr. 132.)
Forst de Battaglia, Otto, *Johann Nestroy*, Leipzig, 1932; Rev. edition München, 1962.
Hillach, A., *Die Dramatisierung des komischen Dialogs. Figur und Rolle bei Nestroy*, München, 1967.
Kraus, Karl, *Nestroy und die Nachwelt*, in: *Die Fackel*, Wien, 1912.
Rommel, Otto, *Johann Nestroy*, in vol. 15 of *Sämtliche Werke*, Wien, 1930.

English adaptation and translations
The Matchmaker. (Based on *Einen Jux will er sich machen*.) By Thornton Wilder, in: *Three Plays*, New York, 1957.
A Man full of Nothing (*Der Zerrissene*).—*The Talisman.—Love Affairs and Wedding Bells* (*Liebesgeschichten und Heiratssachen*), translated by Max Knight and Joseph Fabry, New York, 1967.

Carl Spitteler

Carl Spitteler

by WERNER GÜNTHER

Carl Spitteler was born in Liestal, near Basle, on April 24, 1845. His father, who had played an active role in the *Sonderbundskrieg*, was a high official in both cantonal and federal circles. The boy began his education in schools at Liestal and Berne, before moving to the "literary-humanist" *Obergymnasium* in Basle, where he studied under both W. Wackernagel and Jacob Burckhardt. He later read law and theology at the Universities of Basle, Zurich and Heidelberg, and after overcoming considerable difficulties, was ordained—without, however, taking up office as a priest. From 1871 to 1879 he worked as a private tutor in Russia. Then, on his return to Switzerland, he took up a position in a girls' school in Berne, as a teacher of history. He completed *Prometheus and Epimetheus* in 1880, but when this achieved no recognition, he was compelled to go on teaching, this time at the *Progymnasium* in Neuveville, where he remained for four years. Here he married a Dutch girl, Maria Op den Hooff.

He spent several years after this in journalism, with the *Grenzpost* in Basle, as well as with the *Thurgauer Zeitung and the Basler Nachrichten,* and from 1890–92 acted as editor of the *Neue Zürcher Zeitung.* This period also saw the birth of *Literarische Gleichnisse.*

The death of his wife's parents brought financial independence, and Spitteler moved with her and their two daughters to Lucerne, in order to devote himself completely to literature. It was by the Lake of Lucerne that *Olympischer Frühling* and *Prometheus der Dulder* were created. In December 1914, the author delivered in Zurich a lecture entitled "Our Swiss Standpoint", which brought him a great deal of criticism and hostility from Germany. In 1919, mainly through the special intercession of Romain Rolland, Spitteler was awarded the Nobel Prize. He died in Lucerne on December 29, 1924, a few months before his eightieth birthday.

O NE can distinguish four stages in the development of Carl Spitteler's reputation as an artist. The first runs from *Prometheus und Epimetheus* to *Olympischer Frühling,* i.e. approximately between 1880 and 1905. During this period he received little or no response from critics. The second (roughly 1905–20) is one of growing fame. It began with the clarion call of the musician and conductor Felix Weingartner, in *Carl Spitteler,*

Ein künstlerisches Erlebnis (1904), and was crowned with the award of the Nobel Prize, in 1919, together with a number of introductory and analytical studies of his work. The third period embraces two decades, beginning shortly before the death of the poet, and is characterised chiefly by some extremely sharp criticism. The final period, which brings us up to the present day, is one of a certain degree of alienation from Spitteler—a respectful but, one feels, almost ceremonial silence surrounds his name, tending here and there towards embarrassment, and even the celebration of his centenary (1945) failed to mitigate the situation. Is this the temporary obscurity into which the names of so many great authors fall immediately after their deaths, and from which they eventually arise in a stronger light? It is difficult to be a prophet here, but it does seem doubtful that critics will ever come to full agreement about the greatness of Spitteler.

For what is questioned is not, as it once was with Gotthelf, the outer form, but rather the innermost nature of the work, the genuineness of his creative personality. The critical attacks which hit deepest are those directed not only against this or that idiosyncrasy which may give offence, but against the very essence of his art. Has Spitteler's poetry a foundation of artistic maturity and integrity? That is the question; and the difference between the critics who affirm this and others who concur only with strongest reservations seem to indicate that any overall agreement is far away. Spitteler himself knew that he would never be widely read. His main creations are mythical or mythically adorned epics, and the epic is no longer fashionable—at least not in the garish compounds of myth and realism, phantasy and pessimism which Spitteler evolved. Thus the problem remains one for a small number of initiates and for those with a critical interest.

Fundamentally, the question of the origin of his poetry revolves around the essentially lyrical nature of his creativeness : lyrical, that is, in the modern aesthetic sense, applied to the unconscious, emotional sources of art. Writers of epics and dramatists must also be lyrical in this sense if they wish to be truly poetic, as Spitteler himself recognised :

"In every poet there hides, by definition, a lyricist, as there is in the dramatist and in the author of epics".[1]

Even his most unwavering supporters and apostles admit that Spitteler was not a born lyricist. He called himself a "geborener Epiker", an epic writer of cosmic, mythological and symbolic poetry. By "forfeiting lyricism", he claimed, possibly hoping thereby to blunt any future criticism, one can achieve "epic greatness". He described his own ballads, thus censuring them too strongly, as "Formgymnastik", or "early drafts for a projected future epic"; even his *Schmetterlinge* he defined as "optimistic lyricism" rather than *Gefühlslyrik*; and elsewhere he insists, "My verse does not set out to be musical" for the reason that his soul itself is steeped in music—"My soul was and is my lyricism".[2] He even speaks of a "contempt for language" :

"Language has no naturalness, it is an artificial and quite loathsome means of conveying poetic images."[3]

These and other of his pronouncements are not always, of course, to be taken literally. Yet one thing remains certain : we will find not lyrical outpourings in Spitteler's work. The question is, does he possess instead lyricism in its broader sense : that lyricism of the epic, sublime, brimming over with the fullness of man? He attributes to himself two qualities : first, the fundamentally epic predisposition—joy in the outward splendour of life, taste for adventure, a strong belief in the richness and variety of events, the vast possibilities of the world; and secondly, in contrast, the need for something more ethereal, the reluctance to be limited to and to draw his poetry from normal routine existence. Unlike Mörike, whom, significantly, he here quotes, he longs to build "a higher, broader arch, up and away from the real".[4] His wish is not to indulge in "analysis of the soul", in the manner of the novelist ("The novelist is no epic poet, he is the opposite"), but to escape "nach oben", "far above the surface of the earth into unrestricted heights", where one can treat Gods with "Übermut"—bravado—and even with a touch of irony.[5] It is on the basis of these two elements that critics have propounded Spitteler's greatness : he has been called a realistic poet and a visionary. But the big question remains—whether these two factors alone can produce a great poet, without that "little invisible and indefinable something" which "gives a work of art eternal salvation".[6] This "something" is precisely that hidden nucleus of lyricism of which we spoke, which nourishes all art and without which true art cannot subsist.

Could the absence of this in Spitteler perhaps be connected with the undeniable role of the will in his work, to which he himself admits, and even deliberately stresses? In a sort of "fever of the will" he took, as a young man, the "Entschluss zur Poesie", the conscious decision to be a poet, after renouncing what appear to have been his natural talents, music and painting. True, he speaks of "visitations" in the form of poetic images, which does assume an unconscious, intuitive process of creation, and it would be an error to discount this. Yet at the same time, one senses clearly the part played by the will, which frequently gives to his poetry an air of unnaturalness and strain, extending even to a sort of violence against both subject-matter and language. The fact is, poetry only rarely allows itself to be dictated to : that being when the intuitive faculty is firmly at the artist's command. For intellectuality, artistry and personal elements tend to appear at times when intuition falters. In Spitteler's case, this is undoubtedly the cause of the overemphasis on autobiography in certain passages, and of their excessively hard realism, just as it is the source of the allegories, the exaggerated personification and the violence of the language.

Spitteler's *Weltanschauung* presents us with huge difficulties. It was against Spitteler the philosopher and not the artist that Edith Landmann, a protagonist of Stefan George, directed her attack, still during the poet's lifetime. "It is absurd for a poet to give himself over to Ananke"[7] was the centre of her criticism. And in truth, despite his joy in the richness of life, despite his epic "Übermut", Spitteler's work conceals an abyss of pessimism. In his view, the tragedian may look up from his individual calamity into a moral world-order, but the epic poet looks down, through the sunshine of the outer world, into hollow darkness.[8] Such pessimism, of course, was rife at the time. Like Nietzsche, like Jacob Burckhardt, Spitteler had been weaned on the thoughts of Schopenhauer, and had reached the position of the convinced non-Christian, denying the world and scorning mankind. For all Christian beliefs about the next world, as well as for all "philosophical sleight-of-hand", he had nothing but angry contempt. His symbol for the cruel meaninglessness of the world is the unfeeling automaton, behind whom and in whom, in *Olympischer Frühling*, Ananke, "der gezwungene Zwang",[9] lies concealed.

As an antidote to this basic meaninglessness, Spitteler emphasises the sublime resignation of great men (Prometheus, Hercules), while showing pity for suffering and, above all, maintaining his faith in beauty, art and imagination. This belief in beauty amidst the decay of moral order puts him somewhat in line with the "Absolute" poets of his time, who, lacking a faith, and yet thirsting for one, clung to their own creative forces, and, like the young Nietzsche, found justification for the world only as an aesthetic phenomenon. Yet none of them had gone as far as Spitteler, who removed the soul from the Universe, reducing it to a gigantic laboratory of physics and chemistry, the "Weltenmühle".[10]

Of course, a pessimistic *Weltanschauung* does not necessarily have to be anti-aesthetic. It becomes so only when it puts a curse, as it were, upon the creative impulse, and distorts the artist's perception of true human values. This is what happened to Spitteler. Admittedly, Edith Landmann did not see it in this way, for she praised him as an artist while referring to his work as "a monument to the hopelessness of mankind". However, strictly speaking, the hopelessness of man is also the hopelessness of the artist, and Spitteler was severely handicapped by his view of the world : not only did it prevent him from considering and portraying sympathetically such important character-types as the mother-figure or the saint, but, moreover, it not infrequently distorted his concept of the complete human being, thereby depriving his work of any true "heroes". We may cite Gottfried Keller's judgement of Spitteler :

"If only the poor man would use his talent and his strong imagination to create some really human poetry, he would be one of the best."

Again, in a letter to C. F. Meyer, Keller sums up his opinion in the brief but telling phrase : "he is embarrassed by the simple and the human".

Spitteler did not regard man and his soul with much seriousness, but, in fact, only what Goethe called "heiliger Ernst" can raise life on to the eternal plane. Certainly, Spitteler had a powerful imagination at his command, but it was from this, his most valuable asset, that he removed the driving force—the belief in the dignity of man. If he possessed basic insights of great worth, but failed to fill this framework with living poetry, it was due to deficiencies in his intuitive faculty, and hence in the source from which this is fed—that is, the quality of humanity. In Spitteler, both these qualities lacked a firm root, and were therefore too weak to combine effectively in order to resist non-artistic forces. Both as man and as poet he was a creature of contradiction. His greatness lies in the amount he managed to squeeze out of this rather barren nature.

The most perfectly tuned strings of his lyre were, obviously, those where the least room was given to any anti-artistic strains. Generally speaking, we can distinguish three factors which helped in this. First, his work is capable of achieving an enchanting purity whenever the cosmic vibrations in his soul produce images which stem from a genuinely serious conception of human life, and whenever human forces are facing one another with defiance or serenity, notwithstanding the tragic surroundings in which they may exist.

In a second way, purity is often attained through Spitteler's child-like nature. "Il y a un mot qui vous expliquera tout en moi, ni grand homée, ni homme célèbre, ni poète, ni citoyen. ni rien— seulement... un enfant." Indeed, perhaps no word can get nearer to the true Spitteler, and if this is remembered, much of his work becomes clearer. Even in his poetry, he often plays like a child, and yet the cosmic visionary and the child form complementary opposites, acting and reacting together, witnesses to the breadth of his nature.

The third realm in which Spitteler is at home is that of the sophisticate, the man-of-the-world. Although he strikes a discordant note in his rather limited, puppet-like portrayal of the lower classes (e.g. in *Conrad der Leutnant*), on the other hand he finds precisely the right tone when describing the atmosphere of a court, as for instance the ultra-refinement of Versailles in *Der Neffe des Herren Bezenval*. It was no accidental that he found such brilliant words to write of the French classical era. The aristocratic manners which he acquired in Russia suited his temperament perfectly, endowed as he was with wit, elegance and natural self-assurance.

It is an idle question to ask whether Spitteler wrote better poetry in his introvert or his extrovert vein. The true poet, as he creates, must always be introspective, for at that time he is inhabiting an imagined world, belonging only to himself; according to the degree in which he can adapt this world to normal reality, he may become more outward-looking. Even as a "realist", Spitteler remained an introvert.

A far more important question than this for the critic is that of the choice of theme. Spitteler gained much by restricting the number of subjects he treated to a minimum, and one cannot reproach him at all for this. Richness of artistic imagination, so Jacob Burckhardt had taught him, shows itself not in the number of themes one can invent, but in the mastery of one important motif, treated in various different ways. His Promethean epics, *Imago, Gustav, Der Neffe des Herrn Bezenval, Conrad der Leutnant*, all pertain to the theme of greatness, or the recognition of greatness. It is also touched upon in *Mädchenfeinde*, as well as in several scenes of *Olympischer Frühling*. Greatness, in his view (and not only artistic greatness) entails the renunciation of happiness, especially of happiness through love, and is bought at a terrible price. This theme, which had occupied the Romantics, had been clearly formulated by Schopenhauer, and subsequently appeared in many forms. It is certainly the stuff of tragedy, and has enormous artistic potential, but it is still nevertheless doubtful whether Spitteler did the right thing in devoting so much of himself to it. For quite clearly, in his case, the theme stems far less from the joy and suffering of a warm human heart than from the defiance and self-assurance of his own ego. With so much preoccupation with the self, the danger was that he could easily slip into a consciously intellectual or over-personal art-form. This is the case with, for instance, the novel *Imago*, where Spitteler definitely succumbs to the temptations of writing biography. His treatment of human experience is most effective and memorable in those works where he clothes it in mythology (e.g. *Prometheus*) or else sets it in an idyllic, if rather bitter atmosphere (as in *Gustav* or *Mädchenfeinde*).

Spitteler's genuine pathos reveals itself most clearly in *Prometheus und Epimetheus* (1880). It is easy to list the faults of this early poem : its imbalance, the decline of artistic standards in the second half, the lack of inner motivation in certain episodes, imprecision in the drawing of Prometheus' character, the rational element : above all, the allegories, the excessive length of the work and the monotonous iambic metre, maintained with iron discipline, to the point where it obstructs the search for fresh imagery. It is much more difficult to say why, despite all its faults, the book remains a work of art (if not an "eternal" work as Romain Rolland claims).

"Und sprach ein Lied mit dunkler, weichumhüllter Stimme",[11] says the poet and minstrel in the castle of King Epimetheus. Like the audience there, we are gripped by Spitteler's "Lied" and we, too, see "auf dem dunklen Grunde heller leuchten all die lebensvollen Bilder".[12] If we are to understand logically why we are so moved, we must first of all appreciate the powerful harmony between the mythical atmosphere and the poetic expression : in other words, the artistic unity of the work. This is particularly true of the first half, where there issues, from a huge reservoir, a flood of vision which cannot be denied expression. There are lapses and errors, because the intuitive source lacks balance and consistency, but usually the right tone is found, in tune at the deepest level with both theme and mood.

A second reason for our involvement is the profound belief in the soul which pervades the work. It is not simply the fact that he altered the character of Prometheus which is important—that is the prerogative of any poet—but that he gave him such primitive majesty, such austerity and solid faith in himself. It is the contrast between the basically sombre, almost dull, mood of the poem, and the shining strength of this conviction which gives the book its strange attraction. When we remember this, the criticism that the personality of Prometheus is too vague becomes less important. He

lives by his faith in his own soul, upright and blameless, hard with
himself, but mild with his brother; the tension of his love for the
Goddess of his soul pulsates through the work, bringing it alive even
during the long scene in the wilderness, where Prometheus under-
goes tough physical labour and guards his master's flocks.

These two factors, the basic atmosphere and the faithfulness to
an idea, form the cross-threads of the poetic fabric; and at certain
points, the whole lights up, as if it were prose suddenly becoming
poetry—for example, in the famous scene where Prometheus meets
his Goddess at the top of the mountain, and offers himself to her.
Another scene which is rightly well known is the description of
Pandora's descent to earth : she imagines herself as a mortal woman,
"enduring in her dreams human desires and human suffering", sees
herself in the role of a wife at the side of a loving man, happily
undergoing need, worry, fatigue and illness, and comes to regard
the misery and death of mankind as less bitter than her "desolate
existence, removed from the world and all its pains".

Or again, consider King Epimetheus' conversation with his friend
before the marble statue representing a man leaning on his club
and staring enraptured at the little box he is holding aloft in his
right hand. The irony is that King Epimetheus himself will not
recognise Pandora's box when the peasants bring it to him a little
later. Or, finally, there is the moving scene when, after Epimetheus
and the Behemoth, to cheers from the crowd, have exchanged their
coats as a sign of friendship, the poet suddenly lifts the veil from
the enormous graveyard, ruled by "Proserpina with the soulful
eyes". Here, merciful sisters comfort the souls of the dead, still
trembling from "the dreadful illness of being", and now descending
to the realm of Proserpina while, in Adam's dark cave, the father
of all men and his son Atlas sit, spurning sleep and peace, formula-
ting plans to improve the lot of mankind. They will not listen to
the Goddess, who tells them to rest, for there is no cure for the
world, the taste of the earth's crust is bitter . . . Then from the land
of men they hear a great shout of jubilation. What, has a saviour
been born? Has God taken pity upon his world? The father sends
his son to discover the truth, but when Atlas reappears, he spits
contemptuously upon the floor. What was the cause of the jubilation? "One man has swopped his smock with another !" Thereupon
Adam tears his plans and his books page from page, saying to his
son : " 'True enough, why should we sow? All we shall reap here is
shame, if we spend ourselves any more upon these creatures.' Thus
he spake and they departed in peace to their eternal home."

To sum up Spitteler's first work, one is tempted to employ the words spoken by Pandora when she meets a shepherd boy, who is painting on a canvas the fields, mountains and woods, the clouds and the birds :

"And all drawn with few strokes, somewhat childish and groping, with no certainty; here and there an object changed its form, bushes and hedges becoming lambs; but always there reigned an inward strength, and soul led the gentle lines from the dark foreground with its rough shadows towards the distant, fragrant, hazy land. . . ."

Written in his old age (in 1924), *Prometheus der Dulder*, by his own admission a "second book on the same theme", has only the dark and bitter shadows of the foreground, but lacks the "distant, fragrant, hazy land" behind. The earlier work is more appropriate to its theme, and therefore more solid. One may perhaps describe the change as the move from "poet" to "artist", but in doing so, the usual connotations of value judgement must be removed from these terms. For in this case, in calling him an "artist" we mean that the original creative or "poetic" impulse (which is more or less unconscious, and automatically finds the right verbal expression for its message) has yielded to a *conscious* application of artistic methods : in other words, as the intuitive power decreases, the so-called outer form assumes more importance. In a perfect work of art, the distinction is removed and "artist" and "poet" become one, although one can still—e.g. with Gotthelf—sometimes accuse the poet of "artistic" errors. Naturally, there are almost as many transgressions as there are works of art, for the perfectly blended work is an extreme rarity. In Spitteler's *Dulder*, the effect of the more intellectual approach is felt in three fields : the versification, the "realistic" style, and the overall structure.

In the first *Prometheus*, the hero, escaping from the noisy feast, seems almost lost in the "secret" which drifts up out of the valleys; hour after hour he strides up and down, till the snow buries the land under a soft white carpet and the forest looms black and white under the stars. He is trembling with expectation, listening, peering, staring at the entrance to the forest. When the austere woman suddenly appears, the scene continues in silence. Yet underneath, life is bubbling through its veins.

In the second *Prometheus*, the defiance and restlessness of the hero—who takes a much more active, central role—are depicted in a more plausible fashion. However, it often happens that, to achieve this, too many words are required, and what he says does not make the scene any more impressive; the Goddess, too, loses much of the bewitching power of her beauty, by talking too hastily and too long, and the lines which describe her entry are too round-about and vague, hindered by the demands of rhyme. The magic has gone.

However, in *Dulder*, too, there are many moments of individual beauty. The quest for a wider symbolism certainly bears much fruit, especially in the various secondary motifs which have been well chosen and delightfully executed; we can point, for instance, to the seductive fan which the Angel of God played with, as if casually, as he asks Prometheus a second time to renounce his soul; or the "bird of doom", who glides like a ghost from the forest as the Goddess Soul hurls her curse upon the Angel, on his kingdom, Epimetheus and the whole cowardly race of man; or, finally, there is the Goddess's vision of the future : "I hear the river of life, gush-ing through the caverns...", etc., to which Prometheus, slurring his words like a drunkard, gives not only the reply to which the Goddess counsels him : "Ich !", but the committed "Ich Alle !"

What we have said so far offers enough pointers as to how *Olympischer Frühling* should be judged. Here Spitteler, following all kinds of "experimental works" and practice "on the silent piano", attempted to bridge the gulf between mythology and sym-bolism on the one hand and realistic poetry on the other. He was trying to fill a cosmic vision with human colour and life. The undertaking required great caution, to say the least, and the result was bound to contain weaknesses. The reasons for this are easily enumerated : first, because Spitteler was tempted to confuse the epic element with mere adventure stories; secondly, because the deeper human insights were too readily lost sight of, obscured by the bitterness of the poet's general outlook; and thirdly, because, in any case, the work could never really hold together, the "realistic" element being conceived far too much in terms of the external, thus robbing the world of the Gods of a large part of its mythical flavour. Even apart from all this, there is still another problem inherent in the basic idea : how could he produce a satisfactory end-ing, after all the high-spirited wedding celebrations of the new set of Gods? We know how uncomfortable the poet felt about this problem. In the final version of 1910, he split the ending into two sections, "Ende und Wende", originally the last quarter of the first version, becoming "Der hohen Zeit Ende" and "Zeus"; but the division is purely superficial.

Yet how should he finish off the work? With the fall of the Gods at the end of the modern era? That would require a much longer epic—and where would he find the material for it? Spitteler had long before cut himself off from the greatest source of fresh (and real!) experience : the world of man is forbidden to the Gods. Although there was nowhere else to find the material he required for effective poetic conflicts, it would have gone against his basic premises to come too close to the human sphere. "Des Lebens Zweck ist Schmutz" patters the rain, in his Dionysus-song, "im Stein ist Wahrheit";[13] and on the Morgenberg it brings to the Gods the terrible message : "Kein Raum von Ewigkeit, den nicht der Jammer füllte".[14] Zeus himself learns to his cost what it is to become involved with the "human breed", and henceforth his wish is to suffocate the entire human "horde" in a gigantic cloak and to set a hound upon the lord of the earth! We are left wondering, then, what good Hercules, the "complete human being", can do as he strides towards earth.

Spitteler, sensibly enough, restricted himself to showing us only the Olympic "spring". What might happen in the "summer" and the "autumn" we cannot tell—nor, perhaps, could the author. After the exciting high nuptials, is what follows simply a sort of Olympic banality, no longer worth recording? The theme, which has begun splendidly enough, tails off into nothing. The "basic impulse" of *Olympischer Frühling*, the "need for unlimited elbow-room for the creative imagination" carried in it the seeds of its own destruction. When, towards the middle of the work, the "hohe Zeit", the huge "spring feast of the earth", begins, the ground suddenly falls away from under the poet's feet. What for Spitteler was the central core—the string of colourful adventures—appears to the sensitive reader as no more than richly imaginative ornamentation, while the part which for us has the most artistic weight—i.e. the opening poems *Auffahrt* and *Hera die Braut*—was almost, so the poet tells us, absent-mindedly omitted, at a time when he was without the advice of his friend Jonas Fränkel.

What raises *Die Auffahrt* to such poetic heights can be summed up in three main principles. For one thing, the theme of the ascent of the Gods, from Erebos, up the "Morgenberg", to Mount Olympus, with their detour through Heaven, springs from a blissful vision : there is a flavour of pure art about this journey. Then again, the scenery here is still clearly described and easily imagined : mostly an Alpine landscape seen through fresh eyes. And finally, most important : while the Gods are generally unnamed, we can conceive of them as one unit, and their opponents likewise. Because of this, Spitteler's poetic vision is able to emerge at full strength, not yet diverted or disturbed by other conflicting forces. Is it not remarkable that out of almost a thousand crudities of language in

Olympischer Frühling, an exceedingly small number fall in the first half? For here the poet, much more than the artist, was at work.

Structurally the most powerful scene in the whole book, and one to which the three principles mentioned also apply, is, unquestionably, the confrontation between the old and the new Gods. The latter have already seen Hades, which they passed by on their climb. And with horror they recognise the "scheussliche Lawinenbett"[15] which is made even more ghostly by the white bones, the overhanging medlar-trees, and the deep silence broken only by the trickling of water. As they rest by the fountain, they find, carved in wood, the names of the earlier Gods who had also passed by long ago. They too, engrave their names. . . . Climbing further, during which time an argument over who is to be their king reveals jealousies and hate, they come upon flagstones which have been worn smooth by the steps of Gods, walking this way since time immemorial. "Wie ist die Welt vom Alten", sighs a voice, "Für welchen Jammer hat sie Raum bereits enthalten".[16] Like an echo, booming from the chasm, come the words "Kein Raum von Ewigkeit, den nicht der Jammer füllte",[17] and suddenly the old Gods come rushing towards them. The two groups speak together. The older Gods are envious; once more they climb up and down the "golden ladder of memories"; alternately silent and weeping bitterly, they hand each other the "giant miracle flowers" of memory, while in their tears is reflected the shining Olympus. The new Gods make their reply : we lay groaning in the prison of night while you enjoyed sunshine, pleasures and light; "uns aber schwingt Anankes Schaufel heut nach oben".[18]

Then, like a ghost, Orpheus the seer appears, and all stand back to give him space. His eyes are fixed and glazed, he gazes into the very core of the world, into the heart of eternity. How the world was created, whence evil came, he does not know . . . "I was there, and no more". Shattered, the new Gods stare after the exhausted prophet as he leaves, "ein Unheil ahnend, das die Schwingen weiter spannt".[19] Thereupon, Prometheus appears, pride in his face. Lamentation is not worthy of immortal Gods, he says. Man's body rots away from his soul, his mind and body are destroyed by death, but Fate attacks the Gods only outwardly. "Value, pride, self-assurance, these dwell inside me." He does not drink from the treacherous fountain, thus avoiding the trap of anger. He moves on "as if his path were concern of Fate, not his own".

Kronos, the king, arrives, seated on a charger, his sword hanging from the pommel of his saddle. He shakes his defiant lion's head, and seeing the group of new Gods, flies into a rage. So, any young upstart can aspire to his heritage! ... "I know I have not been conquered. Only treachery has brought me low." (This is the treachery of his daughter Hera.) He turns about, whipping on his army in an attempt to retake Olympus by storm. But the earth trembles, an avalanche sweeps down the valley, and the whole army is carried off in a whirlwind of rocks. The king stands firm for a few moments, and hurls his curse upon whoever shall marry his daughter : may he never find honour upon the throne, nor love in any bed. Then, like a mighty oak falling, he disappears with his charger into the abyss—watched in helpless confusion by the new Gods. Bitterly they reflect upon what one day will be their fate, too—"Why? For what reason? To what purpose?" Despondently, they flop to the ground, awaiting Ananke's command. When nothing happens, they humbly continue their journey.

In such scenes, Spitteler produces the genuine epic atmosphere, steeped in deepest emotion and humanity. These are the visions of a great poet, and the language used is correspondingly effective. For their sake, we must acknowledge *Olympischer Frühling* as a work of art. The second part, *Hera die Braut,* has its living moments, too, scenes which in their own way possess great depth. (For example, there is the union of guilt and lust on Zeus' wedding-night.) However, this section is generally overshadowed by the hardness and cruelty of Hera's character, and by her ultimate treachery.

Genuine pathos, where the particular and the universal become fused, is also to be found in the occasional poem where Spitteler, having achieved a certain level of poetry, manages to sustain it; not, however, in the "visual" lyric of *Schmetterlinge,* nor yet in the more acoustic one of the *Glocken—und Gras-lieder,* where one sees and hears little more than the occasional sally into higher poetry. In the *Balladen* and the *Literarische Gleichnisse,* more undulating strains are to be perceived, though the latter will certainly not be appreciated first and foremost for their lyricism. Even here, however, one still finds no wholly perfected pieces. Only rarely does Spitteler manage to achieve the tonal contrasts of the true literary ballad, so well demonstrated by Goethe.

It is chiefly in the two stories, *Gustav* and *Die Mädchenfeinde,* that the childlike playfulness of Spitteler's "idyllic" temperament reveals itself. In *Gustav* (1892), the theme of greatness is developed out of a not unalluring idyll, which one would scarcely connect with the early satirical *Kleinstadtroman* (never published by Spitteler) on which it is based. A girl imparts to a young artist, who has failed as a medical student, the most precious gift a woman can give to a man—the belief in his vocation. The work certainly has many charming touches, but its basic structure lacks maturity, thus hampering any real refinement of language.

Artistically much more important is the Novelle, *Die Mädchenfeinde* (1907). Only at intervals is this story of a boys' world threatened by the intrusion of the poet's adult personality. As a whole, its evenness of tone, its sureness of touch in the depiction of the child mind, and the power and spontaneity of its epic pictures compel admiration. In his "Früheste Erlebnisse", Spitteler conjures up the prime of his early years with love and moderation, tinged with a sort of bashfulness. In *Die Mädchenfeinde*, boyhood is transmitted on to a higher, more idealised, yet still semi-realistic plane. Thus the idyll, a delightful vision of youthful souls awakening, is embedded in an apparent commonplace of events and in a landscape intimately familiar to the poet. The Novelle is a summer's ramble, a summer's rapture. Yet, over the nimble alertness, the innocence and artlessness of child experience, there hovers the reflection of another ramble, of another, somehow deeper sensual rapture : the gently gliding entry into maturer human experiences. The story strides with consummate skill up the narrow ridge where the innocent child world is overtaken by disillusioned adolescence. Adults play a part in the story only in so far as the plot requires them, and yet they provide a meaningful framework, since the experiences of the youngsters overflow into their domain. The obvious antithesis to the world of child joy is the crazy student. Through this human oddity Spitteler has expounded with extraordinary acuteness his pet theme of the suffering artistic genius.

The mundane temperament of the poet at last reveals itself in engaging fashion in the long story *Der Neffe des Herrn Bezenval* (1889). This is a historical novel set at the time of the French Revolution. Just as in Conrad Ferdinand Meyer's *Amulett*, a young Swiss arrives in Paris and gets himself entangled in love and politics. The theme is the development of a somewhat gauche but morally upright young idealist into a fully aware adult, who finally sacrifices himself for the sake of his convictions.

In *Conrad der Leutnant* Spitteler is dealing with a world far outside his natural sphere. The story was an "art gageure", a challenge to the despised guild of naturalists. It was an attempt to attack his opponents with their own weapons, having first refined them—or so he believed. Refined, that is, not in terms of psychological analysis, which Spitteler considered inartistic and anyway superficial, but through the acceptance of the formal laws of classical tragedy—in particular the French.

With this technique, it is only immediately before the dénouement that he unites the main dramatic themes, imposing upon himself the unity of character and perspective, as well as a regular time-sequence, in order to achieve the most intense involvement possible in the plot. There are two main reasons why the attempt was doomed to failure. As a poet, Spitteler had little feeling for ordinary human love. The popular heart remained amazingly alien to his own. The individual was after all for him not sufficiently noble to warrant any creative interest, *sui generis*. This being so, how could the material he chose ever have provided him with a poetic stimulus? Moreover, Spitteler's self-imposed principles only increased the disparity. For the figures do not live in their own right, but only in order to do justice to a preconceived idea of plot and character. From the outset they are treated like puppets. For the problems of authority and the generation-gap to be presented clearly, and so that the plot will develop in a terse and compact fashion, Conrad's father, who is immersed in ineluctable gloom, must appear to his son and daughter as a loathsome monster. And Conrad himself in his rank of lieutenant must appear as almost childishly obsessed in his hunger for power. Any subtle nuance in the story's fabric is thus precluded, and one is immediately struck by the glaring artificiality, even affectedness, of the work. Between the two main characters, father and son, no single spark of intimacy is ever kindled. There is therefore no basis on which tragic suspense can breed.

Imago, by Spitteler's own admission, was "not just a work of art, but . . . 'life-blood' ". Yet he was "nauseated by this Sisyphus-like toil in prosaic filth". How, one may ask, can life-blood become nauseating? How can "life-blood" transform itself into prosody? If Spitteler preferred to present his innermost spiritual life in a "veiled and disguised" way, why then so sudden and naked a confession? Some personal thorn, some extra-artistic motive must surely have been at work. Was it some insuppressible grudge, a wound that refused to heal—an almost pathological need for revenge? This suspicion is now confirmed by what we know of the work's origins : there could anyway be no other answer to the question. *Imago* was an unfortunate book not only for the author but also for the sensitive reader—in fact, one of the most unedifying among the better-known works of contemporary literature.[20] "The love story of Felix Tandem" (Spitteler published his first two works under this pseudonym) "in the year when he wrote Prometheus". This is Spitteler's own definition. Certainly a love story of a very strange kind ! One lover between two women, one earthly, one unearthly, both with the same face, and after a fight in which he makes a fool of himself, he devotes himself completely to the unearthly. Prometheus with fainting fits—so one might just as well dub it! Not a Prometheus in an imaginary, mythical world, but a Prometheus "among the democrats", in a bourgeois environment. However, what once—in Prometheus' human world, ruled by Epimetheus the king—was a general depiction of human weakness and stupidity, is developed in *Imago* into a biting satire of bourgeois society : "Idealia" as the mirror image of a complacent bourgeoisie flowing with "ideals" but in fact selfish and narrow.

This satire is not charmingly presented, but quivering with scorn and resentment. Resentment is the word, perhaps, which most accurately characterises the work. Resentment on the one side, delusions of grandeur—one cannot avoid the expression—on the other. And this implies the presence of an element which makes the work profoundly unartistic : the personal, the all too personal. The satire is born out of resentment, as is the hero's anguish when he is prevented from loving the woman. The hero is simply not a human being, but the marionette-like creation of the poet's resentful, almost monomanic, mind—a mind which here turns the vacuum of a growing sense of inferiority and aversion into a euphoria of artificial characters, without ever finding a way to translate its own "lifeblood" into any redeeming artistic form.

In his essay on Spitteler, C. A. Bernouilli pronounced that *Imago* was at best an instinctive and violent "Aufschrei", and at worst a completely artificial creation.[21] One is bound to go along with this verdict, adding, too, that there are strains in this "outcry" which cast a shadow on the poet's human decency.

This essay is a considerably shortened version of Professor Werner Günther's (Neuchâtel) important essay on Carl Spitteler, which appeared in *Dichter der neueren Schweiz* (Francke Verlag, Berne, 1963). It was translated by E. M. W. Maguire, B.A.(Oxon.).

ANNOTATIONS AND TRANSLATIONS

1. *Aesthetic Writings*, p. 171.
2. *Autobiographical Writings*, p. 300.
3. *Aesthetic Writings*, p. 71.
4. *Autobiographical Writings*, p. 281–82.
5. *Aesthetic Writings*, p. 185.
6. *Aesthetic Writings*, p. 466.

7. Viz. *Carl Spittelers poetische Sendung,* Schweizer Monatshefte fur Politik und Kultur, 3 vol. (1923).

8. *Aesthetic Writings,* p. 193.

9. Literally, "the compelled compulsion".

10. The world-mill.

11. And spake his song in dark velvet tones.

12. Against the sombre background shining a world of teeming images.

13. Life's purpose is dirt. The truth is in the stone.

14. Not an inch in eternity which is not filled with anguish.

15. The terrible bed of the avalanche's debris.

16. What has become of the world of the Ancients! For what anguish it has already left a space!

17. See 14.

18. But now Ananke's shovel swings us upwards.

19. Foreseeing the doom which will spread its wings ever wider.

20. It testifies to the original fame of the novel that Sigmund Freud published a "Periodical for the application of Psychoanalysis to the Humanities" under the title of *Imago* from 1912. One of the editors, Dr. Hanns Sachs, praised Spitteler's novel, as early as 1913, as a manual for the phenomenon of the Oedipus-complex.

21. C. A. Bernouilli cit. by R. Matzog-Schmauss, *Prometheus-Fate. Essays about Carl Spitteler,* 1930, p. 87.

BIBLIOGRAPHY

Gesammelte Werke in neun Bänden, vermehrt um zwei Geleitbände, Zürich, 1945–1958. Herausgeber: G. Bohnenblust, W. Altwegg, R. Faesi.

Briefe von Ad. Frey und C. Spitteler, Hsg. von Lina Frey, Frauenfeld, 1933.

C. Spitteler, *Laughing Truths,* 1927.

C. Spitteler, *Selected Poems,* 1928.

O. Kluth, *Carl Spitteler,* 1918 in French.

E. Boyd, *Studies of Ten Literatures,* 1923.

R. Gottschalk, *Carl Spitteler,* 1928.

F. Weingartner, *Carl Spitteler. Ein künstlerisches Erlebnis,* 1904.

Th. Roffler, *Carl Spitteler. Eine Literarische Feststellung,* 1926.

R. Faesi, *Spittelers Weg und Werk,* 1933.

J. Fränkel, *Carl Spitteler. Hundigungen und Begegnungen,* 1945.

W. Frels, *Eine Bibliographie Spittelers in "Die Schöne Literatur",* 1925.